Abraham Lincoln's Path to Reelection in 1864

Our Greatest Victory

Fred J. Martin, Jr.

AuthorHouse™
1663 Liberty Drive
Bloomington, IN 47403
www.authorhouse.com
Phone: 1-800-839-8640

Published by AuthorHouse 12/30/2013

ISBN: 978-1-4918-3531-9 (sc)
ISBN: 978-1-4918-3530-2 (hc)

Library of Congress Control Number: 2013921167

My father, Fred J. Martin, and my mother, Dorothy Alkire Martin;

Dr. Allen D. Breck, History Department, the University of Denver;

Dr. Frank T. Edgar, History Department, Culver Stockton College, Canton, Missouri;

William Lee Miller, author, statesman, and friend.

The Cover

Abraham Lincoln with eyeglasses and compass symbolizes both his foresight and vision coupled with his ethical and moral sense. The blind memorandum penned by Lincoln on August 23, 1864 as allies and advisors warned him it was unlikely that he would be reelected and enemies alleged he was a tyrant who would not yield his office even if defeated. It reads: "This morning, as for some days past, it seems exceedingly probable that this administration will not be reelected. Then it will be my duty to so cooperate with the President-elect as to save the Union between the election and the inauguration; as he will have secured his election on such ground that he cannot possibly save it afterward. A Lincoln." Lincoln had folded and sealed it asking his cabinet to sign it unseen, which they did. With his reelection he opened and shared the memorandum with members of his cabinet.

CONTENTS

INTRODUCTION

The 1864 reelection of Abraham Lincoln ended sixty years of slave power rule in the United States, saved the Union, and paved the way for the abolition of slavery. It guaranteed Northern victory in the Civil War and led Congress to reconsider and pass the Thirteenth Amendment, sending it to the states for ratification. Lincoln's victory rooted out the cancer of slavery, by then accepted as the cause of the Civil War.

The reelected Lincoln in his post-election message to Congress said it best:

"The most reliable indication of public purpose in this country is derived though our popular elections. Judging by the recent canvass and its result, the purpose of the people, within the loyal States, to maintain the integrity of the Union, was never more firm, nor more nearly unanimous … The extraordinary calmness and good order with … millions of voters … at the polls give strong assurances of this."

Abraham Lincoln shaped his own reelection as president in 1864. His reelection sustained democratic government and highlighted the ballot as the fulcrum of freedom and democracy. The Civil War erupted because the South had refused to accept Lincoln's election as president. His presidency ended the South's sixty years of dominance of the Congress, the Supreme Court, and the nation and renewed the Union.

This book uses the words Lincoln crafted in speeches, messages, and letters—his words—as the superstructure so the reader can follow his path. Lincoln wrote virtually all of these words. He wrote and spoke to educate and to gain popular understanding, pressing consistently for freedom, equality and justice. Lincoln's presidency reignited equality in the nation as proclaimed in the Declaration of Independence.

Elections establish a nation's direction and reaffirm its values. It is more than two candidates or two teams battling to win. Had Lincoln not effectively challenged Senator Stephen A. Douglas in the Freeport debate—costing him his race for Senate—Lincoln likely would not have become president in 1860. Lincoln's "House Divided" speech and his stand against the expansion of slavery made him our president.

Douglas L. Wilson, in the prologue to *Lincoln's Sword: The Presidency and the Power of Words*, explains, "Eventually it began to be recognized that Lincoln's unsuspected literary talent was having a decisive effect in shaping public attitudes and was a telling factor in the success of his policies." Thus, this book begins with a biographical perspective building on Lincoln's ethical and educational development.

Lincoln built his political career by exploring issues in forceful language that hit home with the people. As his own thought and direction matured, he spelled out his views for the people, harvesting the faith and confidence of the citizenry. This powerful grass-roots strength stood as an unbreachable popular barrier when the radicals within his own party attempted to prevent his nomination for a second term.

Important words are quoted from those who sustained, contested or opposed Lincoln. A candidate scales such heights with determination and courage on a path strewn with obstacles. It has been said a senator is one who rises in the morning, looks in the mirror, and sees the next president. Among contemporaries, senators, publishers, cabinet officers, and capitalists viewed themselves as superior or coveted the job.

Lincoln's heritage and his chief virtue was a boundless capacity to read and learn, and share his quest. When he was but twenty-three, Lincoln walked six miles to get a copy of Samuel Kirkham's *English Grammar*, which ends with a discussion of the figures of speech. He developed as a master of elocution and an exceptional writer, with moral, ethical, and intellectual power that undergirded his pathway to political success.

Lincoln's first text in "blab" school, William Scott's *Lessons in Elocution*, included forty-nine speeches, nineteen from Shakespeare, including a number that Lincoln memorized, such as the soliloquy by King Claudius on his guilt for having murdered Hamlet's father. Lincoln also studied gifted orators, including Henry Clay and Daniel Webster. His reading included many authors and works from *Aesop's Fables* to the Bible.

From his mother, Nancy Hanks Lincoln, came strong memory, acute judgment, and knowledge of the Bible, for she was known to recite and sing verses. From his father, Tom Lincoln, came great strength, an ability to tell a story or crack a joke, and sociability both truthful and honest. As Abe Lincoln matured, books and words became his driving passion. His path diverged from the laboring priorities of his father.

Differences continued to develop between father and son, especially after Nancy died. Yet his stepmother, Sarah Bush Johnson Lincoln, sided with Abe in his desire for learning. Abe objected to being hired out by his father, who worked him like a slave. As Abe turned increasing to his reading, the differences grew because their values increasingly diverged. For Abe, his way forward was through books and not behind the plow.

Abe struggled with religion, politics, and moral and ethical precepts. Taking Henry Clay as his role model, he rejected prevailing Jacksonian political views. This was compatible with Lincoln's rise in electoral politics. He was from the beginning an advocate of public works. His success hinged on restoring government, building a loyal military command, establishing a currency, and reestablishing solvency.

While lacking administrative experience, Lincoln developed as the nation's commander in chief and increasingly with each new challenge. He showed a strong hand constructing his cabinet. Salmon P. Chase, a Jacksonian, a weak choice for Treasury, was essential as Lincoln needed the radical Chase from Ohio every bit as much as he needed the conservative William Seward and Seward's constituency in New York.

James Riley's account of slavery in its grim terms was a formidable influence on Lincoln. This authentic narrative was published in 1815 and republished some eighteen times by 1860. This harrowing white captain's account told of the suffering, slavery, and freedom that he and his crew suffered at the hands of nomadic North African Arabs. Riley subsequently advocated gradual emancipation for slaves:

> I have now learned to look with compassion on my enslaved and oppressed fellow creatures; I will exert all my remaining faculties in endeavors to redeem the enslaved, and to shiver in pieces the rod of oppression … I am far from being of opinion that they should all be emancipated immediately, and at once. I am aware that such a measure would not only prove ruinous to great number of my fellow-citizens, who are at present slave holders, and to whom the property descended as an inheritance; but that it would also turn loose … a race of men incapable of exercising the necessary occupations of civilized life, in such a manner as to ensure to themselves an honest and comfortable subsistence; yet it is my earnest desire that such a plan should be devised … as will gradually … wither and extirpate the accursed tree of slavery, that has been suffered to take such deep root.

In *Lincoln: The Biography of a Writer*, Fred Kaplan quotes the passage cited above. It accounts in good measure for Lincoln's cautious evolution of emancipation. Henry David Thoreau and James Fenimore Cooper both praised Riley's account. Abraham Lincoln included it in his 1860 campaign biography—along with *Pilgrim's Progress* and the Bible—as among the books that had shaped his youthful development.

Since Lincoln never joined a church his religious views were obscure. Professor Rick Gilkey wrote at my request on current research on ethical behavior and Lincoln. Gilkey holds a joint appointment at Emory University on the faculty of the Goizueta Business School as a professor in the practice of organization and management, and in the school of medicine as an associate professor of psychiatry. Gilkey wrote:

> In his classic work *The Individual and his Religion*, Harvard Psychologist Gordon Allport described the difference between beliefs and practices that were intrinsic versus extrinsic. Contrasting those differences in religious behavior, Allport described extrinsic religion, as one focused on social needs—the need for status, group support, and social advancement. Such religiosity is a means to an end.
>
> In contrast those who practice intrinsic religion see their faith as an end not a means, and affiliate with like-minded people who use deeply held inner beliefs as organizing principles by which they live their lives. As the only American President who did not have a formal religious affiliation, Abraham Lincoln clearly practiced a faith based on intrinsic principles. His critique of formal church affiliated religion, where he described the gap between espoused morality and practiced morality, was based on his intrinsically held religious and moral convictions.
>
> In our neuroscience research with executive leaders subjects where we examined the neural substrates of morality (Robertson, D. C., Snarey, J., Ousley, O., Harenski, K., Bowman, F. D., Gilkey, R., and Kilts, C. (2007). The neural processing of moral sensitivity to issues of justice and care. *Neuropsychologia*, 45, 755–766) reinforces this view of Lincoln's ethics by confirming that a moral response involves activations of neural regions associated with early autobiographical memory, personal sense of identity, and

> social emotional circuits particularly those associated with social reasoning and perspective taking (empathy).
>
> These cognitive and emotional processes are part of moral capacity that develops in early phases of life as an interaction of genes and experience. In the case of Lincoln, we would infer that through his primary relationships, ongoing interactions and myriad of experiences that started very early in his life, Lincoln developed a very strong intrinsic base of moral convictions that were both deeply held and devotedly practiced.

Lincoln crafted his positions and expressed them eloquently using his gift for language. His early efforts paved the way, and his reelection in 1864 was a culmination. He pressed popular government in peace and in time of war, rejecting the rule of monarchs, czars and supreme leaders. His work focused on his compelling words of freedom, equality, and justice, equally vital today as when he wrote 150 years ago.

Lincoln had, in effect, educated himself and developed his ethical and moral outlook. His insight into the mind of the people—both North and South—led him to speak and write in a manner that opened the minds of the voters to inevitable change. In a sense, the formula he used to educate himself, he applied to the electorate. He adopted policies after careful deliberation and shared them to ensure popular acceptance.

Our founding fathers relied heavily upon the study of natural law by John Locke, the English philosopher. Locke had relied upon Richard Hooker's *Of the Laws of Ecclesiastical Polity*. Hooker elaborated a theory of law, based on fundamental natural law governing the universe as the expression of God's supreme reason. Hooker studied the thirteenth-century Councilior Movement within the Roman Catholic Church.

Cardinal Nicholas of Cusa and the German archbishop John Krebs of Bernkastle on the Moselle allied with Pierre d'Ailly, the chancellor of the University of Paris, a bishop, and later cardinal. They proposed democratic reform in the then-universal Roman Catholic Church to restore the power of the council and subordinate papal power. Their efforts failed, yet their thinking came to life in the reformation.

Lincoln subscribed to the union as perpetual built on the sovereignty of the people. His words define a Union based on the premise that all men are created equal. While the story of the killing of his grandfather Abraham, who had fought in the Revolution, was most intensely engraved in his mind, he never showed animosity toward Indians, and declared unceasingly for equality of all as basic to the nation.

Lincoln pointed a direction calling for a Union undivided and with slavery on the road to extinction. Lincoln told his law partner, William Herndon, that in his "House Divided" speech he used "some universally known figure expressed in simple language … that may strike home to the minds of men in order to raise them up to the peril of the times." His presidential messages, addresses, and letters continued this theme.

As a young reporter on *The Denver Post*, I was a stringer for *Editor and Publisher*, a publishers' trade journal, in addition to my Post reporting work. My assignment was to cover the press covering the President Dwight Eisenhower's pre-inauguration presidential team then in Denver. Coupled with later experience in Washington and attendance at national political conventions I gained insight into government.

Lincoln had no press secretary and was his own spokesperson. My experience—covering state legislatures, working with Congress, and meeting presidents—highlighted for me the contrast between Lincoln's ways and those of his successors. Lincoln's mastery of words, his understanding of human nature, and his keen identification with the common people has yet to be equaled among his successors.

President Lincoln handling of patronage cast a wide political net with a keen eye on wants of members of Congress. He did not bow to the demands of Weed and Seward for control, but worked closely with

Postmaster Blair and others. This way Lincoln developed the delegate strength for renomination, sidestepping the services of Justice David Davis and Thurlow Weed, yet drawing them into the campaign.

Lincoln adroitly isolated Samuel P. Chase, his secretary of the Treasury, and the radicals who sought to prevent his renomination. He had given Chase rein on patronage appointments, but curbed the power when it proved an impediment to his nomination. Lincoln had skillfully built his Republican party base—later the so-called the Union party—even drawing in recalcitrant conservatives and radicals for the campaign.

The healing process began, as the radicals came to see they could not displace Lincoln as the nominee. Furthermore, it was clear that Lincoln could defeat McClellan and would not step back from emancipation. Lincoln had always kept the door open for the radicals. Concurrently he also took pains to maintain his conservative base. He effectively summed up the 1864 election in his December message to Congress:

"The most reliable indication of public purpose in this country is derived though our popular elections. Judging by the recent canvass and its result, the purpose of the people, within the loyal States, to maintain the integrity of the Union, was never more firm, nor more nearly unanimous than now … Not only all those who supported the Union ticket … but a great majority of the opposing party also, may be fairly claimed to entertain, and to be actuated by, the same purpose.

"It is the voice of the people now, for the first time, heard upon the question. In a great national crisis … unanimity of action among those seeking a common end is very desirable—almost indispensable … In this case the common end is the maintenance of the Union; and, among the means to secure that end, such will, through the election, is … declared in favor of such constitutional amendment."

Lincoln's 1865 inaugural speech speaks even today: "With malice toward none; with charity for all; with firmness in the right, as God gives us to see the right, let us strive on to finish the work we are in; to bind up the nation's wounds; to care for him who shall have borne the battle, and for his widow, and his orphan—to do all which may achieve and cherish a just and lasting peace among ourselves, and with all nations."

The voice of the people, as echoed in their ballots, was no more acceptable to the slave power South in 1864 than in 1860. This loss of power, coupled with dread of more universal suffrage, ignited a reaction. Confederate intelligence worked to defeat Lincoln. A plot to kidnap Lincoln, hatched by their intelligence, to take him to Richmond, and force him to negotiate didn't work. An alternative resulted.

Lincoln's words and those of Shakespeare echoed differently in the mind of John Wilkes Booth. The Confederate intelligence group operated from the home of Mary Surratt and was led by Booth. Mary's son, John Surratt, was the conduit for funds and directions from the Confederate hierarchy in Richmond and in Canada. The plot was the ultimate effort to reject the will of the people expressed by ballot.

It is ironic that Lincoln's words in the mind of Booth made Lincoln a tyrant in the image of Shakespeare's Julius Caesar. While Booth had acted in many a Shakespeare play, it was the role of Brutus in which he cast himself when he fired the shot that killed Lincoln. Fearing equality and Negro voting, Booth acted with his confederates. He chronicled his deed and purpose as he met death attempting to flee south.

It is ironic that the valued words of Lincoln, much predicated on the works of Shakespeare, would provide an ultimate lesson. While the public harkened to the words of Lincoln—and the lessons of Shakespeare echoed through the halls of history—the traitorous and tyrannical mind read hate. Lincoln's words give a crucial lesson for the freedom-seeking people of the world confronting tyrants today.

CHAPTER I

THE MATURING LINCOLN: A KENTUCKY HERITAGE

"I am naturally anti-slavery," Abraham Lincoln wrote. "If slavery is not wrong, nothing is wrong. I cannot remember when I did not so think, and feel."[1]

The Revolutionary War gave birth to the United States, the world's first functioning democracy. When the war ended, many, especially veterans, headed west to expand this new democracy in a challenging frontier. Armed with their long rifles, the men and hardy pioneer women and children first moved on horseback or on foot. A trickle reached a crescendo and then became a flood as settlers swept over the Appalachian Mountains and down the Ohio River to the rich western lands.

The principles of freedom and equality were a paradigm based upon the conviction that people could govern themselves. President Abraham Lincoln would declare the Union perpetual and would fight to renew the basic principles of equality and the rights of man. Abraham Lincoln as president would overturn an unjust slave system in which one man could own another. His election as president—and, most important, his reelection in 1864—would renew this legacy of equality and freedom.

The future president was named for his grandfather, Abraham, a Revolutionary War captain shot by an Indian in 1786 while taming

Kentucky land. The Indian attempted to grab Abraham's young son, Thomas. But Thomas's older brother, Mordecai, raced to the cabin, took up a rifle, and shot the Indian, saving Thomas. This left Abraham's widow, Bathsheba, a niece of Daniel Boone, her sons, Mordecai, Josiah, and Thomas, and her daughters, Mary and Nancy, to make their way.[2]

Speaking of his grandfather, the future president wrote in 1854, "The story of his death by the Indians, and of Uncle Mordecai, then fourteen years old, killing one of the Indians, is the legend more strongly than all others imprinted upon my mind and memory." Yet he was neither anti-Indian nor vindictive. The English law of descents had been repealed, but Mordecai, by common consent, managed the bulk of his father's property, although inheritances went equally to each of the children.[3]

President Lincoln's father, Thomas, was a wandering labor boy, working at times in harness with slaves rented out by their masters. Tom Lincoln, unlike the slaves, kept his earnings, and likely came to see the slaves as fellow creatures. He apprenticed as a carpenter and at age twenty-six married Nancy Hanks. She had come to Kentucky in the arms of her single mother. The intensity and fervor of Nancy Hanks—often called Nancy Sparrow at cabin religious meetings—caught the eye of Tom Lincoln.

Tom was fresh back from one of his trips to New Orleans when he and Nancy were wed on June 6, 1806. As a married man assuming new responsibilities, Tom settled into the carpentry trade in Elizabethtown. When a daughter was born in 1807, Nancy christened her Sarah after her cousin, who became like a sister to Nancy when rescued from Indian captivity. Dennis Hanks praised the mind and heart of his maternal cousin, with whom he had been brought up in the Sparrow sanctuary.[4]

Former senator turned historian, Alfred J. Beveridge, said of Nancy Hanks, "But the qualities of her mind and character were impressed more distinctly than was her physical appearance. All remember that she was uncommonly intelligent; had 'Remarkable Keen perception,' as

Dennis Hanks put it [to Herndon]. Dennis waxed enthusiastic about the mind and heart of his maternal cousin with whom he had been brought up in the Sparrow sanctuary calling her shrewd and smart."[5]

Hanks described both Nancy and Tom: "Her memory was strong ... her judgment was acute almost. She was spiritually & ideally inclined --not dull—not material—not heavy in thought—feeling or action. Thomas Lincoln ... could beat his son telling a story—cracking a joke ... a good, clean, social, truthful & honest man, loving like his wife everything and everybody. He was a man who took the world easy—did not possess much envy. He never thought that gold was God."[6]

As 1807 ended, Thomas moved fourteen miles to a three-hundred-acre spread in the "Barrens" on the south fork of Nolin Creek, known as the Sinking Spring Farm. In 1808 Tom, Nancy, and Sarah moved to Nolin Creek. Tom cut logs from the forest and built a modest cabin with only a hard-packed dirt floor. Abe was born in 1809 in this Nolin cabin and named for the slain Grandpa Abraham. As he grew, Abe would trail his father in the fields and hear Nancy sing Bible verses while doing chores.[7]

Tom and Nancy attended Long Run Baptist Church, where Ben Lynn preached. He had a long association with the antislavery Baptists associations that adopted resolutions condemning slavery as an evil. The slave patroller, Christopher Bush, was a neighbor. Bush's duties becoming demanding, Tom Lincoln was drafted to assist, but stayed only one term, suggesting an inclination against slavery. Abe wrestled with all and likely developed his conviction that slavery was wrong.[8]

Tom often recounted the story of the death of Grandfather Abraham, the resulting hardship, and his trips to New Orleans. When strangers and neighbors stopped, Abe often too boldly took hold of the conversation, and Tom sometimes cuffed him for his brashness. Abe fetched water or tools for his father and absorbed the talk as he trailed Thomas doing his chores. After three years on this rugged, stony clay soil, Lincoln moved on to their Knob Creek farm, where they stayed until Abe was seven.

The Kentucky years were good years for young Abe. Even when in the White House, he could recall every detail of the land and the farms. He delighted in recounting events and places when a visitor would bring up early life in Kentucky. Abe grew up on the Knob Creek farm and spent time in the blab schools run by Zachariah Riney and Caleb Hazel, learning to read and write. On nearby Louisville and Nashville Pike, Lincoln met peddlers, politicians, and even soldiers from the Battle of New Orleans. [9]

A clergyman recalled Lincoln saying:

> I remember how, when a mere child, I used to get irritated when anybody talked to me in a way that I could not understand. I don't think I ever got angry at anything else in my life. But that always disturbed my temper. … I can remember going to my little bedroom, after hearing the neighbors talk … with my father, and spending … the night walking up and down, and trying to make out … the exact meaning of some of their, to me, dark sayings.
>
> I could not sleep, though I often tried to, when I got on such a hunt after an idea, until I had caught it; and when I thought I had got it, I was not satisfied until I had repeated it over and over, until I had put it in language plain enough, as I thought, for any boy I knew to comprehend. This was a kind of passion … and it has stuck by me, for I am never easy now, when I am handling a thought, till I have bounded it north and bounded it south and bounded it east and bounded it west.[10]

A neighbor then in Kentucky, and later a friend in New Salem, Mentor Graham significantly influenced Lincoln's life in both places. Graham showed promise as a student, and his father, Jeremiah, had a brother, Robert, a learned doctor. So Mentor's parents sent him to live with the childless Robert and his wife. Mentor would ride behind Robert on his horse and recite his lessons. The more intellectually endowed Robert proved just the right teacher for Mentor.[11]

Mentor told of an incident remembered because it brought an abrupt halt to the drinking of alcohol by his father. Free haying was underway on land called barrens. A knot of hay cutters gathered at the door of a nearby cabin, drawn by childish cries of distress. They found that a man in a drunken rage had killed his wife. Tom and young Abe happened by. The affected Abe took the weeping girls by the hands and begged them not to cry. The men took the husband to town.[12]

The Lincolns left Kentucky in 1816. An 1860 biographical sketch by John Locke Scripps quoted Lincoln as saying the move was "partly on account of slavery; but chiefly on account of the difficulty of land titles in KY." Indiana, unlike Kentucky, had a more transparent system of land titles. Settlers could mark off their homesteads, then go to the federal land office and pay to secure their claims. And they did not have to compete against farmers who had slave labor.

Tom Lincoln loaded family household goods, his tools, and his savings—converted into barrels of whiskey—on a flatboat he had built. His flatboat flipped in the freezing waters of the Rolling Fork River, pitching him and his belongings overboard well before he could reach and cross the Ohio River. Tom salvaged what he could, including whiskey, and crossed over to Indiana. Tom left his goods in the custody of a pioneer after choosing and marking a site on Little Pigeon Creek.

Back in Kentucky, Tom and Nancy, along with young Sarah and Abe, crossed the Ohio with their bagged goods, bringing two horses so father and son could ride one and mother and daughter the other. Tom obtained an ox-pulled wagon to carry the salvaged whiskey and goods to Little Pigeon Creek. There he pitched a pole-shed, common on the frontier. An open-faced dwelling, it was constructed from a combination of poles, limbs, leaves, and mud, and required a fire on the open side, especially in severe weather. It lacked windows and had a mud floor.

Abe, big for his age, was put to work with an ax. Again according to the account by Scripps, Abe remembered that for the next fifteen years he was "most constantly handling that most useful instrument." To clear the land meant chopping down trees, digging up stumps, cutting out brush and roots, and burning much of the detritus. Then there was the planting, weeding, cultivating, harvesting, and care and butchering of the animals. Tom Lincoln eventually built a typical one-room frontier cabin with a loft, where Abe and Dennis Hanks slept.[13]

Hardly had the Lincolns settled into this eighteen-by-twenty-foot structure when the milk sickness struck. First it hit the recent arrivals, Thomas and Betsy Sparrow. Nancy nursed them as they sickened and died. By late September Nancy, at thirty-six, also took sick and soon died as Tom, Sarah, and nine-year-old Abe sadly watched. Gone all too soon was her tender touch. Much has been said of the effect on Abe and Sarah, but nothing of the surely staggering blow the loss of his wife was to Tom.

In her last days, Nancy called her children to her bedside and told them to grow up and be good—and to be good to their father. Surely she knew her love would be missed and how much she meant to Tom, who had in the past wrestled with depression. Tom built a coffin and buried her on the hillside. Lonely months followed for Tom, Sarah, Abe, and Dennis Hanks. Within a year, Tom headed to Kentucky to court Sarah Bush Johnston, a thirty-year-old widow.[14]

Tom told Sarah he now had no wife and she had no husband. Tom said he wanted a marriage now. When she said she had debts, he paid them. They were married on December 2, 1819. Sarah packed her three children, her belongings, and some furniture. Tom loaded everything into a wagon pulled by four horses and they traveled to Little Pigeon Creek. There Sarah, struck by Tom's children's condition, scrubbed them. She prodded Tom to add a floor for a more livable cabin.

Her feather bedding replaced the cornstalk bedding Tom, Sarah, and Abe had been using. She introduced a measure of civilization to their frontier life. Most important, she mothered Abe and Sarah. Tom stated that Abe now had enough "eddicatin"; Sarah stood strong for Abe's bent to read and learn. Abe showed her love and respect, more so than her own son did. As she later said, Abe never gave her a cross word, and, "I never saw another boy get smarter and smarter as Abe did."[15]

Abe wrestled with the fire and brimstone preaching of the frontier evangelists. After hearing a sermon, Lincoln would mount a stump and deliver it to neighborhood youngsters. He would imitate the preacher and his listeners would cry or shout. Abe digested the words, yet he never found in them reason to join any church. He matured from a rawboned youth into a man of great strength who could sink an ax, lift, wrestle, jump, run, and hurl, besting his companions.

Abe read all the books he could get. His mind and body developed in tandem with an intense concentration focused on poetry and prose. At age sixteen, he sculled a couple of lawyers out to a boat on the Ohio River. When he lifted their trunks onto the boat, each threw him a half dollar. This was more than Abe had ever earned, even with one coin lost in the river. A new horizon of enhanced opportunity emerged, well beyond the thirty-one cents a day he earned butchering.

Abe's river taxi offended two Kentucky ferryboat men, who sought judgment. They alleged Abe taking passengers to a mid-river ship violated Kentucky law. Justice of the Peace Samuel Pate dismissed the case outright. Lincoln successfully contended that he took passengers midstream, not to Kentucky. This awakened Abe's interest in the law, and he would often scull over and observe Kentucky trials. Three years later Abe, like his father, would raft down the Ohio and Mississippi rivers.[16]

In 1829, Tom Lincoln, ever restless and fearing the milk sickness, pulled out of Indiana. With Dennis Hanks and Levi Hall, both married to stepsisters of Abe, Tom relocated to Macon County on the Sangamon River in Illinois. It was here that young Abe helped build their cabin and plant the first crops. Abe mastered the art of inserting the wedge, striking it, and splitting logs into rails. These rails made Lincoln "the rail splitter" candidate in the election of 1860.[17]

In 1831, Lincoln, John Hanks, and John Johnston, his stepbrother, were bringing a flatboat down the Sangamon River, headed for New Orleans. The boat high-centered on the milldam at New Salem. Lincoln bored a hole in the bow, drained the water, freed the boat, and patched the hole. When Lincoln returned, Denton Offutt, who had contracted for the trip, opened a store and hired Lincoln as the clerk. Lincoln's frontier humor—with a share of vulgarity—made him a celebrity.[18]

The world's largest economies in the year Lincoln settled in New Salem were China and India. An industrial crescendo was driving growth in Europe and sending floods of immigrants to the United States, while opening global trade routes. European nations were moving ahead of the Asian nations and were providing a significant market for raw materials including the South's export-driven cotton crop, which reached $29 million annually. One-third of the South's population was black slaves.

Initially Europeans had introduced slavery in the Americas. But in the early 1800s, New York City emerged as the world's slave trading capital and a national financial center. A ban on slave trading was not enforced. Profitable slave vessels were funded chiefly in New York and launched from New England ports. Sugar, heavily labor intensive, was a magnet. Imported slaves were taken primarily to Cuba and Brazil. Others were brought directly to Charleston or smuggled into New Orleans.[19]

Abe Lincoln studied intensively the nation's politics of this time. Andrew Jackson triumphed over President John Quincy Adams. A frontier soldier, Jackson's victory over the British in the Battle of New Orleans made him a national hero. Yet Abe rejected Jacksonian democracy and chose to follow the famed Kentucky Whig, Senator Henry Clay, whom he idolized. Like Clay, Lincoln favored the national bank, the protective tariff, and federal support for roads, canals, and rivers.[20]

Lincoln, describing himself as "a strange, friendless, uneducated, penniless boy," struggled to forge a new life in New Salem, a tight-knit frontier community. Nearly one-half the residents were Grahams or Greens. Lincoln, accepted from the beginning as if he were family, often boarded among these neighbors. The women would mother him, even sewing and patching his ill-fitting and badly worn clothes. He would pitch in on the chores. Soon Lincoln knew just about everybody around.[21]

Stories about the strong, lanky Lincoln were legion. His wrestling with Jack Armstrong won him the approval of the wild Clary Grove Boys led by Armstrong. When clerking, he shared a bed with another clerk, William G. Green. Years later Green visited the White House, and President Lincoln introduced him, saying Green had helped him learn to read and write. Justice of the Peace Bowling Green said, "There was good material in Abe, and he only wanted education."

Lincoln had told John Pitcher, a circuit lawyer, "The things I want to know are in books. My best friend is the man who'll get me a book I ain't read." Lincoln's interest in the law was fostered by attending court sessions when Bowling Green presided. Another neighbor, Abner Y. Ellis, recalled that Lincoln used to say, "He owed more to Mr. Green for his advancement than any other man and I think well he may say." In fact, Ellis said that Bowling Green was almost a second father to Lincoln.

Green, Ellis added, used to say that Lincoln was a man after his own heart. Squire Green, Dr. John Allen, Bill Green, Jack Kelso, their wives, and others treated Lincoln as family. When Bowling Green died, Lincoln was asked to give the eulogy. Overwhelmed with grief, he broke into tears and couldn't finish. This showed his deep respect for Green. While clerking, Lincoln obtained a copy of the *Blackstone's Commentaries*, which he digested, and this further enhanced his interest in law.[22]

In 1832, Governor John Reynolds called out the militia to halt Indians crossing back into Illinois in what was called the Black Hawk War.

Lincoln's company elected him captain, a pleasing honor for a man with no military training. Fortunately they never had to fight. When Lincoln's month of obligatory service ended, he and John Todd Stuart both reenlisted as privates. The much better educated Stuart recognized Lincoln's potential, lent him books, and encouraged him to study law.[23]

Lincoln Elected Legislator

A lawyer and a strong Whig, Stuart pressed Lincoln to run for the legislature. In his first race in 1832, Lincoln was defeated, but came back to win in 1834 with Whig and Democratic votes. In the 1832 race for the legislature, Lincoln had only a month to campaign on his return from his military service. Little known in Sangamon, a large county, he lost. Yet in New Salem, where he was known, he carried 277 of 300 votes cast, showing the overwhelming regard of his neighbors.

The final paragraph of Lincoln's campaign flyer outlines his future hopes: "Every man is said to have his peculiar ambition. Whether it be true or not, I can say the one that I have no other so great as that of being truly esteemed of my fellow men, by rendering myself worthy of their esteem. How far I shall succeed in gratifying this ambition is yet to be developed. I am young and unknown to many of you. I was born and have ever remained in the most humble walks of life."[24]

With his finances low, Lincoln in 1833 was appointed postmaster under the administration of President Andrew Jackson. Lincoln was assured he did not have to give up his principles; he had said, "If I have to surrender any thought or principle to get it I wouldn't touch it with a ten foot pole." Lincoln kept scrupulous account of post office monies. He had access to newspapers. His fortunes improved when John Calhoun, county surveyor and a Democrat, offered him a job as his deputy.[25]

Lincoln also had boarded at the tavern of John Rutledge, New Salem's senior merchant. The debating club at the Rutledge Tavern helped

Lincoln develop as a politician and learn issues. Lincoln found Rutledge's daughter Ann attractive. Ann sadly died of typhoid fever. Stressed by his efforts to master the law and the grief, Lincoln suffered a severe bout of depression in 1835. Ann's death most likely brought to the surface memories of his mother's death during his youth.[26]

His extensive reading gave him insight into aristocracy, monarchy, and democracy. He viewed monarchy as the antithesis of democracy. Lincoln also digested a wide range of newspapers, books, and poetry, including favorites William Shakespeare, Robert Burns, and Lord Byron. Shakespeare's thought and illumination of a quality of human equality, monarchs included, gave insight into human nature through the characters in his plays. The bard's thought significantly impacted Lincoln.

Another Lincoln friend, Jack Kelso, exhibited a passion for fishing, Shakespeare, and the poet Burns. Kelso fished and drank whiskey and recited Shakespeare. Shakespeare shredded the prevailing "divine right of kings" doctrine, forcefully illustrating the common humanity of kings and showing how kingly lust for power spawned murder, travesty, and tyranny. Lincoln's concept of democracy embodied a distrust of kingly rulers and monarchy.

Shakespeare leveled his characters—king or commoner—and placed them within community. In a world where monarchs ruled, Shakespeare significantly redefined the playing field. Once in the White House, Lincoln in conversation with artist Francis B. Carpenter, as reported by Carpenter, said of Shakespeare, "It matters not to me whether Shakespeare be well or ill acted; with him the thought suffices." The bard's thought was to echo through the politics and policies of President Lincoln.

Lincoln identified a social and political essence in the works of the great bard, but singled out one passage. Carpenter quoted him as saying that "seems to me the choicest part of the play. It is the soliloquy of the king, after the murder. It always struck me as one of the finest touches of nature in the world." Lincoln launched into "O! My offense is rank, it smells to heaven."

As if the mode of his own thought, Lincoln then turned to Shakespeare's *Richard III*, which he then quoted further: "Now is the winter of our discontent made glorious summer by this sun of York; and all the clouds that lour'd upon our house in the deep bosom of the ocean buried." Lincoln may have been contemplating the rivalries of his own day, for he declared, "Now, this is all wrong. Richard, you remember, had been, and was then, plotting the destruction of his brothers, to make room for himself." As Lincoln moved toward the election of 1864, similar plotting in both the North and South confronted him.

Shakespeare proved a tutor for Lincoln as to the nature of ambition and rule.

Just as Shakespeare knocked whatever props remained of the divine right of kings, he used exposure most effectively in bringing royalty down to earth.

Human nature ruled as fault and folly came to light in Shakespeare's poetry. Lincoln perceived the same in the men and circumstances around him.[27]

Squire Bowling Green pushed Lincoln to make a second legislative run. Highly respected in the community, Green knew politics. In 1834, Green and several other Democrats offered to open the way. He pledged to get some Democratic candidates out of the race if Lincoln ran. Lincoln feared this would hamper his friend Stuart. But Stuart told him to run. Stuart said he could and would handle his own race, and he did. Both went on to victory. Lincoln ran a grassroots campaign.

Given that preachers and churches were a major force in frontier politics, Lincoln's lack of any church affiliation was an obstacle. Vigorous in his own defense, he made it clear that he was no scoffer at organized religion. The trust and confidence of Lincoln's network of loyal friends helped him override the handicap. Yet Lincoln professed that he could not understand how any church could fail to condemn slavery or could support a proslavery candidate.

Lincoln, while not a Calvinist, held that the future was predestined. As for his views on church affiliation, he told a congressman, "When any church will inscribe over its altar, as its sole qualification for membership, the Savior's condensed statement of the substance of both law and Gospel, 'Thou shalt love the Lord thy God with all thy heart, and with all thy Soul and with all thy mind, and thy neighbor as thyself,' that church will I join with all my heart and all my soul."[28]

After the election of 1834, Lincoln concentrated on the study of law under the guidance of Stuart. He took to the woods, reading with solitary concentration and becoming all but antisocial. That fall he received his license to practice from the Illinois Supreme Court. In March 1837, Lincoln, then age twenty-eight, with debts over one thousand dollars and only seven dollars to his name, moved from New Salem to Springfield on a horse borrowed from Mentor Graham. Lincoln entered law practice as a partner with Stuart.

Lincoln pulled up at the Springfield general store, where Joshua Speed was clerking. Asking about a bed and bedclothes, he allowed as how he could not pay the seventeen dollars asked. Speed then offered to share his double bed. Lincoln took his saddlebags upstairs, came back down, and delightedly said, "Well, Speed, I'm moved." Thus began Lincoln's closest lifelong friendship, for he and Speed confided in each other when it came to their personal lives as well as their views on politics.[29]

Lincoln was the second-youngest legislator among the members, mostly Southern born. He caught on to the mode of doing business that was heavily dependent upon personal influence. A legislative session rubs across many lines, providing legislators a wide-ranging introduction to the issues of the day, and Lincoln was one to absorb all. Vandalia, the capital, while primitive, outclassed New Salem by a long shot, and came alive during the legislative sessions as liquor flowed freely.

At the legislature, Lincoln struck up his lifelong friendship with Orville H. Browning and Mrs. Browning. Lincoln spent many evenings at the Browning home, talking with Mrs. Browning, who saw in Lincoln attributes that would make for future greatness. Browning, however, was lukewarm toward Lincoln as a presidential candidate. He initially favored Bates in 1860, and did not favor Lincoln's reelection. Browning was elected to serve out the senatorial term of Senator Stephen A. Douglas.

Browning regularly was in and out of Lincoln's White House, often seeking help for his various law clients. Included among the clients, some of questionable loyalty, were those who sought permits to import cotton. In his diary Browning also chronicled his carriage rides with Mary Lincoln. Browning had badly wanted the Supreme Court justiceship that went to Judge David Davis. Browning's diary recorded his activities and his relationship with the Lincolns over the years.

A rather inconspicuous freshman legislator, Lincoln initially followed Stuart's leadership yet keenly studied his colleagues. His colleagues often asked Lincoln to draw up legislation. He wrote reports for the Committee on Public Accounts and Expenditures. His own first bill, to limit jurisdiction of justices of the peace, however, died in the Senate. He did introduce and get passed a measure authorizing a toll bridge over Salt Creek. His increasing skills put him much in demand.

Lincoln wrote anonymous dispatches for the *Sangamon Journal* in Springfield, showing an early and keen understanding of the vital role of newspapers in an era of a partisan press. Lincoln believed that policy based upon the will of the people would prevail. This, in his view, made newspapers a key link and means to educate the electorate and ensure a strong basis for wise policy. As his political skills matured, his mastery of press relations helped promote his political success.

While Lincoln achieved little in his first term, he acquired a reputation for sound judgment and linked into the network of legislators, lobbyists, judges and attorneys. As a Whig he supported the state bank and bonds to fund canal development, especially the Chicago to La Salle Canal connecting the Illinois River and the Great Lakes. Early on he had determined a developing society needed both banking and a medium of exchange for purchase and sale, all of which he supported.

In seeking reelection in 1836, Lincoln said, "I go for all sharing the privileges of the government, who assist in bearing its burthens." He added, "Consequently I go for admitting all whites to the right of suffrage, who pay taxes or bear arms, (by no means excluding females)." It was a time when excluding blacks was hardly an issue, for the Illinois constitution of 1818 limited voting to white male inhabitants. Yet Lincoln made the point that the vote for women would come in due time.

In his run for a second term—more confident than before—Lincoln this time spoke in towns, villages, and rural areas. Whig candidate Robert L. Wilson of Athens praised Lincoln's "skill and tact in offensive and defensive debates, presenting the arguments with great force and ability, and boldly attacking the questions and positions taken by opposing candidates." Wilson added, "He would borrow nothing and never ask favors." Lincoln was mastering the art of politics.[30]

Keeping his mode light, Lincoln gained stature as the leading Whig in his district. He urged internal improvements and advocated they be funded from federal land sales. On August 1, 1836, Lincoln handily won reelection, running well ahead of the Whig ticket. For one who had cut his way, ax in hand, through the wilderness, supporting internal improvements had proven to be his ticket to political success. He had matured as a Whig in the mold of Henry Clay.

Lincoln also denounced capitalists, who "generally act harmoniously and in concert, to fleece the people" and politicians, "a set of men who … are, taken as a mass, at least one long step removed from honest men."

Lincoln added swiftly, "I say this with the greater freedom because, being a politician myself, none can regard it as personal." Lincoln displayed ethical conviction, but knew that among his colleagues were those who abused the system for their personal gain, thus betraying their trust.[31]

Lincoln pressed economic development, knowing it required banks, investment, and capital. He argued that Jackson's subtreasury detrimentally bled capital out of circulation. Lincoln wanted canals and railroads funded, and he had learned that bank deposits provided the capital for urgently needed development loans. This economic lesson would serve Lincoln well as a war president when funding the war machine and industrial development were keys to Civil War victory.

Speaking in 1839 in the hall of the House of Representatives at Springfield, Lincoln summed up the Whig arguments against the subtreasury. As contrasted with a national bank, Lincoln said the subtreasury would "injuriously affect the community by its operation on the circulating medium, be a more expensive fiscal agent, and would be a less secure depository of the public money."

He contended that keeping money in circulation rather than locked up better served the public, noting, "By the Sub-Treasury, the revenue is to be collected, and kept in iron boxes until the government wants it for disbursement; thus robbing the people of the use of it, while government does not itself need it, and while the money is performing no nobler office than of rusting in iron boxes. The natural effect of this change of policy, every one will see, is to reduce the quantity of money in circulation."

Lincoln further explained that the "revenue is to be collected in specie," asserting:

> Now mark what the effect. … By all estimates … there are but between 60 and 80 millions of specie in the United States. The expenditures of the Government for the year 1838 … were 40 millions. Thus … if the whole revenue

> be collected in specie, it will take more than half of all the specie in the nation. … By this means more than half of all the specie … is thrown into the hands of … office-holders, and other public creditors … leaving … 14 1/2 million to get along … with less than one-half the specie …
>
> The general distress thus created, will … be temporary, because whatever change may occur in the quantity of money … time will adjust … but while that adjustment is progressing, all suffer more or less, and very many lose everything that renders life desirable. … What I have been saying as to the effect … relates to the whole country.

Lincoln reviewed the nation's fiscal history and concluded that forty years with the national bank was superior to the period under the Jacksonian sub-treasury system.[32]

The law designating Vandalia the Illinois state capital expired in 1839. Sangamon County politicians wanted the capital in Springfield. Lincoln and Springfield-area legislative colleagues—called the Long Nine because of the height of each—traded votes for internal improvement projects. Their support for a canal or railroad link between Chicago and the Illinois River outflanked legislative competitors from the southern part of the state who opposed the expenditures a move would entail.

The bargain sewed up northern county votes. Lincoln had led bargaining that also loosed a flood of projects throughout the state. He defended the bargain fiercely as a key to the votes needed to move the seat of state government to Springfield. This $14 million appropriation left the state with massive debt and offended many Lincoln friends. Yet he and the Sangamon delegates were honor bound to support it. The debt hung over Illinois until paid off in 1880.[33]

Southern states were calling on Northern states for resolutions expressing that they "highly disapprove of the formation of abolition societies" and calling "the right of property in slaves is sacred to the slave-holding states by the federal government, and they cannot be deprived of that right without their consent." Lincoln and another of the Long Nine, Dan Stone, courageously voted against these policy resolutions even as they passed the House 77–6 and the Senate 18–0.

This doctrine, expressed by South Carolina's John C. Calhoun, held the right of property in slaves as sacred. Lincoln contended this was contrary to the true meaning of the Declaration of Independence and the Constitution. Lincoln and Stone protested, "Slavery is founded on both injustice and bad policy." This was an extremely bold statement of conscience given the overwhelming rejection of antislavery views in south and central Illinois and in the nation generally.

Lincoln and Stone also condemned the abolitionists, stating that their doctrine tended to increase rather than abate the evils of slavery by adding "one hundred fold to the rigors of slavery." Lincoln believed slavery, if it were contained, would die out over time, and he claimed this was the vision of the framers of the Constitution. Abolition was expanding in the North, and people in the South, fearing slave rebellion, were even demanding the hanging of abolitionists.

Lincoln unflinchingly addressed this subject, "The Perpetuation of Our Political Institutions," in 1838 before the Young Men's Lyceum at Springfield. He spoke some three months after a mob at Alton shot and killed the young abolitionist editor, Elijah P. Lovejoy, burning the warehouse where he had his press. Lincoln warned against "increasing disregard for law which pervades this country which substitutes passion for the sober judgments of the courts."

He continued:

> I know the American people are much attached to their government. … I know they could suffer much for its sake and would not think to exchange it. Yet, notwithstanding

> of this, if the laws be continually despised and disregarded, if their rights to be secure in their persons and property, are held by no better tenure than the caprice of a mob, the alienation of their affections from the Government is the natural consequence; and to that, sooner or later, it comes. …
>
> When I so pressingly urge a strict observance of all the laws, let me not be understood as saying there are no bad laws, nor that grievances may not arise, for the redress of which, no legal provisions have been made. … But I do mean to say, that, although bad laws … should be repealed as soon as possible, still while they continue in force, for the sake of example, they should be religiously observed. … There is no grievance … a fit object of redress by mob law.

Lincoln, strongly grounded in his own family heritage, turned to the powerful influence the "scenes of the revolution had upon the passions of the people, as distinguished from their judgment" and which were fading with time. They—the revolutionary forebears—"were the pillars of the temple of liberty; and now, that they have crumbled away, that temple must fall unless we, their descendants, supply their places with other pillars, hewn from the solid quarry of sober reason."[34]

Meanwhile, Lincoln's law partner Stuart became a candidate for Congress. In 1838, while Stuart ran for Congress, Lincoln ran for the legislature, yet did a fair amount of the heavy lifting, hitting hard at Stuart's opponent, Stephen A. Douglas, and the Democrats in Washington. With interest running high and hard times blamed on Democrats, Lincoln had an open field. Lincoln campaigned for Stuart while he ran for reelection. Lincoln managed it all, including most of their law practice.

Lincoln voraciously read newspapers and letters and wrote as "A Conservative" for the *Sangamon Journal*. Those who opposed President Martin Van Buren's economic policies called themselves Conservatives.

Thus, Lincoln branded Douglas a radical and called his positions utopian. Lincoln had a major responsibility to advocate and clarify the views of his party on issues. Here we see the genesis of two decades of sparring between the two men.

Most particularly Lincoln singled out "the Utopian scheme of an exclusive specie currency, involving the destruction of all banks—and the dangerous doctrine that all incorporated institutions, and all contracts between the State and its citizens, can be changed or annulled at the pleasure of the Legislature." Both Stuart and Lincoln won in 1838 and again in 1840, as Lincoln matured into an Illinois Whig leader. Douglas angrily protested the assault on his private, moral, and political character.

Lincoln again spoke against the sub-treasury scheme adopted after the Bank of the United States charter was not renewed, detailing allegations of corruption. Lincoln fought a bill to throw off the fourteen northern counties of Illinois to Wisconsin. Lincoln contended that Illinois needed a port on the Great Lakes as well as on the Ohio and Mississippi rivers. Meeting judges, lawyers, public officials, office holders, and politicians expanded his network and enhanced his skills as a politician.[35]

A trust was developing between Lincoln and a man nine years younger, William H. Herndon, who also had clerked and boarded with him and with Joshua Speed, and who aspired to become a lawyer. All three belonged to the lyceum of men who met and read what they had written, focused on current issues. In the election of 1840, Lincoln took the stump for Whig presidential candidate William Henry Harrison, often speaking opposite Stephen A. Douglas.

During the election of 1840, women emerged overwhelmingly on the Whig side as participants. Political stirrings among women, although they could not run for political office or vote, were encouraged in the Whig heartland, as women assisted in rallies, parades, and picnics, and with home-made banners. While Lincoln had previously made a bow to the women while campaigning, Democrats decried Whig efforts, saying political participation was not an activity for a respectable woman.

Whigs carried the state for Harrison, but Democrats took the legislature, relying on imported Irish canal-zone workers, whose votes were questioned. The legislature next approved a Douglas bill that threw out four circuit court judges and set up five new state supreme court judges. Douglas was named to the state Supreme Court, which promptly ruled the canal-zone votes legal. Whigs, Lincoln included, charged the independent judiciary had been destroyed by Douglas's legislation.[36]

CHAPTER II

THE AMBITIOUS MARY TODD, MARRIAGE, AND CONGRESS

Among the Long Nine was Ninian W. Edwards, son of the first Illinois governor, US senator, land speculator, and merchant. The Edwards family had come from Maryland through the Cumberland Gap to Kentucky and then to Illinois. Ninian had married Elizabeth Todd, a daughter of Robert Todd of Lexington, Kentucky, whose younger sister, Mary Todd, came to live with them. Todd's grandparents had fought in the American Revolution, and Robert Todd was a captain in the War of 1812.

Lincoln met the twenty-two-year-old, plump, and sharp-tongued Mary Todd, aggressive, well educated, and politically savvy. Mary spoke and read French and burned with political ambition that rivaled Lincoln's. Mary was decisive, and, as Elizabeth Edwards pointed out, Lincoln hung on her words. The aspiring Mary sensed that this "tall Kentuckian" would be most likely to achieve the ambitions both shared. Mary had known the famed Henry Clay, whom both admired.

In 1841, Abraham Lincoln and Mary Todd agreed to marry. But the Edwards, Ninian and Elizabeth, told Mary that Lincoln was lacking in social graces. They contended an engagement to Lincoln would result in throwing her life away. Mary defended Lincoln, arguing that he had an extremely bright future. Edwards sowed doubt with Lincoln, who backed away from the relationship. Mulling over his feelings toward Mary, he said telling her he loved her while doubtful was wrong.

"The social ideals of the Edwardses differed radically from Lincoln's. Ninian W. Edwards 'was naturally and constitutionally an aristocrat,' wrote one of his colleagues in the state legislature, 'and he hated democracy … as the devil is said to hate holy water.' There was no meeting of minds between him and the man who was to become the embodiment of American democracy."

For some months, Lincoln walked the streets in melancholy, devastated.

Lincoln knew he had failed to keep his pledged word; he had betrayed himself and hurt Mary. Buried in melancholy, he turned to Dr. Anson G. Henry and corresponded with a Cincinnati doctor whom Dr. Henry had suggested. His whole self-worth was on the line. Lincoln determined to write Mary, telling her that he did not love her and therefore could not marry her as he had pledged he would.[37]

Joshua Speed would have none of it. Throwing the letter in the fireplace, he told Lincoln, "If you have the courage of manhood, go see Mary yourself; tell her if you do not love her, tell her so; tell her you will not marry her."

Lincoln went to see Mary and after an hour returned, telling Speed, "When I told Mary I did not love her, she burst into tears and almost springing from her chair and wringing her hands as if in agony, said something about the deceiver being himself deceived. It was too much for me. I found the tears trickling down my own cheeks. I caught her in my arms and kissed her."

Lincoln had recommitted himself, but had yet to reconcile with Mary to the point where they were together again. In agony, Lincoln journeyed to Kentucky to spend time with Speed and his family. Speed's mother presented him an Oxford Bible. Soon to marry, Speed too approached marriage with trepidation. Lincoln, back in Illinois, offered advice.

After his marriage, Speed professed happiness, encouraging Lincoln, who wrote, "Since then (the fatal 1st of January, 1841) it seems to me I should have been entirely happy, but for the never-absent idea that there is one still unhappy whom I have contributed to make so." Then Lincoln revealed a great deal about his own state of mind: "That kills my soul." In another letter to Speed, Lincoln referred to Mary Todd anew when he said the subject continued painful for him:

> In that ability you know I once prided myself as the only or chief gem of my character; that gem I lost—how and where you know too well. I have not yet regained it; and until I do, I cannot trust myself in any matter of much importance. I believe now that had you understood my case at the time as well as I understood yours afterward, by the aid you would have given me I should have sailed through clear, but that does not now afford me sufficient confidence to begin.[38]

Mrs. Simeon Francis, the *Sangamon Journal* editor's wife, also believed Lincoln had fame ahead and that her friend Mary Todd was an accomplished and brilliant woman and a good match. She brought the two together in her parlor and said, "Be friends again."

That summer of 1841, Lincoln shifted into a law partnership with Stephen T. Logan, a rather unkempt but extremely able lawyer. Logan proved the able mentor well schooled in the law that Lincoln then needed.[39]

At this time, James Shields challenged Lincoln to a duel over an "insulting" letter allegedly written by Mary Todd and her friend, Julia Jayne, for which Lincoln took responsibility. Lincoln, given the choice of weapons, chose broad swords. Lincoln and Shields journeyed across the Mississippi to Missouri with their seconds. This near duel was avoided as their seconds negotiated a solution each accepted. Lincoln never would discuss the matter but it taught him not to condone sarcastic letters.[40]

Another wedding was set—one without delay—for November 4, 1842. Lincoln ran into Ninian W. Edwards, telling him he and Mary were to be married that day. Edwards retorted that Mary was his ward and would be married at his house. Asking Mary if it were true, she said yes, and preparations got under way at the Edwards home. Elizabeth Edwards told Mary if she insisted on a wedding that day they would make the best of it, adding, "Do not forget that you are a Todd."

Groomsmen James H. Matheny and Beverly Powell and bridesmaids Julia Jayne and Ann Rodney, with a handful of family and friends, gathered. To preside, Edwards brought in the Reverend Charles Dresser, rector of the Episcopal Church whose rectory the Lincolns later purchased as their first house. The newly married Abe and Mary first boarded at the Globe Tavern. They purchased the Dresser house not too long after, as Mary was not well gaited for boardinghouse living.[41]

Their first son, named Robert after Mary's father, was born August 1, 1843. A second, Edward Baker Lincoln, was born in 1846 and named for Lincoln's good friend Edward Baker. Yet Lincoln—who like others thought nothing of riding his horse and buggy thirty miles a day—still looked like a farmer. He continued to milk and fork hay for their cow as Mary cooked and laundered, helped by a hired girl when she had one, although Mary's quick temper resulted in a rapid turnover.

Lincoln, with a wife and family, decided against another run for the legislature after 1842, turning aggressively to the law. A Kentucky slave owner, Robert Matson, bought land near the cabin of Thomas Lincoln. Matson brought slaves from Kentucky, returning them after harvest and bringing others. He kept a free Negro, Anthony Bryant, as overseer and brought Bryant's wife and four children. Bryant's common-law wife and housekeeper one day threatened Bryant's wife, Jane.

Bryant heard the exchange and raced to Oakland, where he found Hiram Rutherford, a doctor, and Gideon M. Ashmore. That night, Bryant, with his wife and four children, fled to the Ashmore home.

Matson testified before Justice of the Peace William Gilmore that Bryant and his family were Matson's property. They were arrested and locked up in the county jail. Matson hired Usher F. Linder, a former legislator, to represent him. Orlando B. Ficklin was retained on behalf of Bryant and his family.

Gilman said he lacked jurisdiction and turned the Bryants over to the sheriff. Matson, however, was arrested and convicted for living unlawfully with a woman not his wife. Matson sued Rutherford and Ashmore, asking damages for unlawfully holding his slave property. Rutherford asked Lincoln to represent him, but Lincoln said he had been consulted by Linder and therefore could not represent Rutherford. Eventually Lincoln freed himself, but Rutherford then declined his services.

Rutherford eventually hired Charles H. Constable as his lawyer. Matson expected to win by showing he had no plans to locate the family in Illinois. Matson added Lincoln who made an intense inquiry into the facts, made no attack on the defense and admitted outright that if Matson had brought the Bryant family to Illinois to work them as slaves they were entitled to freedom. State supreme court justices William Wilson and Samuel Treat were the trial judges who heard the case.

Carl Sandburg in *The Prairie Years* quotes a Coles Country lawyer, D. F. McIntyre, who reported Lincoln asserting that the whole case hinged on one point:

> Were these Negroes passing over and crossing the State, and thus, as the law contemplates, in transitu, or were they actually located by consent of their master? If only crossing the state the law did not free them, but if located, even indefinitely, by the consent of their owner, their emancipation logically followed. …
>
> Every person in the court room was curious to hear what reasons he could or would assign, on behalf of this

> slaveholder, to induce the court to send this mother and her four children back into lives of slavery. But strange to say Lincoln did not once touch upon the question of the right of Matson. ... His main contention was that the question of the right of the Negroes to their freedom could only be determined by a regular habeas corpus proceeding.

"Mr. Lincoln," Judge Wilson asked, "your objection is simply to the form of the action by which ... this question should be tried, is it not?"

"Yes sir," he said.

Judge Wilson then asked, "Now, if this case was being tried on issue joined in a habeas corpus, and it appear there, as it does here, that this slave owner had brought this mother and her children, voluntarily, from ... Kentucky, and had settled them ... do you think as a matter of law that they did not thereby become free?"

Lincoln replied, "No, sir, I am not prepared to deny that they did."

Linder argued that the slaves were Matson's chattel property, protected by the federal Constitution, and could not be taken from him. Lincoln did not. The court then declared Jane Bryant and her four children "are discharged from the custody as well of the Sheriff as of Robert Matson and all persons claiming them as slaves and remain free from all servitude whatever ... from hence forward and forever." This allowed her to return to her husband, who already was free.

Matson left and did not pay Lincoln.

The bulk of some five thousand cases Lincoln handled were mostly mundane matters that involved divorce, debt, contract, and property issues. Some attorneys, such as Ohio's Salmon P. Chase and Lyman Trumbull, did handle many cases involving blacks. Lincoln devoted his law practice to run-of-the-mill cases that came his way. Six years before,

Lincoln had won freedom for a slave girl sold in Illinois, but he did not, as Chase did, focus intently on such cases.[42]

Lincoln and his law partner, Stephen T. Logan, both aspired to run for Congress. Their partnership ended, as Logan wanted to bring in his twenty-year-old son. Lincoln had benefited because his knowledge of the law matured while studying under Logan.

Lincoln approached William Herndon about a partnership, to the younger man's surprise. Lincoln said, "Billy, I can trust you if you can trust me." These two, of very different temperament, shook hands and hung out a shingle in Springfield.[43]

In the election of 1844, Lincoln campaigned hard for Kentucky senator Henry Clay, the Whig candidate for president. Mary Lincoln had known Clay as an idolized neighbor since she was raised in Lexington. She even told him that she expected someday to be Mrs. President. While Clay did not win, Lincoln emerged stronger than ever as a Whig leader. Lincoln not only spoke in favor of Clay but on behalf of his own reelection to a fourth term in the Illinois House of Representatives.

A proponent of the mercantilist economy, Clay had campaigned for an increase in tariffs to foster industry in the nation, the use of federal funding for infrastructure, and a strong national bank. Clay opposed the annexation of Texas, fearing it would inject the slavery issue into the forefront of politics. Clay opposed both the Mexican American War and Manifest Destiny. His positions, coupled with the fact that he was a slave owner even though opposed to slavery, cost him the election.[44]

Lincoln, in 1843, —egged on by Mary Lincoln—expressed a desire to run for Congress as an entry point into national politics. She aspired to be another Dolley Madison, whose first husband was a Todd. Lincoln wrote to Richard S. Thomas, a Whig lawyer who in Virginia, IL, "Now if you hear any one say that Lincoln don't want to go to Congress, I wish you as a personal friend of mine, would tell him you have reason to believe he is mistaken. The truth is, I would like to go very much."[45]

Voters had sent his former law partner, Stuart, to Washington in the two previous elections. Thus, it appeared whoever received the Whig nomination would win. Both John J. Hardin and Edward D. Baker also wanted the nomination. Lincoln held Baker in high regard, as his second son was named for Baker. English born and an exceptionally good political speaker, Baker and Lincoln enjoyed a warm friendship. Both men had lifted themselves from their early poverty.

The two strenuously sought the endorsement of Sangamon County Whigs. Baker outmaneuvered Lincoln, much to the chagrin of Mary Lincoln, who berated her husband for not fighting hard enough. Thus, in successive congressional races, Lincoln supported Hardin, then Baker. Baker later became a US senator from Oregon, immediately volunteered when the Civil War broke out, and was killed fighting at Balls Bluff. Hardin had been killed in the Mexican War.

The Kentucky-born Hardin, a third cousin of Mary Lincoln, was also popular with the Whigs in the district. Hardin's father had been a US senator. While Lincoln relished his captaincy in the Black Hawk War, Hardin had the rank of major general. He not only studied law at Transylvania University in Lexington, Kentucky, he had clerked for the Kentucky supreme court chief justice. Unlike Baker and Lincoln, Hardin was hardly an orator, yet he had a quick wit and a keen mind.

As it turned out, Hardin captured the Whig congressional nomination for 1844. As Lincoln defined it they had an understanding that Hardin would run in 1844, Baker in 1846, and Lincoln in 1848, with each to serve a single term. This was embodied in the Pekin resolution adopted at the Whig convention of 1843 in Pekin, Illinois. Hardin evinced a desire to run again in the election of 1848, but Lincoln faced down Hardin in the campaign and won the nomination and election.[46]

Lincoln's ensuing nomination for Congress pitted him against Peter Cartwright, an elderly Methodist evangelist circuit rider. Cartwright branded Lincoln a high-toned Episcopalian and deist whom he claimed had said, "Christ was a bastard." Lincoln defeated the preacher politician handily. His friendships throughout the district gave him an overwhelming advantage. In response to various charges, including infidelity, made by Cartwright, Lincoln responded:

> A charge having got into circulation … that I am an open scoffer of Christianity, I have by the advice of some friends concluded to notice the subject in this form. That I am not a member of any Christian Church, is true; but I have never denied the truth of the Scriptures, and I have never spoken with intentional disrespect of religion in general, or any denomination of Christians in particular. …
>
> I do not think I could myself, be brought to support a man … whom I knew to be an open enemy of, and scoffer at, religion. Leaving the higher matter of eternal consequences, between him and his Maker, I still do not think any man has the right thus to insult the feelings, and injure the morals of the community in which he may live. If … guilty of such … I should blame no man who should condemn me … but I do blame those … who falsely put such a charge … against me.[47]

At the age of thirty-seven, Lincoln went to Washington, a newly elected member of Congress. He was the only Whig from Illinois at the time. It was a family journey. The Lincolns traveled to St. Louis, Missouri, and then by boat to Lexington, Kentucky, where they spent time with Mary's family. They crossed the Allegheny Mountains to Washington. Lincoln took the oath and was seated as a member of Congress. Mary hoped to fulfill her childhood dream by becoming a Washington hostess.

The war with Mexico was nearly over, with Mexico badly beaten. The United States acquired the southwest portion of the continent from the

Texas line to the California coast. As Clay had forecast issues around statehood and slavery dominated in Congress. Lincoln experienced firsthand the power of the slave belt, as members from the South voted nearly unanimously on issues affecting slavery. He also detected a strong sentiment for the Union, but within bounds of slave power rule.

Moving from a shabby hotel, the Lincolns chose Mrs. Ann Sprigg's boardinghouse on the current site of the Library of Congress. Mary Lincoln wanted a house, given her ambitions, which she traced from Dolly Madison. Mary's ambitions to be part of city's social life were thwarted by the boardinghouse quarters, and Mary left for Lexington with the boys. Lincoln allowed as she had hindered him some but wrote he missed her.[48]

Eight members of Congress roomed in Ann Sprigg's house, including Joshua R. Giddings of Ohio, the most radical antislavery member of the House. Lincoln was a hit with colleagues and made a quantum leap in his knowledge of national issues. A prominent abolitionist boarder, Theodore Dwight Weld, related that Mrs. Sprigg, not a slaveholder, hired eight colored servants, all free except three buying freedom. White men kidnapped and sold south one, angering the borders.[49]

Legislation for emancipation in the District of Columbia, including Lincoln's more modest bill, went nowhere. Lincoln's main effort was aimed at President James K. Polk and the legitimacy of the Mexican War. Lincoln laid down an eight-point interlocutory asking the president to inform the House by responding to each, thus seeking to know if the spot where the war began actually was Texas or Mexican territory. Polk simply ignored the interlocutory.[50]

While Whigs generally stood with him, Lincoln caught the sharp edge of criticism, specifically back home in his district, which had sent to war his two predecessors, Hardin and Baker. William Herndon, his law partner and a Whig, was among the critics. Lincoln responded, "You fear that you and I disagree about the war. I regret this, not from any fear that we shall remain disagreed, after you have read this letter, but because if you misunderstand, I fear other good friends will also.

"That vote affirms that the war was unnecessarily and unconstitutionally commenced by the President; and I will stake my life, that if you had been in my place, you would have voted just as I did." Lincoln had voted for Massachusetts Representative George Ashmun's amendment affirming the view. "Would you have voted what you felt you knew to be a lie? I know you would not. … You are compelled to speak; and your only alternative is to tell the truth or tell a lie."[51]

Writing Herndon, Lincoln said, "I just take up my pen to say, that Mr. Stephens of Georgia, a little slim, pale-faced, consumptive man, with a voice like Logan's has just concluded the very best speech, of an hour's length, I ever heard. My old, withered, dry eyes are full of tears yet." Back in the district in a state heavily oriented toward Manifest Destiny, Lincoln's opposition to the war virtually assured that he could not be reelected and would return to his law practice and not to Congress.[52]

Georgia's Alexander Stephens, later the Confederate vice president, had declared, "One of the strangest … circumstances attending this war is, that though it has lasted upwards of eight months, at a cost of many millions of dollars, and the sacrifices of many valuable lives … no man can tell for what object it is prosecuted. And it is to be doubted whether any man, save the President and his Cabinet, knows the real and secret designs that provoked its existence." Lincoln shared this point of view.[53]

Congress debated the indemnity Mexico would pay for the war, which had cost the nation 27,000 dead and $27 million. A newly appointed senator, West Point graduate Jefferson Davis, still on crutches from his war wound and firm in his views, declared, "I hold that in a just war we conquered the larger portion of Mexico and that to it we have a title which has been regarded as valid ever since man existed in a social condition—the title of conquest." Davis wanted an empire extending south.

Davis, on March 17, 1848, declared, "It seems to me that that question is now, how much shall we keep, how much shall we give up, and that Mexico cedes nothing to us." Senator Davis's bill asked Congress to fund ten regiments to garrison the cities and provinces of Mexico until Congress decided what to do with them. It passed the Senate 29–19, but Whigs in the House Military Affairs Committee killed it, aided by Georgia's Howell Cobb and Robert Toombs, who differed sharply with Davis.[54]

Lincoln witnessed the South solid on all measure hitting slavery, but not solid on measures hinging on succession. Not keen on advancing the "fences" to acquire territory, Pennsylvania representative David Wilmot introduced a legislative rider that declared any territory acquired in the Mexican War treaty should be free and not slave territory. Lincoln cast his aye vote repeatedly during his term although the Wilmot provision failed. Slave power votes prevented passage.[55]

With Illinois firmly in support of the war, Lincoln risked his political career challenging President Polk. He demanded the president prove that the spot where the war started was not Mexican territory. He called the slave-owning Polk "a bewildered, confounded, and miserably perplexed man." Lincoln was suspicious when Polk backed off of the "fifty-four forty or fight" Oregon territory/Canadian border but supported Southern efforts to extend the cotton belt to California.

Within the White House, two men—Secretary of State James Buchanan and Secretary of the Treasury Robert J. Walker—strongly urged President Polk to take all of Mexico. Lincoln probably did not know this. He repeatedly confronted the national issues in the context of slave power dominance. Lincoln devoted much of his time to research and study in the Library of Congress. Union sentiment he found among Southern Whigs may have led him later to overestimate their loyalty.[56]

South Carolina senator John C. Calhoun was fading, as Lincoln observed, and the militaristic Davis was being groomed as his heir.

Davis viewed slavery as "a common-law right and property in the service of man." Davis made his views clear,. When President Polk sent Davis a commission, brigadier general of volunteers, Davis returned it, contending only states could grant the commission. As a senator, Davis fiercely advocated southern expansion and states' rights.[57]

Another member in Congress, former president John Quincy Adams, led the fight against the gag rule by which petitions calling for an end to slavery were deemed "un-received." Vigorous for his age, he took a daily swim in the Potomac River. Firm in opposition to slavery, Adams had been a senator, a diplomat, and, for seventeen years since his presidency, a member of Congress. In 1848, as he rose to speak, Adams suddenly keeled over and died. Lincoln was a pallbearer.[58]

Lincoln joined several Whig colleagues to promote General Zachary Taylor for the presidential nomination over Henry Clay. Lincoln had gone to the Whig national convention in Philadelphia, where he saw Taylor nominated with help from Illinois delegates. As he told Herndon, "By many, and often, it had been said they would not abide the nomination of Taylor, but since the deed has been done, they are fast falling in, and in my opinion, we shall have a most overwhelming, glorious triumph."

Lincoln stumped for Taylor, beginning in June and continuing right up to election day. Lincoln campaigned throughout New England. Taylor's opponent, Lewis Cass, had a varied career as a general in the War of 1812, territorial governor of Michigan, Secretary of War under President Andrew Jackson, and United States senator. He resigned to run for president, then went back into the Senate from 1845 to 1848, and in 1856 entered Buchanan's cabinet as Secretary of State. Cass died in 1866.[59]

On a swing through New England, Lincoln pitched the Whig ticket, as did then New York governor and soon to be senator William H. Seward. At a hotel, Lincoln told Seward, "I reckon you are right. We have got to deal with this slavery question, and got to give much more attention to it." On the trains, he saw firsthand the foundries, factories, mills, and shops that enriched the Middle Atlantic states and New England. He studied the political terrain, stopping in Albany to meet Thurlow Weed.[60]

In Illinois, as the state's foremost Whig spokesperson, Lincoln stumped for Taylor. When Taylor won, Lincoln learned a hard political lesson about patronage. Lincoln's bid for Illinois land commissioner failed. The job went to Justin Butterfield, who had not aided Taylor's cause but had the support of Daniel Webster. Once in the White House, Lincoln did not make the same mistake. He rewarded friends and political allies, specifically ensuring that members of Congress were consulted.

Lincoln, given his legislative experience in Illinois, was disappointed because he failed to influence congressional colleagues as he had anticipated. Yet he had been admitted to practice before the Supreme Court. But he was chagrined because many members spoke with greater effect. Back home, Lincoln delved into Euclid's geometry. He studied the six elements and learned what *demonstrate* meant. This provided a philosophical outlook consistent with his pragmatic nature.[61]

CHAPTER III

THE 1850S—A RESURGENT POLITICIAN FIGHTING THE KANSAS-NEBRASKA ACT

President Millard Fillmore signed the Compromise of 1850 giving Texas statehood, organizing New Mexico Territory with popular sovereignty, organizing Utah as a territory, and admitting California as a free state. It also enacted the Fugitive Slave Law and banned District of Columbia slave trade. The authors were Whig Senators Henry Clay, Kentucky, and Daniel Webster, Massachusetts. Young senator Stephen A. Douglas, a Democrat from Illinois, managed the bill for Clay and Webster.

Clay designed the Compromise of 1850 to bridge the North-South divide. When Clay died, Lincoln, giving an eloquent eulogy in 1852 in Springfield, focused on Clay's actions on the question of domestic slavery. Clay, Lincoln noted, was led by his feelings and his judgment to oppose both extremes, North and South. With the nation both prosperous and powerful, he asked, "Could it have been quite all it has been, and is, and is to be, without Henry Clay?" Lincoln then declared:

> He ever was, on principle and in feeling, opposed to slavery. ... He did not perceive that on a question of human rights the Negroes were to be excepted from the human race. And yet Mr. Clay was the owner of slaves. Cast into life where slavery was already widely spread and deeply seated, he did not perceive, as I think no wise man has perceived,

> how it could be at once eradicated, without producing a greater evil, even to the cause of human liberty itself. …
>
> Those who would shiver into fragments the Union of these States; tear to tatters its now venerated constitution; and even burn the last copy of the Bible rather that slavery should continue a single hour, together with their more halting sympathizers, have received, and are receiving their just execration. … But I would also array his name … against the opposite extreme … who, for the sake of perpetuating slavery … ridicule … the declaration that "all men are created equal."[62]

This was a time when attitudes against slavery were firming in the North. In the fall of 1852, Dr. Martin Anderson was called to the University of Rochester. A New Englander and former editor of the *Baptist New York Recorder*, he called repeatedly in the *Rochester American* for restraint on men who were dividing society over the slavery issue. Although he also opposed the institution of slavery, he called upon abolitionists to show respect for the Constitution and the law.

The *Rochester American* called for the civilization of slaveholders, educating them to learn that "degrading influence" perpetuated slavery. The paper claimed a rising standard of common schools would turn slaveholders into freedom-lovers and foreigners into true patriots. Yet the *Rochester American*, like so many, said the value of education ran out before it reached the Negro, arguing that hostility combined with prejudice and cruelty required that the freed slaves be resettled in Africa.[63]

A newly born Republican party developed as former Whigs, anti-Nebraska Democrats, Free Soilers, and Nativists banded together under the Republican banner. Lincoln was concerned whether the new party could include the Nativists without alienating immigrants, Catholics, and others, remained a Whig initially.

Aroused by the passage of the Kansas-Nebraska Act of 1854, Lincoln too joined a crescendo of protest with a rousing speech at Peoria, Illinois, on October 16, 1854.

"This is the repeal of the Missouri Compromise," Lincoln declared. "I think … it is wrong; wrong in its direct effect, letting slavery into Kansas and Nebraska—and wrong it its prospective principle, allowing it to spread to every other part of the wide world, when men can be found inclined to take it." Lincoln feared the repeal of the Missouri Compromise would result in spreading slavery across the nation rather than heading slavery for extinction as he had previously expected.[64]

Lincoln ultimately signed on with the Republicans. Once aboard, he swiftly took a leadership role. The primary objective was legislation that would prevent slavery in the territories. This platform would undergird and unite the diverse and rapidly growing new party, and widen its embrace. This reflected Lincoln's lifelong conviction against the spread of slavery. It denied the Southern argument that slaves were property and could not be barred from the territories.

In Chicago on December 10, 1856, Lincoln took up the mantra: "The Central Idea of the Republic: Let past differences, as nothing be; and with steady eye on the real issue, let us re-inaugurate the good old 'central ideas' of the Republic. … The human heart is with us—God is with us. We shall again be able not to declare, that 'all States as States, are equal,' but to renew the broader, better declaration, including both these and much more, that 'all men are created equal.'"[65]

In the 1856 election, Republicans swept state offices. Yet the state of Illinois gave Buchanan a plurality in the presidential race, and the ruling slave power Democrats retained their hold on the nation. Lincoln scolded Buchanan and ridiculed outgoing president Franklin Pierce, declaring:

> Our government rests in public opinion. Whoever can change public opinion, can change the government, practically just

> so much. Public opinion … has a "central idea" … from which minor thoughts radiate.
>
> That "central idea" in our political public opinion, at the beginning was and, until recently, has continued to be "the equality of men." And although it was always submitted patiently to whatever of inequality there seemed to be as a matter of actual necessity, its constant working has been a steady progress towards the practical equality of all men. The late Presidential election was a struggle, by one party, to discard that central idea, and to substitute … that slavery is right.[66]

At Springfield, Illinois, on June 26, 1857, Lincoln said, "There is a natural disgust in the minds of nearly all white people, to the idea of an indiscriminate amalgamation of the white and black races. … Judge Douglas evidently is basing his chief hope, on the chances of being able to appropriate the benefit of the disgust to himself. … He finds the Republicans insisting that the Declaration of Independence includes ALL men, black as well as white; and … he boldly denies that it includes Negroes."

Lincoln charged that Douglas clung to that hope as a drowning man to the last plank.

> [He] proceeds to argue gravely that all who contend it does do so only because they want to vote and eat, and marry with Negroes … that they cannot be consistent else. Now I protest against that counterfeit logic which concludes that, because I do not want a black woman for a slave I must necessarily want her for a wife. I need not have her for either; I can just leave her alone.
>
> In some respects she is not my equal; but in her natural right to eat the bread she earns with her own hands, without asking leave of anyone else, she is my equal and the equal of

> all others. Taney, and Douglas, contend the founding fathers did not include Negroes as equal. I think the authors of that notable instrument intended to include all men, but they did not intend to declare all men equal in all respects.

Lincoln continued, reiterating consistently his key principle:

> They did not mean to say all were equal in color, size, intellect, moral development, or social capacity. They defined with tolerable directness … in what respects they did consider all men created equal—equal in "certain inalienable" rights, among which are life, liberty, and the pursuit of happiness. This they said, and this meant. They did not mean to assert the obvious untruth, and all were then actually enjoying that equality, nor yet, that they were about to confer it. …
>
> They meant simply to declare the right, so that enforcement of it might follow. … They meant to set up a standard maxim for free society … familiar to all, and revered by all; constantly looked to, constantly labored for, and even through never perfectly attained, constantly approximated, and thereby constantly spreading and deepening its influence, and augmenting the happiness and value of life to all people. … They knew the proneness of prosperity to breed tyrants.[67]

Lincoln used the six elements of Euclidean logic he had mastered as a framework for analysis of issues both in law and in politics. Fragments of a May 18, 1858, speech illustrated this coalescing and articulation of his philosophy. He had spoken alongside such notables as the Honorable John M. Palmer, Col. Mark W. Delahay, and the Honorable J. Gillespie. The *Alton Weekly Courier* reported the positions of the Republican party were set at the Madison County Republican meeting.

While the speakers did not fully agree, they were unanimous in their opposition to the fraudulent attempts of the administration and the slave power contingent to force institutions upon a free people against their consent. This speech contained seeds of the House Divided speech. Lincoln attacked the Dred Scott decision, in which Chief Justice Roger Taney had asserted, first, that a Negro could not sue in the US courts, and second, that Congress could not prohibit slavery in the territories.

Lincoln, named the Republican candidate for the US Senate, gave his House Divided speech at the close of the Republican state convention, June 16, 1858. This was a defining speech—one some had warned him not to give. He defined fundamental policy and articulated his views. Enunciating both the givens and what he would seek, he explained, "If we could first know where we are, and whither we are tending, we could then better judge what to do, and how to do it."

"The House Divided speech," the late Stanford University professor Don E. Fehrenbacher wrote in *Prelude to Greatness: Lincoln in the 1850s*, "represents one of those moments of synthesis which embody the past and illumine the future. Lincoln, who revered his country's historical tradition, believed that the cause he embraced pointed the way to a fuller realization of the ideals upon which the republic had been built—those fundamental to the nation. Enjoying an advantage which accrues especially to founders of new political movements, he experienced little difficulty in squaring partisan commitments with his moral convictions."

In a crucial judgment, Fehrenbacher explained, "But if Lincoln had satisfied himself that his personal ambition accorded with the welfare of his party, he was equally certain that nothing other than unadulterated Republicanism could rescue the nation from the peril into which it had fallen. … In his view, the Republican program offered the only solution to the problems of slavery and sectionalism because it alone recognized the tension between moral conviction and constitutional guarantees, and yielded … to either as the other would allow."

The net result, in Fehrenbacher's view, gave Lincoln a unique option: "He was confronted with no painful choices between expediency and priorities." And it put him in sharp contrast with the position taken by Douglas:

> Douglas insisted … the concept of ultimate extinction conflicted with the promise not to attack slavery in the Southern states. … To Lincoln the two propositions were like lines extending into the future, seemingly parallel, but capable of being brought together gradually and gently. Convinced that slavery was wrong, yet willing to settle for a promise of ultimate extinction, he believed an established policy of restriction would incorporate that promise and bring peace to the nation.[68]

Lincoln postulated, "We are now into the fifth year, since a policy was initiated, with the avowed object, and confident promise, of putting an end to slavery agitation. Under the operation of that policy, that agitation has not only not ceased, but has constantly augmented."

Then Lincoln specified exactly what the situation required and what it would mean: "In my opinion, it will not cease, until a crisis shall have been reached, and passed. A house divided against itself cannot stand. I believe this government cannot endure, permanently half slave and half free. I do not expect the Union to be dissolved—I do not expect it will cease to be divided. It will become all one thing, or all the other."

Lincoln's fundamental conviction was that the Union was the touchstone of constitutional democracy, put in place in opposition to a monarchical world as a beacon of hope, which included putting slavery on the road to ultimate extinction.

In his analysis as to outcome, Lincoln declared, "Either the opponents of slavery, will arrest the further spread of it, and place it where the public mind shall rest in the belief that it is in course of ultimate extinction; or its advocates will push it forward, till it shall become alike lawful in all the States, old as well as new—North as well as South." His expectation that political leaders of the South would equally value the preservation of the Union fell short of the mark.

Lincoln turned to the negative developed in the "machinery" of the Kansas-Nebraska legislation and the Supreme Court's Dred Scott decision: "The new year of 1854 found slavery excluded from more than half the States by State Constitutions, and from most of the national territory by Congressional prohibition. Four days later commenced the struggle, which ended in repealing the Congressional prohibition. This opened the national territory to slavery; and was the first point gained."

Regarding squatter sovereignty, he quoted the legislation: "It being the true intent and meaning of this act not to legislate slavery into any Territory of State, nor exclude it therefrom; but to leave the people thereof perfectly free to form and regulate their domestic institutions in their own way, subject only to the Constitution of the United States. … 'But,' said opponents, 'let us be more specific—let us amend the bill … to expressly declare that the people of the territory may exclude slavery.' 'Not we,' said the measure's supporter, who voted it down."

The Dred Scott case arose involving the case of a black's freedom. His owner had taken him into a free state and then a territory covered by the congressional prohibition. Senator Trumbull, on the floor, asked Senator Douglas, the leading Nebraska bill proponent, if the people of a territory could exclude slavery from their state. He elicited this answer: "That is a question for the Supreme Court." The Supreme Court, as apportioned, was anchored in districts that favored the South.

"The election came. Mr. Buchanan was elected, and the endorsement, such as it was, secured. That was the second point gained. The endorsement, however, fell short of a clear popular majority … and so … was not overwhelmingly reliable and satisfactory. … The Presidential inauguration came, and still no decision of the court; but the incoming president, in his inaugural address, fervently exhorted the people to abide by the forthcoming decision, whatever it might be. Then … the decision came," Lincoln asserted, adding:

> The reputed author of the Nebraska bill finds an early occasion to make a speech … endorsing the Dred Scott decision, and vehemently denouncing all opposition to it. The new President, too, seized the early occasion … to endorse and strongly construe that decision and to express astonishment that any different view had ever been entertained. …
>
> The working points of that machinery are: First, that no Negro slave, imported from Africa, and no descendant of such slave can ever be a citizen of any State, in the sense of that term as used in the Constitution. … This point is made in order to deprive the Negro, in every possible event, of the benefit of this provision of United States Constitution, which declares that—'The citizens of each State shall be entitled to all privileges and immunities of citizens in the several states.'
>
> Secondly, that "subject to the Constitution of the United States," neither Congress nor a Territorial Legislature can exclude slavery from any United States territory. This point was made in order that individual men may fill up the territories with slaves, without danger of losing them as property, and thus to enhance the chances of permanency to the institution through all the future.

Clearly this conflicted with Lincoln's hope for ultimate extinction rather than permanent slavery.

> Thirdly, that whether the holding a Negro in actual slavery in a free State, makes him free, as against the holder, the United States courts will not decide, but will leave to be decided by the courts of any slave State the Negro may be

forced into. … Auxiliary to all this, and working hand in hand with it, the Nebraska doctrine, or what is left of it, is to educate and mold public opinion, at least Northern public opinion, to not care whether slavery is voted down or voted up.

This shows exactly where we now are, and partially also, where we are tending. It will throw additional light on the latter, to go back, and run the mind over the string of historical facts already stated. Several things will now appear less dark and mysterious than they did when they were transpiring. The people were to be "perfectly free" subject only to the Constitution. When the Constitution had to do with it, outsiders could not then see.

Plainly enough now, it was an exact niche, for the Dred Scott decision to afterwards come in, and declare the perfect freedom of the people to be just no freedom at all. Why was the amendment, expressly declaring the right of the people to exclude slavery, voted down? Plainly … adoption … would have spoiled the niche for the Dred Scott decision. Why was the court decision held up? Why even a Senator's individual opinion withheld, till after the Presidential election?

Plainly enough now, the speaking out then would have damaged the "perfectly free" argument upon which the election was to be carried. Why was the outgoing President's felicitation on the endorsement? Why the delay of a re-argument? Why the incoming President's advance exhortation in favor of the decision? These things look like the cautious patting and petting a spirited horse, preparatory to mounting … when it is dreaded that he may give the rider a fall. …

While the opinion of the Court, by Chief Justice Taney, in the Dred Scott case, and the separate opinions of all the

> concurring Judges, expressly declare that the Constitution of the United States neither permits Congress nor a Territorial legislature to exclude slavery from any United States territory, they all omit to declare whether or not the same Constitution permits a state, or the people of a State, to exclude it.
>
> In what cases the power of the states is so restrained by the U.S. Constitution is left an open question, precisely as the same question, as to the restraint on the power of the territories was left open in the Nebraska Act. Put that and that together, and we have another Supreme Court decision, declaring that the Constitution of the United States does not permit a state to exclude slavery from its limits.

Lincoln again turned to the consequence that comes from dropping barriers to slavery:

> And this may especially be expected if the doctrine of "care not whether slavery be voted down or voted up," shall gain upon the public mind sufficiently to give promise that such a decision can be maintained when made. Such a decision is all that slavery now lacks of being alike lawful in all the states. Welcome or un-welcome, such decision is probably coming, and will soon be upon us, unless the power of the present dynasty shall be met and overthrown.
>
> We shall lie down pleasantly dreaming that the people of Missouri are on the verge of making their State free; and we shall awake to the reality, instead, that the Supreme Court has made Illinois a slave State. To meet and overthrow the power of the dynasty is the work now before all those who would prevent that consummation. That is what we have to do. But how can we best do it?

Here Lincoln takes issue with Republicans who would ally with Douglas for this end.

> There are those who denounce us openly to their own friends, and yet whisper us softly, that Senator Douglas is the aptest instrument there is. … They do not tell us, nor has he told us, that he wishes any such object to be effected. They wish us to infer … now that he has a little quarrel with the present head of the dynasty; and that he has regularly voted with us, on a single point, upon which, he and we, have never differed. They remind us he is a very great man. …
>
> But "a living dog is better than a dead lion." Judge Douglas, if not a dead lion for this work, is at least a caged and toothless one. How can he oppose the advances of slavery? He don't care anything about it. His avowed mission is impressing the "public heart" to care nothing about it.
>
> A leading Douglas Democratic newspaper thinks Douglas' superior talent will be needed to resist the revision of the African slave trade.
>
> Does Douglas believe an effort to revive the slave trade is approaching? He has not said so. … But if it is, how can he resist it? For years he has labored to prove it a sacred right of white men to take Negro slaves into the new territories. Can he possibly show that it is less a sacred right to buy them where they can be bought cheapest? And, unquestionably they can be bought cheaper in Africa than in Virginia.
>
> He has done all in his power to reduce the whole question of slavery to one of a mere right of property; and as such, how can he oppose the foreign slave trade—how can he refuse that trade in that "property" shall be "perfectly free"—unless he does it as a protection to the home production? And as

> the home producers will probably not ask that protection, he will be wholly without a ground of opposition. … But, can we … infer that he will make any particular change. …
>
> But clearly, he is not now with us—he does not pretend to be—he does not promise to ever be. Our cause, then, must be entrusted to, and conducted by its own undoubted friends—those whose hands are free, whose hearts are in the work—who do care for the result. Two years ago the Republicans of the nation mustered over thirteen hundred thousand strong … under the single impulse of resistance to a common danger, with every external circumstance against us.

Lincoln concluded, fully cognizant that the strands of his party were loosely woven, "Of strange, discordant, and even, hostile elements, we gathered from the four winds, and formed and fought the battle through, under the constant hot fire of a disciplined, proud and pampered enemy. Did we brave all then, to falter now? Now—when the same enemy is wavering, dissevered and belligerent? The result is not doubtful. We shall not fail—if we stand firm—we shall not fail."[69]

Republicans and Democrats in Congress managed to block the admission of Kansas with a proslavery constitution. Illinois Republicans were outraged when a faction of eastern Republicans, led by *New York Tribune* editor Horace Greeley, wanted to reward Douglas with an uncontested return to the Senate. Greeley's push for Douglas, in effect, would sacrifice Lincoln. Lincoln, strongly supported by Illinois Republicans, saw the move as especially galling, given Douglas's views on slavery.

Greeley had broken with Seward and Weed in 1855. Greeley wanted the Whig nomination for New York governor, and Weed blocked his nomination. Greeley then asked to be the nominee for lieutenant governor, but Weed threw his support to Henry Raymond, editor of the

New York Times. With Raymond presiding over the state senate, this helped ensure that Seward was elected to the Senate and positioned for a planned presidential run.

Raymond had started his career as an editor with Greeley's *Tribune*, and Greeley resented his success with the *Times* and his favor with Weed. The *New York Herald* referred to Raymond as "editor of the junior Seward organ," considering Greeley's *Tribune* the senior organ. This was well before Greeley withdrew from the alliance with Weed and Seward. Weed had been an investor in the *Times*, and increasingly looked to Raymond for the essential editorial support in New York City.

The *Times*, consistently opposing slavery as a "moral, social and political evil," insisted, however, that abolition was for the South—and not the North—to decide. It editorialized, "We have scrupulously abstained from meddling with slavery." Opposing repeal of the Missouri Compromise, the *Times* declared, "the Slaveholding power is preparing for a disruption of the Union, by making the Union while it lasts an instrument of extending and consolidating the Slave Empire."[70]

Illinois Republicans unanimously resolved Lincoln was their "first and only choice" for the Senate. They rejected Greeley's proposal to reward and not oppose Douglas for breaking with Buchanan over Kansas. Greeley contended that failure to reelect Douglas would make northern politicians reluctant to resist Southern demands. Lincoln disagreed, convinced that only halting the spread of slavery would put slavery on the road to extinction. Douglas's proslavery views also ruled him out.[71]

The extremely ambitious Salmon P. Chase viewed himself as the logical Republican presidential candidate in 1856 and in 1860. Senator Chase led opposition to the Kansas-Nebraska Act. He had served as a senator from Ohio (1849–55 and 1861) and as governor (1855–60). He was a former Whig, former Abolition party founder, former Free Soiler, former Know-Nothing, and former Democrat. As a Republican, Chase garnered limited delegate support for the 1860 nomination.[72]

In Illinois, Lincoln told a Chicago audience in 1858, "I think that the Republican Party is made up of those who, as far as they can peaceably, will oppose the extension of slavery, and who will hope for its ultimate extinction." Responding to Senator Douglas, Lincoln said if the party gave up the object for which it had been formed—preventing the extension of slavery—it would disintegrate and fail. He called equality "the father of all moral principle" in the founding fathers.[73]

Lincoln was the Republican candidate for the United States Senate in 1854 and again in 1858 against Douglas. In 1854, when he failed to get a majority in the state senate, he withdrew in favor of anti-Kansas-Nebraska Democrat Lyman Trumbull, to prevent the election of Illinois governor Joel A. Matteson. Positioned as the leading Republican in 1858, Lincoln's challenge to Senator Douglas provided the platform that was the issue that led to the seven debates with Douglas across Illinois.[74]

"Is slavery wrong?" Lincoln asked in closing the debates. "That is the real issue. That is the issue that will continue in this country when these poor tongues of Judge Douglas and myself shall be silent. It is the eternal struggle between these two principles—right and wrong—throughout the world. They are two principles that have stood face to face from the beginning of time."

He had, in his debate with Douglas at Freeport, Illinois, asked a series of related interrogatories. "The one is the common right of humanity, and the other the divine right of kings. It is the same principle in whatever shape it develops itself. It is the same spirit that says: 'You work, and toil, and earn bread, and I'll eat it.' No matter in what shape it comes, whether from the mouth of a king who seeks to bestride the people of his own nation, and live by the fruit of their labor, or from one race of men, as an apology for enslaving another … it is the same tyrannical principle."

Lincoln posed the question, "Can the people of a United States territory, in any lawful way, against the wish of any citizen of the

United States, exclude slavery from its limits, prior to the formation of a state constitution?" When Douglas answered in defense of popular sovereignty and declared a territory could exclude slavery, he took a position in opposition of the Supreme Court's Dred Scott decision and defied Southern claims that slave property could not be excluded.

A friend of Lincoln questioned whether Douglas would adhere to his doctrine of popular sovereignty and declare a territory may exclude slavery. "If he does that," Lincoln replied, "He can never be president."

The friend replied, "But he may be senator."

"Perhaps," Lincoln declared, "but I am after larger game; the battle of 1860 is worth a hundred of this."

Lincoln was correct, as Douglas's spirited defense left Douglas fully alienated from President James Buchanan and his southern allies.[75]

Lincoln won the popular vote, but reapportionment by the Democrats left him without the needed votes in the Illinois state legislature. The result, however, put Lincoln on the national stage. Newspapers North and South printed his remarks. The Young Men's Central Republican Union invited Lincoln to speak on February 27, 1860, in the new Cooper Union Building in New York City. He spoke before jurists, scholars, clerics, and other noted citizens.

Isaac N. Arnold, a member of Congress, wrote, "The argument demonstrating the right of Congress to prohibit slavery in the territories and that such was the understanding of 'our fathers,' who framed the Constitution and organized the government, has never been surpassed. … The effort was so dignified, and exhibited so much learning, and such thorough mastery of the subject, that, coming from a source whence this kind of excellence was not expected, it was a surprise and revelation, and, therefore, made the greater impression."[76]

In his Cooper Union speech, Lincoln referenced Senator Douglas, who, in an article published in *Harper's* magazine and written with historian George Bancroft, declared, "Our fathers, when they framed the Government under which we live, understood the question just as well, and even better, than we do now." Lincoln, disturbed because Douglas's claim took the moral element out of this question, asserted:

> I fully indorse this, and I adopt it as a text for this discourse. I so adopt it because it furnishes a precise and an agreed starting point for a discussion between Republicans and that wing of the Democracy headed by Senator Douglas. It simply leaves the inquiry: "What was the understanding those fathers had of the question mentioned?" What is the frame of government under which we live? The answer must be: "The Constitution of the United States. …" Who were our fathers that framed the Constitution?
>
> I suppose the "thirty-nine" who signed the original instrument. … What is the question … those fathers understood "just as well, and even better than we do now?" It is this: Does the proper division of local from federal authority, or anything in the Constitution, forbid our Federal Government to control as to slavery in our territories. Upon this, Senator Douglas holds the affirmative, and Republicans the negative. … The question … seems not to have been directly before the Convention. …
>
> In 1789, by the first Congress, which sat under the Constitution, an act was passed to enforce the Ordinance of '87, including the prohibition of slavery in the Northwestern Territory. … It went through all its stages without a word of opposition, and finally passed both branches without yeas or nays. … This shows that … no line dividing local from federal authority, nor anything in the Constitution,

properly forbade Congress to prohibit slavery in the federal territory. …

Again, George Washington … then President … approved and signed the bill, thus completing its validity as a law. … The sum of the whole is, that of our thirty-nine fathers who framed the original Constitution, twenty-one—a clear majority of the whole—certainly understood that no proper division of local from federal authority, nor any part of the Constitution, forbade the Federal Government to control slavery in the federal territories. … Such was the understanding of our fathers. …

But enough! Let all who believe … "our fathers who framed the Government … understood … just as well, and even better, than we do now," speak as they spoke, and act as they acted upon. … This is all Republicans ask—all Republicans desire—in relation to slavery. As those fathers marked it, so let it be again marked, as an evil not to be extended, but to be tolerated and protected only because … its actual presence … makes that toleration and protection a necessity.

And now, if they would listen, as I suppose they will not—I would address a few words to the Southern people. I would say to them: You consider yourselves a reasonable and a just people; and I consider that in the general qualities of reason and justice you are not inferior to any other people. Still, when you speak of us Republicans, you do so only to denounce us as reptiles, or … outlaws. You will grant a hearing to pirates or murderers, but nothing … to Black Republicans. …

The fact that we get no votes in your section, is a fact or your making, and not of ours. And if there be fault in that fact, that fault is primarily yours, not of ours and if here be fault in that fact, the fault is primarily yours, and remains until you show that we repel you by some wrong principle or practice. If we do repel you by any wrong principle or practice, the fault is ours, but this brings you to where you ought to have started—to a discussion of the right or wrong of our principle.

If our principle, put in practice, would wrong your section for the benefit of ours … then we are sectional. … Meet us … on the question … and so meet us that something may be said on our side. Do you accept the challenge? No! Then you really believe that the principle which "our fathers who framed the Government under which we live" thought so clearly right as to adopt it … is so clearly wrong as to demand your condemnation without … consideration. …

Some of you are for revising the foreign slave trade; some for a Congressional Slave-Code for the Territories; some for Congress forbidding the Territories to prohibit slavery within their limits; some for maintaining slavery in the Territories; some for Congress forbidding the Territories through the judiciary; some for the "gur-reat purrinciple" that "if one man would enslave another, no third man should object," fantastically called "Popular Sovereignty"; but never a man among you is in favor of federal prohibition of slavery in federal territories, according to the practice of "our fathers who framed the Government under which we live. …" Again, you say we have made the slavery question more prominent than it formerly was. We deny it. … It was not we, but you who discarded the old policy of the fathers. We resisted, and still resist, your innovation; and thence comes the greater prominence of the question. …

In the language of Mr. [Thomas] Jefferson, uttered many years ago, "It is still in our power to direct the process of

> emancipation, and deportation, peaceably, and in such slow degrees, as that the evil will wear off insensibly, and their places be, pari passu, filled by free white laborers. If, on the contrary, it is left to force itself on, human nature must shudder at the prospect held up." Mr. Jefferson did not mean to say, nor do I … [that] the power of emancipation is in the federal government.
>
> The Federal Government, however, as we insist, has the power of restraining the extension of the institution—the power to insure that a slave insurrection shall never occur on any American soil which is now free from slavery.

Turning to the moral issue, Lincoln said:

> Human action can be modified to some extent, but human nature cannot be changed. There is a judgment and a feeling against slavery in this nation, which cast at least a million and a half of votes.
>
> You cannot destroy that judgment and feeling—that sentiment—by breaking up the political organization which rallies around it. … But you will break up the Union rather than submit to a denial of your Constitutional rights. That has a somewhat reckless sound; but it would be palliated, if not fully justified, were we proposing, by the mere force of numbers, to deprive you of some right, plainly written in the Constitution. But we are proposing no such thing.
>
> When you make these declarations, you have a specific and well-understood allusion to an assumed Constitutional right of yours, to take slaves into the federal territories, and to hold them as property. Your purpose, then, plainly stated, is that you will destroy the Government, unless you be allowed to construe and enforce the Constitution as you please, on all

points in dispute. … This, plainly stated is your language. You will rule or ruin in all events. …

An inspection of the Constitution will show that the right of property in a slave is not "distinctly and expressly affirmed. …" Under all these circumstances, do you really feel yourselves justified to break up this Government unless such a court decision as yours is, shall be at once submitted to as a conclusive the final rule of political action? But you will not abide the election of a Republican president! In that event, you say, the great crime of having destroyed it will be with us…!

A few words now to Republicans.… It is exceedingly desirable that all parts of this great confederacy shall be at peace, and in harmony, one with another. Let us Republicans do our part to have it so. Even though much provoked, let us do nothing through passion and ill temper … let us calmly consider their demands, and yield to them if, in our deliberate view of our duty, we possibly can. Judging by all they say and do … let us determine, if we can, what will satisfy them.

The question recurs, what will satisfy them? Simply this: We must not only let them alone, but we must somehow, convince them that we do let them alone. … In all our platforms and speeches we have constantly protested our purpose to let them alone; but this had had no tendency to convince them. … These natural, and apparently inadequate means all failing, what will convince them? This and this only: cease to call slavery wrong, and join them in calling it right. …

Wrong as we think slavery is, we can yet afford to let it alone where it is, because that much is due to the necessity arising from its actual presence in the nation; but can

> we, while our votes will prevent it, allow it to spread into National Territories, and to overrun us here in these Free States? If our sense of duty forbids this, then let us stand by our duty, fearlessly and effectively. Let us be diverted by none...groping for some middle ground between right and wrong....
>
> Neither let us be slandered from our duty by false accusations against us, nor frightened from it by menaces of destruction to the government nor of dungeons to ourselves. Let us have faith that right makes might, and in that faith, let us, to the end, dare to do our duty as we understand it. Let us have faith that right makes might, and in that faith let us to the end dare to do our duty as we understand it.[77]

Lincoln awakened the next day with newfound fame.[78]

The evening after the speech, Lincoln freed himself and went directly to the offices of the *New York Tribune*. There he read proof to ensure that his words were correctly recorded and set. Lincoln knew that accurately reporting his words was important, given his intense preparation and his delivery. This awareness was a prelude to his dealing with the New York press in the difficult times ahead. Lincoln looked upon educating public opinion as an imperative.[79]

Back in Illinois, a "Lincoln for President" boom was underway. In a letter to party chairman Norman Judd, Lincoln said, "I am not in a position where it would hurt much for me not to be nominated for the national ticket, but I am where it would hurt some for me not to get the Illinois delegation." Newspapers were calling for his nomination, and the Republican Party convention decided it would cast a unanimous vote of its national convention delegation for Lincoln.

At the Decatur Republican State Convention, not far from where Lincoln's father had settled, some farmers brought into the hall two old split rails inscribed, "Abraham Lincoln, the rail candidate for Presidency in 1860." The two rails were from a lot of three thousand made in 1830 by Thomas Hanks and Abe Lincoln. His father was the first pioneer in Macon County." Delegates cheered for more than fifteen minutes, and then Lincoln was called to the stand, bringing more cheering.[80]

Chairman Judd, representing Illinois, persuaded the national party to hold the 1860 Republican National Convention in Chicago. This advantaged Lincoln, as there were formidable rivals, especially Seward, but also Chase and Bates. Thurlow Weed, spearheading the Seward campaign, had raised a large war chest. Seward's chief handicap was the fear of Pennsylvania and Indiana Republicans who believed if Seward was nominated, their candidates faced defeat in October state elections.[81]

Judge David Davis, Leonard Swett, Norman Judd, and others formed a strong team at work for Lincoln. Davis arrived in Chicago and found all the candidates except Lincoln had established a headquarters. He rented two rooms at the Tremont House. He organized convention forces, gathering about him Lincoln's lawyer intimates. To each he assigned a specific task to canvass for delegates and report back to him. His strategy was to antagonize no one while getting second-choice pledges for Lincoln.

Lincoln had asked that no promises be made in his name, yet, as Davis said, "Lincoln is not here and we are." Davis, Swett, Judd, and others functioned most effectively for Lincoln. When deemed necessary, they gave implied promises of cabinet posts. Indiana's early vote for Lincoln and a surprisingly strong showing in New England started the ball rolling. Pennsylvania's switch to Lincoln was followed soon after by the Ohio delegation, which clinched the nomination for Lincoln.[82]

Greeley, chairing the Oregon delegation, also worked to undermine Seward. His actions were overshadowed as Indiana voted early and unanimously for Lincoln. In the Pennsylvania delegation, only

Representative David Wilmot, a House colleague of Lincoln, initially supported Lincoln. Senator Simon Cameron had both support and opposition as a favorite son. Representative Thaddeus Stevens wanted Supreme Court Justice John McLean, while others leaned toward Bates.

The delegation caucus agreed to give Cameron their first vote, the second to McLean, and the third to Lincoln, over Bates. This threw the Pennsylvania vote to Lincoln and all but assured him the nomination. Only Wilmot had remained rock solid for Lincoln during the voting.

In the Congress, Lincoln had cast votes repeatedly for the 1846 Wilmot Proviso. The proviso was a bold attempt to prevent the introduction of slavery into territories obtained from Mexico when the Mexican War ended, but it failed to gain the needed votes to be enacted into law. Wilmot proved a stalwart Lincoln delegate at the Chicago convention as the state's delegation pivoted to Lincoln.

Pennsylvanian Alexander K. McClure's book, *Lincoln and Men of War Times*, provides this account:

> The defeat of Seward and the nomination of Lincoln were brought about by two men—Andrew G. Curtin of Pennsylvania, and Henry S. Lane of Indiana, and neither accident nor intrigue was a material factor in the struggle. They not only defeated Seward in an anticipated Seward convention, but they decided the contest in favor of Lincoln against Bates, his only real competitor after Seward.
>
> Curtin had been nominated for governor in Pennsylvania and Lane had been nominated for governor in Indiana. The states in which they would battle were the pivotal states of the national contest. It was an accepted necessity that both Pennsylvania and Indiana should elect Republican governors in October to secure the election of the Republican candidate for President in November.

For Curtin and Lane, a nominee other than Seward was crucial. Neither of their states was Republican. "The call for the convention summoned the opposition to the Democratic party to attend the People's State Convention. … A like condition of things existed in Indiana. To win two key races, the Republicans had to pull the American (Know Nothing) element into their fold.

"If the Republicans failed to elect either Curtin or Lane the Presidential battle would be irretrievably lost. … The one thing that Curtin, Lane, and their respective lieutenants agreed upon was that the nomination of Seward meant hopeless defeat in their respective states. … There was no personal hostility to Seward. … They had no reason whatever to hinder his nomination, excepting the settled conviction that the nomination of Seward meant their own inevitable defeat."

McClure defined the issue: "The single reason that compelled Curtin and Lane to make aggressive resistance to the nomination of Seward was his attitude on the school question, that was very offensive to the many thousands of voters in their respective states, who either adhered to the American organization or cherished its strong prejudices against any division of the school fund. It was Seward's record on that single question … that made him an impossible candidate."[83]

When the balloting began, Seward received 173 1/2 votes to 102 for Lincoln. The remaining votes were divided chiefly among Cameron, Chase, and Bates. On the second ballot, Lincoln's total rose to 181 to 184 for Seward. The third and final ballot resulted in a majority for Lincoln. This was swiftly made unanimous. When the results were announced, a cannon was fired and thousands of attendees let out a deafening roar. Hannibal Hamlin of Maine was nominated for vice president.

Greeley had approached New York governor Edwin D. Morgan when the convention turned to nominating a vice presidential candidate. If Seward had been nominated, Lincoln most likely would have been asked to take the second spot. It was logical to seek someone acceptable to the

Seward men, but Morgan, William M. Evarts, and Weed declined to be consulted. The temper in their refusal indicated contempt for the action of the convention that failed to nominate Seward.

Once Lincoln was nominated, a committee of the Republican National Convention, led by the president of the convention, Representative George Ashmun of Massachusetts, and by the chairs of the various state delegations, traveled from Chicago to Springfield. They called on Lincoln and were graciously entertained by Mrs. Lincoln, who also displayed astute political insight. Ashmun notified Lincoln of his nomination. Ashmun then introduced each of the delegates.

Lincoln asked time to reflect on his nomination. "Deeply, and even painfully sensible of the great responsibility … inseparable from that honor—a responsibility which I could almost wish had fallen upon some one of the far more eminent men … I shall, by your leave, consider more fully the resolutions of the Convention, denominated in the platform, and without unreasonable delay, respond … not doubting now, that the platform will be found satisfactory, and the nomination accepted."[84]

Four days later, Lincoln wrote to Ashmun, "I accept the nomination. … The declaration of principles and sentiments, which accompanies your letter, meets my approval; and it shall be my care not to violate, or disregard it, in any part. Imploring the assistance of Divine Providence … I am most happy to co-operate for the practical success of the principles declared by the convention." Lincoln made clear he would reject compromise on barring of slavery from the federal territories.[85]

Meanwhile the Democrats had their own problems. Douglas faced the wrath of the South and the animosity of Buchanan. The thorn that Lincoln had planted with the Freeport Doctrine proved an irreconcilable division between Douglas and Buchanan, and Buchanan's Southern supporters, who were key to Buchanan's power base. Buchanan stripped Douglas partisans of patronage appointments which undercut fundraising and support for Douglas's presidential aspirations.

Douglas fought back, allying himself with New York banker Augustus Belmont. Belmont, in 1856, had supported Buchanan, but he was refused a coveted ministry to Spain. Belmont, a nephew by marriage of Louisiana senator John Slidell, had proposed elaborate plans for the acquisition of Cuba by the United States. Slidell had urged that Belmont be named ambassador to Naples because from there he could negotiate the arrangements regarding Cuba. Buchanan rejected the move.

Belmont, as a youth in Germany, had been taken in and trained by the Rothschilds, an important European banking family. In 1837, Belmont feared problems with immense loans made in Spain. Spanish stability was threatened, and its monarchy depended upon funds drawn from its colony, Cuba. The Rothschilds, concerned about these drafts, had dispatched Belmont to Cuba to check. When he reached New York on May 14, 1837, he discovered a major financial crisis in the United States.

The Rothschilds' American agent, the firm of J. L. & S. Joseph & Co., had gone under with liabilities of more than $7 million. Belmont stopped to superintend their jeopardized interests. While awaiting instructions, he studied the domestic market and soon realized the tremendous possibilities in the United States. Belmont resolved to make New York his permanent home, postponed his Cuba mission, and set up his own banking company in New York City.

August Belmont and Company was named the new agent for the Rothschilds.

Successful from the beginning, the Belmont firm served as disbursing agent, dividend collector, and news gatherer. Activities of the new house included foreign exchange, commercial and private loans, acceptance of deposits, and the handling of commercial paper. Belmont's association with European capitals attracted the business of major private corporations, railroads, and state and local governments.

To strengthen his position, he accepted Austria-Hungary's offer and became its American consul general. He abdicated this role in 1850 chiefly because of his burgeoning interest in politics. By the time of the Mexican War, his firm was strong enough to underwrite a substantial portion of US Treasury loans. During the presidency of Franklin Pierce, Belmont was named ambassador to the Netherlands, giving him enhanced standing as a diplomat and with the European bankers.

Cuba was a significant political issue in the United States. The island seethed with discontent and required an extensive Spanish military presence. A growing faction favored its acquisition, but for different and contrary reasons. Merchants and bankers believed Cuba would increase in commercial and financial strength. The South viewed it as additional slave territory. Protestants saw an end to the Spanish rule they associated with the Inquisition and religious authoritarianism.[86]

Beneath it all was a more controversial but fundamental reason that was far less visible. From 1800 to 1860, New York City had become the slave-trading capital of the world, and slaveholder ships enriched many a prominent family. This was a highly lucrative three-cornered trade. Ships sailed chiefly from New England to Africa, returning with a cargo of slaves that were delivered mainly to Cuba, where they were held to recuperate from the voyages, pending resale.

Author Ron Soodalter's *Hanging Captain Gordon* chronicles the trial and execution of Nathaniel Gordon in New York in 1862, the only man in history to be hanged for the capital crime of slave trading. Gordon had had no reason to fear hanging two years before, when he sailed from the Congo River with his cargo. Yet with Lincoln recently elected president and the Civil War underway, Gordon was caught during a major turning point in the nation's history.

New York District Attorney James Roosevelt offered Gordon a plea bargain: if Gordon gave up the identities of those who had financed the ship, the government would drop the piracy count and allow him to plead guilty to a lesser count. Soodalter explained Roosevelt's rationale: "This city is the head and front of the slave trade. If defendants could be persuaded to reveal the names of the men behind it, they would be of much more use to the government than by hanging them."

Lincoln had warned that the curse of slavery in the United States was as much the work of the North as the South. Gordon's conviction came after Lincoln replaced the sixty-five-year-old Roosevelt with Delafield Smith. Gordon's wife, pleading on behalf of herself and her children, and Gordon's friends continuously lobbied both Lincoln and Mary Lincoln, even as the Lincolns watched over their dying son, Willie. Lincoln, known to pardon so many, was not moved in the case of the slaver.[87]

On May 2, 1856, Senator Judah P. Benjamin announced his transfer of allegiance from the Whigs to the Democrats. He argued it was a mistake for the South to offer or accept any compromise on the slave question not in the Constitution. Benjamin termed the Constitution a compact based upon the principle of the equality of the states. He said the South was "insulted and mocked" by a compromise to give up its portion of the common territory upon the grounds that it never could use it.

Writing to A. H. H. Stuart, a Virginian and a former secretary of the interior, he said:

> In a recent visit to New York I became satisfied from all that I could see and hear from men whom I had formerly regarded as perfectly sound on Southern questions, that a gulf wide, deep, and I fear, impassable is already opened between the northern and southern Whigs. They will unquestionably form at the North for the next presidential election a grand coalition based exclusively on what they call opposition to the slave power. …

> I see but one salvation for us. I say it to you confidentially, but my honest conviction is that we shall be driven to forming one grand Union party to be made up of the entire South acting unanimously and joining the National wing of the Northern democracy. If this is not done, the North will carry out all the measures of the free-soil Whigs and democrats—and then what becomes of the Union?[88]

In 1860, the Democrats met in Charleston, and Douglas held a strong lead among contenders for the presidential nomination. His delegates, however, failed to gain the needed two-thirds to nominate. With the handwriting on the wall, the Southern delegates walked out in protest against the nomination of Douglas. Later, when the party reconvened in Baltimore, Douglas was nominated. In consequence, the Southern wing, backed by the Buchanan administration, bolted the party.

Senator Benjamin Fitzpatrick of Alabama was selected to run with Douglas but declined. Democratic leaders named Georgia's Senator Hershel V. Johnson as the vice presidential candidate. During the election, Belmont and Johnson corresponded vigorously as they searched for a Union-saving compromise. Later Johnson, as a Confederate legislator, initiated the legislation establishing Confederate intelligence operations in Canada designed to subvert the Union.[89]

The seceding Democrats soon met in Baltimore and nominated Vice President John C. Breckinridge and Oregon senator Joseph Lane on a dissident Democratic ticket. A remnant of pro-compromise, conservative Whigs, along with a number of Know-Nothings who had not gone over to the Republicans, met as the Constitutional Union ticket. They nominated Senator John Bell of Tennessee for president and Edward Everett of Massachusetts for vice president, fielding a third slate.

The Democratic convention, at the request of Douglas, elected Belmont to the twenty-nine-member national committee and named him their chair. Belmont tackled the vital task of fundraising. Committee members and the New York business community failed to respond, many not wanting to alienate the South. This meant the funding requests from other states and for the campaign in New York could not be met. This result severely hampered support for Douglas.

Belmont rightly saw New York at the battleground for the election. Belmont realized that if the three anti-Republican slates ran as one ticket, they could beat Lincoln. Then the New York vote, combined with that of the southern states, would throw the election into the House of Representatives. He laid out the plan before Democrats Horatio Seymour, Dean Richmond, Samuel J. Tilden, Erastus Corning, "Honest John" Kelly, Peter Cagger, William B. Astor, and John J. Astor, among others.

The magnitude of the Douglas defeat stunned Belmont. While Douglas received 29.5 percent of the popular vote, Lincoln received 39.8 percent. Lincoln received 180 electoral college votes, while Douglas received twelve: three from the fusion ticket in New Jersey and nine from Missouri. Douglas had battled with all he had, seeking to turn the tide, but it was not enough. When secession loomed, Douglas fought for compromise in the Senate, yet he forcefully sustained Lincoln and the Union.[90]

Chapter IV

The Election of 1860: Republicans Nominate and Elect Lincoln

Once nominated, Lincoln invited Maine's Hannibal Hamlin, the vice presidential nominee, to meet him in Chicago. In Chicago, Lincoln told Hamlin he could name a New Englander to the cabinet. Hamlin picked Gideon Welles, a Connecticut editor and war Democrat, whom Lincoln would name as Secretary of the Navy. Lincoln also invited scores of elected officials and politicians to Springfield and corresponded with scores more. Others either wrote or came for a visit.[91]

Douglas had taken the stump and campaigned vigorously; Lincoln had not. Yet Lincoln closely monitored political developments, watching and studying state by state. He also took a strong hand in assessing, supporting, and guiding politicians in crucial states. To Pennsylvania, he dispatched Davis and Swett to check and report on whether the fragile Republican coalition would give Governor Curtin sufficient support to win his crucial October election, a key hurdle for Republicans.[92]

Mary Lincoln not only proved an able and enlightened hostess, she read extensively, especially Kentucky newspapers. She could and did calculate votes. She also held strong feelings about politicians, especially those who had opposed Lincoln. Mary had a far less forgiving nature than was characteristic of Lincoln. She was outspoken in her judgment of the men in the political spectrum, and she was not shy when it came to making her views known.

Lincoln and Mary often reviewed the political landscape together, and she followed political and social issues. Coming from an aristocratic family, Mary was both well educated and strong willed. It is not surprising that their marriage was rocky. But as even William Herndon noted, "The domestic hell of Lincoln's life is not all on one side." Often Mary had to cope alone as Lincoln traveled the legal circuit or retreated into his own preoccupations with thought, work, and study.

Mary's hospitality surprised many politicians who made their way to Springfield. Mary, temperamental and subject to mood swings, had a firm grasp on the mind of the South. She took seriously the threats and dangers to be faced as the Lincolns confronted the reality of a rejection of the Lincoln presidency by the South. Viewing her own role as "Mrs. President," Mary also knew she would face scrutiny and envisioned an impending need to dress and entertain accordingly.[93]

Lincoln enlisted two young men, John G. Nicolay and John Hay, to act as secretaries and handle the flood of correspondence. As Lincoln read incoming letters, he would roll them, tie them with string, and insert them into his desk cubbyholes. Some years after his assassination, Oliver Barratt, an Illinois lawyer and collector, found the desk with much of the bundled mail in place. Many threatening letter were among them. Many similar letters came to the Lincoln home during the pre-inaugural days.

Carl Sandburg brought to light some of the more extreme letters in *Lincoln Collector: The Story of Oliver R. Barrett's Great Private Collection*. Perhaps Mary had read some as they were delivered. With no Secret Service for protection, Lincoln simply tucked them away.

> Abraham Lincoln Esq
> Sir, You will be shot on the 4th of March 1861 by a Louisiana Creole (as) we are decided and our aim is sure. A young Creole

> Washington, D.C.
> November 14, 1860
> Dear Sir, Caesar had his Brutus! Charles the First his Cromwell And the President may profit from their example. From one of a sworn Band of 10 who have resolved to shoot you from the south side of the Avenue in the inaugural process—on the 4th March 1861. Vindex
>
> Sir, This is to inform you that there is a club of 100 young men in this place who have sworn to murder you. Jos Bradley, Jos Roints, Make O-Brien

Another from Billmore, Louisiana, dated November 5, 1860, read:

> Old Abe Lincoln
> God damn your god damned old Hellfired god damned soul to hell god damn you and goddam your god damned family's god damned hellfired god damned soul to hell and god damnation god damn them and god damn your god damn friends to hell god damn their god damned souls to damnation god damn them and god dam their god damn families to eternal god damnation god damn souls to hell god damn them and God Almighty God damn Old Hamlin to[o] to hell God damn his God damned soul all over everywhere double damn his God damned soul to hell.
>
> Now you God damned old Abolition son of a bitch God damn you i want you to send me God damn you about one dozen good offices. Good God Almighty God damn your God damned soul and three or four pretty Gals God damn you
>
> And by so doing God damn you
> Will Oblige   Pete Muggins[94]

At this time intrigue was rampant in Washington and in Southern state capitals. Virginian John B. Floyd, Buchanan's secretary of war, bolstered federal arsenals In the South by shipping heavy ordinance there. Connecticut's Isaac Toucey, a Southern sympathizer and secretary of the navy, dispatched navy ships to far-flung oceans. Georgia's Howell Cobb resigned as secretary of the Treasury, and Interior Secretary Jacob Thompson, an Alabaman and later a Confederate agent in Canada, left also.

In late 1860, with the Buchanan administration in turmoil, Secretary of State Lewis Cass resigned his post. Jeremiah S. Black was shifted from his post as attorney general to replace Cass at State, and Edwin M. Stanton was named attorney general. Secretary Floyd fled when his traitorous conduct was discovered. Joseph Holt of Kentucky, a loyal Union man, was named in place of Floyd. New Yorker John A. Dix was named to Treasury. Dix learned that Cobb had left the treasury empty.

Stanton, Holt, and Dix, all strong Union men, gave the government a new tone.

The War Department, under Holt, was no longer a bureau of insurrection.

Cooperating with General Winfield Scott, Holt refused to give plans of forts and reports on armament and supplies to conspiring members of Congress. The essential precautions of General Scott were implemented in every possible way. Holt guided the weak and vacillating Buchanan with considerable firmness.

In these final days of the Buchanan administration, Southern-leaning cabinet officers and Southern members of Congress initially stayed in place to forestall action that would prepare the incoming administration to act against secession. Buchanan dispatched the *Star of the Sea* with supplies for Major Robert Anderson at Fort Sumter on December 31, 1860. Thompson slipped away the following day after first alerting South Carolina that the supplies had been dispatched.

Buchanan yielded to a demand from New York financial institutions that no financial aid would come without cabinet friends, appointees that they as Union men could trust. This led Buchanan to appoint Dix to Treasury. Dix, confronted by the crisis at hand with South Carolina's secession ordinance and then the firing on the *Star of the Sea* carrying supplies to Fort Sumter, told one of his revenue officials, "If any one attempts to haul down the American flag, shoot him on the spot."[95]

Stanton initiated a cooperative, confidential relationship with Senator Seward, prompting Seward to write Lincoln, "At length, I have gotten a position in which I can see what is going on in the councils of the president. It pains me to learn that things are even worse than is understood. The president is debating day and night on the question whether he shall not recall Major Anderson and surrender Fort Sumter, and go on arming the South." This was bad news for the nation.

Horrified at the extent of Southern influence over Buchanan, Stanton took the extraordinary step of setting up liaisons both with Seward and with Thomas Ewing, another former Whig from Ohio. They did not meet in person, but Stanton relied upon a legal associate, Peter Watson, to liaise with Seward. Stanton's decision gave key members of the Congress a window on the traitorous actions within the administration. Buchanan vacillated and contended he lacked power to act.[96]

Seward contacted General Winfield Scott and learned the entire military establishment consisted of some sixteen thousand soldiers. Scott told Seward many of the best commanders were resigning to join the rebellion. Many West Pointers were loyal to their states and not to the Union. Seward called on the governors of New York and Massachusetts to activate their militias for call on short notice. He also proposed that the government issue small-denomination Treasury bills.[97]

Stanton declared, "No administration has ever suffered the loss of public confidence and support as this has done. Only the other day it was announced that a million of dollars had been stolen from Mr.

Thompson's department. The bonds were found to have been taken from the vault … and the notes of Mr. Floyd were substituted. … Now is proposed to give up Sumter. All I have to say is that no administration, much less this one, can afford to lose a million of money and a fort in the same week."

Seward elaborated, "In regard to February, 1861, I need only say that at the time the secession leaders were all in the Senate and House, with power enough, and only wanting an excuse to get up a resistance in the capital to the declaration of Mr. Lincoln's election and to his inauguration; in other words, to have excuse and opportunity to open the civil war here before the new Administration and new Congress could be in authority to subdue it. … Subversion ruled their passion."[98]

A caucus of Southern senators met and advised secession and a confederacy for their states. The resolution, adopted January 5, was signed by Senators Jefferson Davis and Alert G. Brown of Mississippi, John Hemphill and Louis Wigfall of Texas, John Slidell and Judah P. Benjamin of Louisiana, Alfred Iverson Sr. and Robert Toombs of Georgia, Robert W. Johnson of Arkansas, Clement C. Clay Jr. of Alabama, and David Levy Yulee and Stephen Mallory of Florida. It read:

> Resolved 1. That in our opinion each of the Southern States should, as soon as may be possible, secede from the Union.
>
> Resolved 2. That provision should be made for a convention to organize a Confederacy of the seceding States, the convention to meet not later than the 15th of February, at the city of Montgomery, in the State of Alabama.
>
> Resolved 3. That in view of the hostile legislation that is threatened against the seceding states, and which may be consummated before the 4th of March, we ask instructions whether the delegations are to remain in Congress until that date for the purpose of defeating such legislation.

> Resolved 4. That a committee be appointed, consisting of Messrs. Davis, Slidell and Mallory, to carry out the objects of the meeting.[99]

Benjamin and Jefferson Davis—whose 1847 resolution asked for ten divisions to occupy Mexico until the United States decided what to do with the territory—wanted an independent South. They envisioned an empire stretching southward through Cuba, Mexico, and Central America, and even into South America—where great landowners such as themselves would be the ruling caste. This potential new empire would be supported by a growing slave system they staunchly advocated.[100]

When a provisional congress of Confederates met in February in Montgomery, Alabama, they elected Davis president and Stephens vice president. Davis immediately said the border states would be welcome, "but beyond this, if I mistake not the judgment and will of the people, a reunion with the States from which we have separated is neither practicable nor desirable." This was a crucial pronouncement and drew a sharp line.

Fifteen years after the war, Davis made the point that the South did not rebel, secede, and fight to preserve and extend slavery, but only to maintain the equality of the states. Since the North contended property rights in slaves existed only under exclusive state jurisdiction, Lincoln wisely and correctly asserted that the federal government could bar slavery in the territories. It was clear that Davis's stand ruled out a negotiated peace, since Lincoln held firmly that states could not secede.[101]

A prolonged war appeared inevitable. The Confederates flatly denied the supremacy of the Constitution, denied the truth of the equality clause of the Declaration of Independence, and denied the right of majority rule. These were the touchstones that Lincoln would affirm in his inaugural address, during his presidency, in his campaign for reelection, and in his second inaugural address. He said, "The Chief Magistrate derives all his authority from the people—the source of sovereignty."

In Washington, the House of Representatives had formed the Committee of 33, tasked with preparing a congressional compromise. Extreme Southerners called this effort futile from the beginning. The chair, Ohio's Thomas Corwin, said, "If the States are no more harmonious in their feelings and opinions than these thirty-three representatives, then, appalling as the idea is, we must dissolve, and a long and bloody civil war must follow. I cannot comprehend the madness of the times."

One man, Kentucky senator John J. Crittenden, political heir to the seat of Henry Clay and a compromiser by nature, loomed above the others in efforts to forge the compromise. His plan consisted of a batch of six proposed constitutional amendments. Harkening back to compromises in 1820 and 1850, he believed that the South could be pacified and civil war could be staved off. With a sense of patriotic earnestness he put forward these six proposed amendments:

(1) Slavery would be protected south of the Missouri Compromise borderline in all existing territory and all acquired hereafter;
(2) Congress would have no power to abolish slavery in territory otherwise under its jurisdiction, such as forts or arsenals, when slavery existed in surrounding states;
(3) Amendment 2 would be applied in the District of Columbia;
(4) Congress would have no power under the Interstate Commerce clause of the Constitution or otherwise to regulate or interfere with interstate slave trade.
(5) The federal government would be responsible for compensating slave owners if their attempts to recover fugitive slaves were prevented by violence; and
(6) The five amendments above would be made unalterable by any future congressional action, nor would Congress have the power to abolish slavery in any state where it existed.

Republicans furiously assailed the proposal. The Senate voted it down 20 to 18 in March, following its defeat in the House of Representatives in January.[102]

Efforts initiated in the Senate failed as well, but Treasury Secretary Cobb precipitated a financial crisis. Early in the Buchanan administration, he had bought up the 1868 maturity 6 percent bonds to get rid of the surplus in the treasury. In 1860, Phillip F. Thomas succeeded Cobb. Revenues fell behind expenditures by some $20 million a year as the low tariff act of 1857 impoverished the treasury. It was at this point that President Buchannan named Dix as Treasury secretary.

Faced with a fiscal crisis, the Senate again took up the House-passed Morrill Tariff Bill. The Southern senators—the foremost opponents who previously had defeated it—were now gone. It passed, and President Buchanan signed it into law on March 2, 1861. Two key financial provisions authorized the president to borrow $10 million more and, more important and crucial, to "substitute treasury notes for the whole, or any part of the money … authorized by previous acts."[103]

Gloom prevailed among Lincoln's visitors in Springfield, yet Lincoln asserted, "My own impression is … that this government possesses both the authority and power to maintain its own integrity." Facing reality, he held firmly against secession, adding, "The ugly point is the necessity of keeping the Government together by force as ours should be a government of fraternity. … He [the president] cannot entertain any proposition for dissolution or dismemberment."[104]

CHAPTER V

JOURNEY TO WASHINGTON AND THE INAUGURATION

Lincoln and his secretaries: John G. Nicholay on the right, and John Hay on the left

Lincoln, with his family and a cadre of close friends, began the rail journey from Springfield to Washington. Speaking from the rear of the train readying to leave, Lincoln said, "My Friends: No one, not in my position, can realize the sadness I feel at their parting. … I hope you, my friends, will all pray that I may receive that Divine assistance, without which I cannot succeed, but with which success is certain. Again, I bid you an affectionate farewell." Never in life would he return to Springfield.[105]

At Indianapolis that evening, responding to Governor Oliver P. Morton, Lincoln declined to speak at length but in his remarks said:

> Most heartily do I thank you for this magnificent reception. ... I will only say that to the salvation of the Union there needs but one single thing, the hearts of a people like yours. The people, when they rise in mass in behalf of the Union and the liberties of this country, truly may it be said: "The gates of hell cannot prevail against them."
>
> In all trying positions in which I shall be placed ... I wish you to remember, now and forever, that it is your business, and not mine; that if the union of these States and the liberties of this people shall be lost it is but little to any one man of fifty-two ... but a great deal to the thirty millions of people who inhabit these United States, and to their posterity in all coming time. It is your business to rise up and preserve the Union and liberty for yourselves, and not for me.[106]

Crossing Ohio after a stop in Columbus, the train moved on to Steubenville, where Lincoln remarked briefly, "Encompassed by vast difficulties as I am, nothing shall be wanting on my part, if sustained by the American people and God. ... If I adopt a wrong policy, the opportunity will occur in four years' time. Then I can be turned out, and a better man with better views put in my place." Noting the burden, Lincoln paced himself well and focused on the imperative for popular support.[107]

When Lincoln stopped in New York City, Mayor Fernando Wood, irascible and unpredictable, properly hosted the president-elect in the Governor's Room at City Hall after a reception at Astor House. Prodding Lincoln to avoid war and compromise, Wood said, "Present political divisions sorely afflicted" New York City and endangered its "commercial greatness." Lincoln gracefully agreed with Wood's sentiment and adding a crucial caveat, provided the Union "can be preserved."[108]

In New Jersey, Lincoln harkened back to his childhood:

> May I be pardoned if, upon this occasion, I mention that away back in my childhood, the earliest days of my being able to read, I got hold of a small book, such a one as few of the young members have ever seen, *Weems' Life of Washington*. I remember all the accounts there given of the battlefields and struggles for the liberties of the country, and none fixed themselves … so deeply as … here at Trenton, New Jersey.
>
> "I am exceedingly anxious that thing—that something that held out a great promise to all of the people of the world to all time to come—I am exceedingly anxious that the Union, the Constitution, and the liberties of the people shall be perpetuated in accordance with the original idea for which that struggle was made, and I shall be most happy indeed if I shall be an humble instrument in the hands of the Almighty, and of this, his chosen people, for perpetuating the object.[109]

Before the New Jersey State Assembly, Lincoln said, "I shall do all that may be in my power to promote a peaceful settlement of all our difficulties. The man does not live who would do more to preserve it, but it may be necessary to put the foot down firmly. … Received as I am by the members of a Legislature, the majority of whom do not agree with me in political sentiments, I trust that I may have their assistance in piloting the ship of State through the voyage, surrounded by perils."[110]

In Philadelphia at Independence Hall on February 22, the anniversary of President George Washington's birthday, his hosts suggested that the task of restoring peace was in his hands. Lincoln responded:

> I can say in return, sirs, that all the political sentiments I entertain have been drawn … from the sentiments which originated … from this hall. I have never had a feeling, politically, that did not spring from the sentiments embodied in the Declaration of Independence. …
>
> It was not the mere matter of separation of the colonies from the motherland, but that sentiment in the Declaration of Independence which gave liberty, not alone to the people of this country, but hope to all the world, for all future time. It was that which gave promise that in due time the weight would be lifted from the shoulders of all men and that all should have an equal chance. This is the sentiment embodied in the Declaration of Independence.
>
> Now, my friends, can this country be saved upon that basis? If it can, I will consider myself one of the happiest men in the world if I can help to save it. If it can't be saved upon that principle, it will be truly awful. But, if this country cannot be saved without giving up that principle—I was about to say I would rather be assassinated on this spot than to surrender it.

Lincoln concluded by declaring, "Now, in my view of the present aspect of affairs, there is no need of bloodshed and war."[111]

Lincoln made his last speech on his journey before the Pennsylvania legislature in Harrisburg. "It is not with any pleasure that I contemplate the possibility that a necessity may arise in this country for the use of the military arm." Lincoln knew that civil war loomed as the likely outcome. Secession was rearing its head across the South. He was aware the so-called compromise options were hardly acceptable, short of turning his back on the platform on which he was elected. He noted:

"While I am exceedingly gratified to see the manifestation … of your military force here, and exceedingly gratified at your promise here to use that force upon a proper emergency … I desire to repeat, in order to preclude any possible misconstruction, that I do most sincerely hope that we shall have no use of them—that it will never become their duty to … shed fraternal blood. I promise … so far as I may have wisdom to direct, if so painful a result … it shall be through no fault of mine."[112]

A crescendo of assassination threats against Lincoln reached a peak in Baltimore, a slaveholding city, with a large class of people threatening rebellion. Railroad detective Allan Pinkerton warned Lincoln that armed men were plotting an attempt on his life. Then General Scott and Senator Seward sent Seward's son, Fred, with a warning that a Baltimore plot had been hatched. Thus, Lincoln agreed that he would covertly travel on a night train through Baltimore and to Washington.

As a result, Lincoln was subject to fraudulent newspaper reporting at the hands of Joseph Howard. Howard asserted that Lincoln slinked through Baltimore in a Scotch outfit, and described the episode in scandalous terms. Howard was a former secretary of Reverend Henry Ward Beecher, pastor of the famed Brooklyn Plymouth Church. Yet Howard failed in his account to report the threats of the mobs and the vicious and vulgar assassination threats otherwise reported in the press.[113]

Telegraph wires were cut. Lincoln went by train to Philadelphia and transferred in Baltimore onto a waiting train to Washington. While agreeing to the travel arranged by railroad officials, he later said, "I did not then, nor do I now believe I should have been assassinated, had I gone through Baltimore as first contemplated, but I thought it wise to run no risk where no risk was necessary." Representative Elihu B. Washburne met him, and they went to the Willard Hotel to meet Seward.[114]

Other issues beyond the pledge to bar slavery from the territories contributed to Lincoln's electoral victory. In the Northwest, support in favor of homestead legislation was significant. In the Far West, it was support for the Pacific Railroad with overland mail to California and Oregon. Lincoln carried Oregon with some 5,500 votes to 5,000 for Breckinridge–Lane and 3,900 for Douglas. In California his 40,000-vote plurality barely topped 38,000 for Douglas and 34,000 for Breckinridge.

In his inaugural address, Lincoln again addressed the apprehension of the South over a Republican administration: "Indeed, the most ample evidence to the contrary…is found in nearly all the published speeches of him who now addresses you." Turning to the slavery question, he said, "I have no purpose, directly or indirectly, to interfere with the institution of slavery, in the states where it now exists. I believe I have no lawful right to do so, and I have no inclination to do so."

Next he turned to the Republican platform: "Resolved, That the maintenance inviolate of the rights of the States, and especially the right of each State to order and control its own domestic institutions according to its own judgment exclusively, is essential to that balance of power on which the perfection and endurance of our political fabric depend; and we denounce the lawless invasion of any State or Territory, no matter under what pretext, as among the gravest of crimes."

As for adherence to the law, Lincoln said:

> And while I do not choose now to specify particular acts of Congress as proper for all, both in official and private stations, to conform to, and abide by, all those acts which stand un-repealed, than to violate any of them. … Yet with all this scope for precedent, I now enter upon … the brief constitutional term of four years, under great and peculiar difficulty. A disruption of the Federal Union, heretofore only menaced, is now formidably attempted.

> I hold, that in contemplation of universal law, and of the Constitution, the Union of these States is perpetual … implied, if not expressed, in the fundamental law of all national governments. … Continue to execute all the express provisions of our national Constitution, and the Union will endure forever—it being impossible to destroy it, except by some action not provided for in the instrument itself. … One party to a contract may violate it … but does it not require all to lawfully rescind it?

Stating he would neither affirm nor deny that some, using any pretext, sought to destroy the Union, he appealed to those who were grounded in the Union and its benefits, saying, "Will you hazard so desperate a step, while there is any possibility that any portion of ills you fly from, have no real existence? … Think if you can, of a single instance in which a plainly written provision of the Constitution has ever been denied. … Plainly, the central idea of secession is the essence of anarchy."

"One section of our country believes slavery is right, and ought to be extended while the other believes it is wrong, and ought not to be extended," Lincoln declared. "This is the only substantial dispute. … Physically, we cannot separate. … This country, with its institutions belongs to the people who inhabit it." Turning to proposed amendments that would make explicit implied powers to bar national interference with domestic institutions in states, he said he would not object.

"The Chief Magistrate derives all his authority from the people, and they have conferred none upon him to fix terms for the separation of the States." Lincoln explained this as the law by which he was bound, adding, "His duty is to administer the present government, as it came to his hands, and to transmit it, unimpaired by him, to this successor. Why should there not be a patient confidence in the ultimate justice of the people? Is there any better or equal hope in the world?"

In closing, Lincoln reached out, North and South:

> In your hands, my dissatisfied fellow countrymen, and not in mine, is the momentous issue of civil war. The government will not assail you. You can have no conflict, without being yourselves the aggressors. You have no oath registered in Heaven to destroy the government, while I shall have the most solemn one to "preserve, protect and defend" it. I am loth to close. We are not enemies, but friends. We must not be enemies.
>
> Though passion may have strained, it must not break our bonds of affection. The mystic chords of memory, stretching from every battlefield, and patriot grave, to every living heart and hearthstone, all over this broad land, will yet swell the chorus of the Union, when again, touched as surely they will be, by the better angels of our nature.

This note was softer than a harsh statement in his first draft, building on a suggestion from Seward to better express the moment.[115]

After taking the oath of office, Lincoln, balancing former Whigs and Democrats, named William H. Seward secretary of state; Salmon P. Chase secretary of the Treasury; Simon Cameron secretary of war; Edward Bates attorney general; Montgomery Blair postmaster; Caleb B. Smith secretary of the interior; and Gideon Welles secretary of the navy. The former Whigs were Seward, Smith, Bates, and Lincoln. The former Democrats were Chase, Cameron, Blair, and Wells.

Lincoln told those who feared the cabinet would lack cohesion due to personal rivalries, "No, gentlemen, the times are too grave and perilous for ambitious schemes and personal rivalries. I need the aid of all of these men. They enjoy the confidence of their several states, and sections and they will strengthen the administration. It will require the utmost skill, influence, and sagacity of all of us to save the Republic; let us forget ourselves and join hands like brothers."[116]

In the summer of 1862, Vice President Hamlin complained, "The slow and unsatisfactory movement of the Government do not meet with my approbation, and that is known, and of course I am not consulted at all, nor do I think there is much disposition in any quarter to regard any counsel I may give much if at all." Seward also objected because he believed Chase and Blair had the lion's share of the patronage. He and Weed fought hard for a stronger hand in patronage.[117]

Against this backdrop, Lincoln had chosen a politically inclusive cabinet. He recognized he had won with a plurality. Because Republicans were a minority, he reached for a governing majority coalition. He gave recognition both to former Whigs and anti-Nebraska Democrats. Lincoln forged a stronger base by pulling in the factions. He hoped to reconcile the men who called upon him or wrote letters supporting or opposing specific candidates.

Lincoln made wise political choices. Functionally, it was a cabinet hardly well equipped to manage the nation's greatest crisis. Realizing all that, but still attempting to hold the government together, Lincoln opted for the broad reach. He had chosen from among his competitors for the nomination. Having named Seward for the State Department, he was all but forced to give Chase the Treasury. Lincoln reluctantly turned to Cameron for war secretary after an initial offer was withdrawn.

The importance of Pennsylvania required it be represented in the cabinet. Cameron wanted the Treasury, but an ethical cloud hung over him. The state's leaders eventually joined in support of Cameron for war secretary to protect Pennsylvania's interests in railroads, iron, and steel. Noting at the time he already had appointed Seward and Bates, both old-line Whigs like himself, Lincoln expressed a desire to add Cameron for the reason that he formerly was a Democrat.[118]

Seward proposed foreign war to hold the nation together and to stem secession. Lincoln rejected this. Chase revealed his lack of financial acumen and a weak understanding of finance. An avowed

Jacksonian, Chase was slow to confront early fiscal challenges. Cameron and Smith proved incompetent. By choosing Blair over Henry Winter Davis, Lincoln earned undying resentment from Davis. As a member of Congress, Davis persistently attacked Lincoln and opposed his policies.

Francis P. Blair Sr., a Kentucky journalist, had been a member of the brain trust of President Andrew Jackson and editor of the *Washington Globe*. His son Montgomery was prominent in Maryland. Another son, Frank Jr., was a power in Missouri politics. Lincoln selected Montgomery Blair over Representative Davis, looking to the Blair influence to help hold the border states. Davis had led Republican efforts in Maryland and had the support of his cousin David Davis.

Due to the death of his father and family hardship, Salmon Chase, born in 1808 in Cornish, New Hampshire, grew up as the ward of his uncle, an Episcopalian bishop in Ohio. He graduated from Dartmouth College in 1828 and moved to Washington, DC, to teach while studying law. Despite Federalist roots, Chase embraced President Jackson and the sub-treasury, yet held strong antislavery convictions. He gravitated to the Free Soil party and then the Republican Party.[119]

To encompass their political diversity Lincoln needed both Chase and Seward in his cabinet. The formidable Seward-Weed wing and the radical pro-Chase elements vied with each other for the upper hand in Republican politics and in patronage. Seward opposed the appointment of Chase. Greeley and Sumner battled equally hard to keep Seward out. Greeley was embittered because Seward ally Thurlow Weed had engineered the defeat of Greeley as senator from New York.[120]

Seward, vexed over failing to get his way on cabinet appointments, wrote to Lincoln and withdrew his name. Seward's note reached Lincoln on March 2. Lincoln held it over the weekend and on Monday, March 4—Inauguration Day—wrote to Seward, "I feel constrained to beg that you will countermand the withdrawal. The public interest, I think, demands that you should; and my personal feelings are deeply enlisted in the same direction." Seward agreed the next day to remain.[121]

A correspondent described how Lincoln's refusal to strike Chase from the cabinet triggered rage on the part of Weed, who declared, "Mr. Chase had been placed in the cabinet to control the patronage and appointments in the city and State of New York, to prevent Governor Seward from controlling the appointments, and to deprive him [Weed] of all power and influence." This likely was the impetus for Seward's attempt to withdraw from the cabinet, as the issue festered during Lincoln's term.

Lincoln named Chase more because he was a radical Ohio man than to back up the anti-Seward men in New York, although Lincoln had pledged justice to all. Lincoln did need both Seward and Chase, and he clearly did not want either to have the whole game. Lincoln did not find in Chase the qualities of a great financier, but politically he was essential. Chase, as a Democrat-turned-Republican with a strong following in Ohio and in the Northwest, balanced off former Whigs in the cabinet.[122]

Seward offered support to modify the Republican platform call for a ban on slavery in the territories, even as his wife pleaded with him not to take that position. Lincoln bluntly declared the ban key to his election, and he rejected modification. His task now was to build an alliance in support of the Union. Seward and Weed thought it best to convene governors. Weed said, "I am unwilling to see a united South and a divided North. With wisdom and prudence we can unite them."

Lincoln was quick to give a firm and direct reply: "Should the convocation of Governors of which you speak seem desirous to know my views on the present aspect of things, tell them you judge from my speeches that I will be inflexible on the territorial question. ... But my opinion is, that no State can in any way lawfully get out of the Union without the consent of the others; and that it is the duty of the President and other Government functionaries to run the machine as it is."[123]

With the cabinet in place, Lincoln turned to the continuous throng of office seekers, nearly all claiming to have worked for his election. Lincoln wanted faithful and loyal men placed while keeping a keen eye on those pressed by members of the House and Senate. By rewarding the loyal men, Lincoln strengthened his political base. Having suffered disappointment under President Taylor, Lincoln was all the more aware of the imperative to ensure justice for those who supported him.

Lincoln dealt with patronage, knowing that except for a few Whig years, it had been the province of Democrats, and chiefly Southern Democrats. Now triumphant, hungry Republicans thronged into Washington. Lincoln said at one point he was so busy filling rooms at one end of the house that he hardly had time to stem the crisis at the other end. Naming Republicans to office, replacing disloyal office holders, and working to hold the border states in the Union tasked him to the limit.[124]

Faced with the immediate question of reinforcing Fort Sumter and the garrison under Major Robert Anderson, Lincoln, at a March 9 cabinet meeting, asked each member for his views in writing. Within the cabinet, only Blair stood firmly for reinforcing Sumter. Chase was for provisioning Sumter only if supplies sent would not result in war—an impossible condition. Seward had all but promised the evacuation of Sumter and therefore opposed sending aid to Major Anderson.

Surprisingly, Bates and Smith were opposed as well, and Cameron advised no, saying, "No practical benefit will result to the country." Wells, too, said no, saying he had doubts. Within Lincoln's cabinet, Montgomery Blair alone said that Sumter must be supplied, and declared he was ready to resign if it was not. On the same day, Confederate commissioners in Washington sent word: "The impression prevails in Administration circles that Fort Sumter will be evacuated in ten days."

Wells credited Francis P. Blair Sr., Montgomery Blair's father and a strong Jackson anti-secessionist, with turning the tide. The senior Blair had been a member of President Andrew Jackson's administration, and was on deck when Jackson put a stop to efforts in South Carolina to nullify the then newly adopted increase in the tariff. Jackson even threatened to hang John C. Calhoun, his vice president during his first term and the leading advocate for secession in South Carolina.

Montgomery Blair had held his ground and Lincoln acted swiftly. "The elder Blair sought an interview with the President, to whom he entered his protest against non-action, which he denounced as the offspring of intrigue. His earnestness and indignation aroused and electrified the President; and touched a responsive chord. The president affirmed from that moment on that an attempt should be made to convey supplies to Major Anderson, and that he would reinforce Sumter."[125]

Lincoln also consulted a young navy captain, Gustavus Fox, a Blair son-in-law soon to be named assistant secretary of the navy. Fox had presented a resupply plan to President Buchanan, who had rejected it. When Fox explained the plan, Lincoln gave orders that led to its implementation. First, he sent Fox to meet with Major Anderson and with South Carolina's secessionist governor, Andrew W. Pickens. Fox reported back to Lincoln that South Carolina expected swift evacuation.

Major Anderson told Fox he was skeptical a relief expedition could be successful. Yet Fox believed it could succeed. Lincoln also dispatched Virginia-born Ward H. Lamon, a trusted friend, and South Carolina-born Stephen A. Hurlburt, both resident in Illinois, to South Carolina. Both found an utter lack of pro-Union sentiment in Charleston. At this point, Seward, communicating chiefly through Supreme Court Justice John A. Campbell, was signaling that Fort Sumter would be evacuated.

Lamon brought word back from the Governor Pickens: "Nothing can prevent war except the acquiescence of the President of the United States in secession. ... Let your President attempt to reinforce Sumter and the tocsin of war will be sounded from every hilltop and valley in the South." Fox returned from Charleston and reported to Lincoln that

Major Anderson's supplies would be used up by April 15, and that he still considered the plan could be implemented successfully.[126]

After a cabinet dinner on March 28 ended, Lincoln asked his cabinet to stay for a secret session on Fort Sumter. He read them a memorandum from General Scott, who advised, "The giving up of Forts Sumter and Pickens may be justified." Montgomery Blair immediately branded this the work of Seward. Yet all rejected the general's advice, and Lincoln called a full cabinet meeting the next day. The agenda at this meeting would be to discuss potential war.

"As to Fort Sumter, I think the time is come to either evacuate or relieve it," Attorney General Bates wrote. Strangely, the secretary of war was absent. Seward held steady: "I would at once, and at every cost, prepare for a war at Pensacola and Texas. I would instruct Major Anderson to retire from Fort Sumter forthwith." The radical Chase opted to maintain Fort Pickens and provision Fort Sumter, while Smith sided with Seward to defend Fort Pickens and evacuate Sumter as politically risky.

Postmaster General Montgomery Blair was explicit: he would hold Fort Pickens and fight "the head and front of the rebellion" at Fort Sumter. It was three and three. Yet Lincoln held his cards close and said nothing publicly as to his intent, yet he made his move. He dispatched Fox to New York and wrote out an order for the secretaries of war and the navy to ready an expedition, which, Lincoln wrote later, "was intended to be ultimately used, or not, according to the circumstances."[127]

On April 1, Lincoln received from Secretary Seward a document entitled, "Some Thoughts for the President's Consideration." Seward called for a declaration of war against Spain and France unless they would meet demands he would frame. In a brash power play, a bid to take power and leadership into his own hands, Seward presented a fivefold analysis:

> First. We are at the end of a month's administration, and yet without a policy, either domestic or foreign. Second: This …

> is not culpable and it has been unavoidable. The presence of the Senate with the need to meet applications for patronage has prevented attention to other and more grave matters. Third: But further delay to adopt and prosecute our policies for both domestic and foreign affairs would not only bring scandal on the administration, but danger upon the country.
>
> Fourth: To do this we must dismiss the applicants for office. But how? I suggest that we make the local appointments forthwith leaving foreign or general ones for ulterior and occasional action. Fifth: I am aware that my views are … perhaps not sufficiently explained … built upon the idea of a ruling one, namely, that we must CHANGE THE QUESTION BEFORE THE PUBLIC FROM ONE UPON SLAVERY, OR ABOUT SLAVERY, for a question upon UNION OR DISUNION.
>
> For Foreign Nations I would demand explanation from Spain and France … at once. I would seek explanations from Great Britain and Russia, and send agents into Canada, Mexico, and Central America, to rouse a vigorous continental spirit of independence on this continent against European intervention. And, if satisfactory explanations are not received from Spain and France … convene Congress and declare war. … But whatever policy we adopt, there must be an energetic prosecution of it. For this purpose it must be somebody's business to pursue and direct it incessantly.

The implication was that there was no policy and that the nation was drifting. "Either the President must do it himself, and be all the while active in it, or devolve it upon some member of the Cabinet," Seward continued. "Once adopted, debates on it must end. It is not in my especial province. But I neither seek nor assume responsibility." Seward clearly looked to be designated.[128]

The essence of Seward's power play, Lincoln artfully refuted in a same-day reply: "Since parting with you I have been considering your paper dated this day. … At the beginning of the month, in the inaugural, I said, 'The power confided to me will be used to hold, occupy, and possess the property and places belonging to the government, and to collect the duties and imposts.'" Lincoln had asserted his intent to maintain the Union and not to surrender federal posts and property.

Then Lincoln reminded Seward of the series of steps he had taken, and that Seward had been consulted and had concurred in the steps:

> This had your distinct approval at the time; and, taken in connection with the order I immediately gave General Scott, directing him to employ every means in his power to strengthen and hold the forts, comprises the exact domestic policy you now urge, with the single exception that it does not propose to abandon Fort Sumter.
>
> Again I do not perceive how the reinforcement of Fort Sumter would be done on a slavery or party issue, while that of Fort Pickens would be on a more national and patriotic one. The news received yesterday in regard to St. Domingo certainly brings a new item within the range of our foreign policy; but up to that time we have been preparing circulars and instructions to ministers and the like, all in perfect harmony, without even a suggestion that we had no foreign policy.

"Upon your closing proposition," which Lincoln repeated, quoting it from the letter, Lincoln was emphatic in declaring that he was to be the master, and not his secretary of state, asserting, "I remark that if this must be done, I must do it. When a general line of policy is adopted, I apprehend there is no danger of its being changed without good reason, or continuing to be a subject of unnecessary debate; still, upon points arising in its progress I wish, and suppose I am entitled to have the advice of all the cabinet." While remaining open to advice, Lincoln clarified the issue.[129]

Wells that day received documents that Lincoln had signed at Seward's request. "Without a moment's delay," Wells said, "I went to the President with the package in hand." Wells then learned that Seward, with army captain Montgomery Meigs and naval lieutenant David Porter, had put documents before Lincoln that placed Porter in command of the *Powhatan*, detaching it from the Sumter mission, contrary to Wells's order sending the *Powhatan* to Sumter under Captain Mercer.

Lincoln now had Seward order Porter to return the ship to Mercer, but Porter held to the prior order. When Seward, Porter, and Meigs first approached Lincoln, Porter gave this rationale: "Mr. Wells is surrounded by officers and clerks, some of whom are disloyal at heart, and if the orders for this expedition should emanate from the Secretary of the Navy, and pass through all the department red tape, the news would be at once flashed over the wires, and Fort Pickens ... lost forever. But if you will issue all the orders from the Executive Mansion, and let me proceed to New York with them, I will guarantee their prompt execution."

"But," replied the president, "is this not a most irregular mode of procedure?"

Seward jumped in: "You are commander-in-chief of the army and navy, and this is a case where it is necessary to issue direct orders without passing through intermediaries."

The president with skepticism inquired, "What will Uncle Gideon say?"

"Oh," said Seward, "I will make it right with Wells."

Seward could not make it right with Wells, and the bad feeling ran deep. Gustavus Vasa Fox, who had originated the Sumter plan, wrote to his wife, "Mr. Seward got up this Pensacola expedition and the Prest signed the orders in ignorance and unknown to the dept." Fox, reflecting Wells's anger took strong issue with Seward's actions, and specifically for borrowing Porter from the Navy Department without ever asking.[130]

Lincoln wrote Fox, "I sincerely regret that the failure of the late attempt to provision Fort Sumter should be the source of any annoyance to you. The practicability of your plan was not ... brought to a test. ... I most cheerfully ... declare that the failure ... has not lowered you a particle, while the qualities you developed in the effort, have greatly heightened you, in my estimation. You and I both anticipated that the cause of the country would be advanced by making the attempt."[131]

As Virginia delegates were debating secession, Lincoln invited Judge George W. Summers to meet him. Summers had asked John B. Baldwin to go, but Lincoln found him arrogant. Lincoln told another Virginian, Unionist John Minor Botts, a Whig who served in Congress with Lincoln, that he had wished to make a proposition, "but I fear you are almost too late." Lincoln then explained to Botts the Union plan: "This afternoon a fleet is to sail from the harbor of New York for Charleston."[132]

Lincoln earlier had said he might have to put the foot down firmly. He did precisely that with his decision to provision Fort Sumter. Confederate president Jefferson Davis moved tactically and ordered an attack on Fort Sumter. He contended, "To have waited further strengthening of their position by land and naval forces, with hostile purpose now declared, for the sake of having them 'fire the first gun,' would have been as unwise as it would to strike down an assailant."

Davis had warning from his secretary of state, Robert Toombs, who said, "The firing on that fort will inaugurate a civil war greater than any the world has yet seen. ... At this time it is suicide, murder, and you will lose us every friend at the North. You will wantonly strike a hornet's nest which extends from mountains to ocean; legions, now quiet, will swarm out and sting us to death. It is unnecessary; it puts us in the wrong, it is fatal." History proved Toombs had called it correctly.[133]

Virginia representative Roger A. Pryor expressed distrust in Charleston: "Gentlemen, if Abraham Lincoln and Hannibal Hamlin were to abdicate their office tomorrow, and were to give me a blank sheet of paper whereupon to write the conditions of re-annexation to the Union, I would scorn the privilege of putting the terms on paper. ... And why? Because our grievance has not been with reference to the insufficiency of the guarantees, but the unutterable perfidy of the guarantors."

When Major Anderson declined, on April 12, to accept terms of surrender, and with relief boats due, the bombardment began. After thirty-three hours of bombardment, Anderson accepted the terms of surrender and marched his men out with drums beating, the flag flying, and a fifty-gun salute. The Union forces boarded a relief ship. In Washington, senators and representatives pledged support for the Union.

Lincoln called upon "all loyal citizens," proclaiming:

> I, Abraham Lincoln, President of the United States, in virtue of the power in me vested by the Constitution and the laws, have thought fit to call forth, and hereby do call forth, the militia of the several States of the Union, to the aggregate number of seventy-five thousand, in order to suppress said combinations, and to cause the laws to be duly executed.
>
> I appeal to all loyal citizens to favor, facilitate and aid this effort to maintain the honor, the integrity, and the existence of our National Union, and the perpetuity of popular government; and to redress wrongs already long enough endured. I deem it proper to say that the first service assigned to the forces ... will probably be to repossess the forts, places, and property which have been seized from the Union.

He urged devastation, destruction of, or interference with property be avoided. "And I hereby command the persons composing the combinations aforesaid to disperse, and retire peaceably to their respective abodes within twenty days. … Deeming that the present condition of public affairs presents an extraordinary occasion, I do hereby … convene both Houses of Congress. Senators and Representatives are therefore summoned to assemble at … the fourth day of July, next to determine, such measures … as … the public safety … may seem to demand."[134]

Lincoln, ever holding the ballot as the supreme arbiter, said of the Confederates, "They knew that this Government desired to keep the garrison, and thus to preserve the Union from actual and immediate dissolution—trusting … to time, discussion, and the ballot-box, for final adjustment; and they assailed and reduced the fort for precisely the reverse object—to drive out the visible authority of the Federal Union, and thus force it to immediate dissolution."

Wells, in his diary, recorded that two days before the Sumter attack, he had met Senator Douglas in front of the Treasury Building. Douglas told him the rebels were determined on war and were about to make an assault on Fort Sumter. Douglas urged immediate and decisive measures, considered it a mistake that energetic action had not been taken, and said the dilatory proceedings of the government would bring on a terrible civil war. He said he would stand with the administration.

When Wells proposed they visit the State Department and see Seward, Douglas said, "Then you have faith in Seward. Have you made yourself acquainted with what has been going on here all winter? Seward has had an understanding with these men. If he has influence with them, why don't he use it?" Wells suggested that, since Seward was a member of the administration, nothing could be done without the knowledge of Seward and his associates, and the wise course would be to be frank with him.

Douglas and Wells were received cordially. Seward told them he knew there were reckless men in Charleston, but knew of no way to prevent an assault if those men resolved to make one. Seward, Douglas said, was not earnest, had no heart in this matter, and could not believe the storm was beyond his ability and power to control. Douglas believed that Seward would soon learn that no mere party management or cunning would answer in such an emergency. He said seeing Seward was useless.

Douglas told Wells that Seward had no idea of the necessities of the case, and was, at that moment, carrying on an intrigue with rebel leaders who were deceiving him, while he flattered himself that he was using and could control them. Douglas had witnessed all of this for months, but because he had the confidence of neither party, he was unable to do anything effective. Douglas told Wells he had tried to rally the Democrats, but too many were determined to break up the Union.[135]

Senator Douglas, better than the cabinet, grasped the needs that war demanded, voicing his strong support for the Union: "We must fight for our country and forget all partisan differences. There can be but two parties—the party of patriots and the party of traitors." Douglas strongly concurred with the president's call for 75,000 volunteers. John W. Forney, a Douglas confidant who later became a close Lincoln ally, claimed that Lincoln planned to call Douglas into his cabinet.

Lincoln asked Douglas to return to the Northwest and shore up support for the Union. In a series of speeches, Douglas said, "Every man must be for or against the United States. There can be no neutrals." In another, he said, "May we conduct it, if a collision must come, that we will stand justified in the eyes of Him who knows our hearts, and who will justify our every act." Just a month after a final speech in Chicago, the "Little Giant" died serving the cause of Union and the nation.[136]

The failure of Cameron and Chase to swiftly and decisively mobilize the full force of the economy, its industrial base, and its transportation network delayed war mobilization and prolonged the Civil War. Chase was slow to grasp the imperative that war of this magnitude required of the nation a capacity for monetary policy and a national currency.

Cameron proved equally inept as an administrator and failed to focus on organizing and equipping a military adequate for a prolonged war.

The naming of Chase, a former Ohio governor recently elected to the US Senate, as Treasury Secretary eased temporarily the concerns of party radicals, who remained rebellious over the Seward appointment. The radicals were incensed about Seward because they viewed him as a compromiser. Chase, an antislavery man, was aligned with their demands. Chase, however, never gave up the view that, given his leadership on antislavery issues, he instead of Lincoln merited the presidency.

Alexander Kelly McClure, in *Lincoln and Men of War-Times*, says of Chase, "He never forgave Lincoln for the crime of having been preferred for President over him, and while he was a pure and conscientious man, his prejudices and disappointments were vastly stronger than himself, and there never was a day during his continuance in the Cabinet when he was able to approach justice to Lincoln." McClure adds, "He seems to have been consumed with the idea that he must be Lincoln's successor."[137]

Yet while Lincoln in previous years had spoken forcefully against the Jacksonian sub-treasury, Chase clearly had been coopted by it. Further, Chase took full advantage of the vast Treasury Department patronage, appointing loyalists while reorganizing a disorganized and chaotic department. In addition, Cameron yielded to Chase, allowing him to take the lead role in choosing Union generals. Cameron seemed to think this would strengthen his hand with radicals in Congress.

Chase, convinced of his own rectitude, never understood his own weakness, believing himself much better qualified than Lincoln to be president. Chase remained undecided on whether the Constitution authorized debt financing, and therefore failed to craft urgently needed financial initiatives. He failed initially to propose and press for needed taxation and borrowing authority. Secretary Chase simply did not grasp the urgent need for national finance in 1861.[138]

Before the Civil War, government fiscal operations were transacted with coin, bypassing banks. The coin was held in the sub-treasury and doled out as the government made its expenditures. Thinly capitalized state banks issued paper notes in small denominations for use as a local currency. These notes were heavily discounted when circulated beyond a bank's central location and excessively counterfeited. This led to hoarding of valuable specie (coins) and a shortage.

The majority of state banks were capitalized chiefly with bonds issued by Southern or border states, bonds that had been bought at a discount and carried at face value. As these bonds lost value with the coming of war, many state banks failed. With neither a national currency nor the authority to formulate monetary policy, the crisis deepened. Bankrupt and confronted with a looming financial crisis, the government was nearly brought to its knees by challenging demands of wartime.

The Lincoln administration inherited a bankrupt government. The key revenue source, the tariff, was inadequate, and the government lacked broader taxation authority. Wartime needs required the means for procuring the ships, guns, men, food, and supplies to win an extended war, and the ability to pay soldiers and sailors. Confronted with a growing shortage of gold and silver coinage and no national currency, the question was how the Union would pay its soldiers and suppliers.

Chase discovered the government had less than $2 million on hand, and that sum had been appropriated many times over. The government also faced a projected need for more than $320 million. By stripping away the nation's fiscal and monetary options, the Jacksonians had weakened the Union. Chase summarized the case in July 1961. When the government failed to pay soldiers, they and their families flooded Congress with complaints. This had an adverse effect on recruiting too.

Chase was forced to issue Treasury notes and to sell bonds the market would take only at a discount. This he found distasteful. Given authority by Congress, Chase borrowed $150 million from banks in New York,

Philadelphia, and Boston, but declined to accept deposit credit. Anticipating the loans, Congress had authorized Chase "to deposit any of the moneys obtained on any of the loans in such solvent specie-paying banks as he might select," leaving the funds banked until needed.

Rigidly adhering to the sub-treasury law and unfamiliar with banking practice, Chase demanded the proceeds be deposited in gold in the sub-treasury. This deprived the banks of capital and forced them to curtail lending. Because the gold was not paid over all at once, the banks were able to continue some lending. Then when gold paid into the treasury was disbursed, much was again deposited with the banks. Matters were moving along until December, when two events hit hard.

First, the banks had anticipated borrowing from them would be temporary and that the secretary's financial report would call for a program of adequate taxation. The failure to make this call fueled keen disappointment and threatened the banks. This heightened the suspicion that Secretary Chase lacked the skills essential to funding the nation's wartime needs. Then came the Trent Affair, in which two Confederate commissioners were taken from a British ship en route to England, threatening war.

The immediate effect undermined the credit of the government. This made it impossible for the banks to sell government securities, held in large amounts, except at a large loss. This also cut off a source through which they had been obtaining specie (metal coin). It frightened off depositors, reducing another source of coinage. Even worse, customers began withdrawing their deposits. Some $27 million in specie was withdrawn from New York banks.

To stave off complete depletion, the New York banks suspended all specie payments in mid-December, and banks in other cities speedily did the same. The consequence was a suspension of national treasury payments. On the first day of 1862, the whole scheme of national finance collapsed. This set in motion a debate in the Congress. In an excessively verbose message, Secretary Chase conveyed his assent to the legal-tender clause to be included in legislation.

Since current law required both the government and banks to use gold, needs could not be met with a shrinking supply. Secretary Chase issued more Treasury notes as a partial legal tender. The notes were used when and where they were accepted. Banks could not use these notes as reserves, as inflation ate into their value. This rudimentary state of federal authority prolonged the war by giving the South time before it felt the overwhelming weight of Northern economic might.

A bill by Representative Elbridge G. Spaulding, was reported on January 7, authorized the secretary to issue $150 million in non-interest-bearing Treasury notes in denominations not less than $5. The notes, legal tender for all debts public and private, were to be exchangeable for bonds after five years and redeemable in twenty years at 6 percent interest. The bill passed the House by a vote of 93 to 59 on February 6, and the Senate by 22 to 17, and became law on February 25, 1862.[139]

William T. Sherman, a West Point graduate destined to become one of the North's foremost generals, left a post as superintendent of the Louisiana State Seminary of Learning and Military Academy. Sherman was well aware of the North's demographic advantage. The North had some twenty million people, over four million of which were white males between the ages of fifteen and forty. This was against the South's population of nine million, three million of whom were slaves, and only 1.1 million white males between the ages of fifteen and forty.

Sherman, prior to departing, told a Southern friend:

> You people of the South don't know what you are doing. This country will be drenched in blood, and God only knows how it will end. It is all folly, madness, a crime against civilization! You people speak so lightly of war; you don't know what you're talking about. War is a terrible thing! You mistake, too,

> the people of the North. They are a peaceable people … (but) they will fight. … They are not going to let this country be destroyed without a mighty effort to save it. …
>
> Besides, where are your men and appliances of war to contend against them? The North can make a steam engine, locomotive, or railway car; hardly a yard of cloth or pair of shoes can you make. You are rushing into war with one of the most powerful, ingeniously mechanical, and determined people on Earth—right at your doors. You are bound to fail. Only in your spirit and determination are you prepared for war. In all else you are totally unprepared, with a bad cause. …
>
> At first you will make headway, but as your limited resources begin to fail, shut out from the markets of Europe as you will be, your cause will begin to wane. If your people will but stop and think, they must see in the end that you will surely fail.

Sherman returned to the North. Eventually his brother, Ohio senator John Sherman, obtained for him a commission in the regular army. Firm in his loyalty to the Union, he nevertheless sternly refused any involvement with politics.[140]

Benjamin Butler told Lincoln he could not successfully fight without Democrats. Lincoln commissioned Butler a general, and likewise commissioned Nathaniel Banks, a former Speaker of the House and governor of Massachusetts, who later replaced Butler in New Orleans. Lincoln offered Colonel Robert E. Lee the command of Union armies, but Lee resigned and took up arms with the Confederacy in Virginia. Lincoln viewed Lee and the other officers who allied with the Confederates as traitors.

Ohio governor William Dennison lacked an adequate militia organization as he faced the problem of organizing and equipping hordes of volunteers. Dennison appointed Captain George B. McClellan to command the Ohio militia. McClellan had left the military and at the time was an official of the Ohio and Mississippi Railroad. Dennison had wanted Major Irwin McDowell of General Scott's staff, but yielded to influential Cincinnati citizens who wanted McClellan.

Back on December 27, 1860, McClellan, in a letter marked "private," had written to his friend, Samuel L. M. Barlow, "In a conversation with a very intelligent Republican, from Indiana, this morning I put to him the direct question whether he & his friends are willing to run the Missouri Compromise line to the Pacific & to repeal the Personal Liberty Bills." From the beginning McClellan's political positions were destined to bring him into conflict with the Lincoln administration.

McClellan looked to a middle ground as he explained: "They (his sources) would gladly to the first & more than the second—that they were perfectly willing that when a fugitive slave was rescued, or impediments thrown in the way of his arrest & return, that the country should pay his full value. I am sure that this is the feeling of the Republican Party in the West. More than this—the feeling of all people here is that the North West will do justice to the South if they give us time."

McClellan cautioned the South not to go off half-cocked and listen only to the "Republican politicians at Washington (who from the nature of the case, cannot represent the present feeling of the North)." Yet he made it clear that "we will meet the consequences unitedly, let it be war or peace—but the general opinion is that it will be war … the South has much to ask that the North ought to & would grant—at the same time we think that in many things the South is in the wrong."

On May 3, McClellan was named to head the Department of Ohio, which consisted of the military administration of Ohio, Indiana, and Illinois, with headquarters in Cincinnati. The department later extended into the western counties of Virginia and Pennsylvania. Urged by

Dennison, McClellan moved his troops across the Ohio River into West Virginia. His Ohio and loyal Virginia troops defeated Confederates in the first battle of the war. McClellan was named a major general in the regular army.

General McClellan's success in the West Virginia campaign led General Scott to recommend him to command the Army of the Potomac. McClellan, a West Point graduate, took command on July 27 and demonstrated talent for organizing and training. His knowledge of the geography, the railroad routes, and the strategic importance of the areas proved valuable. He reached out to organize all of the various Union military commands and lay out a plan for concerted action.[141]

Lincoln previously had known of McClellan as an Illinois Central Railroad vice president. Lincoln had done legal work for the railroad. Little was recorded of any personal views each might have had of the other. Lincoln, however, did know that McClellan had put the railroad's private car at the disposal of Douglas during the 1858 senate race. McClellan also rode in the car with Douglas at the time of the Lincoln-Douglas debates. Lincoln likely viewed the Douglas connection as an asset.

With many of the nation's generals going South, Lincoln and the Northern governors culled the military talent that remained loyal. Some West Point officers who had left the military, such as Grant and Sherman, would eventually emerge. Yet initially Lincoln was chiefly dependent for military advice upon the aging Mexican War hero, General Winfield Scott. Soon, however, McClellan turned on Scott, seeing the aged war hero as an impediment to his efforts to command the army.

In April 1861, Washington faced the threat of imminent invasion. Massachusetts dispatched its militia to Washington through Baltimore, where anti-war protesters attacked the soldiers. The clash killed both soldiers and rioters. This forced the Union to temporarily reroute soldiers coming as reinforcements for Washington. Insurrection in Maryland threatened to halt the flow of troops and leave the nation's capital defenseless.

Lincoln sent the following message to Governor Thomas H. Hicks and Baltimore mayor George W. Brown: "Gov. Hicks, I desire to consult with you and the Mayor of Baltimore relative to preserving the peace of Maryland. Please come immediately by special train. … Answer forthwith." Brown came immediately, but Hicks was away and did not get word. Hicks wrote to Lincoln, protesting against landing more troops at Annapolis, and suggested the British minister, Lord Lyons, be asked to mediate.

Seward, at Lincoln's direction, replied, "No domestic contention … ought, in any case, to be referred to any foreign abritrament." Lincoln said, "The national highway thus selected by the Lieutenant General has been chosen" in consultation with citizens of Maryland. Mayor Brown, accompanied by three citizens, George W. Dobbin, John C. Brune, and S. T. Wallis, were told by Lincoln:

> You … come here to me and ask for peace … and yet have no word of condemnation for those who are making war on us.
>
> You express great horror of bloodshed, and yet would not lay a straw in the way of those who are organizing … to capture this city. The rebels attack Fort Sumter, and your citizens attack troops sent in defense of our government. … And yet you would have me break my oath and surrender the Government … I have no desire to invade the South; but I must have troops to defend this Capital. … There is no way but to march across, and that they must do.[142]

Reverdy Johnson, a former Whig, senator, and attorney general under President Zachary Taylor, wrote to Lincoln, "The existing excitement and alarm … of my own State and of Virginia are owing … to an apprehension that it is your purpose to use the military force, you are assembling in this District for the invasion of these States."

Lincoln reluctantly replied, fearing his reply would create misunderstanding. "I do say the sole purpose of bringing troops here is to defend this capital. I do say I have no purpose to invade Virginia, with them or any other troops, as I understand the word invasion. But suppose Virginia sends her troops, or admits others through her borders, to assail the capital, am I not to repel them?"

Johnson shared the supposedly confidential letter with pro-Confederate Supreme Court justice John A. Campbell of Alabama, and it found its way to Jefferson Davis. Johnson had been a Peace Convention delegate.[143]

On April 24, 1861, 9,244 of the roughly thirty thousand voters of Baltimore cast their ballots for the only ticket offered, "States Rights." They voted in secessionist members of the Maryland legislature, scheduled to meet in a few days. Governor James Hicks, however, called the legislature into session in Frederick, a Unionist community. The strong secessionist tide—strong in eastern Maryland—was ebbing, and Hicks, bucking strong pressures, refused to call a secessionist convention.

Facing criticism raining down on him from the North, Lincoln instructed General Scott:

> The Maryland Legislature assembles tomorrow at Annapolis; and, not improbably, will take action to arm the people of the state against the United States. The question has been submitted to me, and considered by me, whether it would not be justifiable, upon the ground of necessary defense, for you, as commander in chief of the … Army, to arrest, or disperse the members of the body.
>
> I think it would not be justifiable; nor, efficient for the desired object. First, they have a clearly legal right to assemble;

> and, we cannot know in advance, that their action will not be lawful, and peaceful. And if we wait until they have acted, their arrest, or dispersion, will not lessen the effect. ... Secondly, we cannot permanently prevent their action. If we arrest them, we cannot long hold them ... and when liberated they will immediately re-assemble and take their action.
>
> I therefore conclude that it is only left to the commanding general to watch, and await their action, which, if it shall be to arm their people against the United States, he is to adopt the most prompt, and efficient means to counteract, even, if necessary, to the bombardment of their cities—and in the extremist necessity, the suspension of the writ of habeas corpus.

As it turned out, upon assembling the Maryland legislature appointed a committee to confer with the president.[144]

Ardor cooled as it became evident that secession would result in a devastating trade loss for Baltimore. At the same time, more Union regiments crossed Maryland. Next a military department was established under General Benjamin F. Butler. General Scott ordered two regiments to Relay House, eight miles from Baltimore. Butler then advanced a thousand troops into Baltimore and stacked arms on Federal Hill. Scott rebuked him, fearing a clash with local militia could undermine Lincoln's efforts.

Butler—a man who voted fifty-seven times for Jefferson Davis at the Charleston Democratic Convention—was in the vanguard of Union efforts in Maryland. Butler, in 1860, had been a candidate for governor of Massachusetts and had polled six thousand proslavery votes out of total of 169,000 votes cast. Yet using Lincoln's order to Scott that in the face of resistance he might "suspend the writ of habeas corpus," Butler used the suspension and arrested Ross Winans.[145]

Winans, a native of New Jersey and an extremely wealthy member of the Maryland legislature, favored secession. An inventor, Winans had developed the first successful locomotive on the Baltimore and Ohio Railroad and also invented a steam gun designed to cut down infantry with its rapid-fire cannon. Winans shrewdly retained Reverdy Johnson to represent him in this case. Johnson appealed to Lincoln, who turned the case over to Seward, who agreed to free Winans.[146]

Lincoln removed Butler from Maryland and gave him command of Fortress Monroe in Virginia. He gained increased notoriety when he declared slaves coming into his lines were contraband, gave them food and clothing, put them to work, and refused to send them back into slavery. "The Negro," Butler ruled, "must now be regarded as contraband … since every able-bodied hand, not absolutely required on the plantations, is impressed by the enemy into military service as a laborer."[147]

The Union commander at Fort McHenry, General George Cadwalader, dispatched a squad of soldiers who roused and arrested John Merryman at his Maryland home. This resulted in a clash between Chief Justice Roger Taney of the US Supreme Court and President Lincoln. Taney lived in Baltimore, and attorneys for Merryman, denying his guilt for treason, gained a writ of habeas corpus from Taney, who demanded that Cadwalader appear before him and bring Merryman.

General Cadwalader sent a staff officer, who said the general was preoccupied with pressing matters, adding, "He has further to inform you that he is duly authorized by the President of the United States in such cases to suspend the writ of habeas corpus for public safely. This is a high and delicate trust and it has been enjoined upon him that it should be executed with judgment and discretion." He said further response awaited word from the President.

Taney was incensed when the officer did not deliver John Merryman and inquired, "The commanding officer declines to obey the writ?" To which the officer responded, "After making the communication my duty is ended and my power is ended." He left. At that point, Taney ordered "that an attachment forthwith issue against General George Cadwalader for a contempt in refusing to produce the body of John Merryman according to the demands of the writ of habeas corpus."

Taney sent a US marshal to serve the writ on General Cadwalader, but he was not received at the fort. Taney, when apprised of this, said, "It is a plain case, gentlemen, the President, under the Constitution and laws of the United States, cannot suspend the privilege of the writ of habeas corpus, nor authorize any military officer to do so." While claiming legal authority for sending the marshal, he noted he could not act in the face of a force "notoriously superior."[148]

CHAPTER VI

COMMANDER IN CHIEF: GOVERNING, MOBILIZING, FUNDING, AND FIGHTING

In Washington, General Scott proposed his Anaconda Plan that would blockade coastal ports, send forces down the Mississippi River, and seal off the Confederacy. Scott believed the blockage would deprive the citizenry of goods and manifest latent Union sentiment. Scott believed this would lead to a resolution of the difficulties within a year. Scott argued against any effort to invade the South at any point, as this would further reduce the possibilities of a settlement.[149]

On May 21, 1861, the Confederate congress accepted an invitation from Virginia and voted to move their capital to Richmond. The decision had significant political and military implications. The Northern press demanded that the Confederates not be allowed to meet in Richmond. After a cabinet meeting on June 29, plans were formulated for an attack designed to prevent the move. General Irvin McDowell was ordered to attack Manassas, even as he pleaded for more time to train his troops.

The result was a Union defeat in the Battle of Bull Run, which ignited exultation and overconfidence in the South. It brought despair and renewed determination in the North. The next day Lincoln signed a bill for the enlistment of 500,000 three-year volunteers. This meant commissioning a vast number of officers as well. While a remorseful Greeley called for peace on rebel terms, Lincoln promptly summoned

McClellan to command Union forces and strengthen the defenses of Washington.

Lincoln, in a memorandum of military policy suggested by the Bull Run defeat, invoked a broad range of actions. First, he said, "Let the plan for making the Blockade effective be pushed forward with all possible dispatch." Others included the need to drill, discipline, and instruct troops; reorganization of those who fought at Manassas; and a call for volunteers to come forward swiftly. As for Baltimore, he said, "Let Baltimore be held, as now, with a gentle, but firm, and certain hand."[150]

McClellan took counsel consistently with Samuel L. M. Barlow, an influential Democrat. Regarding the pressure to go on the attack, McClellan wrote to Barlow and urged:

> Speaking of an advance let me beg of you not to be impatient. … I am more anxious to advance than any other person in this country—there is no one whose interests would be so much subserved by prompt success. … I feel … the issue of this struggle is to be decided by the next great battle. …
>
> I owe it to my country & myself not to advance until I have reasonable chances in my favor. The strength of the Army of the Potomac has been vastly overrated. … It is now strong enough & well disciplined enough to hold Washington. … But, leaving the necessary garrisons … I cannot yet move in force equal to … the enemy. … I will pay no attention to popular clamor … make the Army strong … & effective enough to give me a reasonable certainly that, if I am able to handle the form, I will win the first battle.[151]

Writing Secretary Cameron, he took aim at the premature element at Bull Run:

> The most important affair, that of Bull's Run, was a serious reverse for us—this result was plainly due to the fact that our army, raw, unorganized and inexperienced, attacked the enemy in his chosen position—had the case been reversed we should have been successful. … The policy of the rebels has been … to remain on the defensive & receive our attack in their positions chosen & fortified beforehand. …
>
> There is a vast difference between the degree of preparation required to resist an attack successfully, & that needed to assault entrenched positions. … So long as I retain my present position I must claim to be the best judge of the time to strike—I repeat, what you already know, that no one is more anxious to terminate speedily this fratricidal war than I am. … One of our chief difficulties is the scarcity of instructed staff officers.[152]

The defeat showed that the cost of the war would far exceed initial expectations of the Treasury Department. Chase turned to Jay Cooke, an experienced state and national loan agent and a native of Ohio. Cooke had opened the banking house of Jay Cooke and Company in Philadelphia. Chase had known Cooke's father, Eleutheros Cooke, and his brother, Henry. Henry, editor of the *Ohio State Journal*, had warmly espoused Chase's political causes, becoming a counselor and intimate social friend.

Henry's newspaper drew financial support from brother Jay. Jay Cooke also paid traveling expenses and the cost of banquets when John Sherman campaigned to succeed Chase in the US Senate. Henry Cooke came to Washington for the inauguration of the new administration, and prolonged his stay to closely monitor developments. At the request of Jay, Henry kept his brother fully abreast of events, and especially the pressing and growing demands on the treasury.

Jay Cooke evaluated prospects for an office in Washington, and told Henry to get promises of business for the banking office, saying, "Tell

Governor Chase that I hold myself at his service and, pay or no pay, I will do all I can to aid him in Treasury matters. I feel, however, that if he would give me a chance I could show him a way to raise money." In a special session in 1861, Congress opened the door for Cooke when on July 17 it authorized the borrowing of $250 million.

A young reporter from the *Philadelphia Inquirer* had been sent to cover the expected push from Manassas to Richmond. The young man, named Painter, was caught behind Confederate lines. Pretending to be a hospital attendant, he escaped, caught a wounded army horse, and rode to Washington. To avoid army censorship, he took a train to Philadelphia. Berated for not following the army to Richmond, he explained that Union military were in full retreat back to Washington.

Bulletins issued by the paper brought an irate crowd threatening to wreck the offices. When the news was confirmed, the crowd backed down. Jay Cooke, a near neighbor acting on his own, immediately toured the banking district and within a few hours had collected pledges of two million dollars for the government. "The undersigned agree," Cooke's prepared paper said, "to advance the Secretary of the Treasury the following sums for a period of sixty days with six per cent interest."[153]

Cooke's move anticipated action by Chase. Chase decided on a similar round of calls on New York and Boston bankers. Cooke had raised the money with the newly authorized 7.3 percent interest Treasury notes as security. Chase, working with Assistant Treasurer John J. Cisco, made an appeal to the Chamber of Commerce in New York and implored bankers and capitalists to subscribe to the notes. They swiftly contracted to advance $50 million on his warrants.

Cooke said, "Having become favorably known to Mr. Chase, and as the result of some correspondence, he stopped on his journey to New York and called to see me, inviting me to go with him to meet the Associated Banks and to aid him in the negotiation of the $50 million he required immediately. I went to New York with him and was present at all the meetings with the presidents of the Associated Banks, giving him my advice and all the aid I could in that transaction."

This made the 7–30s (7 percent for 30 years) famous in the hands of Jay Cooke. It was only after Jay Cooke effectively developed a system of advertising and distributing the bonds in vast quantities to the general public that they gained acceptance. Cooke had learned from previous experience with funding during the Mexican War. His efforts continued during the war and he later worked with Treasury secretaries William P. Fessenden and Hugh McCulloch [154]

Lincoln called for Congress to convene July 4, 1861, in an extraordinary session. In a special message he reviewed the actions of the seceding states, the seizing of federal property, and the firing on Fort Sumter. He charged:

"A disproportionate share of the Federal muskets and rifles had somehow found their way into these (seceded) states, and had been seized to be used against the government. Accumulations of public revenue lying within them had been seized. ... The navy was scattered in distant seas. ... Officers of the Federal army and navy had resigned in great numbers; and of those resigning a large number had taken up arms against the government."

Turning to the Confederate attack on Fort Sumter, Lincoln described the situation:

> In this act, discarding all else, they have forced upon the country, the distinct issue: "immediate dissolution, or blood." And this issue embraces more than the fate of these United States.
>
> It presents to the whole family of man, the question whether a constitutional republic, or a democracy—a government of the people, by the same people—can, or cannot maintain

> its territorial integrity, against its own domestic foes … whether discontented individuals, too few in numbers to control administration … upon the pretenses made in this case … or arbitrarily, without any pretenses … break up their government, and thus practically put an end to free government upon the earth.
>
> So viewing the issue, no choice was left, but to call out the war power of the Government; and so to resist force, employed for its destruction, by force, for its preservation. The call was made and the response was most gratifying; surpassing, in unanimity and spirit, the most sanguine expectations. Yet none of the States commonly called Slave states, except Delaware, gave a regiment through regular State organizations … Of course the seceded States … gave no troops.

Turning to Virginia, he said:

> The people … have thus allowed this giant insurrection to make its nest within her borders; and the government has no choice left but to deal with it, where it finds it. In the border States—in fact the middle states—there are those who favor a policy which they call "armed neutrality"—that is, an arming of those states to prevent the Union forces passing one way, or the other, over their soil. This would be disunion completed. …
>
> Soon after the first call for militia, it was considered a duty to authorize the Commanding General, in proper cases, according to his discretion, to suspend the privilege of the writ of habeas corpus; or, in other words, to arrest, and detain, without resort to the ordinary processes and forms of law, such individuals as he might deem dangerous to the public safety. This authority has purposely been exercised but very sparingly.

> The whole of the laws which were required to be faithfully executed, were being resisted, and failing of execution, in nearly one-third of the States. Must they be allowed to finally fail of execution, even had it been perfectly clear, that by the use of means necessary to their execution, some single law, made in such extreme tenderness of the citizen's liberty, that practically, it relieves more of the guilty, than of the innocent, should, to a very limited extent, be violated?
>
> To state the question more directly are all the laws, but one, to go unexecuted, and the government … go to pieces, lest that one be violated? Even in such a case would not the official oath be broken, if the government should be overthrown, when it was believed that disregarding the single law, would tend to preserve it? But it was not believed that this question was presented. It was not believed that any law was violated.

Lincoln explained the provision of the Constitution:

> "The privilege of the writ of habeas corpus, shall not be suspended unless when, in cases of rebellion or invasion, the public safety may require it," is equivalent to a provision—is a provision—that such privilege may be suspended when, in cases of rebellion, or invasion, the public safety does require it. Now it is argued that the Congress, and not the executive, is vested with the power. But the Constitution itself, is silent as to which or, who is to exercise the power. …
>
> The forbearance of this government had been so extraordinary and so long continued, as to lead some foreign nations to shape their action as if they supposed the early destruction of our national union was probable. While this … gave the Executive some concern, he is now happy to say that the sovereignty and right of the United States are now

everywhere practically respected by foreign powers; and a general sympathy with the country is manifested throughout the world.

It is now recommended that you give the legal means for making this contest a short, and a decisive one; that you place at the control of the government, for the work, at least four hundred thousand men and four hundred million dollars. The number of men is about one tenth of those of proper ages within the regions where, apparently, all are willing to engage; and the sum is less than a twenty third part of the money value owned by the men who seem ready to devote the whole.

It might seem … to be of little difference whether the present movement at the South be called "secession" or "rebellion." The movers well understood the difference. … They invested an ingenious sophism, which, if conceded, was followed by perfectly logical steps … to the complete destruction of the Union. … With rebellion thus sugar coated, they have been drugging the public mind of their section until they have brought good men to a willingness to take up arms against the government. …

The sophism derives much—perhaps the whole—of its currency, from the assumption, that there is some omnipotent, and sacred supremacy, pertaining to a State. … Our States have neither more, nor less power, than that reserved to them, in the Union, by the Constitution. … What is now combatted, is the position that secession is consistent with the Constitution—is lawful and peaceful. … This is … a People's contest … to elevate the condition of men … to afford all an unfettered start.

It may be affirmed, without extravagance, that the free institutions we enjoy, have developed the powers, and

> improved the condition, of our whole people, beyond any example in the world. ... So large an army as the government has now on foot, was never before known, without a soldier in it, but who had taken his place ... of his own free choice.

Noting that popular government had been called an experiment, he said the American people had settled the successful establishment and administration of it.

> One still remains—its successful maintenance against a formidable attempt to overthrow it. It is now for them to demonstrate to the world, that those who can fairly carry an election can also suppress a rebellion—that ballots are the rightful, and peaceful, successors of bullets. ... When ballots have fairly, and constitutionally decided, there can be no successful appeal, back to bullets; that there can be no successful appeal, except to ballots themselves, at succeeding elections.
>
> Such will be the great lesson of peace; teaching men that what they cannot take by an election, neither can they take it by a war—teaching all the folly of being the beginners of war. As to ... the course of the government ... after the rebellion ... the Executive deems it proper to say, it will be his purpose then, as ever, to be guided by the Constitution, and the laws; and that he probably will have no different understanding of the powers, and duties ... expressed in his inaugural.
>
> It was with the deepest regret that the Executive found the duty of employing the war-power, in defense of the government, forced upon him. He could but perform this duty, or surrender the existence of the government. No compromise, by public servants could ... be a cure ... but that no popular government can long survive a marked precedent, that those who carry an election, can only save

> the government ... by giving up the point, upon which the people gave the election.[155]

As in Maryland, the struggle was fierce in Missouri, and difficult in West Virginia and Kentucky. Lincoln, fighting secession intrigue and sympathy, knew the strategic importance of the border states. He did not want a line at the Ohio River. Lincoln understood Kentucky Union sentiment and initially steered clear of emancipation. The resulting gain was twenty-four loyal states with 21,611.422 whites and 342,212 slaves against eleven states with 5,115,790 whites and 3,508,131 slaves.

Lincoln biographer John G. Nicolay gives a detailed account of events:

> In Kentucky, the political strife was deep and prolonged. The governor twice called the legislature together to initiate secession proceedings; but that body refused compliance, and warded off his scheme by voting to maintain the State's neutrality. Next the governor sought to utilize the military organization known as the State Guard to effect his object. The Union leaders offset this ... by enlisting several Union regiments.
>
> At the June election nine Union congressmen were chosen, and only one secessionist; while in August a new legislature was elected with a three-fourths Union majority. Other secession intrigues proved equally abortive; and ... in September, Confederate armies invaded Kentucky ... the Kentucky legislature invited the Union armies of the West into the State to expel them, and voted to place forty thousand Union volunteers at the service of the President.

As Virginia voted to join the Confederacy, the forty-eight counties north of the Allegheny Mountains and adjacent to Pennsylvania and Ohio rejected the action at Richmond, repudiated secession, and formed a loyal provisional state government. Congress then acted to create the state of West Virginia, and Lincoln signed the measure into law, although with some misgivings as to whether the action complied with the Constitution. Nevertheless, it was an essential war measure.[156]

In Missouri, Lincoln secretary John G Nicolay reported that a Confederate plot to seize the Jefferson Barracks in St. Louis, with sixty thousand stands of arms and a million and one half cartridges, was prevented by General Scott. A company of regulars under Captain Nathaniel Lyon, a loyal officer with strong antislavery convictions, took possession of the barracks under orders from Scott. A Union safety committee of leading St. Louis citizens strongly supported Captain Lyon.

A state convention, initially called to pass a secessionist act, instead elected a majority of Union delegates who voted down secession. Governor Claiborne F. Jackson then ordered the state militia into camps with plans to take Missouri out of the Union by military action. Lyon surrounded the camp, and the militia surrendered, curbing the planned treason. President Lincoln authorized raising ten thousand Union volunteers and gave Lyon authority to proclaim martial law.

The legislature, in session at Jefferson City, used its three-fourths secession majority to pass a military bill giving Jackson control of the militia and state financial resources. On June 11, Lyon, promoted to brigadier general by Lincoln, met with Jackson in St. Louis. The governor demanded sole military control coupled with the neutrality of Missouri. Lyon insisted on federal military control. The governor rushed back to Jefferson City and burned bridges along his route of retreat.

General Lyon embarked by steamboat to Jefferson City. He carried a regular artillery battery and several battalions. Moving swiftly up the Missouri, he took possession of the capital and put the rebels to flight. The loyal members of the Missouri State Convention were called into session. They acted to constitute a loyal state government. This action maintained the local civil authority throughout the Civil War, apart from occasional Confederate incursions from nearby Arkansas.[157]

Lincoln appointed John C. Fremont major general and placed him in command of the Northwest with headquarters in St. Louis. Initially Lincoln had wanted to name Fremont, the 1860 Republican presidential nominee, minister in London, but Seward held firm for Adams and urged Fremont for secretary of war. Fremont, a former army lieutenant with no experience in war, proved utterly unfit for either post. Reports of both corruption and a lack of planning and command surfaced.

The expectation was that Fremont would not only hold Missouri, but would mobilize the increasing number of northwest state regiments to split the Confederacy with a thrust down the Mississippi. "From the first, Fremont failed in promptness, in foresight, in intelligent supervision; and, above all, in inspiring confidence and attracting assistance and devotion. His military administration created serious extravagance and confusion … distrust and resentment."

General Lyon found his forces depleted as three-month enlistments expired and his appeals for help went unanswered. He led a last-ditch bayonet charge against three times as many Confederates. Lyon was killed in the resulting Battle of Wilson's Creek, thus forcing Union forces to retreat. This weakened public support for Fremont. Lincoln tried to buttress the command by asking General David Hunter to serve on Fremont's staff, although this failed to change Fremont.

As Lincoln maneuvered to save Fremont, Fremont opened a quarrel with the Blair family, especially Frank Blair, a crucial Union leader in Missouri, and his father, Francis P. Blair. The elder Blair had been instrumental in Fremont's 1856 nomination for president. Increasingly aware that he was losing confidence among civil and military leaders in the Northwest, Fremont took a far more drastic step and proclaimed martial law throughout Missouri without consulting the president.

"All persons who shall be taken with arms in their hands within these lines shall be tried by court-martial, and if found guilty will be shot," Fremont declared. "The property, real and personal, of all persons in the State of Missouri who shall take up arms against the United States, or who shall be directly proven to have taken an active part with their enemies in the field, is declared to be confiscated to the public use; and their slaves, if any they have, are hereby declared freemen."

Lincoln swiftly but firmly, wisely, and diplomatically overruled Fremont:

> My Dear Sir: Two points in your proclamation of August 30 give me some anxiety. First, should you shoot a man, according to the proclamation, the Confederates would very certainly shoot our best men in their hands in retaliation; and so, man for man, indefinitely. It is therefore, my order that you allow no man to be shot under the proclamation, without first having my approbation or consent.
>
> Second, I think there is great danger that the closing paragraph, in relation to the confiscation of property and the liberating slaves of traitorous owners, will alarm our Southern Union friends and turn them against us; perhaps ruin our rather fair prospect for Kentucky.

As a master political strategist with a keen understanding of the vital role the border states would play in saving the Union—and knowing consideration of the slavery question was premature—Lincoln said, "Allow me, therefore, to ask that you will, of your own motion, modify that paragraph so as to conform to the first and fourth sections of the act of Congress entitled, 'An act to confiscate property used for insurrectionary purposes,' approved August 6, 1861, and a copy of which act I herewith send you. This letter is written in a spirit of caution, and not of censure. I send it by a special messenger, in order that it may speedily reach you."

Fremont refused the president's request to act. Counting on the political support for his actions, Fremont said: "If I were to retract it of my own accord, it would imply that I myself thought it wrong, and that I had acted without the reflection which the gravity of the point demanded."

Lincoln responded: "Your answer, just received, expresses the preference on your part, that I should make an open order for the modification, which I very cheerfully do." Yet Fremont had distributed two hundred copies of his proclamation in spite of Lincoln.[158]

Fremont's wife, Jesse Hart Benton, daughter of Senator Thomas Hart Benton, showed up at the White House and gave Lincoln a tongue-lashing. She demanded Lincoln's correspondence with the Blairs regarding Fremont, which Lincoln declined to give her. Responding by letter to Mrs. Fremont, Lincoln said:

> It is not exactly correct, as you say, you were told by the elder Mr. Blair, to say I sent Post Master General Blair to St. Louis to examine into that Department, and report.
>
> Blair did go, with my approbation, to see and converse with Gen. Fremont as a friend. I do not feel authorized to furnish you with copies of letters in my possession without the consent of the writers. No impression has been made on my mind against the honor or integrity of Gen. Fremont; and I now enter my protest against being understood as acting in any hostility toward him.

Lincoln elaborated on his views in a letter to his friend, Senator Orville H. Browning.

> Yours of the 17th is just received, and coming from you, I confess it astonishes me. That you should object to adhering to a law, which you had assisted in making, and presenting to me, less than a month before, is odd enough. … But this is a very small part, Genl. Fremont's proclamation, as to confiscation of property, and the liberation of slaves, is purely political, and not within the range of military law. … The proclamation in the point in question is simply "dictatorship."

> It assumes that the general may do anything he pleases—confiscate the lands, and free the slaves of loyal people, as well as of disloyal ones. And going the whole figure I have no doubt would be more popular with some thoughtless people, than that which has been done!

Lincoln then asserted:

> But I cannot assume this reckless position; nor allow others to assume it on my responsibility. You speak of it as being the only means of saving the government.
>
> On the contrary it is itself the surrender of the government. Can it be pretended that it is any longer the government of the U.S.—any government of Constitution and laws—wherein a General, or a President, may make permanent rules of property by proclamation? What I object to, is, that I as President, shall expressly or impliedly seize and exercise the permanent legislative functions of the government. So much as to principle; now as to policy. …
>
> No doubt the thing was popular in some quarters, and would have been more so if it had been a general declaration of emancipation. The Kentucky Legislature would not budge till that proclamation was modified; and Gen. Anderson telegraphed me that on the news of Gen. Fremont having actually issued deeds of manumission, a whole company of our Volunteers threw down their arms and disbanded.

Lincoln made a crucial point:

> I think to lose Kentucky is nearly to lose the whole game.
>
> Kentucky gone, we cannot hold Missouri, nor, as I think Maryland. These all against us, and the job on our hands is

> too large for us. We would as well consent to separation at once, including the surrender of this capitol. On the contrary, if you will give up your restlessness for new positions, and back me … on the grounds upon which you and other kind friends gave me the election, and have approved in my public documents, we shall go through triumphantly.[159]

At the same time Lincoln was contending with demands for guns to arm new recruits, but with limited supply. Writing Indiana governor Oliver P. Morton, he explained, "We are doing the best we can. You do not receive arms from us as fast as you need them; but it is because we have not near enough to meet all the pressing demands; and we are obliged to share around what we have, sending the larger share to the points which appear to need them the most."[160]

Lincoln found himself on the horns of a dilemma. Radical members of Congress and Western governors supported Fremont's proclamation, calling it a firm measure for prosecuting the war. Trusted sources, including Attorney General Bates, said Fremont stood in the way of efforts to unify Missourians. Others said Fremont lacked the ability to command, surrounded himself with corrupt individuals, and failed to protect pro-Union Missourians from the marauding Confederates.

It was clear that Fremont chose not to bow to the president's policy direction and tried to politically outflank him. Lincoln, in late October, became persuaded that Fremont had to go when Fremont failed to move his troops against the Confederates. Some complained about the dismissal of Fremont, contending Democratic generals were untouched. Lincoln gave instructions to General Scott, who drafted Special Order Number 18, which was sent by Lincoln to General S. R. Curtis. It stated, "Headquarters of the Army, October 24, 1861, Major-General Fremont, of the U.S. Army, the present commander of the Western department of the same, will, on the receipt of this order, call Major-General Hunter, of the U.S. Volunteers, to relieve him temporarily in that command, when he [Major-General Fremont] will report to General Headquarters, by letter, for further orders. Winfield Scott."

This was enclosed with a letter that was addressed by Lincoln to Curtis: "On receipt of this … you will take safe, certain, and suitable measures to have the enclosure addressed to Major General Fremont, delivered to him, with all reasonable dispatch—subject to those conditions only, that if, when Gen. Fremont shall be reached by the messenger … he shall then have, in personal command, fought and won a battle, or shall then be actually in a battle, or shall then be in the immediate presence of the enemy, in expectation of a battle."[161]

Lincoln sent the letter to General Curtis in the hands of Leonard Swett, who reported:

> Tuesday morning I went immediately to Genl. Curtis. … We found numerous obstacles to the delivery. … The trouble of delivery was to get some reliable man, who had legitimate business inside General Fremont's lines. Captain [Ezekiel] Boyden … and Capt. [Thomas J.] McKinney were selected. McKinney, dressed as a farmer, rode two nights and a day and arrived … at 5 AM.
>
> After waiting five hours, and learning that there was no immediate prospect of battle, he applied at headquarters for admission. The aid … told him he must make known his errand. He declined, stating he must see the Gen'l & could confer with no one else. … Finally he was admitted. When the Gen'l read the order he said excitedly: "Sir, how did you get through my lines," when informed the Gen'l dismissed him.

An aide instructed him not to tell in camp about the order. "In a few moments more he came back again asking if Hunter knew of this. To this … he responded as directed that a messenger had gone by Sedalia to give him a duplicate." Swett said the messenger was detained in camp, but using an overheard password and old order from General Curtis, made his way to Hunter, and on the next day about noon found him. Fremont ordered all his men to arms and Hunter to march overnight to join him in battle next morning.

"When morning came, Fremont issued his Farewell Address and left without giving any information about the Gov (ernment) property. There went with him, his bodyguard, 50 Indians and a paymaster with between 200,000 and 300,000$." Swett added, "The paymaster was arrested here last night and has some of the money. Hunter on taking command sent cavalry scouts for from 30 to 40 miles but in all directions from 30 to 40 miles but … there was no enemy."

More damaging, Swett also reported, "Let me tell a few more things which I have tried to investigate candidly & believe to be true. Gen'l Fremont has talked about his signature to unlawful orders being above the law & to be obeyed. The German people have talked about making him Dictator. Some of his officers in quite high standing have talked so too." Lincoln had accurately gauged the situation and had used Swett rather than the military to ensure that his orders were delivered.[162]

Fremont's removal caused an explosion of anger in the West. This same sentiment prevailed among abolitionists and radical members of Congress. *Cincinnati Gazette* editor Richard Smith warned Chase, "The West is threatened with a revolution," because the "public consider that Fremont has been made a martyr." Then he asked, "Is it not time for the President to stop and consider, as this is a government of the people, whether it is not unsafe to disregard and override public sentiment?"[163]

Historian George Bancroft differed. "Your administration has fallen upon times, which will be remembered as long as human events find a record. I sincerely wish to you the glory of perfect success. Civil war is the instrument of Divine Providence to root out social slavery; posterity will not be satisfied with the result, unless the consequences of the war shall effect an increase of free states. This is the universal expectation and hope of men of all parties."

Lincoln replied, "I esteem it a high honor to have received a note from Mr. Bancroft, inclosing … proceedings of a New York meeting, taking measures for the relief of Union people of North Carolina. I thank you, and all others participating, for this benevolent and patriotic movement. The main thought in the closing paragraph of your letter is one which did not escape my attention, and with which I must deal in all due caution, and with the best judgment."[164]

On November 15, Lincoln replied to a delegation of Baltimore citizens, who asked for fair participation by the mechanics and laboring men of Baltimore in supplying material and provisions. Lincoln said he deplored the madness of those citizens who had destroyed the Baltimore and Ohio Railroad, the Northern Pennsylvania Railroad, and the railroad from Baltimore to Philadelphia in a single night. The government was working diligently to restore those great avenues.

"I congratulate you upon the declaration which the people of Baltimore and Maryland have made in the recent election, of their recent approbation of the federal government, and of their enduring loyalty to the Union," Lincoln said. He called their wish for participation in supplying the Union "reasonable and just," adding, "I am sure that every member of the Administration will cheerfully … carry them out so far as it can be done consistently with … prudence and economy."[165]

Meanwhile, Lincoln wrote to Major General Henry Halleck, now commanding in the Department of Missouri, "As an insurrection exists in the United States and is in arms in the State of Missouri, you are hereby authorized and empowered to suspend the Writ of Habeas Corpus within the limits of the military division under your command and to exercise martial law as you find it necessary in your discretion to secure the public safety and authority of the United States."[166]

Lincoln's annual message to Congress December 3, 1861, began:

> In the midst of unprecedented political troubles, we have cause of great gratitude to God for unusual good health, and abundant harvests. … A disloyal portion of the American people have … been engaged in an attempt to divide and destroy the Union. A nation which endures factious domestic division, is exposed to disrespect abroad; and one party, if not both, is sure … to invoke foreign intervention …
>
> The principal lever relied on by the insurgents for exciting foreign nations to hostility … is the embarrassment of commerce. … It is not my purpose to review our discussions with foreign states, because whatever might be their wishes … the integrity of our country, and the stability of our government, mainly depend … on the loyalty, virtue, patriotism and intelligence of the American people. … I venture to hope … we have practiced prudence and liberality toward foreign powers. …
>
> Since … it is apparent that here … foreign dangers necessarily attend domestic difficulties, I recommend that adequate and ample measures be adopted for maintaining the public defenses of every side.

Lincoln specifically asked for fortifications with arms depots on the Great Lakes, and the construction of a railroad to connect to the loyal regions of East Tennessee and North Carolina. Kentucky, he suggested, would cooperate and select the most judicious line.

Turning to Treasury, Lincoln said operations have been conducted with signal success.

> The patriotism of the people has placed at the disposal of the government the large means demanded by the public

> exigencies. Much of the national loan has been taken by citizens of the industrial classes, whose confidence in the country's faith, and zeal for their country's deliverance from present peril, have induced them to contribute … the whole of their limited acquisitions …
>
> This fact imposes peculiar obligations to economy in disbursement and energy in action. … It is gratifying to know that expenditures made necessary by the rebellion are not beyond the resources of the loyal people, and to believe the same patriotism which has thus far sustained the government will continue to sustain it till Peace and Union shall again bless the land.

Lincoln turned to the report of the secretary of war regarding the numerical strength of the army.

> I refer to the creditable degree of discipline already attained by our troops. … It is gratifying to know that the patriotism of the people has proved equal to the occasion, and that the number of troops tendered greatly exceeds the force which Congress authorized. … The recommendation of the Secretary for an organization of the militia upon a uniform basis, is a subject of vital importance to the future safety of the country, and is commended to the … attention of Congress.
>
> The large addition to the regular army, in connection with the defection that has so considerably diminished the number of its officers, gives peculiar importance to his recommendation for increasing the corps of cadets to the greatest capacity of the Military Academy.

Similarly, Lincoln called for a more perfect organization of the navy, virtually recently brought into service, asking for additional grades and calling the present organization of the navy "defective and unsatisfactory."

Lincoln noted the geographical imbalance in the apportionment of the Supreme Court, and the lack of circuit courts in much of the nation. With three vacancies, two of them in the South, Lincoln said he was reluctant to appoint replacements, as those named likely could not or would not serve. A remedy, he suggested, would call for reapportionment of the Supreme Court, and provide for a system of circuit courts apportioned across the nation and ready to serve newly admitted states.

Turning to the current condition of statute law, Lincoln noted the Congress had enacted some five thousand bills and joint resolutions since the government was formed. "It seems to me very important," he said, "that the statute laws should be made as plain as possible, and be reduced to as small a compass as may consist with the fullness and precision of the will of the legislature and the perspicuity of its language." He said better administration would result from recodification.

> The last ray of hope for preserving the Union peaceably expired at the assault upon Fort Sumter. ... What was painfully uncertain then, is much better defined and more distinct now; and the progress of events is plainly in the right direction. The insurgents confidently claimed a strong support from north of Mason and Dixon's line; and the friends of the Union were not free from apprehension on the point. This, however, was soon settled definitely and on the right side.
>
> Little Delaware led off right from the first. Maryland was made to seem against the Union. Our soldiers were assaulted, bridges were burned and railroads torn up within her limits; and we were many days ... without the ability to bring a single regiment over her soil to the capital. Now, her bridges and railroads are repaired ... her people, at a regular election,

> have sustained the Union, by … a larger … vote than they ever before gave to any candidate, or any question.
>
> Kentucky, too, for some time in doubt, is now decidedly, and, I think, unchangeably, ranged on the side of the Union. Missouri is comparatively quiet; and I believe cannot again be overrun by the insurrectionists. These three states … neither of which would promise a single soldier at first, now have an aggregate of not less than forty thousand in the field for the Union.

He noted that after a somewhat bloody struggle, the Union people of West Virginia were masters of their country.

> Lieutenant General [Winfield] Scott has retired from the … army. … The retiring chief repeatedly expressed his judgment in favor of General McClellan for the position; and in this the nation seemed to give a unanimous concurrence. The designation of General McClellan is … in considerable degree the selection of the Country as well as of the Executive; and hence there is … reason to hope there will be given him, the confidence, and cordial support … without which he cannot serve the country.

As for labor:

> It is the effort to place capital on an equal footing with, if not above labor, in the structure of government. It is assumed that labor is available only in connection with capital; that nobody labors unless somebody else, owning capital, somehow by the use of it, induces him to labor. This assumed it is next considered whether it is best that capital shall hire laborers, and thus induce them to work by their own consent, or buy them, and drive them to it without their consent.

> Labor is prior to, and independent of, capital. Capital is only the fruit of labor, and could never have existed if labor had not first existed. Labor is the superior of capital, and deserved much the higher consideration. Capital has its rights, which are as worthy of protection as any other rights. … The error is in assuming that the whole labor of community exists within that relation.

Lincoln concluded, "There is not … any such thing as the free hired laborer being fixed to that condition for life."

Lincoln stoutly defended the free laborer: "No men living are more worthy to be trusted than those who toil up from poverty—none less inclined to take, or touch, aught which they have not honestly earned. Let them beware of surrendering a political power which they already possess, and which, if surrendered, will surely be used to close the door of advancement against such as they, and to fix new disabilities and burdens upon them, till all of liberty shall be lost."[167]

Given the questionable loyalty of federal personnel, the administration had turned to private citizens to purchase military supplies. Equipping and arming the newly expanded military had challenged Cameron and the navy's Wells, tasked with weeding out disloyal men and finding loyal replacements. Cameron selected Alexander Cummings as special agent for the purchase of supplies in New York City. Cummings had been Cameron's link with Weed, who also was recruited.

Cummings had helped to found the Philadelphia *North American* and the *Evening Bulletin* and was the founding publisher of *The New York World*, first published on June 14, 1860. With Cummings spending weeks in Washington and in New York, the *World* faced financial problems. Cummings facilitated the merger between what was to become Manton Marble's *World* and James Watson Webb's *New York Courier and Enquirer*. Next he managed to get Webb an appointment as minister to Brazil.

The *World* started as a nativist, Protestant paper with a conservative Republican editorial policy. When the *World* met with financial problems, Cummings tried to enlist Weed as editor. Weed declined because he did not have an editor to replace him at his *Albany Evening Journal*. A Weed partner, Fred Seward, went to Washington with his father and Associate Editor George Dawson was named Albany, New York, postmaster. His efforts failed and stockholders dumped Cummings.

Marble gained control of the *World*, and sought Weed as editor, hoping this would end financial problems. Weed, and other Republicans Marble approached, declined. Marble turned to Barlow, a New York lawyer and investor who was a leading New York Democrat and a confidant of McClellan. Representative Fernando Wood, the city's former mayor, also invested. Cummings failure and Marble's success allowed Marble to remake the *World* into the voice of the Democratic opposition.

It was after the defeat of Clement Vallandigham for governor of Ohio in the October 1863 elections that Marble induced Barlow to buy out Wood, not wanting Democrats to be linked to peace democracy or the Copperheads. Marble celebrated Vallandignam's defeat, arguing it showed the party was not antiwar. His independent policies, however, gave way as Marble, influenced by Barlow, threw his support to General McClellan and sharply criticized Secretary Stanton.

Democratic leaders coopted the *World*. Their Albany Regency faction, led by Dean Richmond and Erastus Corning of the New York Central Railway, merged their *Albany Argus*, with the *World*. August Belmont also invested. Marble remained editor in chief. He and Barlow brought in important allies like Samuel J. Tilden, a prominent railroad lawyer. Marble wrote to Democrats throughout the Union asking that they form party clubs, send political information, and distribute the *World*.

The *World*'s circulation climbed, making it fifth among the metropolitan dailies.

Journalists and politicians joked that Belmont, Barlow, and Tilden ran the *World* with assistance from Marble. The Belmont-Marble correspondence reveals many instances of Belmont providing ideas for editorial policy and management. When Belmont in 1863 founded the Society for the Diffusion of Political Knowledge, he looked to the *World* as his personal printing press for the literature.

"Pamphleteers attacked the rising war debt, the government's military strategy, and the Republican Party's centralizing project and agitated for a negotiated peace and a revocation of emancipation. Belmont also promoted these ideas in the *World*." Marble's vengeance centered on the campaign to unseat President Lincoln, and he stepped up the pace of his regular correspondence with McClellan as a potential candidate. Marble and Barlow were closely allied and corresponded regularly.[168]

Benjamin Wood bought the *New York Daily News* in 1861 with backing from his brother, Mayor Fernando Wood. It was an openly antiwar newspaper and became the political organ for the mayor. *New York Times* editor Henry Raymond backed Lincoln, but hewed to a conservative Republican editorial policy. The *New York Evening News*, edited by William Cullen Bryant, had cut loose from an alliance with the Albany Regency Democrats, shifting to support of radical Republicans. Greeley's *Tribune* increasingly shied away from Lincoln and criticized his war policies.[169]

The *New York Herald* and Greeley's *Tribune* were the most widely circulated and thus most potent New York papers. James Gordon Bennett's *Herald* was the strong second. Educated as a Scottish Roman Catholic seminarian, Bennett, declining holy orders, immigrated and in 1823 landed in Charleston, South Carolina. The *Charleston Courier* hired him. His arrival coincided with a slave insurrection that terrorized white citizens. Coincidentally, Fernando Wood was then in Charleston.

Bennett moved to New York and increasingly became politically active. In 1826, he was rising in the Tammany Hall's Democratic ward committee in the city's first ward. On cue from Amos Kendall, a Jackson confident, who organized American Telephone and Telegraph Co., Bennett viciously attacked the Second Bank of the United States. He supported Martin Van Buren over John C. Calhoun, which he calculated would further his career, but this effort failed to yield results.[170]

In Congress, the Committee on Government Contracts called Cummings to testify. Weed's name came up, but he was undertaking a European diplomatic mission and avoided the hearings. The chair, Representative Henry Laurens Dawes, "found (Cameron) hopelessly leagued with rats and scoundrels, playing politics and furthering his own Pennsylvania organization at Federal expense." In the hearings, Dawes reviewed the naval purchases and declared Wells acted with honesty.

Wells was criticized for giving his wealthy brother-in-law, Governor Edwin E. Morgan, responsibility of buying ships with a 2.5 percent commission, which some in Congress branded excessive. Yet the ships Morgan bought were good ships obtained at the lowest possible current price. This contrasted with the sharply criticized performance of Cummings. During the April crisis, Cummings was responsible for buying supplies for troops rushing to the defense of Washington.[171]

When contrasting the first year of the Lincoln administration and the final year of the Buchanan Administration, Dawes declared "that somebody has plundered the public Treasury well nigh in that single year as much as the entire current yearly expenses of the Government, which the people hurled from power because of corruption." Dawes spoke of Cummings telling the House committee he had no vouchers to put in evidence, going further, as quoted in the *Congressional Globe*:

"On the 21st of April, in the city of New York, there was organized a corps of plunderers upon the Treasury, and $2,000,000 was put at the discretion of a poor unfortunate—honest, I think—but entirely incompetent editor of a newspaper. He went straightway to purchase linen pantaloons and straw hats and London porter and dried herrings and such like provisions for the Army, including Hall's carbines, until he has used up $240,000 … and then he got scared and stopped."

Cameron's mistakes stoked criticism. Cameron, to blunt critics, called for arming slaves—the final straw that forced Lincoln to remove him. Wells, writing in his diary, said Cameron's retirement was "not wholly for the reason that was given out, but for certain loose matters of contracts, and because he had not the grasp, power, energy, comprehension, and important qualities essential to the administration of the War Department … to say nothing of his affiliation with Chase."[172]

Representative Stephen Baker, a Republican from New York, was among a number of members critical of Chase. As quoted in the *Congressional Globe*, he said:

> With all due deference to the opinion of the able and intelligent chairman of the Committee on Commerce, I think that high functionary committed a very grave political mistake when he sought a position for which he is not qualified, and resigned his seat in the Senate for the privilege of virtually wielding the civil patronage of government.
>
> The state of our finances is the most important subject that can engage our attention. … I propose directing the attention of this House … and in so doing it will be necessary to criticize the management of our finances. In this purpose I have no design to cast any imputation upon the character of the Secretary of the Treasury. I most emphatically differ in opinion … from the ardent and eloquent gentleman from Illinois [Elihu B. Washburne] as to his [Chase's] masterly financial ability.
>
> I accord him legal and political sagacity; but, looking to the deplorable condition of the Treasury and public credit,

> I fail to see any evidence of financial skill or ability. … He has fumbled over it for ten months, and it lies prostrate. It only requires the touch of a master to make it spring into full, vigorous, and abundant life. … It is with pain and humiliation that I mention … the credit of the Government has sunk so low that it cannot purchase … supplies at fair market prices.[173]

In the emerging and evolving industrial age, the national imperative remained a government able to harness and focus the resources of the nation to suppress the rebellion. This required a government loyal in purpose and able to mobilize the resources under the leadership of the president as commander in chief. Lincoln, confronted with the magnitude of the need, tasked his cabinet with finding loyal and able men to revitalize government.

President George Washington and his secretary of the treasury, Alexander Hamilton, had emerged from the Revolutionary War fully aware of the new national needs. Hamilton had proposed a military sufficient to maintain the nation, a bank of the United States to provide for currency and monetary policy, and an adequate government structure. Much of what he initiated died during the subsequent sixty years of slave power rule, predicated on limited government.

During the administration of President Andrew Jackson, both the Bank of the United States and federal regulation of the fur trade were eliminated. Senator Thomas Hart Benton of Missouri and Representative Churchill C. Cambreleng of New York, an associate of John Jacob Astor, were instrumental in these actions, along with Martin Van Buren. The demise of the Philadelphia-based bank shifted the financial power center of the nation from Philadelphia to New York's state banking system.

The Albany Regency, led by Marin Van Buren, was the creative spirit that maintained banks and politics in a most intimate union. In 1829 Van

Buren, elected New York governor, sponsored a law authorizing a system of state banks under a safety fund. He then resigned the governorship and headed for Washington. He joined the Jackson administration and was part of the attack that killed the Bank of the United States. This resulted in a void that became a political thorn for Lincoln.

In 1796, Washington had established the federal fur factory system, which supplied goods to Indians at cost, protecting them against exorbitant charges and raw alcohol from private traders. Dismantling this system turned the fur trade over to Astor's American Fur Company. Astor hired Benton as general counsel. Eliminating the bank took away the government's capacity to provide currency and ensure bank credit. Exclusive metallic money—hoarded in times of crisis—was inadequate.[174]

The slavery issue, raised anew by Cameron in his annual report in December 1861, abruptly called for the enlistment of freed slaves in the army and navy. Cameron's report was rushed by telegraph to newspapers, blindsiding Lincoln. Lincoln immediately ordered Postmaster Montgomery Blair to have all copies recalled and replaced it with a milder version. Cameron had seized on the issue of arming Negroes in an attempt to save his job, but Lincoln made him withdraw it.[175]

Cameron's advocacy for arming Negroes had the support of Edwin M. Stanton, who penned the key paragraph in the proposal. Stanton, soon to replace Cameron, had been on the verge of partnership with Samuel L. M. Barlow, wealthy New York lawyer, investor, and Democratic power broker. Cameron's conclusion squared with Stanton's convictions. Strangely, it also served Barlow's purpose of fostering a quarrel within the administration.

In a subsection of the July 4 report, Cameron said, "Those who make war against the Government justly forfeit all right of property, privilege, and security derived from the Constitution and laws against which they are in armed rebellion; and as the labor and service of their slaves constitute the chief property of the rebels, such property should share the common fate of war. … It is as clearly the right of the Government to arm slaves, when it may become necessary, as it is to use gunpowder taken from the enemy."[176]

Struggling to hold Kentucky, Maryland, and Missouri in the Union, Lincoln knew the report was counterproductive and inflammatory. Further it undermined Lincoln's initiative for compensated emancipation in Delaware, relations with the three border states, and the will of white soldiers "fighting only for the Union." Lincoln, contrary to Stanton, focused his own report on support for the Union and declaring that secession violated the Constitution.

Cameron's tenure at the War Department ended on January 11,1862. Lincoln wrote to Cameron, "As you have more than once expressed a desire for a change of position, I can now gratify you, consistently with my view of the public interest. I therefore propose nominating you to the Senate, next Monday, as minister to Russia." Two days later Lincoln nominated Edwin M. Stanton as the Secretary of War. He proved strong for the Union and opposed to slavery.[177]

In November 1861, a major incident that threatened war with England engaged the president. Known as the Trent Affair, it arose when Capt. Charles Wilkes of the US Navy halted a British mail packet ship and ordered the arrest of Confederate commissioners James Mason and John Slidell, transferring them from the packet to his *San Jacinto*. The action drew public commendation, but endangered relations with England, where it was viewed as a violation of sovereignty.

"Amidst the wild excitement created by this international interlude, the President alone maintained an imperturbable calmness and composure," Ward Hill Lamon reported.

> From the very first … he regarded the capture … as unwise and inexpedient. He was heard to say repeatedly that it

> would lead to dangerous complications with England. "Unfortunately," he said, "we have played into the hands of that wily power, and placed into their grasp a whip with which to scourge us."
>
> When interrogated … as to whether it was not a great humiliation to surrender the captured Commissioners … Mr. Lincoln replied, "Yes, it was the bitterest pill I have ever swallowed. There is, however, this counterbalancing consideration, that England's triumph will not have a long tenure … After our war is over … we shall be powerful enough to call her to an account and settlement."

Seward prepared a paper yielding to the British demand to give up the commissioners. Lincoln said he would try a hand at a paper opposed, but concluded to give them up. Chase called and said he and Stanton had discussed the issue, and Stanton believed the arrest was legal and could be sustained by international law. Lincoln said Stanton had been rude to him in the past but asked Chase to bring in Stanton, who came and presented his views, which Lincoln asked be put in writing.

It was when Stanton presented his views that Lincoln said,"'Mr. Stanton, this is a time of war, and you are as much interested in sustaining the government as myself or any other man. This is no time to consider mere party issues. The life of the nation is in danger. I need the best counselors. … I have every confidence in your judgment, and have concluded to ask you to become one of my counselors. The office of the Secretary of War will be vacant, and I want you to accept the position. Will you do it?' Stanton, shocked, said: 'Why, Mr. President, you take me by surprise. … Give me a day or two …' Two days later he accepted."[178]

Congress, which investigated the initial actions of the War Department, issued the following censure: "Resolved, that Simon Cameron, late Secretary of War, by investing Alexander Cummings with the control of large sums of the public money, and authority to purchase military supplies without restriction … when the services of competent public officers were available … has adopted a policy highly injurious to the public service, and deserves the censure of the House."

Lincoln then filed an unexpected response:

> The insurrection which is yet existing in the United States, and aims at the overthrow of the federal Constitution and the Union, was clandestinely prepared during the winter of 1860 and 1861, and assumed an open organization in the form of a reasonable provisional government. … On the 12th day of April 1861, the insurgents committed the flagrant act of civil war by the bombardment and capture of Fort Sumter, which cut off all hope of immediate conciliation …
>
> Immediately afterward all the roads and avenues to this city [Washington] were obstructed, and the capital was put into the condition of siege. The mails in every direction were stopped, and the lines of telegraph cut off by the insurgents, and military and naval forces, which had been called out by the government for the defense of the Washington, were prevented from reaching the city by organized and combined treasonable resistance in the State of Maryland …
>
> Congress had indefinitely adjourned. There was no time to convene them. It becomes necessary for me to choose whether, using only the existing means, agencies, and processes … I should let the government fall at once into ruin, or availing myself of the broader powers conferred by the Constitution in cases of insurrection, I would make an effort to save it. … I thereupon summoned my constitutional advisers, the heads to departments to meet.

Lincoln said he, with the cabinet's "unanimous concurrence," directed an armed cutter to protect coastal marine and especially California treasure ships. He ordered the purchase or charter of various ships. He further directed several officers "to take the advice and obtain the aid and efficient services of … Edwin D. Morgan, the governor of New York, or, in his absence, George D. Morgan, William M. Evarts, R. M. Blatchford and Moses H. Grinnell, who were … especially empowered."

Lincoln continued:

> On the same occasion I directed that Governor Morgan and Alexander Cummings … should be authorized by the Secretary of War, Simon Cameron, to make all necessary arrangements for the transportation of troops and munitions of war … until communications by mails and telegraph should be completely re-established between the cities of Washington and New York. No security was required to be given by them, and either of them was authorized to act …
>
> I authorized and directed the Secretary of the Treasury to advance, without requiring security, two millions of dollars of public money … to be used in meeting such requisitions. … The several departments of the government … contained so large a number of disloyal persons that it would have been impossible to provide safely, through official agents only, for the performance of the duties thus confided to citizens favorably known for their ability, loyalty and patriotism …
>
> I recall these transactions now because my attention has been directed to a resolution which passed the House. … Congress will see that I should be wanting equally in candor and in justice if I should leave the censure expressed in this resolution to rest exclusively or chiefly upon Mr. Cameron. The same sentiment is unanimously entertained by the heads of departments, who participated in the proceedings which the House of Representatives has censured.

> It is due to Mr. Cameron to say that, although he fully approved the proceedings, they were not moved nor suggested by himself, and that not only the President but all the other heads of departments were at least equally responsible with him for whatever error, wrong or fault was committed in the premises.

Lincoln's statement defending Cameron and his allies protected and cemented their loyalty in the Republican Party in Pennsylvania, important for the election of 1864.

Cameron approvingly wrote from St. Petersburg on June 26, 1862, "I must begin this my first letter from Russia, by thanking you for your Message to Congress, in relation to the N(ew) York agencies. It was a good act, bravely done. Right, in itself, as it was, very many men in your situation, would have permitted an innocent man to suffer rather than incur responsibility. I am glad to see that the leadings papers of Europe speak of it, in high terms, as an act of nobleness."[179]

Stanton stepped into a War Department historically run by field commanders who acted nearly independently of the secretary and the president. The field commanders—often with strong support in the states—looked on the department as a nuisance or as clerks. Generals such as McClellan and Fremont took policy into their own hands. Yet they demanded more men, weapons, and supplies. It was vital to provide support for a growing military.

Stanton's objective was to provide the military power to win the war. Stanton also told Edward Atkinson in June 1862 that he had concluded that each day of war added strength to the abolitionist argument. He, like Lincoln, knew the Union army marched to the tune of Northern opinion. As events transpired, opinion in the army shifted. Soldiers were coming to see the need to deprive the South of the productivity of slaves and to enlist the freed slaves in the military.

Lincoln backed Stanton as he swiftly reformed the department. Congress was persuaded to give him two more assistant secretaries.

Stanton named his trusted colleague, Peter Watson, and John Tucker, a Pennsylvanian. He retained Thomas A. Scott, a former superintendent of the Pennsylvania Railroad, who later left to head that railroad and who gained fame as mentor to Andrew Carnegie. The appointments showed that Stanton understood the military's reliance on railroads.

Stanton reduced the earlier call for volunteers, chiefly to allow time to organize the army and to ensure the recruits could be adequately equipped and trained. Stanton organized a War Department that could cope. He cultivated members of Congress, specifically members of the congressional Committee on the Conduct of the War.

A new challenge emerged when the July military draft failed to produce enough men, requiring a supplementary call even as governors asked the draft be postponed.

Pleased to have a capable war secretary, Lincoln supported Stanton's reform of the department's bureaucratic structure. This included more clerks, messengers, and laborers and more noncommissioned officers on the staff of the adjutant general. His new assistant secretaries, Watson and Tucker, proved both efficient and effective in their work. The experienced Scott, tasked with supervision of railroads, organized the efficient movement of supplies and troops.

Stanton, McClellan, and Quartermaster General Montgomery Meigs negotiated a rate formula that prevented gouging by the railroads for the transport of wartime material. Stanton ordered standardized track gauges, freight-car procedures, and signaling systems. Stanton named Edward S. Sanford, president of the American Telegraph Company, as military supervisor of the telegraph. Stanton demanded rigid censorship. Watson screened journalists to ensure both their loyalty and that reporting did not expose military information.[180]

In early January 1862, McClellan resigned as president of the eastern division of the Ohio and Mississippi Railroad, noting in a letter to

Barlow, "I sent my resignation … so I am no longer a railroad man—but strongly suspect I will be back in some occupation in civil life when this rebellion is over." Commenting on Stanton's appointment to succeed Cameron, he called it "a most unexpected piece of good fortune, & I hope it will produce a good effect in the North."[181]

Viewing Secretary Stanton as an ally, McClellan, in late January 1862, laid out his strategic plan, centered on military and political objections that eventually proved the dividing line for the election of 1864. McClellan's ties to Barlow and the deliberate nature of his military movements fueled opposition in the Committee on the Conduct of the War. Stanton, who had backed away from a lucrative law partnership with Barlow, initially supported McClellan, who wrote to Stanton:

"I assumed command of the troops in the vicinity of Washington on Saturday July 27, 1861, 6 days after the Battle of Bull Run. I found no army to command, a mere collection of regiments cowering on the banks of the Potomac, some perfectly raw, others dispirited by their recent defeat. Nothing … had been done to secure the southern approaches to the Capital … nothing had been done to defend the avenues to the city on the northern side of the Potomac."

Turning to the present, he said:

> The Capital is secure against attack—the extensive fortifications erected by the labor of our troops enable a small garrison to hold it against a numerous army; the enemy have been held in check; the State of Maryland is securely in our possession; the detached counties of Virginia are again within the pale of our laws; & all apprehension of trouble in Delaware is at an end; the enemy are confined to the positions … occupied before 21 July …
>
> More than all this, I have now under my command a well-drilled & reliable Army to which the destinies of the country

> may be confidently committed. This Army is young, & untried in battle, but it is animated by the highest spirit, & is capable of great deeds. That so much has been accomplished, & such an Army created in so short a time from nothing will hereafter be regarded as one of the highest glories of the Administration & the nation.
>
> Many weeks, I may say many months, ago this Army of the Potomac was fully in condition to repel any attack;—but there is a vast difference between that & the efficiency required to enable troops to attack successfully an Army elated by victory, and entrenched in a position long since selected, studied, & fortified.

McClellan had done his work well. An observer in the Crimean War, he learned firsthand of the slaughter that modern weapons fired from entrenched positions could inflict on attackers.

> In the earliest papers I submitted to the Presdt I asked for an effective movable force far exceeding the aggregate now on the banks of the Potomac—I have not that force ... Even when in a subordinate position I always looked beyond the Army of the Potomac; I was never satisfied in my own mind with a barren victory, but looked to combined & decisive operations. When I was placed in command of the Armies of the U.S. I immediately turned my attention to the whole field of operations. ...
>
> I confess that I did not then appreciate the absence of a general plan which had before existed, or did I know that utter disorganization & want of preparations pervaded the western armies. I took it for granted that they were nearly, if not quite, in condition to move towards the fulfillment of my plans—I acknowledge that I made a great mistake.

Strategically, McClellan had wanted East Tennessee occupied and the railroad running below the Cumberland Gap cut.

> I sent at once, with the approval of the Executive, officers I considered competent to command in Kentucky & Missouri—their instructions looked to prompt movements. I soon found that the labor of creation & organization had to be performed there—transportation, arms, clothing, artillery, discipline—all were wanting; these things required time to procure them; the Generals in command have done their work most creditably—but we are still delayed.
>
> I had hoped that a general advance could be made during the good weather of December—I was mistaken. My wish was to gain possession of the Eastern Tennessee Railroads as a preliminary movement,—then to follow … immediately by an attack on Nashville & Richmond. … I have ever regarded our true policy as … fully preparing ourselves & then seeking for the most decisive results;—I do not wish to waste life in useless battles, but prefer to strike at the heart.

In analyzing the two plans—a direct attack south upon the enemy's entrenched positions at Manassas or an operation in the lower Chesapeake Bay, McClellan favored the second. The first, he said, involved moving his vast army over nearly impassable roads against entrenched enemy positions. The second, he said, provided the shortest route to Richmond, and roads usable in all seasons.

Furthermore, supplies for the army could come on the waterways of the area.

As to the first of the two plans, McClellan explained, "In this latitude the weather will for a considerable period be very uncertain, & a movement commenced in force on roads in tolerably firm condition will be liable, almost certain, to be much delayed by rains & snow. It will therefore be next to impossible to surprise the enemy, or take him at a disadvantage by rapid maneuvers;—our slow progress will enable him to divine our purposes & take his measures accordingly."[182]

Lincoln defended McClellan against congressional charges that he was a proslavery Democrat and who urged him to attack. Lincoln wanted an attack on Richmond from Manassas that would keep Union forces between Confederate forces and Washington. A loss of the capital would be catastrophic for the nation and could result in foreign intervention. Stanton, was put off by McClellan's response, and steadily moved away from his initial support for him.[183]

CHAPTER VII

THE UNDERCURRENT OF ELECTIONS; POLITICS AND MCCLELLAN'S POLITICS; THE PRESS AND THE ARMY

Radical representatives and senators, angered over Union defeats at Bull Run and Ball's Bluff, organized the Committee on the Conduct of the War. Upset over too many Democrat generals, the firing of Fremont, and the pace of the war, three senators and four representatives named to form the committee were tasked to look into all phases of the Civil War. Radical members also took issue with McClellan as a proslavery Democrat who failed to take the initiative in battle.

In the Senate, Vice President Hamlin named Republicans Benjamin F. Wade, Ohio, and Zachariah Chandler, Michigan; and Democrat Andrew Johnson, Tennessee. House Speaker Galusha Grow of Pennsylvania chose Republicans George W. Julian, Indiana; John Covode, Pennsylvania; and Daniel W. Gooch, Massachusetts; and Democrat Moses Fowler Odell, New York. The committee held hearings behind closed doors and targeted McClellan, his political stand, and his strategy.[184]

Congress challenged Lincoln on the question of whether seceded states remained as states or not. Restless and impatient radicals contemplated vengeance. Greatly concerned that Lincoln would seek to restore the status quo, on February 11, 1862, Senator Charles Sumner of Massachusetts introduced resolutions calling for "subjugation through emancipation."

Sumner's resolutions undermined Lincoln's reconstruction plan and Lincoln's position that secession was illegal.

In his first resolution, Sumner declared, "That any vote of secession, or other act by which any State may undertake to put an end to the supremacy of the Constitution ... is inoperative and void ... and when sustained by force it becomes a practical abdication ... of all rights under the Constitution, while the treason which it involves still further works an instant forfeiture of all those functions and powers essential to the continuous existence of the State as a body politic." From that time forward, Sumner asserted, "the territory falls under the exclusive jurisdiction of Congress."

A second resolution stated, "Any combination ... assuming to act in the place of such State, attempting to ensnare or coerce the inhabitants into a confederation hostile to the Union, is rebellious, treasonable, and destitute of moral authority; and that such combination is an usurpation incapable of any constitutional existence and utterly lawless."

A third stated, "That the termination of a State under the Constitution necessarily causes the termination of those peculiar local institutions which, having no origin in the Constitution, or in those natural rights, which exist independent of the Constitution, are upheld by the sole and exclusive authority of the State."

Sumner, a leading Senate Republican, was proposing to annihilate state governments in rebel states, punishing the loyal and the disloyal, and Lincoln said he would veto the resolutions.

Senator James Dixon of Connecticut then introduced this resolution: "That all acts or ordinances of secession, alleged to have been adopted by any legislature or convention of the people of any State, are as to the Federal Union absolutely null and void. ... They do not, in any degree, affect the relations of the State, wherein they purport to have been adopted, to the Government of the United States, but are as to such Government acts of rebellion, insurrection, and hostility."

The resolution declared that acts of secession were "on the part of the individuals engaged therein, or giving assent thereto; and that such States are, notwithstanding such acts or ordinances, members of the Federal Union and as such are subject to all the obligations and duties imposed upon them by the Constitution of the United States; and the loyal citizens of such States are entitled to all the rights and privileges thereby guaranteed or conferred."

Congress adopted the Dixon resolution.[185]

With the defeat of his resolutions, Sumner declared support for the Wade-Davis Bill for reconstruction under Congress: "Sir, as it now stands, I am unwilling that emancipation shall depend upon the will of any one man, be he President or Senator. I wish to place (it) under the highest sanctions which our country knows."

Wells said that Sumner, apart from international law and treaties, was "impulsive and unreliable, and when his feelings were enlisted, imperious, dogmatical, and often unjust."[186]

When Union forces recaptured enough of Tennessee, Lincoln turned to the question of its administration. He ran head on into the congressional debate over reconstruction. Despite disagreements and debate in Congress, the president acted on his own, naming Senator Andrew Johnson military governor. Appointments in other states followed. Lincoln's decision was controversial, but he was careful to appoint officials acceptable to Congress.

General William Nelson, who had entered Nashville with Buell's army, warned, "Do not send Andy Johnson here in any official capacity. He represents a party! Let him come as Senator if he wants to. He is too much embittered to entrust with a mission as delicate as the direction of a people under the present circumstances."

Assistant Secretary of War Thomas A. Scott, also in Nashville, agreed. He suggested to Stanton it would be better to select a "wise and prudent man" for the post, adding, "While I know of no man personally I would rather see in that position than Mr. Johnson, yet I believe that it would not be a prudent appointment at this time."

Yet it was Mrs. Lincoln who bitterly opposed the appointment. Elizabeth Keckley described how Mrs. Lincoln prided herself on her ability to read character. Keckley said that she overheard Mary Lincoln tell her husband, "He is a demagogue, and if you put him in power, Mr. Lincoln, mark by words. You will rue it some day."[187]

In March 1862, Lincoln in his message to Congress urged cooperation with any state that might adopt gradual emancipation with compensation. He said the cost of this war would purchase all the slaves at fair value in any named state. He argued it deprived the South of a hoped-for independence among seceding states and the belief that, once achieved, Southern independence would entice Northern slave states to join them. "To deprive them of this hope, substantially ends the rebellion."[188]

A joint resolution of Congress declared, "The United States ought to co-operate with any State which may adopt gradual abolishment of slavery giving to such State pecuniary aid, public and private, produced by such change of system." A further resolution of April 14 ordered the printing of ten thousand copies of the message and resolutions. None of the border states, however, accepted Lincoln's earnest plea for the attention of Congress and the people for compensated emancipation.

When the *New York Times* intimated the plan would fail on the score of expense, Lincoln wrote to Raymond, "I hope you will reconsider this. Have you noticed … that less than one half-day's cost of this war would pay for all the slaves in Delaware, at four hundred dollars per head?—that eighty-seven day's cost of this war would pay for all in Delaware, Maryland, District of Columbia, Kentucky, and Missouri at the same price?" Raymond replied that the *Times* since had sustained the message.[189]

On March 11, Lincoln relieved McClellan from command of military departments other than the Potomac, as active operations of the Army of the Potomac would require his presence and supervision. The order consolidated commands west of a north-south line through Knoxville, Tennessee, under General Halleck and a mountain department under General Fremont. The president instructed that "prompt, full and frequent reports will be expected of all and each of them."

Rebutting McClellan directly, Lincoln asked, "'Do you really think I should permit the line from Richmond, via Manassas Junction, to this city to be entirely open, except what resistance could be presented by less than twenty thousand unorganized troops?' This is a question which the country will not allow me to evade." The president raised the question of how many troops McClellan had. McClellan had originally reported 108,000 and now was reporting only 85,000.

"I suppose the whole force which has gone forward for you, is with you … and if so, I think it is the precise time for you to strike a blow. By delay the enemy will relatively gain upon you … faster, by fortifications and re-enforcements, than you can be re-enforcements alone. And, once more let me tell you, it is indispensable to you that you strike a blow. I am powerless to help this. The country … is now noting … the present hesitation … is but the story of Manassas repeated."[190]

In May, Major General David Hunter, commanding the Department of the South at Hilton Head, South Carolina, imposed martial law as a military necessity on the states of South Carolina, Georgia and Florida, for having taken up arms against the United States. He declared, "Slavery and martial law in a free country are altogether incompatible; the persons in these three States—Georgia, Florida and South Carolina—heretofore held as slaves, are therefore, declared forever free."

Lincoln swiftly issued his own proclamation, declaring "that the government of the United States had no knowledge, information, or belief, of an intention on the part of General Hunter to issue such a proclamation. … And further, that neither General Hunter, nor any other commander, or person, has been authorized by the Government of the United States, to make proclamations declaring the slaves of any State free; and that the supposed proclamation … is altogether void."

Lincoln turned to the resolution adopted by Congress calling for national cooperation "with any State which may adopt a gradual abolishment of slavery, giving to such State pecuniary aid, to be used by such State in its discretion to compensate for the inconveniences, public and private produced by such changes in the system." Lincoln said the resolution adopted by large majorities of both branches of Congress stood as a definite and solemn proposal.

"You cannot if you would, be blind to the signs of the times. I beg of you a calm and enlarged consideration of them, ranging, if it may be, far above personal and partisan politics. This proposal makes common cause for a common object, casting no reproaches upon any. It acts not the Pharisee. The change it contemplates would come gently as the dews of heaven, not rending or wrecking anything." Then Lincoln added an earnest appeal: "Will you not embrace it?"[191]

Lincoln wrote to *New York Herald* publisher James G. Bennett, "Thanking you again for the able support given by you, through the *Herald*, to what I think is the true cause of the country, and also your kind expressions toward me personally, I wish to correct an erroneous impression of yours in regard to the Secretary of War. He mixes no politics whatsoever with his duties, knew nothing of Gen. Hunter's proclamation; and he and I … got up the counter proclamation."

The *Herald* had speculated that divisions in the cabinet related to Hunter's proclamation might require change, dismissing Seward and Chase "because they have given up the nigger business," and Welles also because he wanted only to be allowed "'to dose in peace.' Who, then, remains? Only Secretary Stanton, to whom both Seward and

Chase have thrown their dirty linen—the newspapers and the niggers." Bennett replied, telling Lincoln he had a mind to visit him.[192]

On June 10, 1862, Lincoln transmitted to Congress a copy of a treaty for the suppression of the African slave trade. The treaty between the United States and Britain was negotiated between Secretary Seward and Lord Lyons, and signed by both nations. Lincoln added, "It is desirable that such legislation as may be necessary to carry the treaty into effect should be enacted." Congress passed the needed implementation act on July 11.[193]

On February 4, Lincoln had granted a two-week stay of execution for Nathaniel Gordon, indicted and convicted for being engaged in the slave trade. Gordon's family and friends intensively pressed President Lincoln and his wife, Mary. Lincoln said he was bound to reject the application for a change to life imprisonment. He urged Gordon to abandon all hope of human pardon and "refer himself alone to the mercy of the common God and father of all."[194]

Both Fremont and McClellan asked more troops. Lincoln wrote to Fremont, "I do not say you have not done all you could. I presume you met unexpected difficulties; and I beg you to believe that as surely as you have done your best, so have I. … I am only asking of you to stand cautiously on the defensive, get your force in order, and give such protection as you can to the valley of the Shenandoah, and to Western Virginia. Have you received the orders? Will you act upon them?"[195]

Brigadier General Carl Schurz, at Fremont's headquarters, wrote, "When you ordered Gen. Fremont to march from Franklin to Harrisonburg, it was absolutely impossible to carry out the order. The army was in a starving condition and literally unable to fight. … It is … a very fortunate circumstance that Gen. Fremont did not succeed in placing himself across Jackson's line of retreat; for Jackson's force was so much superior … that he probably would have been beaten."[196]

At the same time, a delegation of progressive Friends called upon the president and presented a memorial praying him to decree the emancipation of slaves. In reply, the president said it was a relief to be assured that the deputation were not applicants for office, his chief trouble coming from that class of persons. He cited slavery as the next most troublesome, and agreed that slavery was wrong. He questioned whether a degree of emancipation could be enforced in the South.

One of the delegates, Oliver Johnson, responded decisively: "True, Mr. President, the Constitution cannot now be enforced at the South, but you do not on that account intermit the effort to enforce it, and the memorialists are solemnly convinced that the abolition of slavery is indispensable to your success." William Barnard, another, expressed sympathy and an earnest desire that Lincoln might, under divine guidance, free the slaves and thus save the nation from destruction.

Congress acted to repeal a previous currency provision. The president objected and sent it back to the Senate:

> The bill proposes to repeal the existing legislation, prohibiting the circulation of bank notes of a less denomination than five dollars within the District of Columbia, without permitting the issuing of such bills by banks not legally authorized to issue them. In my judgment, it will be found impracticable, in the present condition of the currency, to make such a discrimination.
>
> The banks have suspended specie payments; and a legal sanction given to the circulation of the irredeemable notes of one class of them will almost certainly be so extended, in practical operation, as to include those of all classes, whether authorized or unauthorized. If this view be correct, the currency of the District, should this act become a law, will certainly and greatly deteriorate, to the serious injury of honest trade and honest labor.

> This bill seems to contemplate no end which cannot be otherwise more certainly and beneficially attained. During the existing war it is peculiarly the duty of the national government to secure to the people a sound, circulating medium. This duty has been … satisfactorily performed, in part at least, by authorizing the issue of United States notes, receivable for all government dues except customs, and made a legal tender for all debts, public and private, except interest on public debt.
>
> "The object of the bill submitted to me, namely, that of providing a small note currency during the present suspension, can be fully accomplished by authorizing the issue of United States notes made necessary by the circumstances of the country, of notes of a similar character, but of less denomination than five dollars.

The effect of Secretary Chase's demand that the banks remit funds to the federal sub-treasury was stripping the banks of gold, and resulting in the shortage.

"Such an issue," Lincoln explained, "would answer all the beneficial purposes of the bill; would save a considerable amount to the treasury in interest; would greatly facilitate payments, to soldiers and other creditors, of small sums; and would furnish to the people a currency as safe as their own government."

Lincoln was addressing a Congress skeptical about the issuance of the notes, but also very much aware that they lacked an alternative.[197]

Senator Reverdy Johnson reported to President Lincoln as a special agent appointed by the Department of State. His assignment was to report on foreign consul complaints against the military proceedings under General Benjamin Butler in New Orleans. In his reply, Lincoln told Johnson of existing limitations:

> So far, for want, mainly, of adequate military force, little has been done but to obtain the possession of this City & the Country, immediately surrounding it.
>
> Whatever Union feeling (& it is said to have been extensive—) there was … has been subsided, & principally, from an impression that it is the purpose of Govt to force the Emancipation of slaves. This impression grows, in a great measure, from the course of Genl. Phelps. … Depend upon it, my Dear Sir, that unless this is at once corrected, this State cannot be, for years, if ever, reinstated in the Union. (General Phelps was the military governor of Arkansas and Louisiana.)
>
> Please pardon me for believing this is a false pretense (that Union feeling is being crushed out by the course of General Phelps). The people of Louisiana—all intelligent people everywhere—know full well, that I never had a wish to touch the foundation of their society, or any rights of theirs. With perfect knowledge of this, they forced a necessity upon me to send armies among them, and it is their own fault, not mine, that they are annoyed by the presence …
>
> And might it not be well for them to consider whether they have not already had time enough to do this? They very well know that the way to avert all this is simply to take their place in the Union upon the old terms. If they will not do this, should they not receive harder blows rather than lighter ones? You are ready to say I apply to friends what is due only to enemies. I distrust the wisdom of the sincerity of friends, who would hold my hands while my enemies stab me.[198]

In June, Lincoln traveled to West Point for consultations with General Scott, who summed up the meeting in a memorandum:

> I consider the numbers & positions of Fremont & Banks, adequate to the protection of Washington against any force the enemy can bring by the way of the Upper Potomac, & the troops at Manassas junction, with the garrisons of the forts on the Potomac & of Washington, equally adequate to its protection on the South.
>
> The force at Fredericksburg seems entirely out of position, & it cannot be called up … by McClellan, from the want of rail-road transportation, or an adequate supply train, moved by animals. If, however, there be a sufficient … vessels, at hand, that force might reach the head of York River … to aid in the operations against Richmond. … The defeat of the rebels … or their forced retreat … combined with our previous victories, would be a virtual end of the rebellion.

In the final battle of Seven Days at Malvern Hill, Lee lost heavily as artillery cut down his men. McClellan then retreated to Harrison's Landing, losing men and material. McClellan appealed to Stanton in a shocking and insubordinate telegram, closing, "If I save this Army now I tell you plainly that I owe no thanks to you or any other persons in Washington—you have done your best to sacrifice this Army." Lee was angered too, but because McClellan had withdrawn from the peninsula successfully.

Edward S. Sanford, telegraph supervisor at the War Department, did not relay McClellan's final sentence. Lincoln replied, "Save your Army at all events. … It is the price we pay for the enemy not being in Washington." Lincoln also was implored by another noted Democrat, August Belmont, the party chairman, who urged that Stanton be replaced by General Halleck, saying this would appeal to Democrats and firm up support among the Democrats for the policies of President Lincoln.[199]

This was a time when General McClellan expressed both anger and disgust at the direction from Washington. With more candor and force than at any time during the war, McClellan not only gave vent to his political views, but was unsparing in his criticisms of Secretary Stanton and Generals Pope and Halleck. In letters to Samuel Barlow, the New York Democratic leader, McClelland was unsparing in attacks on the Lincoln administration and his disdain for the president as well.[200]

McClellan handed a letter to Lincoln at Harrison's Landing, Virginia:

> I cannot but regard our condition as critical and I earnestly desire, in view of possible contingencies, to lay before your Excellency, for your private consideration, my general views concerning … the rebellion; although they do not strictly relate to the situation of this Army or strictly come within the scope of my official duties. These views amount to convictions … deeply impressed upon my mind and heart.
>
> Our cause must never be abandoned; it is the cause of free institutions and self government. The Constitution and the Union must be preserved, whatever may be the cost in time, treasure and blood. If secession is successful, other dissolutions are clearly to be seen in the future. Let neither military disaster, political faction or (sic) foreign war shake your settled purpose to enforce the equal operation of the laws of the United States upon the people of every state.
>
> The time has come when the Government must determine upon a civil and military policy, covering the whole ground of our national trouble. The responsibility of determining, declaring and supporting such civil and military policy and of directing the whole course of national affairs in regard to the rebellion must now be assumed and exercised by you or our cause will be lost. The Constitution gives you power sufficient even for the present terrible exigency.
>
> This rebellion has assumed the character of a War; as such it should be … conducted upon the highest principles known

> to Christian Civilization. It should not be a War looking to the subjugation of the people of any state. … It should not be … a War upon population; but against armed forces and political organizations. Neither confiscation of property, political executions … territorial organization of states or forcible abolition of slavery should be contemplated.

In this confidential letter, McClellan sought to direct policy on the conduct of war:

> In prosecuting the War, all private property and unarmed persons should be strictly protected; subject only to the necessities of military operations. All private property taken for military use should be paid or receipted for; pillage and waste should be treated as high crimes; all unnecessary trespass sternly prohibited; and offensive demeanor by the military toward citizens promptly rebuked.
>
> Military arrests should not be tolerated, except … where active hostilities exist; and oaths not required by enactments—Constitutionally made—should be neither demanded nor received. Military government should be confined to the preservation of public order and the protection of political rights. Military power should not … interfere with the relations of servitude, either by supporting or impairing the authority of the master; except for repressing disorder. …
>
> Slaves contraband under the Act of Congress, seeking military protection, should receive it. The right of the Government to appropriate permanently to its own service claims to slave labor should be asserted and the right of the owner to compensation therefore should be recognized. This principle might be extended upon grounds of military necessity and security to all the slaves within a particular state; thus working manumission in such state.

McClellan, in this letter dated July 7, 1862, declared that "in Missouri, perhaps in Western Virginia also and possibly even in Maryland the expediency of such a military measure is only a question of time." It was reported that Lincoln had quietly pocketed the letter to be read later, but that it was this letter that led Lincoln to begin drafting the Emancipation Proclamation. General McClellan's views were in opposition to Lincoln's.

The general's letter continued:

> A system of policy thus constitutional and conservative, and pervaded by the influences of Christianity and freedom, would receive the support of almost all truly loyal men, and would deeply impress the rebel masses and all foreign nations, and it might … commend itself to the favor of the Almighty. Unless the principles governing the further conduct of our struggle shall be made known and approved, the effort to obtain requisite forces will be almost hopeless.
>
> A declaration of radical views, especially upon slavery, will rapidly disintegrate our present armies. The policy of the Government must be supported by concentrations of military power. The national forces should not be dispersed in expeditions, posts of occupation and numerous Armies; but … collected into masses and brought to bear upon the Armies of the Confederate States; those Armies … defeated, the political structure … they support would … cease to exist.
>
> In carrying out any system of policy … you may form … will require a Commander in Chief of the Army; one who possesses your confidence, understands your views and who is competent to execute your orders by directing the military forces of the nation to the accomplishment of the objects by you proposed. I do not ask that place for myself. I am willing

> to serve you in such position as you may assign me and I will do so as faithfully as ever subordinate served superior.
>
> I may be on the brink of eternity and as I hope forgiveness from my maker I have written this letter with sincerity toward you and from love of my country.

When McClellan handed this confidential letter to Lincoln, he was taking counsel with important Democrats. Key was Barlow, as they corresponded extensively, and Fernando Wood, who visited, urging him to be a candidate for president in 1864. The visits and the letter compromised McClellan.[201]

McClellan wrote to his wife, "His Excellency was here yesterday & left this morning. He found the army anything but demoralized or dispirited—in excellent spirits. I do not know to what extent he has profited by his visit—not much I fear, for he really seems quite incapable of rising to the height of the merits of the question & the magnitude of the crisis. I will enclose … a copy of a letter I handed him, which I would be glad to have you preserve carefully as a very important record."[202]

The summer of 1862 was a very dark period of the war, as General McClellan took a 160,000-man, well-equipped army into Virginia, vowing to take Richmond. After severe fighting, he returned to Washington. Lincoln told Frank B. Carpenter, "Things had gone on from bad to worse, until I felt that we had reached the end of our rope on the plan of operations we had been pursuing; that we had about played our last card, and must change our tactics or lose the game."[203]

Issues of slavery and runaway slaves led Lincoln to sanction General Butler's policy labeling those within Union lines "contraband." Secretary Stanton informed Butler the president "is of the opinion that, under the law … they [runaway slaves] cannot be sent back to their masters; that, in common humanity, they must not be permitted to suffer for want of food, shelter or other necessaries of life … they should be provided for … and those capable of labor … set to work and paid wages."[204]

Artist Frank B. Carpenter harbored a desire to paint the first reading of the Emancipation Proclamation before the cabinet. Referred to Lincoln by representatives Schuyler Colfax and Owen Lovejoy, Carpenter and Lincoln agreed on the project. Through the courtesy of the President and Mrs. Lincoln, the White House state dining room was provided as a studio. Carpenter and Lincoln conversed freely during the six-month project, and Carpenter had access to Lincoln's private office.

Before the election of 1864, Henry Raymond published *The Life and Services of Abraham Lincoln*, and included the anecdotes and reminiscences of Carpenter, who quoted Lincoln: "I now determined upon the adoption of the Emancipation policy; and, without consultation with, or the knowledge of the Cabinet, I prepared the original draft of the Proclamation; and, after much anxious thought, called a Cabinet meeting upon the subject." This was in late July or early August of 1862.

"All were present, although Secretary Blair came in late. He asserted that issuing the proclamation could cost the Administration the 1862 elections. Nothing … was offered that I had not already fully anticipated and settled in my own mind, until Secretary Seward spoke. Said he:—'Mr. President, I approve of the Proclamation, but I question the expediency of its issue at this juncture. The depression of the public mind, consequent upon our reverses, is so great.'"

Seward explained, "I fear the effect of so important a step. It may be viewed as the last measure of an exhausted Government—a cry for help. … His idea, said the President, was that it would be considered our last shriek on the retreat." As the president told it, Seward concluded, "I suggest, sir, that you postpone its issue until you can give it to the country supported by military success, instead of issuing it, as would be the case now, upon the greatest disaster of the war."

Carpenter quoted Lincoln further: "The wisdom of the view of the Secretary of State struck me with very great force. It was an aspect of the case that, in all my thought upon the subject, I had entirely overlooked. The result was, that I put the draft of the Proclamation aside, as you do your sketch for the picture, waiting for a victory. From time to time I added or changed a line, touching it up here and there, waiting the progress of events." Thus, he waited until victory at Antietam.

Carpenter asked if there was not some opposition within the cabinet. Lincoln said Blair thought it would cost them the fall elections. There were reports that Smith believed they would lose Indiana, which they did. When Carpenter asked how Blair felt about it later, Lincoln replied, "Oh, he proved right in regard to the fall elections, but he is satisfied that we have since gained more than we lost." It was a political gamble, but Lincoln believed that the time and the proclamation were right.

On August 22, Greeley published in the *Tribune* "The Prayer of Twenty Million," editorially declaring:

> We think you are strangely and disastrously remiss … with regard to the emancipating provisions of the new Confiscation Act. … We think you are unduly influenced by … fossil politicians … from the Border Slave States. … We think timid counsel in such a crisis calculated to prove mistaken. … We complain that the Confiscation Act … is habitually disregarded …
>
> Mr. President, there is not one disinterested, determined, intelligent champion of the Union cause who does not feel that all attempts to put down the Rebellion and at the same time uphold its inciting cause are preposterous and futile. … I close as I began … that what an immense majority of the Loyal Millions of your countrymen require of you is a frank, declared, unqualified, ungrudging execution of the laws of the land.

Lincoln responded with a letter sent to Greeley on August 22:

> I have just read yours of the 19th … to myself through the New-York Tribune. If there be in it any statements, or assumptions of fact, which I may know to be erroneous, I do not, now and here, controvert them. If there be in it any inferences which I may believe to be falsely drawn, I do not now and here, argue against them. If there be perceptible in it an impatient and dictatorial tone, I waive it in deference to an old friend, whose heart I have always supposed to be right.
>
> As to the policy I "seem to be pursuing" as you say, I have not meant to leave any one in doubt. I would save it (the Union) the shortest way under the Constitution. The sooner the national authority can be restored; the nearer the Union will be "the Union as it was." If there be those who would not save the Union, unless they could at the same time save slavery, I do not agree. … If there be those who would not save the Union unless they could … destroy slavery, I do not agree. …
>
> My paramount object in this struggle is to save the Union, and is not either to save or to destroy slavery. If I could save the Union without freeing any slave I would … and if I could save it by freeing all the slaves I would … and if I could save it by freeing some and leaving others alone I would. … What I do about slavery, and the colored race, I do because I believe it helps to save the Union; and what I forbear, I forbear because I do not believe it would help to save the Union.
>
> I shall do less whenever I shall believe what I am doing hurts the cause, and I shall do more whenever I shall believe doing more will help the cause. I shall try to correct errors when shown to be errors; and I shall adopt new views so fast as they shall appear to be true views. I have here stated my purpose according to my view of official duty; and I intend

> no modification of my oft-expressed personal wish that all men everywhere could be free.

He signed it "A. Lincoln."[205]

Greeley printed Lincoln's letter in the *Tribune*, and editorialized, "I never doubted … that you desire, before, and above all else, to re-establish the now derided authority … of the Republic. I intended to raise only this question—Do you propose to do this by recognizing, obeying, and enforcing the laws, or by ignoring, disregarding, and in effect denying them?" Greeley's editorial policy proved throughout the Civil War to be antagonistic and a burden for Lincoln.[206]

The president, as commander in chief, ordered McDowell, Banks, and Fremont to cut off Jackson at Port Royal, as they had 40,000 men against Jackson's 17,000 men. Jackson escaped up the valley, but bloodied Fremont and Shields in a rearguard action before escaping to join Lee. Lincoln then brought General John Pope from the West to command the Army of Virginia, combining troops under Banks, Fremont, and Shields. Since the other three outranked him, Fremont immediately resigned.[207]

Pope assumed command in late July. Pope had scored two victories in Western battles. In addressing the men of his new command, Pope bred resentment when he praised his Western forces and disparaged the Eastern forces. General Lee swiftly attacked Pope's army. When the Army of Virginia met the massed forces of Generals Lee and Jackson in the second Battle of Bull Run, Pope was soundly defeated. General McClellan's forces failed to aid Pope.

Prior to the battle, Lincoln wired McClellan, "What news from direction of Manassas Junction?" McClellan offered options when he replied, "I am clear that one or two courses should be adopted. First to concentrate all our available forces to open communication with Pope. Second to leave Pope to get out of his scraps & at once use all our means to make the capital perfectly safe. No middle ground will now answer. Tell me what you wish me to do & I will do all in my power."

Lincoln wired back, "I think your first alternative, to wit, to concentrate all our available forces to open communication with Pope, is the right one. But I wish not to control. That I now leave to Gen. Halleck, aided by your counsels."

Lincoln, thinking the two armies would link up, was mystified by McClellan's words "leave Pope to get out of his scraps." Part of Pope's command was defeated at Cedar Mountain. Then in the second Bull Run, Lee and Jackson met and whipped Pope, who simply failed to understand the battlefield situation.

"Lee's achievement in his second strategic offensive was even more remarkable than in his first. Less than a month earlier the main Union army had been only twenty miles from Richmond. With half as many troops as his two opponents [Pope and McClellan], Lee had shifted the scene to twenty miles from Washington, where the rebels seemed posed for the kill." Lee outmaneuvered and psyched out both Union generals and carried the war North, to the shock of the nation.[208]

Lincoln's biographer Nicolay describes the situation:

> The defeat of Pope became final and conclusive on … August 30, and his telegram announcing it conveyed an intimation that he had lost control of his army. … President Lincoln had … to confront a most serious crisis … with what began to look like a serious conspiracy among McClellan's officers against Pope, with Pope's army in a disorganized retreat upon Washington, with the capital in possible danger … and with a … half-mutinous cabinet …
>
> On Monday, September 1, repressing every feeling of indignation, and solicitous only to make every expedient

> contribute to the public safety, he called McClellan from Alexandria to Washington and asked him to use his personal influence with the officers who had been under his command to give … support to Pope … and McClellan at once sent a telegram in this spirit. On September 2 … he gave a verbal order … that Major-General McClellan be placed in command … for the defense of the capital.
>
> Mr. Lincoln made no concealment of his belief that McClellan had acted badly toward Pope and really wanted him to fail; "but there is no one in the army who can man these fortifications and lick these troops of ours into shape half as well as he can," he said. "We must use the tools we have; if he cannot fight himself, he excels in making others ready to fight." It turned out … Washington had been exposed to no real danger.

Members of Congress objected to recalling McClellan. Within the cabinet, Chase had drawn up a letter to the president also signed by Stanton and Smith. It urged the "immediate removal of … McClellan." Bates drafted a similar document, contending, "It is not safe to entrust to Major General McClellan the command of any of the armies of the United States." Wells and Blair declined to sign. In a cabinet session, and in answer to words from Chase, Lincoln was distressed, precisely because he knew they were earnestly sincere.[209]

George Kimball, serving in Company A, Twelfth Massachusetts Volunteers, recounted:

> The men were scattered about in groups, discussing the events of their ill-starred campaign, and indulging in comments … decidedly uncomplimentary to those who had been responsible for the mismanagement. Suddenly, while these mournful consultations were in full blast, a mounted officer … reined up enough to shout, "Little Mac is back here on the road boys!"

> From extreme sadness we passed in a twinkling to a delirium of delight. … Whenever General McClellan appeared among his troops … it was the signal for the most spontaneous and enthusiastic cheering I ever listened to. … McClellan had always been fortunate … to excite enthusiasm among his troops, but demonstrations at this time took on an added … emphasis from the fact that he had been recalled to command after what the army believed to be an unwise and unjust suspension.[210]

On September 7, Christians of all denominations meeting in Chicago adopted a memorial in favor of national emancipation. The Rev. William W. Patton and the Rev. John Dempster presented it to the president, who said:

> The subject presented … is one upon which I have thought much for weeks past, and may I say even for months. I am approached with the most opposite opinions and advice, and that by religious men who are equally certain they represent the divine will …
>
> I am sure that either the one or the other class is mistaken in that belief, and perhaps in some respects both. I hope it will not be irreverent for me to say that if it is probable that God would reveal his will to others, on a point so connected with my duty, it might be supposed he would reveal it directly to me; for, unless I am more deceived in myself than I often am, it is my earnest desire to know the will of Providence in this matter. And if I can learn what it is I will do it!
>
> These are not, however, the days of miracles … I must study the plain physical facts of the case … and learn what appears to be wise and right. The subject is difficult and good men do not agree. … Would my word free the slaves when I cannot even enforce the constitution in the rebel States?

He added, "I raise no objections against it on legal or constitutional ground; for as commander-in-chief … I suppose I have a right to take any measure which may best subdue the enemy. Nor do I urge objections of a moral nature."

The delegates countered that good men differed, but truth was somewhere, and a matter of solemn moment for the president to ascertain. They said the memorial contained facts, principle, and arguments appealing to the intelligence of the president and his faith in Divine Providence; that he could not deny that the Bible denounced oppression as one of the highest of crimes, and threatened divine judgments against the United States.

The president rejoined: "I admit that slavery is the root of the rebellion, or at least its sine qua non. The ambition of the politicians may have instigated them to act, but they would have been impotent without slavery as their instrument. I will also concede that emancipation would help us in Europe, and convince them that we are incited by something more than ambition. I grant further that it would help somewhat at the North, though not as … you and those you represent imagine."

Emancipation, he said, would weaken the rebels by drawing off their laborers—a matter of great importance. "But," he added, "I am not so sure we could do much with the blacks. If we were to arm them, I fear that in a few weeks the arms would be in the hands of the rebels; and indeed thus far we have not had arms enough to equip our white troops." He further noted it would be a serious loss if some 50,000 Union soldiers from the border-states went over to the rebels as a result. I do not think they all would—not so many indeed as a year ago, or as six months ago—not so many today as yesterday. … Let me say one thing more: I think you should admit that we already have an important principle to rally and unite the people in the fact that constitutional government is at stake."

The delegates agreed that the value of constitutional government was indeed a grand idea, but contended the people knew that nothing else had put constitutional government in danger but slavery.

The two clergy urged good sense in drilling, arming, and using black as well as white troops. They urged that desertions would be replaced two to one by the increased spirit in the North. They said the struggle had gone too far and cost too much in treasure and blood to allow a partial settlement: "Let the line be drawn at the same time between freedom and slavery, and between loyalty and treason." They said the sooner the North knew who its enemies were, the better for the cause.

"Do not misunderstand me," President Lincoln responded, "because I have mentioned these objects. They indicate the difficulties that have thus far presented my action in some such way as you desire. I have the matter under advisement. And I can assure you that the subject is on my mind … more than any other. Whatever shall appear to be God's will I will do. I trust that, in the freedom with which I canvassed your views, I have not … injured your feelings."[211]

General Lee could not successfully attack the formidable defense of Washington, and instead invaded Maryland. Lee and Jefferson Davis had considered the risks and decided potential gains outweighed the risks. Lee hoped to feed and reequip his worn-down army with urgently needed supplies, including boots, munitions, and food, from the farms, factories, and towns of Maryland and Pennsylvania. He also wished to avoid battles in Virginia during the harvest season.[212]

Confederate Major General John G. Walker quoted Lee:

> In ten days from now, if the military situation is then what I confidently expect … after the capture of Harper's Ferry, I shall concentrate the army at Hagerstown, effectually destroy the Baltimore and Ohio road, and march to this point. … That is the objective point of the campaign. You remember … the long bridge over the Susquehanna, a few miles from Hagerstown.
>
> Well, I wish effectually to destroy that bridge, which will disable the Pennsylvania railroad for a long time. With the

> Baltimore and Ohio in our possession, and the Pennsylvania railroad broken up, there will remain to the enemy but one route of communications with the West, and that very circuitous by the way of the Lakes. After that I can turn my attention to Philadelphia, Baltimore, or Washington, as may seem best for our interests …
>
> "You doubtless regard it hazardous to leave McClellan practically on my line of communication, and to march into the heart of the enemy's country? Are you acquainted with General McClellan? He is a very able general but a very cautious one. His enemies among his own people think him so. His army is in a very demoralized and chaotic condition, and will not be prepared for offensive operations—or he will think so—for three of four weeks.[213]

A successful campaign might also induce European powers to recognize the Confederacy. Lee wrote to Davis on September 8 that a proposal for peace backed by Southern soldiers on Northern soil "would enable the people of the United States to determine at their coming elections whether they will support those who favor a prolongation of the war, or those who wish to bring it to a termination." Lee shrewdly assessed both opposing generals and Union politics.

His Pennsylvania operation emboldened by Jackson's capture of Harper's Ferry, Lee concentrated his army at Sharpsburg, Maryland, and decided to fight. As it turned out, Lee had only three or four days before McClellan, with some 70,000 men reinforced to 80,000 and no longer demoralized, was cautiously searching for Lee. Two of his soldiers, in a field near Frederick, found a copy of Lee's orders, showing Lee's army fragmented. Due to this unique stroke of luck Lee's battle plan fell into his hands, but McClellan failed to push through the mountain passes and destroy Lee before he could reassemble his divided army.

McClellan had a good battle plan, with three Union corps on the right, Burnside's large corps on the left, and four Union divisions and cavalry in reserve. But it was poorly executed. The fault was McClellan's, who failed to coordinate the attack. His army went forward in three stages instead of simultaneously, which permitted Lee to shift troops from quiet sectors to meet successive attacks. When his troops did break through, McClellan failed to commit his reserves and counter Lee.[214]

McClellan allowed Lee and his army to escape back into Virginia. Antietam weakened McClellan's hold on the Army of the Potomac. His failure to press the advantage in battle angered his men. Their respect for Lincoln grew. Lincoln had depressingly referred to the Army as "McClellan's body guard." McClellan's slows gave Lincoln the flexibility to replace McClellan. Lincoln had built a government and a war machine, and now needed an aggressive general in command.

Antietam gave Lincoln the victory needed to issue the preliminary Emancipation Proclamation in September 1862, declaring free all black slaves in Confederate territory. Using his authority as commander in chief, he freed the southern slaves as an act of military necessity. The proclamation virtually eliminated the possibility of European recognition of the Confederacy that could have broken the Union blockade of Southern ports.

> I, Abraham Lincoln, President of the United States of America, and Commander-in-chief of the Army and Navy thereof, do hereby proclaim and declare that hereafter, as heretofore, the war will be prosecuted for the object of practically restoring the constitutional relation between the United States, and each of the states, and the people thereof, in which states that relation is, or may be suspended, or disturbed.

Deliberately using legal form, his war measure explained:

> That it is my purpose, upon the next meeting of Congress, to again recommend that adoption of a practical measure

> tendering pecuniary aid to the free acceptance or rejection of all slave-states, so called, the people whereof may then have voluntarily adopted, immediate, or gradual abolishment of slavery within their respective limits; and that the effort to colonize persons of African descent upon this continent, or elsewhere, with their consent ... will be continued.
>
> That on the first day of January in the year ... one thousand eight hundred and sixty-three, all persons held as slaves within any state, or designed part of a state, the people whereof shall then be in rebellion against the United States shall be then, thenceforward, and forever free; and the executive government of the United Sates, including the military and naval authority will recognize and maintain the freedom of such persons in any efforts ... for their actual freedom.

Skeptics had feared that with the proclamation, many Union soldiers would throw down their arms. Lincoln immediately moved against those who would disrupt the draft and discourage enlistment. He declared:

> [It is] necessary to call into service not only volunteers but also portions of the militia by draft in order to suppress the insurrection ... and disloyal persons are not adequately restrained by the ordinary process of law from hindering this measure and from giving aid ... to the insurrection.
>
> Now ... be it ordered, first, that during the existing insurrection and as a necessary measure for suppressing the same, all Rebels and Insurgents, their aiders and abettors within the United States, and all persons discouraging volunteer enlistments, resisting militia drafts, or guilty of any disloyal practice, affording aid and comfort to Rebels against ... the United States, shall be subject to martial law and liable to trial and punishment by Courts Martial or Military Commissions.

> Second. That the Writ of Habeas Corpus is suspended in respect to all persons arrested, or who are now, or hereafter during the rebellion shall be, imprisoned in any fort, camp, arsenal, military prison, or other place of confinement by any military authority or by the sentence of any Court Martial of Military Commission.

Lincoln knew the demands of the military, weakened by desertions, had to be met, and yet believed the time not yet right to mobilize Negro troops.[215]

Governors of the loyal states met at Altoona, Pennsylvania, and eleven or twelve called on the president in Washington, conveying a message of strong support, which was summarized by the *National Intelligencer* of September 27:

> The address expresses, first, a cordial personal and official respect for the President; second, a determination, under all circumstances, to support and maintain his constitutional authority, speaking for themselves and people of their respective states.
>
> Third, pledges their aid in all measures to bring the war to an early termination, and that it should be prosecuted to ultimate victory, unless all rebels voluntarily return to their constitutional duty and obedience. Fourth, congratulates the President upon his proclamation, believing it will do good as a measure of justice and sound policy. Fifth, concludes with a reference to those who have fought our battles.

Lincoln and the governors met for some three hours harmoniously.[216]

In October, Lincoln wrote to General McClellan:

> You remember my speaking to you of what I called your over cautiousness. Are you not overcautious when you assume

> that you cannot do what the enemy is constantly doing? Should you not claim to be at least his equal in prowess, and act upon the claim? As I understand, you telegraphed General Halleck that you cannot subsist your army at Winchester unless the Railroad from Harper's Ferry … be put in working order.
>
> But the enemy does now subsist his army at Winchester at a distance nearly twice as great from railroad transportation as you would have to do without the railroad named. He now wagons from Culpepper C. H. … about twice as far as you would have to do from Harper's Ferry. He is certainly not more than half as well provided with wagons as you are. I should certainly be pleased for you to have the advantage of the railroad … but it wastes the remainder of the autumn …
>
> One of the maxims of war … is "to operate upon the enemy's communications … without exposing your own." You seem to act as if this applies against you, but cannot apply in your favor. … If he make a stand at Winchester … I would fight him there, on the idea that if we cannot beat him when he bears the wastage of coming to us, we never can when we bear the wastage of going to him. … We should not so operate as to merely drive him away. As we must beat him.[217]

On October 23, McClellan transmitted a report of Colonel Robert Williams to Halleck: "I have in camp 267 horses … of these, 128 are positively and absolutely, unable to leave the camp … [due to] consequent lameness and sore backs. … The horses which are sound, are absolutely broken down from fatigue."

Lincoln wrote to McClellan, "Will you pardon me for asking what horses of your army have done since the battle of Antietam that fatigue anything?"[218]

"By order of the president," Lincoln wrote to General Halleck on November 5, the day after the election, "It is ordered that Major General McClellan be relieved from the command of the Army of the Potomac; and that Major General Burnside take the command." He further told Halleck to give command of Burnside's corps to General Hunter; to relieve Major General Fitz-John Porter; and to place General Hooker in command of that corps. Lincoln now assumed the upper hand with the army.[219]

Lincoln fired McClellan both for military and political reasons. As McClellan's Harrison Landing letter showed, he was attempting to dictate policy to the president and was constantly critical of both Stanton and Lincoln. After reading that letter, Lincoln knew he had to review his policies and subsequently drafted the Emancipation Proclamation. McClellan showed contempt for the proclamation despite advice to submit from New York financier William Henry Aspinwall.

Governor J. Gregory Smith of Vermont told Lincoln of a conversation his brother, General William F. (Baldy) Smith, had had with McClellan. McClellan and Smith had been together at West Point. Lincoln related the story to Hay, who recorded it:

> When they went down to the Peninsula their same intimate relations continued, and General talking freely with Smith … until one day Fernando Wood and other [Democratic] politician appeared and … passed some days with McClellan.
>
> From that day … Smith saw … that McClellan was treating him with unusual coolness. … After some days he mentioned this to McClellan, who … told Baldy he had something to show him. He told him that these people who had recently visited … had been urging him to stand as an opposition candidate for President; that he had thought the thing over and had concluded to accept … and had written them a letter giving his ideas on the proper way of conducting the war.

> This letter he read to Baldy, who, after the reading … said earnestly, "General, do you not see that looks like treason, and that it will ruin you and all of us?" After some further talk the General destroyed the letter in Baldy's presence. … Immediately after the Battle of Antietam, Wood and his familiar came again and saw the General, and again Baldy saw an immediate estrangement on the part of McClellan. He seemed to be anxious to get his intimate friends out of the way …
>
> One night Smith was returning from some duty … and, seeing a light in McClellan's tent, he went in. … After everyone was gone he told him those men had been there again and had renewed their proposition, and had written them a letter acceding to their terms, and pledging himself to carry on the war in the sense already indicated. … Immediately thereafter … Smith applied to be transferred from the army. At … the same time others asked the same.[220]

In the midterm elections of 1862, the Republicans took a drubbing, losing the race for governor in New York and New Jersey. Democrats also gained control of legislatures in New York, Illinois, and Indiana, and achieved a tie in Pennsylvania. Republicans managed to retain control of the House of Representatives thanks to their alliance with twenty-five Unionist representatives, chiefly disaffected prowar Democrats. Republicans seats fell from 59 percent to just over 46 percent.

For the congressional seat Lincoln once represented at Springfield, his former law partner John T. Stuart, a Democrat, defeated a key Lincoln ally, Leonard Swett. Anti-black sentiment that overwhelmingly favored forbidding freed slaves from immigrating to the North and preventing black suffrage was a key factor in that race. The *Cincinnati Gazette* declared voters "are depressed by the interminable nature of the war … and the rapid exhaustion of the national resources."

A Democrat won the New York governorship after the Seward/Weed faction's efforts to form a Unionist ticket and nominate General John A. Dix failed. Greeley and his allies successfully nominated abolitionist general James A. Wadsworth, who lost to Democrat Horatio Seymour. New Jersey went Democratic and elected Joel Parker governor. Three key House Republicans, Speaker Glusha A. Grow of Pennsylvania, Roscoe Conkling of New York, and John A. Bingham of Ohio, were all defeated.

In Illinois, Senator Orville Browning would not be reelected, as Democrats won the legislature. Browning had urged Lincoln to hold back the Emancipation Proclamation. Browning had declared in July of 1861, "I would rejoice to see all the States in rebellion return to their allegiance." He said if they did, they would be fully protected "in all their rights, including the ownership, use and management of slaves." He did, however, support abolitionist Representative Owen Lovejoy.[221]

General Carl Schurz wrote a letter after the election, focusing on these alleged facts: "The defeat of the administration is the administration's own fault. … It admitted its professed opponents to its counsels. … It placed the Army, now a great power in the Republic, into the hands of its enemies. … In all personal questions, to be hostile to the party of the government, seemed, to be a title to consideration."

"Three main causes told the whole story," Lincoln declared. "1. The democrats were left in a majority by our friends going to the war. 2. The democrats observed this & determined to re-instate themselves in power, and 3. Our newspapers, by vilifying and disparaging the administration, furnished them all the weapons to do it with. Certainly, the ill-success of the war had much to do with it." While Lincoln said he would not dispute the opinions, he asked for evidence on the "facts."

"The plain facts, as they appear to me are these," Lincoln countered.

> The administration came into power, very largely in a minority of the popular vote. Notwithstanding this, it distributed

> to its party friends as nearly all the civil patronage as any administration ever did. The war came. The administration could not even start in this, without assistance outside of its own party. It was mere nonsense to suppose a minority could put down a majority in rebellion.
>
> Mr. Schurz [now general] was about here then & I do not recollect that he then considered all who were not Republicans, were enemies of the government, and that none of them must be appointed to military positions. … It so happens that very few of our friends had a military education or were of the profession of arms. It would have been a question whether the war should be conducted on military knowledge, or political affinity …
>
> Accordingly I have scarcely appointed a Democrat to a command, who was not urged by many Republicans and opposed by none. It was so as to McClellan. He was first brought forward by the Republican governor of Ohio, & claimed, and contended for at the same time by the Republican Governor of Pennsylvania. I received recommendations from the Republican delegations in Congress, and I believe every one of them recommended a majority of democrats.
>
> But, after all many Republicans were appointed; and I mean no disparagement to them when I say I do not see that their superiority of success has been so marked as to throw great suspicion on the good faith of those who are not Republicans.

In a subsequent letter to Schurz, Lincoln said he had been much dissatisfied with the slowness of Buell and McClellan, but feared that relieving them he would find successors who would do no better. This was his major challenge. "I fear we shall at last find out that the difficulty is in our case, rather than in particular generals. I wish to disparage no one … but I must say I need success more than I need sympathy, and that I have not seen so much greater evidence of getting success from my sympathizers, than from those … denounced as the contrary. It does seem to me that in the field the two classes have been very much alike, in what they have done, and what they have failed to do."[222]

Lincoln also expressed concern for the "fire in the rear" or the activities of antiwar Democrats branded as Copperheads by Ohio Republicans.

With Democrats doing well only in traditionally strong areas, Michigan, California, and Iowa went Republican in the 1862 elections, and the party picked up five Senate seats. What Lincoln saw and most Copperheads did not was the degree to which Democrats were losing ground among the soldiers. The antiwar wing was alienating the soldiers in the Union armies.

These shifts were rapidly becoming evident in the North. The Copperheads were viewed as traitors by the Union soldiers, which gave Lincoln the flexibility to dismiss McClellan. Military setbacks and the Emancipation Proclamation resulted in a reduction in the numbers of enlistees, and led Congress to grant increasing powers through a new draft law. At the same time the Copperheads worked vigorously to generate increasing resistance to the new draft.[223]

Lincoln wrote to Major John J. Key, expressing sympathy over the death of his son. Lincoln, nevertheless, refused to reverse Key's dismissal from the military.

> In regard to my dismissal of yourself … it seems to me you misunderstand me. I did not charge or intend to charge you with disloyalty. I had been brought to fear that there was a class of officers … who were playing a game to not beat the enemy when they could, on some peculiar notion as the proper way of saving the Union. …
>
> When you were proved to me, in your own presence, to have avowed yourself in favor of that "game," and did not attempt

> to controvert the proof, I dismissed you as an example and warning to that supposed class. I bear you no ill will; and I regret that I could not have the example without wounding you. … But can I now, in view of the public interest, restore you to the service, by which the army would understand that I endorse and approve that game myself?

Lincoln could not and did not.[224]

Chapter VIII

A National Currency; We Cannot Escape History

Don Piatt, an Ohio Whig, recounted this anecdote in a *North American Review* article:

> Amasa Walker, a distinguished New England financier, suggested that notes issued directly from the government to the people, as currency, and should bear interest. This for the purpose, not only of making the notes popular, but for the purpose of preventing inflation, by inducing people to hoard the notes as an investment when the demands of trade should fail to call them into circulation as a currency.
>
> The idea struck David Taylor, of Ohio, with such force that he sought Mr. Lincoln and urged him to put the project into immediate execution. The President listened patiently and said: "That is a good idea, Taylor; but you must go to Chase. He is running that end of the machine, and has time to consider your proposition." Taylor sought the Secretary of the Treasury, and laid before him Amasa Walker's plan. Chase heard him in a cold unpleasant manner, and then said:
>
> "That is all very well, Mr. Taylor; but there is one little obstacle in the way that makes the plan impracticable, and

that is the Constitution." Saying this, he turned to his desk, as if dismissing both Mr. Taylor and his proposition at the same moment. The poor enthusiast felt rebuked and humiliated. He returned to the President, however, and reported his defeat. ... "Taylor!" he exclaimed, "go back to Chase and tell him not to bother himself about the Constitution.

"Say that I have the sacred instrument here at the White House, and I am guarding it with great care." Taylor demurred ... on the ground that Mr. Chase showed by his manner that he knew all about it, and didn't wish to be bored by any suggestion. "We'll see about that," said the President, and taking a card from the table he wrote upon it, "The Secretary of the Treasury will please consider Mr. Taylor's proposition. We must have money, and I think this a good way to get it."

Armed with this, the real father of the greenbacks again sought the Secretary. He was received more politely then before, but was cut short in his advocacy of the measure by a proposition for both of them to see the President. They did so, and Mr. Chase made a long and elaborate constitutional argument against the proposed measure. "Chase," said Lincoln, "down in Illinois I was held to be a pretty good lawyer, and I believe I could answer every point you have made;

"But I don't feel called upon to do it. ... These rebels are violating the Constitution to destroy the Union; I will violate the Constitution, if necessary, to save the Union: and I suspect, Chase, that our Constitution is going to have a rough time of it before we get done with this row. Now, what I want to know is, whether Constitution aside, this project of issuing interest-bearing notes is a good one?"

"I must say," responded Mr. Chase, "that, with the exception you make, it is not only a good one, but the only one open

> to us to raise money. If you say so, I will do my best to put it into immediate and practical operation, and you will never hear from me any opposition on this subject."

This was a stunning turnaround for Chase from his avowed hard-money Jacksonian views. Lincoln often said, "Chase was running the machine" at Treasury. This showed that Lincoln was calling the tune.[225]

In his December 1 message to Congress, Lincoln said:

> The Civil War, which has so radically changed for the moment the occupations and habits of the American people, has necessarily disturbed the social condition, and affected very deeply the prosperity of the nations with which we have carried on a commerce that has been steadily increasing throughout ... half a century. It has, at the same time, excited political ambitions and apprehensions ... throughout the civilized world.
>
> In this unusual agitation we have forborne from taking part in any controversy between foreign states, and between parties and factions in such states. ... We have left to every nation the exclusive conduct and management of its own affairs. Our struggle has been, of course contemplated by foreign nations with reference less to its own merits, than to its supposed and often exaggerated effects and consequences resulting to those nations themselves.

Lincoln turned to the slave trade that had been fostered by financial interests in the North, explaining:

> The treaty with Great Britain for the suppression of the slave trade has been put into operation with a good prospect of complete success. It is an occasion of special pleasure to acknowledge that the execution of it, on the part of Her

> Majesty's government, has been marked with a jealous respect for the authority of the United States, and the rights of their moral and loyal citizens.
>
> A blockage of three thousand miles of seacoast could not be established, and vigorously enforced ... without committing occasional mistakes, and inflicting unintentional injuries upon foreign nations and their subjects. ... All such collisions tend to excite misapprehension. ... I have, so far as possible, heard and redressed complaints ... presented by friendly powers. ... I have proposed to some ... states ... mutual conventions to examine and adjust such complaints.

Lincoln expressed optimism that, while there existed a reluctance among free blacks to move, he believed that opinion in respect to resettlement of freed slaves outside of the United States was improving. He made clear he would decline to move any group without first obtaining agreement from the receiving country to protect all such emigrants in their rights as free men. He noted Liberia and Haiti were the only nations in which colonists of African descent could currently maintain their rights.

"I have favored the project for connecting the United States with Europe by an Atlantic telegraph, and a similar project to extend the telegraph from San Francisco, to connect by a Pacific telegraph with the line which is being extended across the Russian empire," Lincoln said. He added that the immense mineral resources of some territories "ought to be developed as rapidly as possible" to improve the revenues of the government and diminish the peoples' burden.

> The condition of the finances will claim your most diligent consideration. The vast expenditures incident to the military and naval operations required for the suppression of the rebellion have ... been met with a promptitude, and certainty, and the public credit ... maintained. The continuance of the war ... demand your best reflections as to the best modes of

> providing the necessary revenue, without injury to business and with the least possible burdens upon labor.
>
> The suspension of specie payments by the banks … made large issues of United States notes unavoidable. In no other way could the payment of the troops, and the satisfaction of just demands, be so economically, or so well provided for. The judicious legislation of the Congress, securing … these notes for loans and internal duties, and making them a legal tender for other debts, has made them a universal currency; and has satisfied … the … want of an uniform circulating medium.

Lincoln took note that this medium resulted in "saving … the people immense sums in discounts and exchanges. A return to specie payments … compatible with due regard to all interests concerned, should ever be kept in view. Fluctuations in the value of currency are always injurious, and to reduce these fluctuations to the lowest possible point will always be a leading purpose in wise legislation. Convertibility … into coin, is generally the best and surest safeguard against them."

Lincoln then said, "It is extremely doubtful … a circulation of United States notes, payable in coin, and sufficiently large for the wants of the people can be permanently, usefully and safely maintained." Lincoln upped the ante: "Is there, then, any other mode in which the necessary provision for the public wants can be made and the great advantage of a safe and uniform currency secured?" Lincoln had opened the door for the introduction of a national banking system.

"I know of none," he declared, "which promises so certain results, and is, at the same time, so unobjectionable, as the organization of banking associations, under a general act of Congress, well guarded in its provisions. To such associations the government might furnish circulating notes, on the security of United States bonds deposited in the treasury." Lincoln thus advocated a Whig position on the banking system opposed to the hard-money Jacksonians.

Lincoln explained his policy:

> These notes, prepared under the supervision of proper officers, being uniform in appearance and security, and convertible always into coin, would at once protect labor against the evils of a vicious currency, and facilitate commerce by cheap and safe exchanges. A moderate reservation from the interest on the bonds would compensate the United States for the preparation and distribution of the notes and a general supervision of the system. …
>
> The public credit, moreover, would be greatly improved and the negotiation of new loans greatly facilitated by the steady market demand for government bonds which the adoption of the proposed system would create.

This message to a degree harkened back to his early years as a Whig when he supported the Bank of the United States, opposed the sub-treasury, and fought for the Illinois State Bank. Lincoln recognized the need much more swiftly than Chase.

"It is an additional recommendation of the measure, of considerable weight, in my judgment, that it would reconcile, as far as possible, all existing interests, by the opportunity offered to existing institutions to reorganize under the act, substituting only the secured uniform national circulation for the local and various circulation, secured and unsecured, now issued by them." This offered state banks a sounder capital option in place of state bonds that were declining in value.

"That portion of the earth's surface … owned and inhabited by the people of the United States," Lincoln said, "is well adapted to be the home of one national family; and it is not well adapted for two, or more. Its vast extent, and its variety of climate and productions are of advantage, in this age, for one people, whatever they might have been. … Steam, telegraphs, and intelligence, have brought these, to be an advantageous combination, for one united people."

Reiterating the points of his inaugural address, Lincoln said:

> There is no line, straight or crooked, suitable for a national boundary, upon which to divide. … But there is another difficulty. … The great interior region, bounded east by the Alleghenies, north by the British dominions, west by the Rocky Mountains and South by the line along which the culture of corn and cotton meets … will have fifty million people within fifty years, if not prevented by … political folly or mistake. …
>
> This region has no seacoast, touches no ocean anywhere. … But separate our common country into two nations, as designed by the present rebellion, and every man of this great interior region is thereby cut off from … one or more … outlets, not, perhaps by a physical barrier, but by embarrassing and onerous trade regulations. … Our national strife springs not from … the land we inhabit. … There is no possible severing … but would multiply, and not mitigate evils.

On the slavery question, Lincoln delineated the differing views:

> Among the friends of the Union there is great diversity, of sentiment, and of policy, in regard to slavery, and the African race amongst us. Some would perpetuate slavery; some would abolish it suddenly, and without compensation; some would abolish it gradually, and with compensation; some would remove freed people from us, and some would retain them with us; and there are other minor diversities.
>
> Because of these diversities, we waste much strength in struggles among ourselves. By mutual concession we should harmonize, and act together. This would be compromise; but

> it would be compromise among the friends, and not with the enemies of the Union.

He proposed consideration of three amendments to the Constitution:

> These articles are intended to embody a plan of such mutual concession. If … adopted, it is assumed that emancipation will follow.
>
> As to the first article, the main points are: first, the emancipation; secondly, the length of time for consummating it—thirty-seven years—and thirdly the compensation. The emancipation will be unsatisfactory to the advocates of perpetual slavery, but the … time should greatly mitigate their dissatisfaction. The time spares both races from the evils of sudden disarrangement—in fact from … any derangement—while most … disturbed by the measure will have passed away.
>
> Another class will hail the prospect of emancipation, but will deprecate the … time. They will feel that it gives too little to the now living slaves. But it really gives them much. It saves them from the vagrant destitution which must largely attend … and it gives the inspiring assurance that their posterity shall be free forever. The plan leaves each state … to abolish slavery now, or at the end of the century, or at any intermediate time … or by degrees.
>
> It also provides for compensation, and generally the mode of making it. This, it would seem, must further mitigate the dissatisfaction of those who favor perpetual slavery. … Doubtless some of those who are to pay, and not to receive will object. Yet the measure is both just and economical. In a certain sense the liberation of slaves is the destruction of property—property acquired by descent, or by purchase, the same as any other property. …

> The people of the South are not more responsible for the original introduction of this property, than are the people of the North; and when it is remembered how unhesitatingly we all use cotton and sugar, and share the profits of dealing them. … If then, for a common object, this property is to be sacrificed it is not just that it be done at a common charge? And if, with less money … we can preserve … the Union … than we can by war alone, is it not also economical?

Using the cost of war as a further argument, Lincoln suggested, "Let us ascertain the sum we have expended on the war since compensated emancipation was proposed last March, and consider whether, if that measure had been promptly accepted, by even some of the slave States, the same sum would not have done more to close the war, than has been otherwise done. If so the measure would save money, and, in that view, would be a prudent and economical measure."

The cost of compensated emancipation, he said, would be large, but would require no ready cash. He proposed bonds be issued, and given continued growth of the population, the nation likely would have more than 100 million people to share the burden. The nation would reach this goal "if we do not ourselves relinquish the chance, by the folly and evils of disunion, or by long and exhausting war springing from the only … element of … discord among us."

His second article included the clause, "All slaves who shall have enjoyed actual freedom by the chances of the war … shall be forever free." Lincoln said it would be impractical to return to bondage those freed, but for those who had been the slaves of loyal citizens, he proposed compensation to those citizens.

His third article returned to colonization. He said it did not oblige, but merely authorized Congress to aid in resettling freed blacks only with the mutual consent of those freedmen.

"I cannot make it better known than it already is, that I strongly favor colonization," Lincoln said. "And I wish to say there is an objection urged against free colored persons remaining in the country, which is largely imaginary, if not sometimes malicious. It is insisted that their presence would injure, and displace white labor and white laborers. If there ever could be a proper time for mere catch arguments, that time surely is not now. In times like the present, men should utter nothing for which they would not willingly be responsible through time and eternity." This was a formidable pronouncement by Lincoln.

> Is it true, then, that colored people can displace any more white labor, by being free than by remaining slaves? If they stay in their old places, they jostle no white laborers; if they leave their old places, they leave them open to white laborers. Logically, there is neither more nor less of it.
>
> Emancipation, even without deportation, would probably enhance the wages of white labor, and, very surely, would still have to be performed; the freed people would surely not do more than their old proportion of it, and very probably, for a time, would do less, leaving an increased part to white laborers, bringing their labor into greater demand, and, consequently, enhancing the wages of it. … Labor is like any other commodity. … Increase the demand … and you increase the price. …
>
> It is dreaded that the freed people will swarm forth, and cover the whole land? Are they not already in the land? Will liberation make them any more numerous? Equally distributed among the whites of the … country … there would be but one colored to seven whites. … Why should emancipation south, send the free people north? People, of any color, seldom run, unless there be something to run from.

Gradual emancipation and deportation, he said, eliminated the reason.

The recommendations would not stay the war or the Emancipation Proclamation, he said, expressing confidence that adoption of his plan would assist the restoration of the Union. "This plan is recommended as a means, not in exclusion of, but additional to, all others for restoring and preserving the national authority throughout the Union. The subject is presented exclusively in its economic aspect." The plan, he said, rather than relying on force, would cost no blood.

Lincoln noted that this would be permanent constitutional law requiring a two-thirds vote of Congress and ratification by three-fourths of the states, including seven slave states. Gravity, he said, must characterize a message from the chief magistrate to the Congress. He said some in the Congress were his seniors, with more experience. Yet, he explained, given the great responsibility resting on him, they should perceive no want of respect in the earnestness of his message.

> Can we, can they, by any other means … so speedily, assure these vital objects? We can succeed only by concert. It is not "can any of us imagine better …?" Still the question recurs "can we do better?" The dogmas of the quiet past are inadequate to the stormy present. The occasion is piled high with difficulty, and we must rise with the occasion. As our case is new, so we must think anew, and act anew. We must disenthrall ourselves, and then we shall save our country.
>
> Fellow citizens, we cannot escape history. We of this Congress and this administration will be remembered in spite of ourselves. No personal significance, or insignificance, can spare one or another of us. The fiery trial through which we pass, will light us down, in honor or dishonor, to the latest generation. We say we are for the Union. The world will not forget what we say. We know how to save the Union. The world knows we do know how to save it.

Lincoln concluded forcefully with these words: "We—even we here—hold the power, and bear the responsibility. In giving freedom to the slave, we assure freedom to the free—honorable alike in what we give, and what we preserve. We shall nobly save, or meanly lose, the last best, hope of earth. Other means may succeed; this could not fail. The way is plain, peaceful, generous, just—a way which, if followed, the world will forever applaud, and God must forever bless."[226]

"I have just had a long conference with General Burnside," Lincoln wrote to General Halleck. "He believes that General Lee's whole army, or nearly the whole of it is in front of him, at and near Fredericksburg. Gen. B[urnside] says he could take into battle now any day, about, one hundred and ten thousand men; that he does not want more men with him, because he could not handle them to advantage; that he can cross the river in the face of the enemy and drive him away."

Lincoln quoted Burnside as saying the plan was "somewhat risky." Lincoln said, "I wish the case to stand more favorable than this in two respects. First, I wish his crossing of the river to be nearly free from risk; and secondly, I wish the enemy to be prevented from falling back, accumulating strength as he goes, into his intrenchments at Richmond. I therefore proposed that Gen. B[urnside] shall not move immediately."[227]

As Burnside marshaled his forces, the Confederates dug into extremely strong positions on the heights behind Fredericksburg. Burnside's deliberate movements were plagued by delay. General Lee left Burnside free to cross the river. Lee had anticipated the Union crossing and had his troops largely hidden. Meanwhile Burnside's orders demonstrated that he had no fixed plan of battle. In the face of the enemy, his intentions seemed continually changing.

Burnside's forces attempted to storm the heights and faced a withering fire from Lee's entrenched army. Burnside's army sustained a crushing defeat, with the loss of more than ten thousand men. Burnside wanted to renew the attack the next day, but his generals opposed a renewed assault. Navy Secretary Wells recorded in his diary: "The army has recrossed the Rappahannock; driven back, has suffered heavy loss. The shock is great. … I fear the plan was not a wise one."

News of the scope of the Fredericksburg defeat hit Washington. Thirty-two Republicans senators—already full of anger over November election losses—caucused in secret. Lincoln took a big hit in popularity. The war seemed to be interminable as the toll of dead and wounded grew. Gold speculation was rampant and credit tightened. Anger over McClellan's long tenure and failure to win victories exploded along with the perceived incompetence of Burnside.

The senators pressed their attack, singling out Secretary Seward. Alarmed by reports from Chase and others, the senators saw Seward as a back-door influence on Lincoln, thwarting vigorous prosecution of the war. They also targeted Lincoln, charged by Chase and others for not consulting his cabinet. Seward was alleged to have stood tenaciously behind McClellan, even as Democrats were actively working to make him a candidate for president.

Republicans in Congress were irate over significant losses in the midterm elections. Lincoln, nevertheless, had maintained a working majority among remaining Republicans and Union or war Democrats. In caucus the more radical Republicans wanted a Republican to head the army. Their ire had been fed by Chase and to some extent Stanton and Smith. Chase vociferously criticized both Seward and Lincoln for the lack of better coordination and insufficient consultation within the cabinet.

The caucus of radical senators endorsed a demand that the president dismiss Mr. Seward from the cabinet. Late that evening it was withdrawn and another adopted with a plan of action. Twenty-eight senators agreed on a modified resolution stating that public confidence in the present administration would be increased by a change in and partial reconstruction of the cabinet. They underestimated Lincoln's hold of his administration and resolved to send a delegation to call for change.[228]

The senators objected to Seward's letter to Minister Adams in London disparaging emancipation. It said, "It seems as if the extreme advocates of African slavery and its vehement opponents were acting in concert together to precipitate a servile war—the former making the most desperate attempts to overthrow the Federal Union, the latter by demanding an edict of universal emancipation as a lawful and necessary, if not, as they say, the only legitimate way of saving the Union."[229]

In his diary, Secretary Wells said that New York senator Preston King, together with Secretary Seward's son Fred, came to Lincoln's office and presented the resignation of Seward. Fred Seward also resigned from State. King left when the caucus called for the resignation of Seward, and reported this to Seward, who then wrote out his resignation. King informed Senator Collamer, the chair, who notified the president they would call that evening after six. Lincoln said he would meet them at seven.

According to Wells, the president described an evening "spent in a pretty free and animated conversation" with no opposition manifested towards any other cabinet officer than Seward. The president said they charged Seward with indifference and want of earnestness in prosecuting the war. Seward, as a senator and in the administration, had taken a tempered view, which squared with the interests of a significant part of the New York commercial community.

Wells reported that the president "stated how the movement had shocked and grieved him; that the Cabinet he had selected in view of impending difficulties and … responsibilities upon himself; that he and the members had gone on harmoniously, whatever had been their previous party feelings … that in the overwhelming troubles … he had been sustained and consoled by the good feeling and the mutual and unselfish confidence and zeal that pervaded the Cabinet."

Lincoln asserted that "this movement was uncalled for, that there was no such charge, admitting all that was said, as should break up or overthrow a Cabinet, nor was it possible for him to go on with a total abandonment of old friends." The president met with the cabinet and requested members join him and meet the Senate committee that evening. After considerable discussion, Chase expressed reluctance to attend but, finding no graceful way out, relented.

Senators attending the committee meeting were Collamer, Fessenden, Harris, Trumbull, Grimes, Howard, Sumner, and Pomeroy. Wade was absent. The president read the resolutions of the committee and reviewed his interview with the committee and their purpose. He described unity within the cabinet. He explained that all were free to think and to speak as they wished on all subjects, but all had to acquiesce in measures once the issue before them was decided.

Wells's account stated Senator Collamer followed the president and calmly and fairly presented the caucus's views. "They wanted united counsels, combined wisdom, and energetic action." Senator Fessenden "wanted the whole Cabinet to consider and decide great questions, and that no one in particular should absorb and direct the whole Executive action." Senators Grimes, Sumner, Pomeroy, and Trumbull were emphatic and unequivocal, holding firmly in opposition to Seward.

Secretary Blair sustained the president and dissented "most decidedly from the idea of a plural Executive." Secretary Bates took the same view. The president managed his own case and, in the words of Wells, "showed great tact, shrewdness and ability." In response to a query from the president, Collamer and Fessenden declined to join in asking for Seward's resignation. Senator Harris said, "The effect of Mr. Seward's retirement would … be calamitous in the State of New York."

By chairing the meeting, Lincoln moderated the mood of the senators as well as cabinet members. Under these circumstances, it proved difficult for the senators and cabinet members to harshly criticize each other face-to-face.

With Washington alive with rumors, Lincoln again met with his cabinet. Wells recorded, "Chase said he had been painfully affected by the meeting last evening … and told the President he had prepared his resignation. 'Where is it?' Said the President quickly, his eyes lighting up in a moment. 'I brought it with me,' said Chase. … 'Let me have it,' said the President. Something further he wished to say, but the President … did not perceive it, but took and hastily opened the letter. 'This,' he said … 'cuts the Gordian knot. … I see my way clear.'" Lincoln now could keep both secretaries and maneuver to hold sway. Lincoln sent identical letters to each secretary, saying the public interest required that both continue.

Seward immediately resumed his role. Chase said he wanted to sleep on it overnight, as he was taken aback by the way in which the president had so eagerly scooped up his note of resignation. The following Monday, Chase sent two notes to the president. The first suggested that both he and Seward could best serve out of the cabinet. The second said he had reconsidered and would continue to serve. Lincoln, by holding his ground, cemented his disparate cabinet, as he needed them all.

Lincoln met the greatest political challenge to his administration, retaining his mastery for the balance of his term. Had he failed, he would have been a wounded president, and, equally important, his role as commander in chief would have been compromised. Fully in command, he turned back to his primary task of governing. With adroit political management, he continued to wield patronage effectively and cemented loyalty across the spectrum of Union supporters.

The cabinet's work resumed, Wells analyzed the outcome this way: "Seward, assuming to be helmsman, has, while affecting and believing in his own superiority, tried to be patronizing to all, especially soothing and conciliating to Chase, who sees and is annoyed by it. The President feels … under obligations to each, and that both are serviceable. He is friendly to both. He is fond of Seward … he respects Chase, who is clumsy. Seward comforts him; Chase he deems a necessity."[230]

The president mostly deferred to Seward on diplomatic issues. He turned to Chase to learn the current fiscal condition. Chase sat in on daily conferences on cash and credit, credit balances, tax revenue, tariff duties, and future income. At this point the cost of the war had reached two million dollars per day. Chase was not an accredited financier, and the prospect of having to borrow $600 million in 1863 weighed on him. His plea for more aggressive military leadership would, he hoped, reduce costs.

Mary Todd Lincoln

Abraham Lincoln

Mary Lincoln's view differed. Elizabeth Keckley reported:

> Often Mr. and Mrs. Lincoln discussed the relations of Cabinet officers, and gentlemen prominent in politics, in my presence. … She was well versed in human character, was somewhat suspicious of those by whom she was surrounded, and often her judgment was correct. Her intuition about the sincerity of individuals was more accurate than that of her husband. She looked beyond, and read the reflection of action in the future.
>
> Her hostility to Mr. Chase was very bitter. She claimed that he was a selfish politician … and warned Mr. Lincoln not

> to trust him too far. … "Father I do wish you would inquire a little into the motives of Chase." "Mother you are too suspicious. I give you credit for sagacity, but you are disposed to magnify trifles. Chase is a patriot and one of my best friends." "Yes, because it is his interest to be so."

Lincoln, according to Keckley, told his wife, "I fear you are prejudiced against the man."

To which Mary replied, "Mr. Lincoln, you are either blind or will not see. I am not the only one that has warned you against him."

"True, I receive letters daily from all parts of the country, telling me not to trust Chase; but then these letters are written by the political enemies of the Secretary, and it would be unjust and foolish to pay any attention to them."

Keckley said Mrs. Lincoln was equally severe with Seward: "She but rarely lost an opportunity to say an unkind word to him." Lincoln received a letter from Seward and told Mrs. Lincoln he must go see him, prompting Mrs. Lincoln to say, "Seward! I wish you had nothing to do with that man. He cannot be trusted." Lincoln responded, "You say the same of Chase. If I listened to you, I should soon be without a Cabinet." Mary showed no patience with Lincoln's frank, confiding nature.[231]

Both Lincoln and Chase felt the lash as Ohio representative Clement Vallandigham told the House, "Defeat, debt, taxation, and sepulchers—these are the only trophies." And from Joseph Medill of the *Chicago Tribune* came this warning: "Money cannot be supplied much longer to a beaten, demoralized and homesick army. Sometimes I think that nothing is left now but to fight for a boundary." He said soldiers marched in mud and slept on frozen ground and waited for back pay.[232]

Representative Fernando Wood—who as mayor of New York City in 1861 had proposed that New York City secede from the Union and become a free city—wrote to Lincoln, "I was advised by an authority … I deemed … well informed, as well as reliable and truthful that the southern states would send representatives to the next congress, provided that a full and general amnesty should permit them to do so. No guarantee or terms were asked … other than amnesty referred to."

Lincoln replied:

> I strongly suspect your information will prove to be groundless; nevertheless I thank you for communicating it. … Understanding the phrase "the Southern States would send representatives to the next Congress" to be substantially the same as "the people of the Southern States would cease resistance, and would … submit to, and maintain the national authority, within the limits of such states under the Constitution of the United States."
>
> I say that in such case, the war would cease on the part of the United States; and that, if within a reasonable time "a full and general amnesty" were necessary … it would not be withheld. I do not think it would be proper now for me to communicate this … to the people of the Southern States. My belief is that they already know it … they can communicate with me. … Nor do I think it proper now to suspend military operations to try an experiment of negotiations.

Wood replied, "Pardon me, Mr. President, when I say that your reply has filled me with profound regret. It declines what I had conceived to be an innocent effort to ascertain the foundation for information in my possession of a desire in the South to return to the Union. … In compliance with your request, that your letter shall not for the present become public I shall withhold its publication at this time." Lincoln had dealt diplomatically with Wood whose track record was capricious.[233]

As the year ended, Lincoln faced the knotty problem of legislation to create the state of West Virginia. Wrestling with the constitutional requirement for the consent of the legislature to admit West Virginia, Lincoln accepted the vote of the West Virginia legislature, on the grounds that its members had been elected by those who had voted, if not by a majority in Virginia. "We can scarcely dispense with the aid of West Virginia in this struggle; much less can we have her against us."

Lincoln continued, "We have so acted as to justify their hopes; and we cannot fully retain their confidence, and cooperation, if we seem to break faith with them. In fact, they could not do so much for us, if they would. Again, the admission of the new state, turns that much slave soil to free; and thus, is a certain, and irrevocable encroachment upon the cause of the rebellion." Lincoln signed the legislation passed by Congress and strongly pressed by West Virginians.[234]

Keen for success in the Mississippi Valley, yet Lincoln had to give priority to overall policy and to Lee's threat to Pennsylvania. The naval blockade was having its effect, severely constricting the Confederacy financially. Their efforts to seek intervention from Britain and France were all but destroyed when Lincoln followed through and issued the final Emancipation Proclamation. After a day of intensely shaking hands, Lincoln steadied himself and carefully signed.

The Emancipation Proclamation, issued on January 1, 1863, began with Lincoln explaining the basis of his power and authority to issue the proclamation:

> Now, therefore I, Abraham Lincoln, President of the United States, by virtue of the power in me vested as Commander-in-Chief, of the Army and Navy … in time of actual armed rebellion against authority and government of the Unites States, and, as a fit and necessary war measure for suppressing said rebellion. …

> And by virtue of the power, and for the purpose aforesaid, I do order and declare that all persons held as slaves within and designated States, and part of States, are, and henceforth shall be free; and that the Executive government of the United States, including the military and naval authorities thereof, will recognize and maintain the freedom of such persons.

He had specified the proclamation applied only to states or portions thereof in rebellion, as his war power did not extend further.

"And I hereby enjoin upon the people so declared to be free to abstain from all violence, unless in necessary self-defense, and I recommend to them that, in all cases when allowed they labor faithfully for reasonable wages. And I further declare and make known, that such persons of suitable condition, will be received into the armed service of the United States." This bold step opened the door for the induction of former slaves and free blacks as Union soldiers and sailors.[235]

Artist Francis B. Carpenter's Painting: The First Reading of the Emancipation Proclamation: Lincoln & the Cabinet

ABRAHAM LINCOLN AND HIS Emancipation Proclamation

Whereas On the Twenty-second day of September, in the year of our Lord one thousand eight hundred and sixty-two, a Proclamation was issued by the President of the United States, containing among other things the following, to-wit:

"That on the first day of January, in the year of our Lord one thousand eight hundred and sixty-three, all persons held as slaves within any State, or designated part of a State, the people whereof shall then be in rebellion against the United States, shall be then, thenceforward and forever free, and the executive government of the United States, including the military and naval authority thereof, will recognize and maintain the freedom of such persons, and will do no act or acts to repress such persons, or any of them, in any efforts they may make for their actual freedom.

"That the executive will, on the first day of January aforesaid, by proclamation, designate the States and parts of States, if any, in which the people thereof respectively shall then be in rebellion against the United States, and the fact that any State, or the people thereof, shall on that day be in good faith represented in the Congress of the United States by members chosen thereto at elections wherein a majority of the qualified voters of such State shall have participated, shall, in the absence of strong countervailing testimony, be deemed conclusive evidence that such State and the people thereof are not then in rebellion against the United States."

Now, therefore, I, ABRAHAM LINCOLN, President of the United States, by virtue of the power in me vested as Commander-in-Chief of the Army and Navy of the United States in time of actual armed rebellion against the authority and government of the United States, and as a fit and necessary war measure for suppressing said rebellion, do, on this first day of January, in the year of our Lord one thousand eight hundred and sixty-three, and in accordance with my purpose so to do, publicly proclaim for the full period of one hundred days from the day the first above mentioned order, and designate as the States and parts of States wherein the people thereof respectively are this day in rebellion against the United States, the following, to-wit:

ARKANSAS, TEXAS, LOUISIANA (except the parishes of St. Bernard, Plaquemines, Jefferson, St. John, St. Charles, St. James, Ascension, Assumption, Terre Bonne, Lafourche, St. Mary, St. Martin, and Orleans, including the city of New Orleans), MISSISSIPPI, ALABAMA, FLORIDA, GEORGIA, SOUTH CAROLINA, NORTH CAROLINA and VIRGINIA (except the forty-eight counties designated as West Virginia, and also the counties of Berkley, Accomac, Northampton, Elizabeth City, York, Princess Ann and Norfolk, including the cities of Norfolk and Portsmouth), and which excepted parts are, for the present, left precisely as if this Proclamation were not issued.

And by virtue of the power and for the purpose aforesaid, I do order and declare that all persons held as slaves within said designated States and parts of States are and henceforward shall be free; and that the executive government of the United States, including the military and naval authorities thereof, will recognize and maintain the freedom of said persons.

And I hereby enjoin upon the people so declared to be free, to abstain from all violence, unless in necessary self-defence, and I recommend to them that in all cases, when allowed, they labor faithfully for reasonable wages.

And I further declare and make known that such persons of suitable condition, will be received into the armed service of the United States to garrison forts, positions, stations and other places, and to man vessels of all sorts in said service.

And upon this act, sincerely believed to be an act of justice, warranted by the Constitution, upon military necessity, I invoke the considerate judgment of mankind, and the gracious favor of Almighty God.

In testimony whereof, I have hereunto set my name, and caused the seal of the United States to be affixed.

Done at the City of Washington, this first day of January, in the year of our Lord one thousand eight hundred and sixty-three, and of the Independence of the United States the eighty-Seventh.

By the President: ABRAHAM LINCOLN.

WILLIAM H. SEWARD, Secretary of State.

NOTE.—The rest of the slaves were afterwards freed by Legislation and Constitutional Amendments.

The proclamation failed to satisfy many hard-core abolitionists; it met significant approval from the military. Lincoln had delayed because he wanted to be assured approval from the majority of soldiers and sailors. He knew that increasingly the Union military understood that Confederate whites fought while depending upon their slaves to maintain agricultural production back home. The proclamation drew strong support from working people throughout Europe.

August Belmont, as titular Democratic Party head, worked on the upcoming presidential race with Samuel L. M. Barlow, Samuel J. Tilden,

Dean Richmond, and other Democrats as early as 1862. They organized party support for General McClellan as their candidate. Belmont explained his war view: "My own views on our national troubles have never changed. I have looked upon secession as a great political blunder & crime. I shall always remain uncompromisingly opposed to it."[236]

At the 1856 Democratic National Convention in Cincinnati, Louisiana senators John Slidel (an uncle of Belmont by marriage), Judah P. Benjamin, John Bright, and Benjamin Bayard gathered at Barlow's temporary Cincinnati home. Barlow, a wealthy New York corporate lawyer and investor, was Belmont's counsel. When the convention nominated James Buchanan for president, Slidell emerged as a key power behind Buchanan, and Barlow emerged with significant influence.[237]

As Democrats were organizing, two editorial staff members on Marble's *New York World* coined the term "miscegenation" in an elaborate hoax that falsely alleged it was produced by abolitionists. The publication advocated interracial marriage and similar views designed to offend an excessively Negrophobic electorate, aiming to make race the key issue in the 1864 election. The *World* and its Democratic Party backers, Barlow, Belmont, and Tilden, were accused of fostering the pamphlet.

The anonymous pamphlet was entitled "Miscegenation: The Theory of the Blending of the Races, Applied to the American White Man and Negro." Widely reprinted, it was written by *World* staffers David Goodman Croly, the managing editor, and George Wakeman, a reporter. It advocated the intermarriage of whites and blacks, indistinguishably mixed. It alleged that this radical policy, extremely offensive to most whites during Civil War times, represented Republican Party principles.[238]

"The word is spoke at last," said the introduction. "It is miscegenation—the blending of the various races of men—the practical recognition of the brotherhood of all the children of the common father. While the sublime inspiration of Christianity has taught this doctrine, Christians so called have ignored it in denying social equality to the colored man;

while democracy is founded upon the idea that all men are equal, democrats have shrunk from the logic of their own creed."

The introduction went on to assert that "while science has demonstrated that the intermarriage of diverse races is indispensable to a progressive humanity, its votaries, in this country at least, have never had the courage to apply that rule to the relations of the white and colored races. But Christianity, democracy, and science, are stronger than the timidity of prejudice and pride of short-sighed men; and they teach that a people, to become great, must become a composite."

On another front, in an exchange with Lincoln, Tennessee governor Andrew Johnson wired, "The battle of Murfreesborough has inspired much confidence … of the ultimate success of the Government. … If the rebel army could be expelled … and Union sentiment developed without fear or restraint, I still think Tennessee will be brought back into the Union by decided majority.… Eastern portion of the State must be redeemed before confidence can be inspired with the mass of the people …"[239]

Lincoln simultaneously faced a growing challenge in Missouri. He wrote to General Samuel R. Curtis, "One class of friends believe in greater severity, and another in greater leniency, in regard to arrests, banishments, and assessments. As is usual in such cases, each questions the other's motives." Lincoln was bombarded with charges and counter charges from both sides. He urged Curtis to sit down with Governor Hamilton R. Gamble and search for a common ground.

"On the one hand," Lincoln wrote, "it is insisted that Governor Gamble's Unionism, at most, is not better than a secondary spring of action—that 'hunkerism,' and a wish for political influence, stand before Unionism, with him. On the other hand, it is urged that arrests, banishments, and assessments are made more for private malice, revenge and pecuniary interest, than for the public good." He called Gamble "an honest and true man, not less so than yourself."[240]

In the House of Representatives, Clement L. Vallandigham repeatedly voiced strong opposition to the war and to the policies of Lincoln's administration:

> You can never subdue the seceded States. Two years of fearful experience have taught you that. Why carry on the war? If you persist, it can only end in final separation between North and South. And in that case, believe it now, as you did not by former warnings, the whole Northwest will go with the South.
>
> "Believe me, as you did not the solemn warning of years past, the day which divides the North from the South … decrees eternal divorce between West and East. There is not one drop of rain that falls over the whole vast expanse of the Northwest that does not find its home in the bosom of the Gulf. We must and we will follow it, with travel and trade; not by treaty, but by right; freely, peaceably, and without restriction or tribute, under the same government and flag. …
>
> Not believing the soldiers responsible … I have never withheld my vote where their separate interests were concerned. … I have denounced … the usurpations and the infractions … of law and Constitution, by the President and those under him … repeated and persistent arbitrary arrests, the suspension of habeas corpus, the violation of freedom of the mails, of the private house, of the press and of speech, and all … wrongs and outrages upon the public liberty and private right. …
>
> And now, sir, I recur to the state of the Union today. What is it? Sir, twenty months have elapsed, but the rebellion is not crushed out; its military power has not been broken; the insurgents have not dispersed. The Union is not restored; nor the Constitution maintained; nor the laws enforced. …

> Six hundred days have passed; a thousand millions been expended; and three hundred thousand lives lost or bodies mangled; and today the Confederate flag still is near the Potomac.

Vallandigham recounted and panned the fiscal measures, noting, "Money and credit, then you have had in prodigal profusion. And were men wanted? More than a million rushed to arms!" He said more than half melted away after the first campaign, and the president demanded three hundred thousand more for the war and then drafted yet another three hundred thousand for three months. Vallandigham added, "And yet victory, strangely, follows the standard of the foes."

> The war for the Union is, in your hands, a most bloody and costly failure. The President confessed it on the 22nd of September [the Preliminary Emancipation Proclamation], solemnly, officially. … The priests and rabbis of abolition taught him that God would not prosper such a cause. War for the Union was abandoned; war for the Negro openly begun, and with stronger battalions. … With what success? Let the dead at Fredericksburg and Vicksburg answer. …
>
> War … while it lasts, is disunion, and, if it last long enough, will be final, eternal separation first, and anarchy and despotism afterward. Hence, I would hasten peace now, today, by every honorable appliance. … But slavery is the cause of the war. Why: Because the South obstinately and wickedly refused to restrict or abolish it as the demand of the philosophers or fanatics and demagogues of the North and West. Then, Sir, it was abolition … which caused disunion and war. …
>
> Sir, I will not be answered now by the old clamor about "the aggressions of the slave power." That miserable specter … has been exorcised and expelled by debt and taxation and blood. If that power did govern … for the sixty years preceding this

> terrible revolution, then the sooner this Administration and Government return to the principles and policy of Southern statesmanship, the better for the country; and that, sir, is already, or soon will be, the judgment of the people.[241]

In mid-January, Lincoln reviewed his actions and said in his message to Congress: "I have signed the joint resolution to provide for the immediate payment of the army and navy. … The Joint Resolution is a simple authority, amounting … to a direction to the Secretary of the Treasury to make an additional issue of one hundred millions of dollars … for the payment of the army and navy. My approval is given … for the prompt discharge of all arrears of pay due to our soldiers and our sailors."

Lincoln expressed his qualms: "While giving this approval, however, I think it my duty to express my sincere regret that it has been found necessary to authorize so large an additional issue of United States notes, when this circulation, and that of the suspended banks together have become already redundant as to increase prices beyond real values, thereby augmenting the cost of living to the injury of labor, and the cost of supplies to the injury of the whole country."

Lincoln warned of negative consequences:

> It seems very plain that continued issues of United States notes, without any check to the issues of suspended banks, and without adequate provision for the raising of money by loans, and for funding the issues so as to keep them within due limits, must soon produce disastrous consequences. And this matter appears to me so important that I feel bound to avail myself of this occasion to ask the special attention of Congress to it.
>
> That Congress has power to regulate the currency of the country, can hardly admit of doubt; and that a judicious

> measure to prevent the deterioration of this currency, by a reasonable taxation of bank circulation or otherwise, is needed, seems equally clear. Independently of this general consideration, it would be unjust to the people at large, to exempt banks, enjoying the special privilege of circulation, from their just proportion of the public burdens."

Lincoln zeroed in on the imperative for a national currency:

> To raise money by way of loans most easily and cheaply, it is clearly necessary to give every possible support to the public credit. To that end, a uniform currency, in which taxes, subscriptions to loans, and all other ordinary public dues, as well as all private dues may be paid, is almost, if not quite indispensable. Such a currency can be furnished by banking associations, organized under a general act of Congress, as suggested. …
>
> The securing of this circulation, by the pledge of United States bonds … would still further facilitate loans, by increasing the present and … future demand for such bonds. In view of the actual financial embarrassments of the government, and of the greater embarrassments sure to come, if the necessary means of relief be not afforded, I feel that I should not perform my duty by … announcement of my approval of the Joint Resolution which proposes relief only by increasing circulation.

Lincoln urged the measures receive the early sanction of Congress. A measure introduced January 8 to provide ways and means for the support of the government was approved on March 3. It provided for $150 million of US notes for the payment of the army, navy, and other creditors, for not more than $900 million in bonds and $400 million in Treasury notes. It further provided that holders of US notes issued under the act of February 25, 1862, should turn them in for bonds by July 1, 1863.[242]

The act also put a tax on all banks or other institutions issuing notes or bills for circulation or currency. Lincoln wanted a sustained fiscal policy that would more effectively fund the war. This required a common currency, as otherwise the nation could not pay its soldiers and purchase essential supplies and equipment. To establish a currency, the nation had to provide Treasury securities that would adequately capitalize the banks and sustain the currency's value.

David Davis, now a US Supreme Court Justice by appointment from Lincoln, visited the White House and told Lincoln the Illinois legislature, dominated by Democrats, proposed resolutions demanding an immediate cessation of the war unless the Emancipation Proclamation were withdrawn. The conservative Davis, working closely with Thurlow Weed, said both he and Weed also advocated this course as a measure essential for victory in the 1864 election.

Davis urged the president reorganize the cabinet and dump both Chase and Postmaster Montgomery Blair. In response, Lincoln forthrightly declared his policy regarding slavery was fixed and he meant to adhere to it. Furthermore, the question of cabinet changes would be governed by future events. He held his ground.

Lincoln asked Weed to raise political money. On February 19, 1863, he wrote to Weed, "The matters I spoke to you about are important; & I hope you will not neglect them." The matter Lincoln referenced was a need for fifteen thousand dollars in campaign funds. With Lincoln's note in hand, Weed acted swiftly. On the back were the signatures of New York merchants he had contacted. His files showed each one of them had pledged one thousand dollars and delivered the funds.

Pledging $1,000 each he listed Charles Knapp, Marshall O. Roberts, Alexander T. Stewart, Isaac Bell, William H. Aspinwall, Cornelius Vanderbilt, James Mitchell, H. B. Cromwell, Horace Allen, James T. Sanford, Spofford and Tileston, J. F. Winslow, and Secour and Co. Additionally, P. S. Forbes, Russell Sturges, and Henry W. Hubell pledged $1,000 jointly. Obviously, when Weed called at the behest of the president, these key men of the New York financial elite responded.[243]

Secretary Wells in his diary said the funds were to influence the Connecticut and New Hampshire elections. On March 8, Weed wrote to Lincoln, "The Secession 'Petard,' in Connecticut has probably 'hoisted' its own engineers. Thank God for so much." Connecticut Governor Buchingham was reelected, beating Democrat Thomas H. Seymour by a two-thousand-vote majority. His reelection was vital to Lincoln, who needed supportive pro-Union governors like Buchingham.[244]

When Lincoln proclaimed emancipation, the workingmen of Manchester, England, hurting from the cutoff of cotton exports, wrote to Lincoln, declaring, "We rejoice in your greatness. … We honor your free state, as a singular, happy abode for working men. … One thing alone has, in the past, lessened our sympathy with your country and our confidence in it … the ascendency of politicians who not only merely maintained Negro slavery, but desired to extend and root it more firmly."

Lincoln responded, "I know and deeply deplore the sufferings which the workingmen of Manchester and in all Europe are called to endure. … It has been often … represented that the attempt to overthrow this government … built upon the foundation of human rights, and to substitute for it one … exclusively on the basis of human slavery, was likely to obtain favor in Europe. … I cannot but regard your decisive utterance … as an instance of sublime Christian heroism."[245]

General Burnside telegraphed the president in January: "I have prepared some very important orders and I want to see you before issuing them. Can I see you alone if I am at the White House after midnight?" To this, Lincoln replied: "Will see you any moment when you come." At the White House, Burnside presented the president with a series of orders for the dismissal of a number of high-rankings officers. If these were not approved then he, Burnside, wished to resign.

Burnside topped his list with General Joseph Hooker. Burnside's order said Hooker was "guilty of unjust and unnecessary criticisms of the actions of his superior officers … by the general tone of his conversation, endeavored to create distrust in the minds of officers … and having, by omissions and otherwise, made reports and statements which were calculated to create incorrect impressions, and for habitually speaking in disparaging terms of other officers, is hereby dismissed."

Lincoln that morning had called in Secretary Stanton and General Halleck and told them of Burnside's proposed orders, according to an account by General Halleck. The president told them of his decision to relieve Burnside and put Hooker in command. Halleck added that Burnside subsequently joined the meeting and agreed to withdraw his resignation, as Halleck had urged. But the president did not reinstate him.[246]

Lincoln immediately penned a note to Hooker:

> I have placed you at the head of the Army of the Potomac … upon what appears to me to be sufficient reasons. And yet I think it best for you to know that there are some things in regard to which, I am not quite satisfied with you. I believe you to be a brave and skillful soldier, which, of course, I like. I also believe you do not mix politics with your profession, in which you are right. You have confidence in yourself, which is valuable. …
>
> But I think that during Gen. Burnside's command … you have taken counsel of your ambition, and thwarted him as much as you could, in which you did a great wrong to the country, and to a most meritorious and honorable brother officer. I have heard … of your recently saying that both the Army and the Government needed a Dictator. Of course, it was not for this, but in spite of it, that I have given you the command. Only generals who gain success can set up dictators.

> What I now ask of you is military success, and I will risk the dictatorship. The government will support you to the utmost. … I much fear … the spirit … you have aided to infuse into the Army, of criticizing their Commander, and withholding confidence … will now turn upon you. I shall assist you as far as I can, to put it down. Neither you nor Napoleon … could get any good out of an army, while such a spirit prevails. … Beware of rashness, but go forward and give us victories.

In January, Lincoln wrote to General Rosecrans about Confederate cavalry raids:

> In no other way does the enemy give us so much trouble, at so little expense to himself, as by the raids of rapidly moving small bodies of troops (largely, if not wholly mounted) harassing, and discouraging loyal residents, supplying themselves with provisions, clothing, horses, and the like, surprising and capturing small detachments of our forces, and breaking our communications. …
>
> I think we should organize proper forces, and make counter-raids. We should not capture so much of supplies … but it would trouble them more to repair railroads and bridges than it does us. What think you of trying to get up such a corps in your army. Could you do it without any, or many additional troops (which we have not to give you), provided we furnish horses, suitable arms and other appointments?

As was his pattern, Lincoln explained that this was a suggestion and not an order.[247]

Lincoln, responding to a Senate resolution requesting information on a visit of French minister Henri Mercier to Richmond, forwarded Seward's report, which read, "That no suggestions were made to M.

Mercier by the Secretary of State that induced, or were designed or calculated to induce, him to undertake a mission to Richmond in April last, or at any other time." Seward made clear to suspicious senators that Mercier was not empowered to make any representations by this government.

An account by Victor Vifquain supports Seward's statement. Vifquain, with two other Frenchmen, reached Richmond plotting to kidnap Jefferson Davis. Since Davis used a tug to visit Newport and check on the Confederate ironclad, they befriended the tug captain, a Creole, and planned to commandeer the boat with Davis aboard and take him north. When Union forces occupied Newport and McClellan's Virginia forces pulled back to Washington, the Frenchmen aborted their planned plot.

This strange adventure resulted because the Frenchmen enlisted in a regiment in New York City that was disbanded without seeing action. They concocted their plan, traveled south, and were arrested as spies and incarcerated in Libby Prison. The trio convinced authorities that they were not spies. Learning that Minister Mercier was in Richmond, they contacted him and told him they had come to visit Prince Camille Armand de Polignac, a brigadier general in the Confederate Army.

Vifquain and his colleagues, through Mercier, gained access to Judah P. Benjamin, then Confederate acting secretary of state. Mercier told them he came to retrieve a cargo for the Rothschild banking interests. The Rothschilds, prior to war, had bought tobacco in Virginia for the French government. Mercier said he had been granted leave by Secretary Seward to secure the tobacco. He chartered a steamer in Norfolk, came to Richmond, and left as soon as the tobacco was on board.

It was Viscount Maurice de Beaumont, a prince, secretary of the French legation and a cousin of Vifquain, who provided Vifquain and his colleagues with letters of introduction to French consuls in Richmond and New Orleans. When their plot failed, Vifquain and his colleagues escaped north through the Shenandoah Valley. Vifquain reentered Union service and was brevetted brigadier general. He later won the Medal of Honor for valiant action with Union forces at Fort Blakely, MI.[248]

In a letter to Chase dated March 2, Lincoln said, "After much reflection, and with … pain that it is adverse to your wish, I have concluded … it is not best to re-nominate Mr. [Mark] Howard, for collector of internal revenue, at Hartford, Connecticut. Senator Dixon, residing at Hartford, and Mr. Loomis, representative of the district, join in recommending Edward Goodman … and, so far, no one has presented a different name, I will thank you … to send me a nomination … for Mr. Goodman."

Chase speedily replied:

> This morning I received your note directing me to send the nomination proposed by Mr. Dixon and Mr. [Dwight] Loomis & was about replying, when the Senator called & we talked the matter over. The result … was an agreement to call on you … and submit the matter to you for further consideration. I do not insist on the re-nomination of Mr. Howard and Mr. Dixon & Mr. Loomis, as I understand, do not claim the nomination of his successor.
>
> I shall be glad if this shall prove acceptable to you. My only object—and I think you so understand it—is to secure fit men for responsible places, without admitting the right of Senators or Representatives to control appointments for which the President & the Secretary as his presumed adviser must be responsible. Unless this principle can be practically established I feel that I cannot be useful to you or the country in my present position.[249]

Chase noted in his diary that Dixon said he regretted opposing Howard, and he proposed several names. Chase said he had no other candidate than his old friend, James G. Bolles, and Dixon agreed to go along with the nomination. The Senate confirmed Bolles for the post. As in a number of other exchanges, Lincoln insisted that members of Congress have a say. Chase rather self-righteously insisted his only aim was responsible appointees, most of them loyal Chase supporters.

Lincoln, with many soldiers absent without leave, issued a proclamation granting amnesty to those who returned before April 1. It read:

> Whereas evil disposed and disloyal persons … have enticed and procured soldiers to desert and absent themselves from their regiments, thereby weakening … the armies and prolonging the war, giving aid and comfort to the enemy, and cruelly exposing the gallant and faithful soldiers remaining to increased hardship and danger. …
>
> I do therefore call upon all patriotic and faithful citizens to oppose and resist the aforementioned dangerous and treasonable crimes, and to aid in restoring to their regiments all soldiers absent without leave, and to assist in the execution of the act of Congress "for enrolling and calling out the national forces, and for other purposes," and to support the … authorities in the prosecution and punishment of offenders against said act, and in suppressing the insurrection and rebellion.[250]

CHAPTER IX

LINCOLN TURNS A MID-TERM CRISIS TO ADVANTAGE; LEE'S INVASION AIM TO IMPACT UNION POLITICS

Toward the end of the previous year, Lincoln had said to Weed, "Governor Seymour has greater power just now for good than any other man in the country. He can wheel the Democratic Party into line, put down rebellion, and preserve the government. Tell him for me, that if he will render this service to his country, I shall cheerfully make way for him as my successor." Weed delivered the message before Seymour was inaugurated and urged him to accept, but Seymour delayed.[251]

Lincoln followed with a private and confidential letter to the newly inaugurated New York governor in a bid for cooperation. Noting that they were substantially strangers, Lincoln asked Seymour for his cooperation:

> I, for the time being, am at the head of a nation which is in great peril; and you are at the head of the greatest State of that nation. As to maintaining the nation's life, and integrity, I assume and believe there cannot be a difference of purpose between you and me.
>
> If we should differ as to the means, it is important that such difference should be as small as possible—that it should not be enhanced by unjust suspicions on one side or the other. In

> the performance of my duty, the cooperation of your State, as that of others, is needed—in fact, is indispensable. This alone is a sufficient reason why I should wish to be a good understanding with you.

He asked for a long letter in reply, yet Seymour was deliberate and failed to respond in a timely fashion.

Professing preoccupation with pressing duties, Seymour attributed his delay to a desire "to state clearly the aspect of public affairs from the standpoint I occupy. … I assure you that no political resentments, or no personal objects will turn me aside from that pathway I have marked out for myself—I intend to show to those charged with the administration of public affairs a due deference and respect and to yield them just and generous support … within the scope of their constitutional powers."

In March, Lincoln wrote to Tennessee governor Andrew Johnson:

> I am told you have at least thought of raising a Negro military force. In my opinion the country now needs no specific thing so much as some man of your ability, and position, to go to this work. When I speak of your position, I mean that of an eminent citizen of a slave state, and himself a slaveholder. The colored population is the great available and yet unavailed of force for restoration of the Union.
>
> The bare sight of fifty thousand armed, and drilled black soldiers on the banks of the Mississippi, would end the rebellion at once, and who doubts that we can present that sight, if we but take hold in earnest? If you have been thinking of it please do not dismiss the thought.

While there is no record of a reply from Governor Johnson, Lincoln's letter revealed the manpower needs of the military coupled with the growing acceptability of black soldiers.

Congress that same month enacted a national draft law. It created a provost marshal general of the army, as head of a separate bureau in the War Department, to administer the new law. Congress adopted this measure because regiments could not be kept at full strength through volunteers alone, and the states could not meet requisitions for additional troops. Under the law, the nation was divided into enrollment districts and a military provost marshal named for each district.[252]

For fraternizing with Confederates in what looked like a mutiny, the entire 109th Illinois regiment were arrested, disarmed, and put under guard at Holly Springs, Mississippi. Two thousand and one deserters were arrested in Illinois in six months. The arrests came as some forty thousand Democrats massed at Springfield, where US Senator William A. Richardson and Representative S. S. Marshall blasted President Lincoln for violating the ancient right to claim one's own home as a castle of defense.

Indiana governor Morton had telegraphed Lincoln that he expected the Indiana legislature to acknowledge the Southern Confederacy and urge the Northwest break all bonds of law with New England. The Knights of the Golden Circle, a Copperhead organization, claimed one million members, although Senator McDonald heard Lincoln say, "Nothing can make me believe that one hundred thousand Indiana Democrats are disloyal." A counter effort using spies and informers blunted the threat.[253]

General Lee wrote to Mrs. Lee, "I do not think our enemies are so confident of success as they used to be. If we can baffle them in their various designs this year & our people are true to our cause & not so devoted to themselves & their own aggrandizement, I think our success will be certain. But we will have to suffer & must suffer to the end. But will all come right. This year I hope will establish our supplies on a firm basis. On every other point we are strong."

The general identified the key to victory: "If successful this year, next fall there will be a great change in public opinion at the North. The

Republicans will be destroyed & I think the friends of peace will become so strong as that the next administration will go in on that basis. We have only therefore to resist manfully." That was on April 13, 1863. In June, Lee again pressed this very same point, in a letter to Confederate President Jefferson Davis:

"We should neglect no honorable means of dividing and weakening our enemies ... the most effectual mode of accomplishing this object, now within our reach, is to give all the encouragement we can, consistently with truth, to the rising peace party of the North." Lee suggested strategies he believed would undermine Northern support for the war, urging Davis to permit the North to believe that the South would accept peace on the basis of returning to the Union.[254]

Union general Burnside, commanding the Department of Ohio, had issued Order No. 38: "The habit of declaring sympathy for the enemy will not be allowed in this department." Seeking to quell antiwar men, Burnside and his officers became the judges as to whether what was said was treason and whether to lock up the offender. Vallandigham challenged this order on May 1, at Mount Vernon, Ohio, while sharing a platform with representatives Samuel S. Cox and George Hunt Pendleton.

Burnside dispatched a Union officer to record Vallandigham's speech. Vallandigham charged that Burnside's order violated the First Amendment and that "King Lincoln" was thirsty for despotism, rejected Southern peace offers, and waged war only to liberate black slaves. Vallandigham had recently been defeated in his bid for reelection by General Robert C. Schenck, a Republican wounded at Second Bull Run and persuaded by Lincoln, Stanton and Chase to run.

Burnside, without consulting with the War Department or Lincoln, dispatched soldiers in the early morning hours of May 5, broke down Vallandigham's front door, and hauled the former congressman off to prison in Cincinnati. From there Vallandigham wrote, "I am here in a military bastille for no other offense than my political opinions, and the defense of them, and of the rights of the people, and of your constitutional liberties." Ohio Democrats nominated him for governor.

This confronted Lincoln with a major challenge. Copperheads threatened civil war in the Northwest. New York governor Seymour declared the arrest "has brought dishonor upon our country; it is full of danger to our persons and to our homes; it bears upon its front a conscious violation of law and justice." Seymour's statement was read at an Albany rally. Similar gatherings and warnings occurred as Copperheads and their allies organized meetings in states across the Northwest.

Lincoln saw the arrest of Vallandigham as unfortunate but realized he had to see it through. Lincoln ably undercut Vallandigham's status as a martyr when he ordered him sent south into Confederate lines. While the Confederates appeared not overly anxious to receive him, they sent him to Wilmington, North Carolina. There he eventually boarded a blockade-running ship bound for Canada. He settled in Windsor, across the river from Detroit, where he could see Union warships.[255]

On another front, Lincoln, seeking to avoid strife with Indian tribes on the western frontier, initiated a dialogue with Indian chiefs invited to the White House. He told them:

> We have people from all parts of the globe. ... There is a great difference between this pale-faced people and their red brethren, both as to numbers and the way ... they live. We know not whether your own situation is best for your race, but this is what has made the difference in our way of living. The pale-face people are numerous and prosperous because they cultivate the earth.
>
> This is the chief reason of the difference; but there is another. Although we are now engaged in a great war ... we are not ... so much disposed to fight and kill one another as our red brethren. ... I really am not capable of advising you, whether,

> in the providence of the Great Spirit … the great Father of us all, it is best … to maintain the habits and customs … or adopt a new mode of life. … I can see no way … your race is to become as numerous and prosperous … except [by] … the cultivation of the earth.[256]

As requested by the Senate, Lincoln proclaimed a national fast day.

> And whereas it is the duty of nations as well as of men, to own their dependence upon the overruling power of God, to confess their sins and transgressions, in humble sorrow, yet with assured hope that genuine repentance will lead to mercy and pardon; and to recognize the sublime truth, announced in the Holy Scriptures and proven by all history, that those nations only are blessed whose God is the Lord.
>
> And, insomuch as we know that, by His divine law, nations like individuals are subjected to punishments and chastisements … may we not justly fear that the awful calamity of civil war, which now desolates the land, may be but a punishment, inflicted upon us, for our presumptuous sins, to the needful end of our national reformation as a people? It behooves us then, to humble ourselves … confess our national sins, and to pray for clemency and forgiveness.[257]

Lincoln addressed Pennsylvania governor Andrew Curtin's fears of invasion. He told Governor Curtin, "The whole disposable force at Baltimore, and elsewhere in reach, have already been sent after the enemy which alarms you. The worst thing the enemy could do … would be to weaken himself before Hooker, & therefore it is safe to believe he is not doing it; and the best thing he could do for himself, would be to get us so scared as to bring part of Hooker's force away."

Meanwhile, Lincoln's memorandum on Hooker's proposed campaign against Richmond declared, "My opinion is, that just now, with the enemy directly ahead of us, there is no eligible route for us into Richmond." Hooker responded, "I have concluded that I will have more chance of inflicting a serious blow ... by turning his position to my right, and if practicable sever his communication with Richmond."[258]

Hooker contemplated an all-out offensive against Lee's army. Lee had dispatched General Longstreet south to secure supplies and protect the coast, leaving him with some 60,000 men entrenched at Fredericksburg. Hooker had 130,000 at Falmouth on the north side of the Rappahannock River, opposite Fredericksburg. Hooker directed 59,000 men under General Sedgwick to cross the Rappahannock River below Fredericksburg and hold Lee's army there.

A dispatch taken from a captured Confederate courier revealed that Lee had just learned that Union forces were concentrated at Chancellorsville. Hooker, however, delayed until morning. The Sixth New York Calvary reconnaissance toward Spotsylvania Court House in the moonlight scattered Stuart's cavalry and created alarm. The Union men fought their way back to Chancellorsville. The encounter was reported to Hooker, who finally realized the importance of the information.

Hooker led a 42,000-man force up the river, crossing at Chancellorsville, ten miles west of Fredericksburg. His plan was to attack back along the river on Lee's flank and rear. The cavalry corps under General Stoneman was ordered to raid Lee's rear, destroy the railroads and block his lines of communications. To move on Fredericksburg with an unknown force ahead would be hazardous. This changed the whole situation, and without a blow, Hooker, in effect, put himself on the defensive.

Brevet Major General Alfred Pleasonton explained, "The very cavalry under Stuart that Lee depended on ... had been cut off ... and we had it over the signature of General Lee himself that his army had been surprised. General Hooker had it in his power ... to have crushed Lee's army and wind up the war. The Army of the Potomac never had a better opportunity, for more than half its work had been done before a blow had been struck, by the brilliancy of its strategy."[259]

In a daring move, Lee sent Generals Jackson, A. P. Hill, and Stuart on a stealth mission, encircling Hooker's position and falling on his right flank. Had Jackson handled his infantry differently, he would have carried the Union position at the high point of Hazel Grove, but his men were instead cut down by artillery on the grove. From captured Confederates, it was learned that both General Jackson and General Hill had been wounded. Jackson's wounds proved fatal, a major loss to Lee.

General Hooker ordered the Union artillery on Hazel Grove to withdraw across the river. General Stuart, now in command of Jackson's forces, placed his artillery on Hazel Grove, enfiladed the withdrawing Twelfth Corps, and punished the Third Corps. Hooker was wounded when a shell hit the post next to where he was standing. This left him disabled with a concussion. The extraordinary conditions forced the Army of the Potomac back to new positions north from Chancellorsville.

The fighting continued on May 4, but for Hooker personally the battle ended on the third. Yet on the May 2, the Army of the Potomac had comparatively few killed and wounded. The enemy inflicted the greatest injury on May 3, when the Union army lacked a commander. The Confederates lost 22 percent of their force with 13,000 casualties, and the Army of the Potomac lost 15 percent with 17,000 casualties, without positive results. For the Confederates, it was a costly victory.[260]

When word of the disaster reached Lincoln days later, *Sacramento Union* reporter Noah Brooks quoted Lincoln: "My God, my God, what will the country say?" Lincoln soon decided that he would not immediately replace Hooker. Yet he knew the losses, while far more damaging to the Confederates, would further intensify the criticism of his administration and the army and increase resistance to the draft.

Pressing for action at Charleston, Lincoln told General David Hunter and Admiral Samuel F. DuPont, "We still hope that by cordial and judicious cooperation, you can take the batteries on Morris Island and Sullivan's Island, and Fort Sumter. But whether you can or not we wish the demonstration kept up … for a time, for a collateral and very important object. We wish the attempt to be a real one … But if prosecuted as a demonstration only, this must not become public."

John Hay was dispatched to Hilton Head, South Carolina, with an order from Secretary Wells to DuPont "to send all the ironclads … in a fit condition to move, after your present attack … directly to New Orleans." Hay reported, "The General and the Admiral … received the orders … directing the continuance of operations against Charleston. The contrast was very great. … The General was absolutely delighted … the Admiral seemed in low spirits about it."[261]

In a May proclamation, Lincoln reiterated, in line with the statutory requirement, that all able-bodied male citizens and persons of foreign birth who had declared their intention of becoming citizens, between the ages of 25 and 45, were subject to the draft. To avoid misapprehensions, Lincoln declared, "No plea of alienage will be received or allowed to exempt … any person of foreign birth who shall have declared on oath his intention of become a citizen of the United States."[262]

At the same time, Lincoln received a letter from Hooker, who said, "My movements have been a little delayed by the withdrawal of many of the two-years' and nine-months' regiments, and those whose time is not already up it will be expedient to leave on this side of the river. This imposes on me the necessity of partial reorganization. My marching force of infantry is cut down to about 80,000, while I have artillery for an army of about double that number."

On May 14, Lincoln wrote to Hooker that he had thought an early movement would advantage Hooker, but no longer now that the enemy had reestablished communications, regained position, and received reinforcements. Lincoln added, "It does not now appear probable to me that you can gain any thing by an early renewal of the attempt to cross the Rappahannock. I therefore shall not complain, if you do no more, for a time, than to keep the enemy at bay. … Still, if in your own clear judgment, you can renew the attack successfully, I do not mean to restrain you."

Turning to concern among the generals about Hooker, Lincoln warned, "Bearing upon this last point, I must tell you I have some painful intimations that some of your corps and division commanders are not giving you their entire confidence. This would be ruinous, if true; and you should therefore, first of all, ascertain the real facts beyond all possibility of doubt."[263]

On another front, Lincoln replied to members of the Presbyterian General Assembly:

> It has been my happiness to receive testimonies … from all denominations of Christians. They are all loyal, but perhaps not in the same degree. … This to me is most gratifying, because from the beginning I saw that the issue of our great struggle depended upon Divine interposition and favor. If we had that, all would be well. The proportions of this rebellion were not for a long time understood. …
>
> I have acted according to my best judgment. … The views expressed by the committee accord with my own; and on this principle "the government" is to be supported though the administration may not in every case wisely act. As a pilot, I have used my best exertions to keep afloat our ship of State, and shall be glad to resign my trust at the appointed time to another pilot more skillful and successful than I. … In every case the government must be perpetuated.[264]

Lincoln responded to a letter protesting against Vallandigham's arrest formulated by Democrats meeting in Albany, New York. In a masterpiece of political statesmanship, Lincoln took issue with the resolutions of the meeting, led by Erastus Corning, wealthy former member of Congress, land speculator, iron merchant, and railroad kingpin. The protest focused on what was considered the unconstitutional nature of the recent arrest and exile of Vallandigham. Lincoln rejected their view.

"The resolutions, as I understand them," Lincoln, succinctly summarizing them, wrote, "are resolvable into two propositions—first, the expression of a purpose to sustain the cause of the Union, to secure peace through victory, and to support the administration in every constitutional, and lawful measure to suppress the rebellion; and secondly, a declaration of censure upon the administration for supposed unconstitutional action such as the making of military arrests."

Lincoln took the Albany resolution a step further:

> And, from the two propositions a third is deduced, which is, that the gentlemen composing the meeting are resolved on doing their part to maintain our common government and country, despite the folly or wickedness, as they may conceive, of any administration. This position is eminently patriotic, and as such, I think the meeting, and congratulate the nation for it. My own purpose is the same. …
>
> But the meeting, by their resolutions assert and argue, that certain military arrests and proceedings following them for which I am ultimately responsible, are unconstitutional. I think they are not. … But these provisions of the Constitution have no application to the case we have in hand, because the arrests complained of were not made for treason—that is, not for the treason defined in the Constitution, and upon conviction of which, the punishment is death. …
>
> The arrests were made on totally different grounds, and the proceedings following, accorded with the grounds of

the arrests. Let us consider the real case with which we are dealing, and apply to it the parts of the constitution plainly made for such cases. … The insurgents had been preparing for more than thirty years, while the government had taken no steps to resist them. The former had carefully considered all the means which could be turned to their account.

It undoubtedly was a well-pondered reliance … in their own unrestricted effort to destroy Union, constitution, and law … the government would … be restrained by the same constitution and law, from arresting their progress. Their sympathizers pervaded … the government, and nearly all communities. … Under cover of "Liberty of speech," "Liberty of the press" and "Habeas corpus" they hoped to keep … spies, informers, suppliers and aiders and abettors of their cause. …

Yet, thoroughly imbued with a reverence for the guaranteed rights of individuals, I was slow to adopt the strong measurers … I have been forced to regard as … within the exceptions of the constitution, and as indispensable to public safety. … And yet … he who dissuades one man from volunteering, or induces one solider to desert, weakens the Union cause as much as he who kills a union soldier. … Yet this … inducement may be so conducted as to be no defined crime. …

Ours is a case of Rebellion—so called by the resolutions before me—in fact, a clear, flagrant, and gigantic case of Rebellion, and the provision of the constitution that the privilege of the writ of Habeas Corpus shall not be suspended, unless when in cases of Rebellion or Invasion, and public Safety may require it is the provision which specifically applies. … This … is our present case … of Rebellion, wherein the public Safety does require the suspension.

In the latter case, arrests are made, not so much for what has been done, as for what probably would be done. The latter is more for the preventive, and less for the vindictive, than the former. In such cases the purposes of men are much more easily understood, than in cases of ordinary crime. The man who stands by and says nothing, when the peril of his government is discussed, cannot be misunderstood. If not hindered, he is sure to help the enemy. …

Of how little value the constitutional provision … will be rendered, if arrests shall never be made until defined crimes shall have been committed, may be illustrated by a few notable examples. Gen. John C. Breckinridge, Gen. Robert E. Lee, Gen. Joseph E. Johnston, Gen. John B. Magruder, Gen. William B. Preston, Gen. Simon B. Buckner, and Commodore [Franklin] Buchanan, now occupying the very highest places in the rebel war service, were all within the power of the government since the rebellion began, were all well known traitors then as now …

By the third resolution … indicates … military arrests may be constitutional in localities where rebellion actually exists; but that such arrests are unconstitutional in localities where rebellion, or insurrection, does not actually exist. They insist that such arrests shall not be made "outside of the lines of necessary military occupation, and the scenes of insurrection" … as the constitution itself makes no such distinction, I am unable to believe … there is any such … distinction. …

They assert … that Mr. Vallandigham was by a military commander, seized and tried "for no other reason than words addressed to a public meeting, in criticism of … the administration, and in condemnation of the military orders of that general". … But the arrest … was made for a very

> different reason. Mr. Vallandigham avows his hostility to the war ... and his arrest was made because he was laboring ... to prevent the raising of troops, to encourage desertions.

With a master stoke both legally correct and politically wise, Lincoln threw the entire case back to his adversaries:

> Long experience has shown that armies cannot be maintained unless desertion shall be punished by ... death. ... Must I shoot a simple-minded soldier boy who deserts, while I must not touch a hair of a wily agitator who induces him to desert ... I think that in such a case, to silence the agitator, and save the boy, is not only constitutional, but, withal, a great mercy.
>
> I further say, that as the war progresses ... opinion, and action ... in great confusion at first, take shape, and fall into more regular channels; so that the necessity for arbitrary dealing ... gradually decreases. I have every reason to desire that it would cease altogether; and far from the least is my regard for the opinions and wishes of those ... like the meeting in Albany, declare ... to sustain the government in every constitutional and lawful measure to suppress the rebellion.[265]

An Ohio Democratic party convention delegation similarly branded Vallandigham's arrest, imprisonment, pretended trial, and actual banishment in violation of the Constitution. They asserted Vallandigham, when arrested, was a prominent candidate for governor, and that the Democratic Party was fully competent to decide whether he was a fit man. An attempt to deprive them of that right was an unmerited imputation upon their intelligence and loyalty.

The convention resolution declared, "The public safety will be far more endangered by continuing Mr. Vallandigham in exile. If a man ...

believes that from the inherent nature of the federal compact, the war … cannot be used as a means of restoring the Union … but would inevitably result in the final destruction of both the constitution and the Union, is he not to be allowed that right … to appeal to the judgment of the people, for a change of policy, by the … remedy of the ballot box?"

They asserted:

> The people of Ohio, are willing to cooperate zealously with you in every effort warranted by the Constitution to restore the Union … but they cannot consent to abandon those fundamental principles of civil liberty, which are essential to their existence as a free people. In their name we ask, that by a revocation of the order of his banishment, Mr. Vallandigham may be restored to the enjoyment of those rights of which … he has been unconstitutionally deprived.
>
> The undersigned are unable to agree with you in the opinion that the Constitution is different in time of insurrection or invasion from what it is in time of peace & public security.

Lincoln responded:

> I have not expressed the opinion you suppose. I expressed the opinion that the Constitution is different, in its application in cases of Rebellion or Invasion, involving the Public Safety, from what it is in times of profound peace and public security. …
>
> I only add that … the benefit of the writ of Habeas corpus, is the great means through which the guaranties of personal liberty are conserved, and made available in the last resort; and corroborative of this view, is the fact that Mr. V in the very case … under the advice of able lawyers, saw not where else to go but to the Habeas Corpus. But by the constitution

> the benefit of the writ … may be suspended when in cases of Rebellion or Invasion … public Safety may require it.
>
> You ask … whether I really claim that I may override all the guarantied rights of individuals, on the pleas of conserving the public safety. … The constitution contemplates the question as likely to occur … but it does not expressly declare who is to decide it. By implication … I think the man whom … the people have … made the commander-in-chief … is the man who … bears the responsibility of making it. If he used the power justly, the same people will justify him. …
>
> You claim that men may, if they choose, embarrass those whose duty it is, to combat a giant rebellion, and then be dealt with … only if there was no rebellion. The Constitution rejects this view. … I am unable to perceive an insult to Ohio. … I was wholly unaware that Mr. V was at the time … candidate for the democratic nomination for governor. … I am grateful to the state of Ohio for many things, especially for the brave soldiers and officers she has given to the armies.

Turning to the increasing resistance to the war and the draft, known as the fire in the rear, Lincoln said:

> We all know that combinations, armed in some instances, to resist the arrest of deserters, began several months ago; that more recently the like has appeared in resistance to the enrollment preparatory to a draft; and that quite a number of assassinations have occurred from the same animus. Those had to be met by military force, and this again has led to bloodshed and death. …
>
> I solemnly declare … that this hindrance, of the military, including maiming and murder, is due to the course in

which Mr. V has been engaged, in a greater degree than to any other cause; and is due to him personally, in a greater degree than to any other one man. These things have been notorious, known to Mr. V. Perhaps I would not be wrong to say they originated with his special friends and adherents. … He has not been known … to counsel against such resistance.

With all this … the convention you represent have nominated Mr. V. for governor of Ohio; and they and you, have declared the purpose to sustain the national Union by all constitutional means. But … they and you … reserve to yourselves to decide what are constitutional means, and, unlike the Albany meeting, you omit to state … that … an army is a constitutional means of saving the Union against rebellion; or even to intimate that you are conscious of an existing rebellion.

At the same time your nominee for Governor … is known to you, and to the world, to declare against the use of an army to suppress the rebellion. Your own attitude … encourages desertion, resistance to the draft and the like, because it teaches those who incline to desert, and to escape the draft, to believe it is your purpose to protect them, and to hope that you will become strong enough to do so. … It is a substantial hope, and … a real strength to the enemy.

If it is a false hope, and one which you would willingly dispel, I will make the way exceedingly easy. I send you duplicates of this letter, in order that you, or a majority of you, may if you choose, endorse your names upon one of them, and return it thus endorsed to me, with the understanding that those signing, are thereby committed to the following propositions, and to nothing else.

Lincoln listed three propositions, which, when endorsed, would be published.

> 1. That there is now a rebellion in the United States, the object and tendency of which is to destroy the national Union; and that in your opinion, an army and navy are constitutional means for suppressing that rebellion.
> 2. That no one of you will do anything which in his own judgment, will tend to hinder the increase, or favor the decrease, or lessen the efficiency of the army or navy, while engaged in the effort to suppress that rebellion.
> 3. That each of you will, in his sphere, do all he can to have the officers, soldiers, and seamen of the army and navy, while engaged in the effort to suppress the rebellion, paid, fed, clad, and otherwise well provided for and supported.

Lincoln said that publication would itself be a revocation of the order in relation to Vallandigham without embracing any pledge from Vallandighan. Lincoln said he would act chiefly because "I thereby prevail on other influential gentlemen of Ohio to so define their position, as to be of immense value to the Army—thus more than compensating for the consequences of any mistake in allowing Mr. V to return; and so that, on the whole, the public safety will not have suffered by it."

The delegates responded:

> The opinion of the undersigned, touching the questions … in these propositions … have been many times publicly expressed, and are sufficiently manifested in the resolutions … and they cannot suppose that the President expects … they will seek the discharge of Mr. Vallandigham, by a pledge, implying not only an imputation upon their own sincerity and fidelity … but also carrying … a concession of the legality of his arrest, trial and banishment. …

> And they have asked the revocation … not as a favor, but as a right due to the people of Ohio … they do not do this, nor does Mr. Vallandigham desire it, at any sacrifice of their dignity and self-respect. The idea, that such a pledge, as that asked … would secure the public safety sufficiently to compensate for any mistake of the President in discharging Mr. Vallandigham, is … a mere evasion of the grave questions involved in this discussion … and of a direct answer to their demands.[266]

On the war front, in the face of Lee's thrust into Pennsylvania, Lincoln faced panic calls from Alexander McClure in Pennsylvania and New Jersey governor Joel Parker for the reinstatement of General McClellan to command. In a letter to Governor Parker, Lincoln said, "I beg you to be assured that no one out of my position can know so well as if he were in it, the difficulties and involvements of replacing General McClellan in command—and this aside from any imputations upon him."

Charles F. Benjamin, who served both with the Army of the Potomac and in the War Department during the Civil War, reviewed Hooker's appointment and removal. He told of efforts to call General John F. Reynolds to command. He said Reynolds demanded liberty of action beyond what he could reasonably expect and thus declined the command. Reynolds was dropped, and the choice finally came down to Hooker and George G. Meade, with the chances a hundred to one favoring Meade.[267]

Benjamin explained, "Making … allowance for the strength and availability of Mr. Chase, as against Mr. Lincoln or any other civilian candidate, his [Chase's] friends did not conceal from themselves that the general who should conquer the rebellion would have the disposal of the next Presidency." They were on the lookout for the "right military commander," according to Benjamin. Thus, they opened communication with Hooker's friends about his views on the presidency.

Hooker gave them "assurances that … nothing could induce him to accept other than military honors." Chase and his allies were more convinced he was the right man for command, Benjamin reported, adding, "Hooker probably knew of these dickerings. Certainly Stanton did, through a friend in Chase's own circle." Benjamin, said this resulted "by reason of the fixed conviction of the Secretary of War that the former ought not to be chosen in any contingency.

"Stanton knew there were two Hookers ... He knew one as an excellent officer, mentally strong, clever and tireless, and charming (almost magnetic) in address. It was the other Hooker on whom he wished to take no chances." General Lee's invasion of Pennsylvania forced the decision. When Hooker suffered defeat at Chancellorsville, Lincoln grabbed Halleck and raced to the front. Upon his return, he conferred with the secretary of war, concluding that Hooker should be relieved.

General Halleck returned with Hooker's word that Hooker had not sought command and would resign. Halleck was determined the decision would not be reversed as strong measures were used to wring a resignation from Hooker. Stanton feared the impending battle would come before the command transfer. Duplicate copies of the order for change of command, authenticated and addressed to General Meade and Hooker, were entrusted to General James A Hardie, a friend of both.

Equipped with the orders, passes, and money to facilitate his trip, and in civilian dress, General Hardie made his way to Frederick and located Meade's headquarters some miles beyond. Passing through camps thronged with soldiers, many filled with Maryland whiskey, he obtained a buggy and driver. In the early morning he reached Meade, asleep in his tent. Awakened by a general from the War Department, Meade protested the order, urging that Reynolds be named instead of him.

Benjamin explained that Meade quickly realized Hardie had no lawful means to vary the order. The party headed for general headquarters. Hardie broke the news to Hooker, who called in General Butterfield, chief of staff. The four set about finalizing the transfer. When Meade expressed shock at the scattered condition of the army, Hooker showed strong feelings. When Reynolds heard the news, he rushed to headquarters and told Meade he could count on his complete support.

Meade told Reynolds all he had learned from Hooker and Butterfield as to the movements and positions of the two armies. The two of them developed the plan that resulted in the Battle of Gettysburg, which was fought on ground selected by Reynolds. And Hardie and Hooker, after the formal announcement of the change of command, boarded a spring wagon for the railroad station. The train would take Hooker to Baltimore and Hardie back to Washington. Meade bid them goodbye.[268]

In a Confederate strategy conference in Richmond with President Davis and War Secretary James Seddon, Lee contended a reinforced Army of Northern Virginia could invade the North. General James Longstreet had proposed his division reinforce General Braxton Bragg in Tennessee, forcing General Ulysses S. Grant to back off Vicksburg, which Davis wanted. Lee argued it would take months to get troops to Vicksburg, while the June climate would save the day if they could hold out.

Lee said that a successful invasion across the Potomac could inflict a crushing defeat on the North and force the Union hand. Lee argued it would get the Army of the Potomac out of Virginia, open the opportunity to feed and provision his army in Pennsylvania, encourage foreign intervention, discredit Republicans, and perhaps force peace consideration on the North. Lee said his men were riding the crest of victories and "will go anywhere and do anything if properly led."[269]

Lee declared an imperative for encouraging the Northern peace movement, having written Davis, "Conceding to our enemies the superiority claimed by them in numbers, resources, and all the means and appliances for carrying on the war, we have no right to look for exemptions from the military consequences of a vigorous use of these advantages. ... We should not, therefore, conceal from ourselves that our resources in men are constantly diminishing."[270]

Brevet Major-General Henry J. Hunt, chief of artillery, recounted:

> In the Army of the Potomac it was different; the proportion of veterans was much smaller; a cessation of recruiting at the very beginning of active operations, when men were easily obtainable to supply losses in existing regiments, had been followed, as emergencies arose, by new levies, for short periods of service, and in new organizations which could not readily be assimilated by older troops. …
>
> There were special difficulties. The Army of the Potomac was not in favor at the War Department. Rarely, if ever, had it heard a word of official commendation after a success, or of sympathy or encouragement after a defeat … the discharge of 58 regiments had reduced its strength since Chancellorsville by 25,000. … The average strength of army corps and divisions was about half that of the Confederates … the organization … in every way inferior to that of its adversary.[271]

General Meade was not without military assets as he directed the chiefs of engineers and artillery to select a field of battle on which his army might be concentrated. General Reynolds, through swift action and gallantry, chose the decisive field and opened brilliantly the battle that extended for three days. While directing operations, Reynolds was killed by a sharpshooter, a loss for Meade comparable to Lee's loss of General Jackson.

General Hunt explained, "As Meade believed Lee's army to be at least equal to his own, all the elements … were in favor of the Pipe Creek line. But Meade's orders … drawing his corps toward the threatened flank, carried Reynolds to Gettysburg. … Reynolds … was eager for the conflict, and his collision with [General Henry] Heth, assuming the dimensions of a battle, caused an immediate concentration of both armies at Gettysburg."[272]

When General A. P. Hill reported that the federals were in force at Gettysburg, he was instructed to avoid a general battle until Lee could bring up the rest of his forces. Lee had wanted to attack Harrisburg first, believing he could capture stores and munitions, specifically artillery shells, needed for unrestricted firing. Meade, at Taneytown, informed that the Confederates were advancing on Gettysburg, planned an "offensive-defensive line" behind Pipe Creek.

General Longstreet urged Lee "to turn Meade's left, and by interposing between him [Meade] and Washington and threatening his communications. … A battle was a necessity to Lee, and a defeat would be more disastrous to Meade. … Whatever his reasons, he decided to accept the gage of battle offered by Meade, and to attack as soon as practicable. … Meade was engaged personally or by his staff in rectifying his lines, assigning positions … watching the enemy, and studying the field."[273]

"In taking risks, it would not be for his army alone, but also for Philadelphia, Baltimore, and Washington. Gettysburg was not a good strategic position, and the circumstances under which our army was assembled limited us tactically to a strictly defensive battle." In calculating the risk, this was proven the correct course given that the brilliant victory, decisive both to the campaign and to the invasion, had a vast effect on morale at home and abroad, North and South.[274]

Meade, having had a horse shot from under him, closed the second day with a consultation with his corps commanders. It was decided unanimously to hold present lines and wait one day before taking the offensive. "General Lee, on the other hand, failed at Gettysburg because he made his attack precisely where his enemy wanted him to make it and was most fully prepared to received it," confederate major General E. M. Law said in "The Struggle for 'Round Top.'"[275]

"Gettysburg was the turning-point in the great struggle. Together with the fall of Vicksburg, which occurred simultaneously with the retreat of Lee's army toward the Potomac, it inspired the armies and people of the North with fresh courage and stimulated anew the hopes of ultimate success which were visibly flagging under an almost uninterrupted series of reverses to the Federal arms in Virginia, extending over a period of two years," General Law's report explained.

As Grant began his difficult movements south along the Mississippi toward Vicksburg, he benefited from Confederate differences. In a western swing, President Davis visited his commanding generals. Having lost his favorite, General Albert Sidney Johnson, in the Battle of Shiloh, General Joseph E. Johnson, sufficiently recovered from wounds suffered at Seven Pines, was given command of three departments with headquarters at Chattanooga, Tennessee.

General Johnson told President Davis the distance between the armies of Tennessee and Mississippi with different objects and adversaries made combined action impossible. The president insisted the distance of these departments from the seat of government made imperative a command nearer them, in case of an emergency. Johnston contended that failure to heed his warning allowed the effective concentration of federal military and naval resources.[276]

Confederate confidence in Vicksburg was strengthened as Grant's 1962–63 campaign failed to get an east bank base of operations. Thus, Grant conceived a bold plan to march his army down the west bank below Vicksburg. At the same time, Union gunboats ran the batteries at Vicksburg and arrived to the south, positioned to carry Grant's troops across the Mississippi. By mid-May the army was in the rear of Vicksburg, preparing for a regular siege and cutting off Confederate resupply.

Sherman proposed reaching high ground on the east bank, establishing a depot of supplies, and moving from there. Grant, in response, said, "The country is already disheartened over the lack of success on the part of our armies; the last election went against the vigorous prosecution of the war, voluntary enlistments had ceased throughout most of the North and conscription was already resorted to, and if we went back as far as Memphis it would discourage people."

Grant tightened his grip on Vicksburg and sent forces east to capture Jackson, destroy railroads, supplies, and manufacturing facilities, preventing Johnston from reinforcing General John C. Pemberton. Pemberton proposed an armistice. Grant replied, "The useless effusion of blood you propose stopping … can be ended … by the unconditional surrender. … Men who have shown so much endurance and … I can assure you will be treated with all the respect due to prisoners of war."

Surrender enabled Grant to report via Cairo, Illinois, to General Halleck: "The enemy surrendered this morning. The only terms allowed [are] their parole as prisoners of war. This I regard as a great advantage of us. … It saves … several days in the capture, and leaves troops and transports ready for immediate service. Sherman, with a large force, moves immediately on Johnston, to drive him from the State. I will send troops to the relief of Banks, and return the 9th army corps to Burnside."

The victories at Vicksburg and at Gettysburg, Grant said, "lifted a great load of anxiety from the minds of the President, his Cabinet and the loyal people all over the North. The fate of the Confederacy was sealed when Vicksburg fell." Grant concluded there would be much hard fighting with many lives lost in the months ahead, but he asserted the "morale" was with the Union ever after. Of great importance, the Mississippi River was entirely in the hands of the Union forces.[277]

Admiral Samuel P. Lee, in the wake of Union victory, forwarded to Navy Secretary Wells a note from Alexander H. Stephens, Confederate vice president, who, as military commissioner, wrote, "For the purpose of delivering the communication in person and conferring upon the subjects to which it relates, I desire to proceed directly to Washington in the Steamer 'Torpedo' commanded by Lt. Hunter Davison of the 'Confederate States' Navy."

Lincoln replied to Admiral Lee, "You will not permit Mr. Stephens to proceed to Washington, or to pass the blockade. He does not make known the subjects to which the communication … from Mr. Davis relates. … These subjects can only be military, or not military, or both. Whatever … military will be … received, if offered through … military channels … nothing else, will be received by the President … in terms of assuming the independence of the so-called Confederate States."

When President Lincoln learned that Vicksburg had fallen, he wrote to Grant:

> I do not remember that you and I ever met personally. I write this now for the almost inestimable service you have done the country. … When you first reached the vicinity of Vicksburg, I though you should do, what you finally did—march the troops across the neck, run the batteries with the transports, and thus go below; and I never had any faith … that the Yazoo Pass expedition, and the like, could succeed.
>
> When you got below, and took Port-Gibson, Grand Gulf, and vicinity, I thought you should go down the river and join General Banks; and when you turned Northward East of the Big Black, I feared it was a mistake. I now wish to make the personal acknowledgment that you were right and I was wrong.

A staff officer sent by Grant delivered a detailed report, and Lincoln reportedly said, "I guess I was right in standing by Grant, although there was great pressure … to have him removed."[278]

Former president Franklin Pierce—whom Jefferson Davis had served as secretary of war—told a Fourth of July mass meeting of Democrats in Concord, New Hampshire, "Here in these free States, it is made criminal for that noble martyr of free speech, Mr. Vallandigham, to discuss public affairs in Ohio—ay, even here, in time of war the mere arbitrary will of the President takes the place of the constitution," claiming shock that "evil counsels, incompetency and corruption overwhelm our nation."[279]

On the same day, New York governor Seymour—with nineteen of his state guard regiments at Gettysburg—told an audience at the New York Academy of Music that the nation was on "the very verge of destruction," alleging government coercion in seizing our persons, infringing upon our rights, insulting our homes, depriving us of those cherished principles for which our fathers fought." The implication was that he not only opposed the draft but "outrages" should be resisted.

At this point, New York-area manufacturing was profiting from the war. The new dome for the nation's capital was built in New York. Its shipyards were turning out ships—including the famed ironclad *Monitor*—vital to the blockade of the Confederacy. Some shipyards had been building ships for the slave trade, which Lincoln had halted. In a major shift in productivity, New York retooled and out produced the entire Confederacy.[280]

Nine days later—on the heels of Lincoln's Day of Thanksgiving proclamation—New York City was convulsed by anti-draft riots. The draft lottery was initiated on Saturday, and on Sunday working-class families pored over the names. The *New York Herald* reported that wives and mothers "mingled their wildest denunciations against the conscription law." Many had fortified themselves with hard liquor. All of this triggered a determined resolve to prevent the draft.

Thousands of friends, relatives, and sympathizers gathered on vacant lots armed with clubs, staves, cart rungs, and iron pieces. The wrathful began a growing tide of destruction and burning of draft offices. Gathering near Central Park, rioters organized and swiftly patrolled throughout the city. Volunteer firemen, angry over having lost their draft exemptions, joined in driving off the police. The mob focused their rage to halt the draft by destroying draft lists.

Limited numbers of police reserves "were routed and stomped, their bodies stripped, their faces smashed." Homes suspected of providing refuge to fleeing policemen were burned. "Fury at the Metropolitans, building for years, blazed up viciously." Republicans came under attack, and Republican mayor George Opdyke's home was threatened, but Democrats protected it. Fifth Avenue mansions were sacked, looted, and burned.

"Troops began arriving Wednesday evening," a prelude to "a day of atrocities during which crowds had hanged, drowned, and mutilated black men, looted and burned black homes up and down Sixth Avenue, and attacked Republican mansions and Protestant missions. … Bands of Irish longshoremen, with quarrymen, street pavers, teamsters and cart men began chasing blacks, screaming, 'Kill all niggers!' They even burned the 'Colored Orphan Asylum.'"

Thursday evening the rioting ended as some six thousand troops cleared the streets. "Troops assaulted 'infected' districts, using howitzers … to mow down rioters and engaged in fierce building-by-building firefights. Rioters defended their barricaded domains with mad desperation. Faced with tenement snipers and brick hurlers, soldiers broke down doors, bayoneted all who interfered and drove occupants to the roofs, from which many jumped to certain death."

Mayor Opdyke appealed to Secretary Stanton for troops and asked martial law be declared. He also asked that General Butler be placed in command. But Lincoln, keen to avoid offending Democrats, named General John A. Dix, a financier and war Democrat who had served in President Buchanan's cabinet, as the commander of the Department of the East. Bringing in ten thousand troops, Dix, with a major show of force, restarted the draft and restored calm in the battered city.[281]

Thurlow Weed, in police headquarters observing the chaos, wrote, "I was in New York, witnessing scenes which I hope may never occur again." Later he wrote to *New York Times* editor Henry Raymond,

"I concur with you in believing that there are not spires enough in your city to avert the wrath of Heaven, if immediate relief and future protection be not extended to persecuted colored citizens." For relief of those harmed, Weed sent his personal check for $500.[282]

Governor Seymour had asked previously for a postponement of the draft, but Lincoln had said no. Dix, on July 30, asked the governor "whether the military power of the State may be relied on to enforce the execution of the law in case of forcible resistance to it." He added, "I am very anxious that there should be perfect harmony between the Federal Government and that of the State of New York, and if, under your authority to see the laws faithfully executed."[283]

When Dix did not receive a reply by August 12, Dix requested the ten thousand troops and urged the president call out the state militia. Seymour replied on August 15. On the same day Lincoln drafted a letter to the governor, declaring:

> Whereas, by reason of unlawful combinations against the authority of the Government of the United Sates, it has become impracticable, in my judgment, to enforce, by the ordinary course of judicial proceedings, the laws of the United States within. …
>
> Therefore: I, Abraham Lincoln, President of the United States, do call forth the Militia of the State of New York, to aid in suppressing said combinations and opposition to said laws. And I do respectfully request, and direct that, for this purpose your Excellency do forthwith order Major General Sanford, with his command, to report for orders to Major General John A. Dix.

As Seymour cooperated, Lincoln withdrew the proclamation and the draft resumed.[284]

Governor Seymour telegraphed Lincoln: "In view of the uncertainty as to the quotas which may be required from the several Congressional districts … there is a doubt by many as to whether volunteers now recruited will be available to reduce the quotas as they may be ultimately adjusted. This doubt interferes with the recruiting of volunteers. I therefore request that volunteers heretofore recruited and mustered … shall be accepted as substitutes for such conscripts."

Lincoln responded that he did not understand Seymour's dispatch. "My view of, the principle is that every soldier obtained voluntarily, leaves one less to be obtained by draft. The only difficulty is in applying the principle properly. Looking to time, as heretofore I am unwilling to give up a drafted man now, even for the certainty, much less for the mere chance, of getting a volunteer hereafter. … My purpose is to be just and fair; and yet to not lose time."[285]

Representative James C. Conkling wrote to Lincoln, "The unconditional union men of all parties in our state are to hold a Grand Mass Meeting at Springfield [Illinois] on the 3rd day of September next. It would be gratifying to the many thousands who will be present … if you would also meet with them." Lincoln replied on August 20, "Your letter of the 14th is received. I think I will go, or send a letter—probably the latter." A significant object was to counter a previous peace rally.

Lincoln could not get away from Washington, but in a masterful fashion laid his case before the people in an August 26, 1863, letter to Representative Conkling. Conkling read the letter before the massive rally more than 75,000 strong. In the letter, Lincoln explained his rationale:

"There are those who are dissatisfied with me. To which I would say: You desire peace; and you blame me that we do not have it. But how can we attain it? There are three conceivable ways.

> First, to suppress the rebellion by force of arms. This, I am trying to do. Are you for it? If you are, so far we are agreed.

> If you are not for it, a second way is to give up the Union. I am against this. Are you for it? If you are, you should say so plainly. If you are not for force, nor yet for dissolution, there only remains some imaginable compromise. I do not believe any compromise, embracing the maintenance of the Union, is now possible. All I learn leads to a directly opposite belief.
>
> The strength of the rebellion, leads to a directly opposite belief. The strength of the rebellion is its military—its army. That army dominates all the country, and all the people, within its range. Any offer of terms made by any man or men within that range, in opposition to that army, is simply nothing for the present; because such man or men, have no power whatever to enforce their side of a compromise, if one were made to them.

Lincoln asked if a compromise would stop Lee's army. "But no paper compromise, to which the controllers of Lee's army are not agreed, can, at all, affect that army. In an effort at such compromise we should waste time, which the enemy would improve to our disadvantage; and that would be all. A compromise, to be effective, must be made either with those who control the rebel army, or with the people first liberated from the domination of that army, by the success of our own army."

Lincoln assured them no such proposal had been made. He pledged that as the servant of the people if any such proposition shall come to him that it shall not be rejected nor kept secret. "I fully acknowledge myself the servant of the people, according to the bond of service—the United States Constitution; and that, as such, I am responsible to them."

As to the Negro question, he said, "But, to be plain, you are dissatisfied with me about the Negro. Quite likely there is a difference of opinion between you and myself upon that subject. I certainly wish that all men could be free, while I suppose you do not. Yet I have neither adopted, nor proposed any measure, which is not consistent with even your view, provided you are for the Union." Lincoln explained:

> I suggested compensated emancipation; to which you replied you wished not to be taxed to buy Negroes, except in such way, as to save you from greater taxation to save the Union exclusively by other means.
>
> You dislike the emancipation proclamation; and, perhaps, would retract it. You say it is unconstitutional—I think differently. I think the Constitution invests its commander-in-chief, with the law of war, in time of war. The most that can be said, if so much, is, that slaves are property. Is there—has there ever been—any question that by the law of war, property both of enemies and friends, may be taken when needed? And is it not needed whenever taking it, helps us, or hurts the enemy?

As to the use of blacks as soldiers, Lincoln said:

> I know … that some of our commanders … in the field … believe the emancipation policy, and the use of colored troops, constitute the heaviest blow yet dealt the rebellion. … You say you will not fight to free Negroes. Some of them seem willing to fight for you, but no matter. Fight you, then, exclusively to save the Union. …
>
> I thought, whatever extent the Negroes should cease helping the enemy to that extent it weakened the enemy. … Do you think differently?
>
> I thought that whatever Negroes can be got to do as soldiers, leaves just so much less for white soldiers to do, in saving the union. Does it appear otherwise to you? But Negroes, like other people act upon motives. Why should they do

> anything for us, if we will do nothing for them? If they stake their lives for us, they must be prompted by the strongest motive – even the promise of freedom. And the promise being made must be kept.
>
> Peace does not appear so distant as it did. I hope it will come soon, and come to stay; and so come as to be worth the keeping in all future time. It will then have been proved that, among free men, there can be no successful appeal from the ballot to the bullet; and that they who take such appeal are sure to lose their case, and pay the cost. … Still let us not be over-sanguine. … Let us diligently apply the means, never doubting that a just God, in his own good time, will give us the rightful result.[286]

Radical senator Chandler of Wisconsin wrote to Illinois senator Lyman Trumbull, saying he had become convinced Lincoln would not back down on the Emancipation Proclamation. Chandler explained the reason Lincoln would not back down and buttressed his point by noting that Weed might be shaky, but not Lincoln: "This peculiar trait of stubbornness (which annoyed us so much 18 months ago) is now our Salvation." Lincoln "is as stubborn as a mule when he gets his back up."[287]

Thurlow Weed wrote to Raymond, "For the persecution of the Negro there is divided responsibility. The hostility of Irishmen to Africans is unworthy of men who themselves seek and find in America an asylum from oppression. Yet this hostility would not culminate in arson and murder but for the stimulants applied by fanatics. Journalists who persistently inflame and exasperate the ignorant and the lawless against the Negro are morally responsible for these outrages."

Taking a hard line against abolitionists, Weed declared, "In South Carolina ultra Abolitionists have been hailed as the 'best friends' of secession. Practically, they are the worst enemies of the colored man.

Had it not been for the malign influence of these howling fanatics in Congress and with the President, rebellion would not, in the beginning, have assumed such formidable proportions; nor, in its progress, would the North have been divided or the government crippled."[288]

Weed proposed a four point plan: (1) proclaim pardon and amnesty to all engaged in making war upon the government; (2) declare an armistice for ninety days, protecting all traveling to and from North and South; (3) citizens of Confederate States who returned to their allegiance and duties within 90 days, would be restored their rights, privileges, and prerogatives enjoyed before secession; and (4) those who declined would face renewed war and confiscation of property.

Weed said he developed the plan because the Union army was either repulsed or held at bay and badly in need of manpower. He said he submitted it to the President, who requested him to commit it to paper. Writing Lincoln, Weed said, "It makes our record so clearly right, that you stand justified in the eyes of the whole world." Weed said he had support from Stanton and Massachusetts senator Henry Wilson, but not Seward. He said Dean Richmond, an Albany Democrat, favored it.

Weed proposed giving confiscated property to Union soldiers, adding: "In answer to those who may object … I think it quite sufficient to say that in maritime wars this feature has long [been] … practiced. … This, therefore, in all wars upon the oceans and seas of the world, being a part of the law of nations, cannot … be objected to, whereas … the sufferers are in rebellion … and have been warned of the consequences of rejecting the most liberal offers of peace, protection, and prosperity."[289]

When Weed retired as editor of the *Albany Evening Journal*, his longtime political voice, Lincoln wrote on January 29, 1863, "Your valedictory to the patrons of the *Albany Evening Journal* brings me a good deal of uneasiness. What does it mean?"

Weed replied:

> I retired from an apprehension that I was doing more harm than good. I could not remain without remonstrance against a Spirit by which you are persecuted, and which I know will end our Union and Government.
>
> It is impossible, just now, to resist Fanaticism—a Fanaticism which divides the North and deprives you of the support essential, vital indeed, to the Life of the Republic. Its constant cry is: "Give! Give!" and the more you give the more it demands. They accuse me of "opposing the Administration." I answered that falsehood yesterday, and sent Mr. Nicolay a Paper. I have labored to shield the Administration from their persecution.

Weed wanted a more moderate course from Lincoln. [290]

CHAPTER X

COPING WITH NEW YORK; GOVERNOR SEYMOUR, WEED, AND GREELEY; CHALLENGE AT CHATTANOOGA

A chief source of trouble for Lincoln came from *New York Tribune* publisher Greeley. While Lincoln humored him, he was not deceived. Lincoln described Greeley as "a rotten old shoe." Greeley persisted in his feud with former allies Seward and Weed, who had engineered his defeat for the Senate. Lincoln remained aware that Greeley had supported Douglas over him for senator in 1858, tried to make Douglas the 1860 Republican presidential nominee, and hoped to dump Lincoln in 1864.

The bitter feud between the Seward/Weed faction and Greeley constantly challenged Lincoln, who wanted to avoid alienating Greeley, as Weed wrote:

> There is crazy "method" in Greeley's Abolitionism. He has the presidency on his Brain. He ran "Maine Law" into the ground expecting to make himself Governor. His Ambition is mere lunacy, but, unfortunately, I fear he possesses the power to ruin our country. If I could be heard by the same number of readers, I should hope to open their eyes.
>
> This State was ours, in November, by 25,000 majority, with Morgan, and 50,000 with Dix, but he, and his like, would

> have an Abolition issue for Governor, that they might have a Legislature in favor of Greeley or Field for U.S. Senator.

With considerable bitterness, Weed claimed it resulted in the election of Seymour, a Democrat, as governor of New York, adding, "I may not be able to do much good, but all I am belongs to my Country, and to yourself as president."[291]

In the spring of 1863, Greeley, as Weed told Lincoln, was working to find a candidate to replace him. Lincoln asked James R. Gilmore, a New York shipping and cotton merchant who had met with Greeley, "How does Horace feel now?" Gilmore replied, "Somewhat downhearted." When a meeting was suggested, Gilmore said Greeley responded that Lincoln could not be trusted, had failed to give the *Tribune* early information, and was slow alerting him about the Emancipation Proclamation.

Gilmore's account quoted Greeley: "No … I can't trust your 'honest old Abe.' He is too smart for me. He thinks me a damned fool; but I am never fooled twice by the same individual." Greeley insisted Lincoln had the idea that God was managing the war and thought of himself as vice regent. Two more years of this and the country would be ravaged past saving. Furthermore, he said, the only hope was to defeat Lincoln in 1864. He claimed Republican leaders agreed with him.[292]

Lincoln was aware that Chase was angling to replace him as the party's nominee. Even when Chase became an open candidate, Lincoln said of him, "I have determined to shut my eyes so far as possible to everything of the sort. Mr. Chase makes a good secretary, and I shall keep him where he is. If he becomes President, all right. I hope we may never have a worse man. I have observed with regret his plan of strengthening himself." Clearly the Chase matter weighed on him.

Alexander McClure said he had never seen Lincoln unbalanced except in the summer of 1863. Given widespread distrust among Republican leaders, Lincoln knew if discordant elements focused on a single candidate, he could be defeated. McClure said Lincoln detained him one night at the White House until two o'clock in the morning, expressing concern. McClure told Lincoln that Chase could not be the candidate, and that McClure regarded Lincoln's renomination as reasonably certain.

It was midnight at that time, and McClure said he rose to leave, but Lincoln renewed the subject. Lincoln did so again at one o'clock. "By the way, McClure," he said, "how would it do if I were to decline Chase?"

McClure asked, "How could that be done?"

"Well," said Lincoln, "I don't know how it could be done." And he launched into a story about two Democrats running for the state senate in southern Illinois, which in the early years of statehood was almost solidly Democratic.

Debating day after day, both became ashamed of their disgraceful wrangles. So finally they agreed that either should say anything he pleased about the other, and it should not be resented.

On election night, since both lived in the same town, the returns were uncomfortably until a distant precinct where one had expected a large majority reported against him.

The winner told his opponent that, since they had agreed either was free to say whatever he wished, he had done so. The winning candidate had taken the liberty of saying that his opponent had retired from the contest—in other words, the winner had "declined" his opponent, which led to the opponent's defeat. "I think," Lincoln told McClure, with a hearty laugh, "I had better decline Chase." Without saying how, McClure said it was obvious that Lincoln believed he could do it.[293]

Judge Davis, concerned about Lincoln's renomination, was working closely with Swett and Weed, corresponding regularly. Weed,

Swett, and Davis also traded cotton. In March 1864, Davis wrote to Weed, urging more aggressive effort by the president to ensure renomination at the Baltimore convention. Davis also remained on good terms with his cousin and Lincoln foe, Representative Henry Winter Davis, who remained angered because Blair got the cabinet post he had wanted.

"I showed your letter to the President. It pains him when you are not satisfied with what he does," Davis wrote to Weed. "He stated to me that he has the highest esteem for you, knows that you are patriotic, and that it hurts him when he cannot do what you think advisable." Davis said Lincoln's views differed and told Weed, "I think he ought to act, and act promptly, but his mind is constituted differently from yours and mine. We will have to wait for his decision in the important matter."

Weed's political stance was identical in 1862 and in 1863, urging a Republican canvass to learn voter opinion singly for the Union. The clamor for peace among Democrats had reached new levels of intensity. To Weed, this was evident from the 1862 defeat of an Abolition-Republican ticket, while a Union Republican ticket achieved a 30,000-vote majority in 1863. With Lincoln more disposed in 1863 to tolerate the radicals, by 1864 his views shifted as they continued to attack him.

"They will all be against him in '64," Weed wrote to Judge Davis. "Why does he persist in giving them weapons with which they may be able not only to defeat his re-nomination, but to destroy the government?" As the war continued, the conviction developed that no party had the strength to defeat the South. Northern political divisions posed as much of a threat as Confederate arms. Weed resented Chase and demanded a hand in New York Treasury appointments.

Weed wrote to Davis, claiming the Chase appointees in New York had even been blocking an endorsement of Lincoln in the New York legislature. The vast patronage of the federal Treasury made New York a significant stronghold for Chase, even as ugly evidence of corruption, if not treason, in the United States Custom House in New York was aired in Congress. It was alleged that arms and contraband had escaped to the South by collusion of customs officers in the New York office.

Weed, arguing vehemently, told Davis, "And I beg you to say to the President, distinctly and emphatically, that if the Custom House is left in custody of those who have, for two years, sent 'aid and comfort' to the enemy his fitness for President will be questioned." Weed wrote directly to the president, naming persons in the custom house who were drawing government salaries while spending virtually their entire time on the Chase campaign and asked that they be removed.

Weed elaborated: "I informed Mr. Lincoln, when I saw him in November, that the infamies of the Appraiser's Office required the removal of Hogeboom and Hunt, men whose appointments originally, we in vain resisted. … It is not alone that these men are against Mr. Lincoln, but they disgrace the office—a Department everywhere spoken of as a 'Den of Thieves.' Mr. Lincoln not only spurns his friends … but promotes an enemy who ought to be removed." Davis shared this with Lincoln.

Weed asked Davis when the president would remove Hiram Barney, the collector of customs. It was alleged that Barney was managing private investments for Chase. Davis responded that Lincoln intended to remove Barney, and likely appoint Weed ally Abraham Wakeman, the current New York postmaster. Davis explained that Lincoln was embarrassed by the many petitions for Wakeman's appointment but would choose a successor before long. [294]

Concerned about the possible affront to Thurlow Weed, Lincoln wrote, "I have been brought to fear recently that somehow, by commission or omission, I have caused you some degree of pain. … I am sure if we could meet we would not part with any unpleasant impression on either side." Weed replied, "Amid your great and constant responsibilities I regret that you should have been annoyed by any small grief of mine. It is not however, pleasant to be misunderstood." Weed continued:

> I certainly was pained to learn that you regarded my controversy with the N. Y. Tribune as a personal quarrel with Mr. Greeley, in which both were damaging our cause. If, a year or more since, when ultra Abolition was rampant, I had not throttled it, rescuing Republican organizations from its incendiary influences, the North would have been fatally divided and your power to serve the Country as fatally paralyzed. … My quarrels are in no sense personal. …
>
> I am without personal objects or interests. … I have confided unwaveringly, in your Integrity and Patriotism, from the beginning of this Rebellion, the certainty and magnitude of which I foresaw; and I have earnestly and faithfully labored to uphold your administration. … If you will carry our Country safely through its great Trial—and I know you will if you can—I will serve, honor and bless you—with all my strength and my whole heart, as long as Life is given to me.

In the area of foreign policy, Lincoln was distressed by the French intervention in Mexico, specifically because the Confederates were supporting opponents of Benito Juarez. The Union had a very specific problem, as supplies were being smuggled from the northern provinces of Mexico to Confederates in Texas. And the French action was a violation of the Monroe Doctrine. Lincoln, after Vicksburg fell, ordered a drive into Texas despite Grant's wish to attack Mobile. The effort failed.

Weed also became increasingly agitated over the heavy debt burden of the Union, writing to Senator Morgan and urging repeal of the homestead law. "Three years of eventful experience and observation have taught us one priceless … truth, namely, that this Rebellion is sure to result in its own overthrow, in the vindication of our government, and in the restoration of our Union. And the penalty for rebellion will be the inevitable subversion of power that caused it."

This subversion, Weed, said, was the only retribution proportioned to the magnitude of the crime, adding:

> Assuming that we are, no matter at what further cost, and in defiance of all obstacles, to preserve our government and Union, it behooves statesmen to divide their time and thoughts between the present and the future. When the war terminates we shall find that it has cost at least four thousand millions of dollars, three fourths of which amount will remain as a national debt.
>
> Is it not time to grid our fiscal loins, and gather strength to bear this heavy burden? Should we not cast a financial anchor that will enable the Treasury to ride safely through a crisis equal, if not greater, than England ever encountered? After years of discussion and debate, the popular idea of "voting yourself a farm" obtained, and in 1861 the "homestead law" was enacted. The argument … that the government did not need the proceeds of the public lands was then conclusive. Is it so now?
>
> Shall we not, when the din of the war ceases, need every resource to maintain the national credit? In view, therefore, of an approaching momentous financial crisis—a crisis, which if not, so far as possible, seasonably provided for, may prove as severe a trial as the war which may produce it, will not Congress immediately rescue the public domain by a repeal of the homestead law?

He declared, "There is no surer way of fortifying the nation's credit."

Weed and Dean Richmond, a friend, ally, and prominent Democrat, had worked closely with Corning. Corning and Richmond were executive officers of the New York Central Railroad. All three had speculated in land, both West and South. Corning's ironworks manufactured and supplied rails and railroad equipment. This stoked their interest in the public lands. Weed was trading cotton with Leonard Swett, as they knew postwar Europe would want cotton and low tariffs.[295]

From Kansas, Senator James H. Lane and Representative Abel C. Wilder alerted Lincoln to the cruel massacre August 21 of some two hundred men and boys in Lawrence, Kansas. Lane escaped, fleeing in his nightshirt through a cornfield. Lincoln wrote General John M. Schofield, "The severe blow they have received, naturally enough makes them intemperate, even without any just cause for blame, Please do your utmost to give them future security, and to punish their invaders."

Lincoln had placed Schofield in command in Missouri, and had urged him to work with the state's two political factions. Lane and Wilder told Lincoln, "The result of the massacre at Lawrence having excited feelings amongst our people, which makes a collision between them & the military probable, the imbecility & incapacity of Schofield is most deplorable. Our people unanimously demand the removal of Schofield, whose policy has opened Kansas to invasion & butchery."

Schofield told Lincoln, "Since the capture of Vicksburg a considerable portion of the rebel army in the Mississippi Valley has disbanded, and large numbers of men have come back ... some ... under instructions to carry on a guerrilla warfare, and others, men of the worst character, became marauders on their own account. ... Under instructions from the rebel authorities ... considerable bands, called 'Border Guards,' were organized in the counties of Missouri bordering on Kansas."

Their ostensible purpose was protecting those counties against inroads from Kansas, and preventing slaves from escaping from Missouri into Kansas. Schofield stated, "There could be no cure for the evil short of the removal from the counties of all slaves entitled to their freedom, and of the families of all men known to belong to these bands, and others who were known to sympathize with them." Schofield ordered that policy be implemented.

He continued:

> Almost immediately … Quantrill secretly assembled from several of the border counties … about 300 of his men. They met … near the Kansas line about sunset, and immediately marched for Lawrence. … They sacked and burned the town and murdered the citizens in the most barbarous manner. … It is easy to see that any unguarded town … where such a number of outlaws can be assembled is liable to a similar fate, if the villains are willing to risk the retribution which must follow. …
>
> I have strong reasons for believing that the authors of the telegram to you are among those who introduced and obtained the adoption of the Leavenworth resolution, and who are endeavoring to organize a force for the purpose of general retaliation upon Missouri. … I have not the "capacity" to see the wisdom or justice of permitting an irresponsible mob to enter Missouri for the purpose of retaliation, even for so grievous a wrong as that which Lawrence has suffered.[296]

General Schofield explained that those who telegraphed the president had pushed adoption of the revolution, adding: "I have increased the force upon the border … and no effort will be spared to punish the invaders of Kansas and to prevent such actions in the future." On August 31, Lincoln wrote to General Halleck, "It is not improbable that retaliation for the recent great outrage at Lawrence, in Kansas, may extend to indiscriminate slaughter on the Missouri border, unless averted."[297]

Halleck telegraphed to General Schofield, "You will please report whether measures are being taken to prevent hostile collisions on the Kansas border; also whether General Ewing's order to depopulate certain counties in Missouri has been approved or disapproved by you." General Schofield replied that he was at the border to prevent such trouble, and had the order by General Ewing under review, and indicated it would be modified after meeting General Ewing.

As the Kansans planned in detail retaliation against Missouri and recovery of stolen property, General Schofield told the governor of Kansas, "You cannot expect me to permit anything of this sort," assuring them he would make every effort to punish the guilty. In Missouri, radicals contended that the proslavery policies of Missouri governor Gamble, brother-in-law of Attorney General Bates, were paralyzing federal action. The radicals then organized a Committee of Seventy to call on Lincoln.

In Washington, the seventy Missourians—one from each county—were joined by a Kansas delegation, eighteen strong. Still smarting because Lincoln had set aside Fremont's proclamation of emancipation, they voiced three demands: General Schofield should be relieved and General Butler appointed to command in Missouri; Missouri's enrolled militia should be broken up and national forces substituted; and only persons allowed by law should be permitted to cast their ballots.

Delegation chair Charles Daniel Drake, anti-secession legislator and author of notable law treaties, read a prepared address. Lincoln later told John Hay, "They are nearer to me than the other side, in thought and sentiment, though bitterly hostile personally." And he told the delegation, "You gentlemen must bear in mind that in performing the duties of the office I hold I must represent no one section, but I must act for all sections ... in trying to maintain the supremacy of the Government."

He also said, "I will take your address, carefully consider it, and respond at my earliest convenience." Lincoln further explained, "I cannot act on vague impressions," as they had not made specific complaints against Schofield. As to their objections to Governor Gamble, he reminded them that Gamble was governor because he had been selected by their own state convention.

Knowing some branded him a tyrant, Lincoln turned to Schofield's suspension of habeas corpus under his decree. One delegate said, "We thought it would be used against the other side." Lincoln replied, "Certainly you did. Your ideas of justice seem to depend on the application of it. You object to its being used in Missouri. In other words, that which is right when employed against opponents is wrong when employed against yourselves."

Lincoln was aware, as Hay noted, "a certain unreasoning radicalism which pervaded the whole North might … prevent his re-nomination or reelection."

Declining to enter into differences between radicals and conservatives, but willing to hear both, Lincoln said, "The Radicals and Conservatives each agree with me in some things and disagree with me in others. I could wish both to agree with me in all things, for then they would agree with each other and would be too strong for any foe from any quarter. They, however, choose … otherwise; and I do not question their right. I too shall do what seems to be my duty."[298]

Lincoln wrote Schofield, while there was no organized military force in Missouri that was in opposition to the government, the condition of things made it indispensable to maintain the government's military establishment. Laying down a series of injunctions, Lincoln said, "Expel guerrillas, marauders, and murderers, and all who are known to harbor, aid, or abet them. But in like manner, you will repress assumptions of unauthorized individuals to perform the same services."

Writing to Governor Andrew Johnson, Lincoln said, "All Tennessee is now clear of armed insurrectionists. You need not to be reminded that it is the nick of time for re-inaugurating a loyal State government. ... The re-inauguration must not be such as to give control of the State, and it's representation in Congress, to the enemies of the Union, driving its friends into political exile. ... Let the reconstruction be the work of such men only as can be trusted for the Union."

Johnson responded, "It reminds me of calling your attention (to)... the 4th Section of the constitution & and propriety under the section of authorizing the military govt to exercise all power necessary & proper to secure to the people of Tennessee a republican form of govt. ... Such authority emanating from the Prest ... would exert much influence ... here. ... I have taken decided ground for Emancipation. ... Now is the time for settlement of this question. I am for immediate emancipation."[299]

Meanwhile General Rosecrans—inactive since the January Stone's River battle—took after Confederate forces under General Bragg. In his diary, John Hay reported, "The next morning [September 12] he [the president] came into my bedroom ... (and) said: 'Well, Rosecrans has been whipped, as I feared. ... Rosecrans says we have met with serious disaster—extent uncertain.'" In the face of adversity, Lincoln wired Rosecrans, "Be of good cheer. We have unabated confidence in you."[300]

Lincoln wanted federal forces in Chattanooga to hold their position because it kept Tennessee clear of the enemy and broke key communications lines. Lincoln told Halleck, "If you concur, I think he [Rosecrans] would better be informed that we are not pushing him beyond this position; and that, in fact, our judgment is rather against his going beyond it. If he can only maintain this position, without more, this rebellion can only eke out a short and feeble existence."

Rosecrans successfully maneuvered Bragg's troops south of the Tennessee River, toward Chickamauga, Georgia. Reinforced with fresh troops from Mississippi, Bragg pursued and defeated Rosecrans, taking possession of the heights of Missionary Ridge and Lookout Mountain. By occupying these commanding heights overlooking Chattanooga, Bragg outmaneuvered and isolated Rosecrans, controlled his line of supply and threatened his hold on Tennessee.

In a letter to Mary Lincoln at the Fifth Avenue Hotel in New York, Lincoln wrote, "We now have a tolerably accurate summing up of the late battle if at all, only in the fact that we, after the main fighting was over, yielded the ground, thus leaving considerable of our artillery and wounded to fall into the enemies' hands, for which we got nothing in turn. … Gen. Rosecrans telegraph from Chattanooga: 'We hold this point, and I cannot be dislodged, except by superior numbers.'"

The sad news he conveyed to Mary was that she had lost her thirty-two-year-old brother-in-law, General Ben Hardin Helm, married to Mary's younger sister, Emily. Both were favorites of the Lincolns. Lincoln wrote, "We lost, in general officers, one killed, and three or four wounded, all brigadiers; while according to rebel accounts … they lost six killed and eight wounded. Of the killed, one major genl. and five brigadiers, including your brother-in-law, Helm."[301]

Meanwhile, positive political developments occurred. James G. Blaine, chairman of the Maine Union Committee, wired Lincoln on September 14, "Maine sustains your administration by a majority of 15,000," adding later, "Fuller returns magnify our victory. Indications now are that we have carried every county in the State, elected every Senator; secured seven eights of the Representatives and followed up a majority of 20,000 out of a total vote of 100,000." Lincoln sent thanks for the news.

Rosecrans was in deep trouble and required assistance. Charles A. Dana wired from Chattanooga that unless prevented, Rosecrans would retreat. It would have meant the loss of the strategic position, all artillery, and even the army itself. Already the men were on half rations and some ten thousand animals had starved. The enemy prevented a train loaded with ammunition and medical supplies from reaching Union forces, left with barely enough ammunition for a day's fighting.

Given the dark news, Stanton had John Hay awakened Lincoln at the Soldier's Home to bring him to Washington. Chase, Seward, and the president all arrived at the War Department. They read a telegram from General James A. Garfield at Chattanooga, urging reinforcements. Stanton opened the discussion by asking Halleck what reinforcements Burnside could add from the Army of the Cumberland. Halleck responded, "Twenty-thousand men in ten days, if uninterrupted."

Stanton then asked, "When will Sherman's [troops] reach Rosecrans?" Halleck replied, "In about ten days, if already moved from Vicksburg. … Boats have already gone down from Cairo and every available man ordered forward, say from 20,000 to 25,000." General Halleck previously had wired Grant to send all available forces directly to reinforce Rosecrans. Grant had dispatched General Sherman with the Seventeenth Corps, positioning him to advance to Chattanooga.

Stanton declared, "I propose to send 30,000 from the Army of the Potomac. There is no reason to expect that General Meade will attack Lee. … In five days 30,000 could be put with Rosecrans." The president was skeptical that in five days the troops could even reach Washington. The president and Halleck were disinclined to weaken Meade. Chase and Seward urged that Rosecrans be reinforced because of the strategic importance of holding Chattanooga.

Stanton had sent identical telegrams summoning to Washington three key railroad officials: former assistant secretary of war Thomas A. Scott of the Pennsylvania, John W. Garrett of the Baltimore and Ohio, and S. M. Felton, president of the Philadelphia, Wilmington and Baltimore. The three executives calculated distances, running speeds and locations of locomotives and cars. They immediately chose the route for what was to be the fastest troop movement in the nation's history.

"The matter has been carefully investigated," Stanton said, "and it is certain that 30,000 bales of cotton could be sent in that time, and by taking possession of the railroads and excluding all other business I do not see why 30,000 men cannot be sent." Stanton reported, "At 2:30 A.M. on September 24, Meade was ordered … to prepare two army corps, under General Hooker, ready for transport, with five days' cooked provisions, with baggage, artillery, ammunition, horses, to follow."[302]

Responsibility was divided among the three rail executives initially. Scott was dispatched to Louisville to manage the movement south to Bridgeport, near Chattanooga. General Hooker commanded the dispatched troops with orders to take military possession of all railroads and equipment essential to the movement. Within forty-eight hours after Dana's message had reached Stanton, the first trains were moving, and in a great feat of the war, troops began arriving within ten days.

Then followed the trains carrying the camp and field equipment: the wagons, horses, mules, tents, baggage, and supplies. Given the complexity of coordinating the trains from the various railroads, it was a masterful job with all due credit to Stanton. As Hooker cabled, "If you projected the late movement … you may justly claim the merit of having saved Chattanooga to us." Stanton wired Scott at Louisville, "Your work is most brilliant. A thousand thanks … a great achievement."

Even with the perilous situation at Chattanooga, both Lincoln and Stanton were focused on the crucial 1863 elections. Republicans campaigned under the National Union banner with strong support from the War Department. Furloughs were granted so troops could return home and vote. Furloughed regiments cast ballots in Delaware, New York, Kentucky, and Tennessee. Maryland voters went to polls protected by provost marshals.

In the closely watched Ohio race for governor, Union candidate John Brough defeated former representative Vallandigham by 100,000 votes. Vallandigham had slipped across the border from Canada when nominated for governor by the Democrats. Lincoln chose to ignore his return. This race was absolutely crucial, given Vallandigham's antiwar and anti-draft stands. Secretary Stanton arranged matters so that Ohio soldiers could vote in the field.

Regiments were furloughed to Pennsylvania—another key state—to vote. Ailing Governor Curtin reluctantly ran when pressed. He defeated Chief Justice George W. Woodward of the Pennsylvania Supreme Court, who was endorsed by McClellan. Justice Woodward's defeat was a Lincoln victory because the justice had considered the Enrollment and Legal Tender acts as unconstitutional. Curtin was highly regarded by the state's soldiers because of his frequent visits to the wounded.[303]

The Midwest, with Copperhead plots afoot, was troubled. Indiana governor Morton's fear of Copperhead opposition led to General Lew Wallace and others being granted leave to campaign. Soldiers were furloughed.

Election results telegraphed to Lincon showed a smashing victory. The Union ticket swept every loyal state except New Jersey. Even in the border states of Delaware and Kentucky, the Union party won. Springfield, Illinois, came back into the fold. Overall, a Chicago paper labeled it a slaughter of the Democrats.

In the telegraph office, Lincoln eagerly followed the returns. Senator James W. Grimes wired, "As ever Iowa is erect. We have swept the state overwhelmingly." Morton reported, "Returns from country elections in Indiana show an enormous union gain keeping pace with that in Ohio." From Representative James K. Moorhead in Pittsburgh: "Let me congratulate you on the glorious result in Ohio & Penna, who now declare for A. Lincoln in 1864." This was a vital reaffirmation for Lincoln.

Lincoln—concerned with judges releasing draftees using the writ of habeas corpus—suspended the writ by proclamation where "public safety does require that the privilege of the said writ shall now be suspended." He specified suspension in cases of prisoners of war, spies, aiders or abettors of the enemy, those enrolled or drafted or mustered or enlisted in or belonging to the armed forces, deserters, and those resisting a draft or committing any other offense against war service.[304]

With the election past, Lincoln issued a proclamation calling upon the governors of the states to raise and have enlisted 300,000 volunteers: "The term of service of a part of the Volunteer forces of the United Sates will expire during the coming year, and whereas, in addition to the men raised by the present draft, it is deemed expedient to call out three hundred thousand volunteers to serve for three years or the (the duration of the) war, not, however, exceeding three years."

Lincoln addressed those who volunteered: "I further proclaim, that all volunteers thus called out and duly enlisted, shall receive advance pay, premium and bounty ... that all volunteers, thus called ... shall be duly credited or deducted from the quotas established for the next draft ... that if any State shall fail to raise the quota assigned ... then a draft for the deficiency in said quota shall be made ... and the said draft shall commence on the fifth day of January, 1864."[305]

Grant was ordered to proceed to Louisville, Kentucky, for further orders, and Stanton sped westward by train to meet him. Grant's train was pulling out of Indianapolis when a messenger halted it, as Secretary Stanton was arriving and wanted to meet with General Grant. Newly elected Ohio governor John Brough was with Stanton. Stanton dismissed his train, and they rode to Louisville with Grant. This was Grant's first meeting with Brough, who was a friend of his father.

Stanton handed Grant two orders, signed by Lincoln, identical in all but one provision. Both orders created the Military Division of the Mississippi with Grant to command. It encompassed the Departments of Ohio, Cumberland, and Tennessee. The option was whether Grant would choose to keep the besieged Rosecrans in command or replace him with General George Thomas. Grant chose Thomas. Lincoln had delayed any change, fearing an adverse effect on the Ohio election.

Grant immediately wrote out an order taking command, telegraphing it to Rosecrans. Grant then ordered Thomas to take command and hold Chattanooga. Thomas responded, "We will hold the town until we starve." General James A. Garfield later contended Rosecrans would have done better had a proposed presidential candidacy not tempted him. Grant, in Chattanooga, replaced Burnside with General Sherman, who was given command of the Army of Tennessee.

Hooker's troops were halted at Bridgeport, as that was as far as the railroad could take them. If moved into Chattanooga, they could neither be fed nor supplied. Grant reached Stevenson, Alabama, and met Rosecrans heading north. Rosecrans briefed Grant and made what Grant described as excellent suggestions, but left him wondering why they had not been carried out. Continuing on horseback, they reached Chattanooga over all but impassable muddy roads.

After a thorough briefing from General W. F. Smith, Grant initiated military moves that opened up the supply routes to Chattanooga. Coordinated movements captured or drove away Bragg's forward units at the river. Using boats, horses, and mules brought with Hooker's troops, Grant had fresh food, boots, clothing, supplies, and ammunition delivered to Chattanooga. This improved the morale of the existing troops, and newly arrived troops strengthened the hand of Thomas.[306]

The Confederates were equally determined to hold their line at Chattanooga. Jefferson Davis traveled to Bragg's headquarters. He viewed Bragg as a friend and ally and he knew the Confederates needed to hold at Chattanooga. Wedged near the Alabama and Georgia lines, Grant's force posed a threat to cut the South in half. The Confederate goal was to blunt the threat and regain Tennessee and Kentucky, even Vicksburg, and again be in control on the Mississippi.

Lincoln, sick in bed, read a wire from Grant: "Lookout Mountain top, all the rifle-pits in Chattanooga Valley, and Missionary Ridge entire, have been carried and now held by us." Because Bragg had him cornered, Grant knew retreat meant all but certain annihilation and attacked. Union soldiers under Sheridan, without orders, raced up Lookout Mountain, overlooking the valley, turned the tide, and sent Bragg's forces reeling. This was the first time Confederate soldiers had run when routed in battle.

CHAPTER XI

THE GETTYSBURG ADDRESS: THE REELECTION CAMPAIGN OPENS

Prior to the Chattanooga victory, Lincoln delivered his Gettysburg Address. The address, in the view of many, opened his campaign for reelection. Duties of chief orator fell not to Lincoln but Edward Everett, who in 1860 had run for vice president on the Bell-Everett ticket in opposition to Lincoln. Everett had been a US senator, Massachusetts governor, congressman, secretary of state under President Fillmore, minister to Great Britain, and president of Harvard University.

Lincoln had learned of the dedication of the National Soldiers' Cemetery at Gettysburg from a circular mailed to senators, representatives, governors, and cabinet members. Lincoln replied to that circular, saying he too would be present. This prompted David Wills of Gettysburg, acting for the governors of the organizing states, to formally invite Lincoln. They asked that Lincoln, after the major oration, "set apart these grounds to their sacred use by a few appropriate remarks."[307]

At this point Weed's earlier proposal to incent Union soldiers with title to captured land in the south was offset on the radical side by Boston's John Murray Forbes, a staunchly pro-Union railroad investor. Forbes wrote a letter carried by Senator Charles Sumner to the president:

> Bonaparte, when under the republic, fighting despots of Europe, did as much by his bulletins as he did by his bayonets: the two went on together promising democratic institutions to the populations whose leaders he was making war upon.
>
> You have the same opportunity, and greater; for you have enemies North and South, reading our language, whom you can teach. My suggestion, then, is that you should seize an early opportunity and any subsequent chance, to teach your great audience of plain people that the war is not the North against the South, but the people against the aristocrats.

Lincoln was traveling that road and hearing advice urging him to speak out strongly on the merits of democratic institutions.[308]

"Four score and seven years ago," Lincoln intoned at Gettysburg, "our fathers brought forth, upon this continent, a new nation, conceived in Liberty, and dedicated to the proposition that all men are created equal." Lincoln was expressing bedrock conviction stretching back to his earliest years, a conviction that extended and included everybody. "Now we are engaged in a great civil war, testing whether that nation, or any nation so conceived, and so dedicated can long endure."

Turning to his purpose:

> We are met here on a great battlefield of that war. We have come to dedicate a portion of it as a final resting place for those who here gave their lives that that nation might live. It is altogether fitting and proper that we should do this. But in a larger sense we cannot dedicate—we cannot consecrate—we cannot hallow this ground. The brave men, living and dead, who struggled here, have consecrated it far above our poor power to add or detract.

> This world will little note, nor long remember, what we say here, but can never forget what they did here. It is for us, the living, rather to be dedicated here to the unfinished work which they have, thus far, so nobly carried on.

Shifting from the dedication so finely honed, Lincoln pressed upon the living, the nation, that this was not final, but an introduction to the unfinished business of the day. The mission was the perpetuation of democracy and to make equality a reality.

"It is rather for us to be here dedicated to the great task remaining before us—that from these honored dead we take increased devotion—that we here highly resolve that these dead shall not have died in vain; that this nation shall have a new birth of freedom; and that this government of the people, by the people, for the people shall not perish from the earth."[309]

Subsequently, Everett wrote to Lincoln, "Permit me also to express my great admiration of the thoughts expressed by you, with such eloquent simplicity & appropriateness, at the consecration of the cemetery. I should be glad, if I could flatter myself that I came as near to the central idea of the occasion, in two hours, as you did in two minutes. My son who parted from me at Baltimore & my daughter, concur in these sentiments."

Lincoln thanked Everett. "Your kind note of today is received. Of course I knew Mr. Everett would not fail; and yet, while the whole discourse was eminently satisfactory, and will be of great value, there were passages in it which transcended my expectations. The point made against the theory of the general government being only an agency, whose principals are the States, was new to me, and, as I think, is one of the best arguments for national supremacy."[310]

On Dec. 8—the same day on which he sent his annual message to Congress and issued his Proclamation of Amnesty and Reconstruction—Lincoln wrote to Grant, "Understanding that your lodgment at Chattanooga and Knoxville is now secure, I wish to tender you, and all under your command, my more than thanks—my profound gratitude—for the skill, courage, and perseverance, with which you and they, over so great difficulties, have effected that important object."

A month before, Lincoln had written Postmaster Montgomery Blair regarding his brother, Frank, asserting, "The foregoing is what I would say, if Frank Blair were my brother instead of yours."

> I understood you to say that your brother, Gen. Frank Blair, desires to be guided by my wishes as to whether he will occupy his seat in congress or remain in the field. My wish then, is compounded of what I believe will be best for the country, and best for him.
>
> And it is, that he will come here, put his military commission in my hands, take his seat, go into caucus with our friends, abide the nominations, help elect the nominees, and thus aid to organize a House of Representatives which will really support the government in the war [reflecting Lincoln's major concern with Congress]. If the result shall be the election of himself as Speaker, let him serve in that position; if not, let him re-take his commission, and return to the Army.
>
> By a misunderstanding ... I think, he is in danger of being permanently separated from those with whom only he can ever have a real sympathy—the sincere opponent of slavery. It will be a mistake if he shall allow the provocations offered him by insincere time-servers, to drive him out of the house of his own building. He is young yet. He has abundant talent—quite enough to occupy all his time, without devoting any to temper. He is rising in military skill and usefulness.
>
> His recent appointment to the command of a corps, by one so competent to judge as Gen. Sherman, proves this. In

> that line he can serve both the country and himself more profitably than he could as a member of congress on the floor.

Blair served in Congress from March 4 to June 10, 1864, when Samuel Knox managed to defeat him in his campaign to be reelected. Blair returned to the army and was assigned command of the Seventeenth Army Corp on April 23, 1864.[311]

In his annual message to Congress, Lincoln praised the improved condition of national affairs, noting that the Union was "in peace and friendship with foreign powers." Singling out the supplemental treaty with Great Britain for the suppression of the African slave trade, he stated the treaty had been ratified and carried into execution, adding, "It is believed that, so far as American ports and American citizens are concerned, that inhuman and odious traffic has been brought to an end."

Lincoln had fixed Omaha, Nebraska, as the point from which the railroad and telegraph lines would run to the Pacific Ocean. Noting arrangements that had been made with Russia for "a continuous line of telegraph from our Pacific Coast," Lincoln urged favorable consideration by Congress of a telegraph line across the Atlantic, and between Washington and the national forts along the Atlantic seaboard and the Gulf of Mexico, as an effective aid to the diplomatic, military, and naval service.[312]

Lincoln said the mineral resources of Colorado, Nevada, Idaho, New Mexico, and Arizona "are proving far richer than … heretofore understood."

> I again submit to your consideration the expediency of establishing a system for the encouragement of immigration. Although this source of national wealth is again flowing with greater freedom than for several years before the insurrection

> occurred, there is still a great deficiency of laborers in every field of industry. …
>
> The enactment by Congress of a national banking law has proved a valuable support of the public credit; and the general legislation in relation to loans has fully answered the expectations of its favorers. … Since these measures have been in operation, all demands on the treasury have been … met and fully satisfied. Some amendments may be required to perfect existing laws; but no change in their principles or general scope is believed to be needed.[313]

The naval branch's extensive blockage of the coast, Lincoln said, had been increasing in efficiency. The navy consisted of 585 ships completed or near completion, some seventy-five of them armored or ironclad. The armored vessels in service or under construction, he proudly added, exceed those of any other nation. Yet, while those could be relied upon for coastal service and defense, others of greater strength would be needed to maintain the nation's rightful position on the ocean.

Lincoln explained a policy shift:

> The policy of emancipation, and of employing black soldiers, gave to the future a new aspect, about which hope, and fear, and doubt contended in uncertain conflict. According to our political system, as a matter of civil administration, the general government had no lawful power to effect emancipation in any State, and for a long time it had been hoped that the rebellion could be suppressed without resorting to it as a military measure.
>
> It came, and as was anticipated, it was followed by dark and doubtful days. Eleven months having now passed, we are permitted to take another review. The rebel borders are pressed still further back, and by the complete opening of

> the Mississippi the country dominated by the rebellion is divided into distinct parts. … Tennessee and Arkansas have been substantially cleared of insurgent control …
>
> Maryland, and Missouri … only dispute now as to the best mode of removing it. …
>
> Of those who were slaves … full one hundred thousand are now in the United States military service, about one-half … actually bear arms … thus giving the double advantage of taking so much labor from the insurgent cause, and supplying the places which otherwise must be filled with so many white men. So far as tested, it is difficult to say they are not as good soldiers as any. No servile insurrection … has marked … measures of emancipating and arming of blacks. …
>
> These measures have been much discussed in foreign countries, and … the tone of public sentiment there is much improved. At home the same measures have been fully discussed, supported, criticized and denounced, and the annual elections following are highly encouraging to those whose official duty it is to bear the country through the great trial. Thus we have the new reckoning. The crisis which threatened to divide the friends of the Union is past.

With growing confidence in ultimate victory, Lincoln set forth in his message and in a parallel proclamation the means for reestablishing rebellious states in the Union and granting amnesty to persons in rebellion. Citing the presidential power to grant pardons and reprieves, he declared, "Nothing is attempted beyond what is amply justified by the Constitution." While he included the form of an oath, he added, "No man is coerced to take it. The Constitution authorized the Executive to grant or withhold the pardon at his own absolute discretion; and this includes the power to grant on terms, as is fully established by judicial and other authorities."

In his proclamation he provided this oath for repentant rebels:

> I, ______, do solemnly swear, in presence of Almighty God, that I will henceforth faithfully support, protect and defend the Constitution of the United States, and the union of the States thereunder; and that I will, in like manner, abide by and faithfully support all acts of Congress passed during the existing rebellion with reference to slaves, so long and so far as not repealed, modified or held void by Congress, or by decision of the Supreme Court. ...
>
> And that I will, in like manner, abide by and faithfully support all proclamations of the President made during the existing rebellion having reference to slaves, so long and so far as not modified or declared void by decision of the Supreme Court. So help me God.

Ineligible for this oath were former judges, civil and diplomatic officers, those who left Congress, those who resigned high-ranking military posts, and those who served the "so-called confederate government."

In addition, Lincoln went beyond ranking civil and military officials to single out "all who have engaged in any way in treating colored persons or white persons, in charge of such, otherwise than lawfully as prisoners of war, and which persons may have been found in the United States service, as soldiers, seamen, or in any other capacity." Building on the base of loyal citizens with those willing to take the oath, Lincoln laid out a means for restoring the rebellious states to the Union.

Enumerating the states, he said whenever a number of persons not less than one-tenth of those who had voted in the 1860 presidential election had taken the oath and not violated it, such qualified voters could reestablish a government. This government, consistent with the oath and in no way contravening it, would be recognized as the true government of the state, and the government would receive the benefits of the constitutional provision that declared:

"The United States shall guaranty to every State in this union a republican form of government, and shall protect each of them against invasion; and, on application of the legislature, or the executive (when the legislature cannot be convened,) against domestic violence." He explained the state name, boundaries, subdivisions, constitution, and general code of laws, as these existed before the rebellion, could be retained, subject only to the conditions that he had identified and he added:

"Any provision which may be adopted … in relation to the freed people of such State, which shall recognize and declare their permanent freedom, provide for their education, and which may yet to consistent, as a temporary arrangement, with their present condition as a laboring, landless, and homeless class, will not be objected to by the national Executive." He sid the proclamation exempted states that had maintained loyal governments throughout the conflict.

As for members elected to Congress by the restored states, Lincoln said whether those delegates would be seated was a matter exclusively in the hands of Congress. At the same time, he said the proclamation provided a mode by which the national authority and loyal state governments might be re-established, the best that the executive could suggest. He made it clear the details were negotiable; he should not be understood to mean that no other possible mode would be acceptable.

Lincoln ended his message to Congress declaring movements for emancipation in several states were "matters of profound gratulation." Yet, he said, "We must not lose sight of … the war power is still our main reliance … to give confidence to the people in the contested regions. … Hence our chiefest care must still be directed to the army and navy, who have thus far borne their harder part so nobly and well. … We do also honorably recognize the gallant men … who compose them."[314]

Turning to the Missouri situation, Lincoln wrote to Stanton that General Schofield must be relieved from command of the Department of Missouri. "Otherwise a question of veracity, in relation to his declarations as to his interfering, or not, with the Missouri Legislature, will be made with him, which will create an additional amount of trouble, not to be overcome by even a correct decision of the question. The question itself must be avoided."

Lincoln indicated that if Schofield asked to be relieved, it would induce Senator John B. Henderson, a radical, to back off his opposition to a move by the state's other senator, Gratz Brown, to confirm Schofield as major general. Further, Lincoln said he was under obligation to do something for General Rosecrans. Lincoln said he found Henderson and Brown would agree to naming Rosecrans to the command and that the two together "will go far to healing the Missouri difficulty."

Shifting to Louisiana, Lincoln pressed General Nathaniel P. Banks, a former member of Congress and a former Massachusetts governor currently commanding the Department of the Gulf, to galvanize the sputtering Louisiana restoration. "I have all the while," Lincoln said, "intended you to be master as well in regard to reorganizing a State government for Louisiana, as in regard to the military matters of the Department. … I now tell you that in every dispute … you are master."

General Grant issued an order in December manifesting anti-Semitism by expelling Jews from the Department of the Mississippi. Incensed over illicit cotton trading by Jewish merchants, he said, "Jews, as a class, violating every regulation of trade established by the Treasury Department … seem to be a privileged class." About two dozen Jews were expelled from Paducah, Kentucky.

When word of the order reached Lincoln, he immediately moved to revoke it. He had to be shown a copy by a Jewish delegation, for at first he did believe that Grant would issue such an order. Democrats were swift to condemn the "detestable order." Lincoln said, "And so the children of Israel were driven from the happy land of Canaan?" To this the group leader responded, "Yes, and that is why we have come unto Father Abraham's bosom, asking protection."

In a meeting a second delegation, Rabbi Isaac M. Wise of Cincinnati thanked Lincoln for revoking the order. Wise said Lincoln "fully illustrated to us and convinced us that he knows of no distinction between Jew and Gentile, that he feels no prejudice against any nationality, and that he by no means will allow that a citizen in any wise be wronged on account of his place of birth or religious confession." Wise said the president manifested "a peculiar attachment to the Jews."[315]

After Grant achieved a third major victory as his troops broke the siege of Chattanooga and sent the Confederates reeling, he ordered Sherman to move toward Knoxville. Burnside was under siege there from General Longstreet. Learning that Sherman was en route, Longstreet withdrew. Grant said that as a result of these victories, "the loyal portion of the North rejoiced over the double victory; the raising of the siege of Knoxville and the victory at Chattanooga."

This proved a major boon for President Lincoln. He had long wanted the Confederate yoke removed from the persecuted loyal citizens of East Tennessee, who had suffered greatly at the hands of the Confederates. Grant contended victory in Tennessee, combined with the Union victories at Gettysburg and Vicksburg, could have been the last battles fought for the preservation of the Union if the same press freedom had been allowed the people and press in the South as in the North.[316]

Speaking to an Arkansas delegation, Lincoln said he had determined not to appoint a separate military governor. The recently appointed General Frederick Steele, commander of the Department of Arkansas, would be both military governor and commander. Lincoln said that past experience had shown that to have a separate military governor was injurious. He urged swift reorganization of Tennessee under the terms of his amnesty proclamation.[317]

In January 1864, former senator Hershel Johnson, who was Douglas's 1860 vice presidential running mate, wrote to President Davis, "The Cincinnati Enquirer has published a tabular statement of the vote polled, in the late elections of the U.S. It shows that 1,500,000 were cast against the ruling administration in Washington. Is that not evidence of a very strong hostility to Lincoln? It is true, I have no doubt, that they profess to be for... a restoration of the Union."

Confederate leadership had by now concluded that Lincoln was the issue; Lincoln would not negotiate on terms that would perpetuate slavery and recognize Confederate independence. Johnson, currently a Confederate legislator, wrote, "But I am well satisfied, that if Lincoln could be defeated—or the candidate of his party—in the next President election, it would end the war and lead to peace. These elections show strong opposition to Lincoln, especially in the North West states."

Johnson turned to a strategy for the election:

> On these facts, I predicate a single suggestion. It is this: Would it not be wise to have a secret agent in Canada, who by seeking interviews, with the right men of the North & N. West (perhaps it might be better to confine him to the North West) might aid in stimulating & organizing more efficiently that opposition, and securing influences that would result in the withdrawal of the N[orth] Western States from the Union?
>
> Might not a discreet and prudent agent, bring to the support of such a policy, a portion of the press of those states? Might not the experiment be made without compromitting (sic) the Confederate States? There is in the United States a powerful conservative element. At least they call it conservatism & it is conservatism, compared with the rabid and barbarous policy of the Federal administration.

He then asked: "Might not an adroit agent do much to encourage that element? The sword will scarcely end the war. Looking to the relative strength of the two powers and the objects sought … on either side, it is hardly to be expected, that either can conquer a peace. The pen & not the sword will bring peace. … Who shall say … the agency indicated may not put in motion influences that will prepare the way for … negotiation? I have thought much on the subject & I believe the experiment worth being made & … $1,500,000 … expended, would be well spent."[318]

This spawned the Confederate intelligence operation in Canada in the hands of former interior secretary Jacob Thompson of Mississippi (also a former member of Congress) and Clement C. Clay of Alabama, along with James P. Holcombe of Virginia. They reported through Secretary of State Judah P. Benjamin, to a trio led by President Jefferson Davis along with Benjamin and dependent upon General Robert E. Lee for military support and military intelligence.

As Congress was voting a medal of thanks for Grant, the *New York Herald*'s James Gordon Bennett touted Grant for president. Bennett in past elections had supported Andrew Jackson, William Henry Harrison, and Zachary Taylor. This was a shrewd move by the wily Bennett who viewed Grant as a popular independent who could rise above politics. Given Bennett's intense bias against abolitionists, he likely viewed Grant as an alternative to an endorsement of either Lincoln or McClellan.

Bennett said Grant would owe no debts to hack politicians and corrupt machines. He said the history of the Lincoln administration proved civilians were totally unfitted to win the war, but in Grant they would have a champion. Grant, having put down the rebellion, would break from the "cowardly and truckling foreign policy of Lincoln" to force the French out of Mexico and exact $20 million tribute for damage done by British-built Confederate privateers to Union shipping.[319]

Here was Grant, whom Lincoln had never met, and Grant's stock was rising. Congress was resurrecting the rank of lieutenant general, previously bestowed only on President George Washington and General Winfield Scott. Lincoln turned to Representative Elihu Washburne, Grant's hometown friend, asking, "About all I know of Grant I have got from you. I have never seen him. Who else besides you knows anything about Grant?" Washburne suggested J. Russell Jones, a Gelena man.

Lincoln wired Jones, a US marshal at Chicago, to come to Washington. Jones had recently visited Grant in Mississippi. Jones packed and, valise in hand, picked up some letters at his office en route to the train. One was from Grant, responding to Jones's letter urging him to pay no attention to attempts to run him for president. Grant responded that he had as big a job as a man could ask and correspondence received attempting to push him into politics went into the wastebasket.

In Washington, Jones sent word of his arrival and was asked to come at eight o'clock that evening. Jones said the president, without naming Grant, told him he was anxious to talk to somebody from the West. Jones figured he would like to talk of Grant and said, "Mr. President, if you will excuse me for interrupting you, I want to ask you kindly to read a letter that I got from my box as I was on my way to the train." Jones handed Grant's letter to Lincoln, who read it with intense interest.

Jones said that when the president came to the part where Grant said, "it would be impossible for him to think of the presidency as long as there was a possibility of retaining Mr. Lincoln," Lincoln arose, put his hand on Jones's shoulder, and said, "My son, you will never know how gratifying that is to me. No man knows, when that presidential grub gets to gnawing at him, just how deep it will get until he has tried it; and I didn't know but what there was one gnawing at Grant."[320]

On the political front, Lincoln expressed his considerable anxiety about the Custom House in New York City. Writing Secretary Chase, he said, "Mr. Barney has suffered no abatement of my confidence in his honor and integrity; and yet I am convinced that he has ceased to be master of his position." He noted one J. F. Bailey was assumed to be collector de facto, while Barney remained nominally so. Bailey was summoned before a congressional committee investigating his conduct.

Lincoln said Bailey, in advance of the hearing, called upon the chair in an effort to smother the investigation. Bailey said, among other things, "that whatever might be developed, the President would take no action, and the committee would thereby be placed unpleasantly. The public interest cannot fail to suffer in the hands of this irresponsible man." Lincoln proposed sending Barney as minister to Portugal.

Chase responded that he was surprised and pained by Lincoln's letter, adding, "Misrepresentations, I am sure, must have been made to you about the New York Custom House." Chase asked that the president confer with him before taking any action.

Barney actually was a Lincoln appointment. He had come to the 1860 Republican convention as a Chase delegate, but anti-Seward. At the convention, he had switched to Lincoln and raised some $35,000 for Lincoln's presidential race.[321]

In a letter to Governor John A. Andrew of Massachusetts, Lincoln noted, "You are engaged in trying to raise colored troops for the U.S. and wish to take recruits from Virginia … and the loyal governor of Virginia, also trying to raise troops, objects." Lincoln said he could not permit this, having to be fair to all. He added, "If … Massachusetts wishes to afford a permanent home … for all, or even a large number of colored persons who will come … I shall be only too glad to know it."

As the presidential campaign took shape, Lincoln in his messages to Congress, in his proclamations and speeches, and in his letters successfully laid the issues before the public. These were the issues that undergirded the fate of the Union and the outcome of the war. The slavery question loomed ever larger over the political landscape. Party feeling also became increasingly prominent as Lincoln forged a Union party with increasing numbers of war Democrats and Republicans.

Since his election, Lincoln had carefully attended to political appointments, using patronage to build party strength in the states. Lincoln remembered his extensive campaigning for President Zachary Taylor, only to be shut out in his bid for office by another who had not been active. Lincoln looked to a melding of party faithful, radical and conservative, into a supportive party. He also consulted members of Congress, building loyalties and developing support on crucial issues.

As the radicals schemed to make Lincoln a one-term president, Lincoln skillfully used a combination of patronage and a team of political operatives to ensure his renomination, while evolving a broader-based Union party. As early as January, he consulted Francis P. Blair, Gideon Welles, and former Ohio governor William Dennison. Among others in the political loop were Simon Cameron, John Forney, and even Thurlow Weed. This trio produced important newspaper endorsements.[322]

Lincoln was a commanding favorite with the people. He cultivated them in his messages, letters, and interactions with visitors, which he called his public opinion baths. Neither Chase nor the radicals in Congress, bent on replacing Lincoln, would admit to his popularity in the countryside and among small-town editors. Careful in his use of patronage, Lincoln recruited supporters who would make his reelection possible, and he wisely consulted members of Congress.

In January, Lincoln loyalists, many patronage recipients, initiated efforts for endorsements of Lincoln's renomination. Beginning in New Hampshire, The Granite State, Republicans met on January 7 and renominated Governor Joseph A. Gilmore. William E. Chandler, Harvard graduate and chair of the state central committee, subsequently appointed by Lincoln as Navy judge advocate general, successfully moved a resolution endorsing Lincoln that was overwhelmingly affirmed.

Chandler's resolution ended thus: "We, therefore, declare Abraham Lincoln to be the people's choice for reelection to the Presidency in 1864." A second resolution threw a left-handed compliment to Chase:

"Having the fullest confidence in the integrity and financial ability of Hon. Salmon P. Chase … we call upon him, and all other officers … to establish and enforce a rigid system of accountability, and promptly to detect, expose and punish all corruption and fraud."

The New Hampshire resolutions were well publicized beyond New Hampshire. Taking a swing at Chase, the *Albany Evening News*, edited by George Dawson, Albany postmaster, and Thurlow Weed, declared the resolution "deserves to be written in letters of gold." It elaborated, "The people will demand that those who have the administration of the National affairs on their hands shall not only practice economy but promptly 'expose and punish all corruption and fraud.'"[323]

Two days later, Pennsylvania followed, as John Hay recorded: "Cameron has written to the President that the entire Union force of the Pa. Legislature, House and Senate, have subscribed a request that the President will allow himself to be reelected, and that they intend visiting Washington to present it. He says, 'I have kept my promise.'" Cameron had done similarly for President Andrew Jackson when he too wanted a second term; Lincoln had suggested the same and Cameron delivered.[324]

Next came Connecticut, where Lincoln faced a raging feud over patronage between Governor Buckingham, Mark Howard, and Calvin Day, who leaned toward Chase on the one hand, and US senator James Dixon, Collector James F. Babcock of the Port of New Haven, and Postmaster Nehemiah D. Sperry of New Haven, who leaned toward Lincoln. Secretary Wells failed to heal this split. Lincoln distributed the major share of the patronage to Dixon's partisans, who in turn delivered for Lincoln.

The Howard group was strong in the Union League, a political organization, but Dixon's group drew strength from his hold on patronage. Howard wrote Wells pleading for equal recognition. He wanted to hold up the presidential question pending a resolution. At the February 17 convention, Buckingham was renominated for governor, but Babcock took control of the presidential question. A full slate of delegates selected pledged to give Lincoln "united support" for renomination.[325]

The Democratic Party, so long allied with the Southern interests, made every effort for a policy that left slavery in place and kept up a chorus of loud and constant criticism leveled at Lincoln and his supporters wherever they touched the slavery issue. For no matter what Lincoln did about slavery, it was too much for the Democrats and too little for the radical Republicans. Rivalries within the Republican Party similarly continued to challenge Lincoln's renomination.[326]

The sanctimonious Chase viewed himself as much better qualified than Lincoln for the presidency and considered Lincoln inferior in intellect and character. Chase used the patronage of the Treasury and actively encouraging his partisans in his own interests. He sent word that he was not seeking the nomination, but could not refuse if called. Lincoln, while fully cognizant of these efforts, yet remained aloof. Biding his time, he knew an immediate firing of Chase would create political harm.

A February 8, 1864, circular said so long as no effort was made to forestall "political action of the people," friends of the government would do well to focus on putting down the rebellion. But it declared, "party machinery and official influence" were being exercised to perpetuate the administration, forcing "friends of the Union and of freedom … to assert themselves." It further contended that reelecting Lincoln was impossible and undesirable given the influences opposed to him.

The circular boldly espoused the view of the radicals in Congress—one Chase continually pressed on his own behalf—that even if reelection of Lincoln were possible, it was undesirable given his tendency toward "compromise and temporary expediency," likely to be stronger in the second term than in the first. It said patronage had been extended and abused under Lincoln's administration, thus requiring that Lincoln be restricted to one term to preserve the republic.

Previously in congressional caucus, Representative Henry Winter Davis and Senator Charles Sumner had attempted to get a committee formed with the hope to express congressional opinion and delay the nominating convention. Together with radical members, they wanted to prevent a second term for Lincoln. Knowing a stop Lincoln effort made in open session would breed opposition, they attempted—as did the Chase committee—to do an end run around the Lincoln forces, but to no avail.

The February circular advocating the nomination of Secretary Chase over Lincoln went out signed by Kansas senator Samuel C. Pomeroy, and distributed to the press. Chase wrote to Lincoln, "It is probable that you have already seen a letter … in the Constitutional Union … & reprinted in the Intelligencer this morning, written by Senator Pomeroy, as chairman of a Committee of my political friends. I had no knowledge of the existence of this letter before I saw it in the Union."

The *New York Herald* took note of the connection between Senator Pomeroy and James M. Winchell, a New York banker alleged to have written the circular, and their interest in the Hannibal and St. Joseph Railroad. Under the Pacific Railroad Act, the Secretary of the Treasury was empowered to authorize federal subsidies for railroads already in operation that could become branches. Pomeroy requested Chase's views on including his line, and Chase gave an affirmative response.

Bennett's *Herald* reported, "It appears to us that this circular may after all be only a political double entendre. … It may mean the Presidency and it may mean the Pacific Railroad. If the Pacific Railroad wants anything from Congress, Mr. Chase is certainly the best man for it to run as far as Congress goes. But whatever the Circular means it has started considerable excitement in the Republican Party, and embarrasses … those … who were going to re-elect old Abe anyhow."[327]

The Republican National Committee, under the leadership of Senator Morgan, issued a call for a national convention to nominate candidates for president and vice president. They designated Baltimore as the site for the convention and June 7 as the date. Chase backers and congressional radicals exerted every effort to delay the convention until some three months later. Their aim was more time to sidetrack the renomination of Lincoln in favor of another candidate.[328]

The radicals were anything but unanimous in support for an alternate candidate, yet repeatedly accused Lincoln of indecisiveness that had proven costly and had prolonged the war. Yet Lincoln had moved decisively, obtaining the men and material to win the war and to restore the Union. The radicals also declared reconstruction the prerogative of Congress and not the president. More extreme radicals insisted that seceded States had committed political suicide.

Justice David Davis, writing to Weed, labeled Chase's withdrawal "a mere sham, & disgracefully done. The plan is to get up a great opposition to Lincoln through Fremont & others & represent when the convention meets, the necessity of united effort, & that any body can unite, except Lincoln, & then present Chase again." Attuned to the political situation. Davis hit the core of Chase's statement, saying: "Look at the meanness in not saying one word about Mr. Lincoln."

Chase wrote to Lincoln:

> A few weeks ago several gentlemen called on me & expressed their desire, which, they said, was shared by many earnest friends of our common cause, that I would allow my name to be submitted to the consideration of the people in connection with the approaching election. I feared that any such use … might impair my usefulness as Head of the Treasury Department & I much preferred to continue … free from distracting influences. …
>
> We had several interviews. After consultation, and conference with others, they expressed their united judgment that the

> use of my name as proposed would not affect my usefulness in my present position, and that I ought to consent to it. I accepted their judgment as decisive, but at the same time told them distinctly that I could render them no help, except what might come incidentally from the faithful discharge of public duties, for these must have my whole time.
>
> I said also that I desired them to regard themselves as not only entirely at liberty, but as requested, to withdraw my name from consideration wherever, in their judgment the public interest would be promoted by so doing. The organization of the Committee, I presume, followed these conversations; but I was not consulted about it; nor have I been consulted as to its actions; nor do I even know who compose it. … I have thought this explanation due to you as well as to myself. …
>
> For yourself I cherish sincere respect and esteem; and, permit me to add, affection. Differences of opinion as to administrative action have not changed these sentiments; nor have they been changed by assault upon me by persons who profess themselves to spread representations of your views and policy. You are not responsible for acts not your own; nor will you hold me responsible except for what I do or say. … Great numbers now desire your reelection.[329]

Lincoln responded, "Yours of yesterday … was duly received; and I write … to say I will answer … more fully when I can find the leisure to do so." Some six days later, Lincoln responded more fully, suggesting he had little to say: "My knowledge of Mr. Pomeroy's letter having been made public came to me only the day you wrote; but I had, in spite of myself, known of its existence several days before. I have not yet read it, and I think I shall not. I was not shocked or surprised."

Lincoln, in a discrete but direct reply, explained that "because I had knowledge of Mr. Pomeroy's Committee, and of secret issues which I supposed came from it, and of secret agents who I supposed were sent out by it, for several weeks. I have known just as little of these things as my friends have allowed me to know. They bring the documents to me, but I do not read them—they tell me what they think fit to tell me, but I do not inquire for more." Yet he closely tracked the Chase movement.

"I fully concur with you," he wrote, "that neither of us can be justly held responsible for what our respective friends may do without our instigation or countenance; and I assure you, as you have assured me, that no assault has been made upon you by my instigation, or with my countenance. Whether you shall remain at the head of the Treasury … I will not allow myself to consider … other than my judgment of the public service." He concluded, "I do not perceive occasion for a change."

As talk centered on the Chase circular, Indiana held its state convention on February 23, and former governor Cyrus M. Allen introduced two resolutions to be considered as one. The first endorsed President Lincoln and the war, and the second renominated Governor Morton. Pandemonium burst out. An attempt was made for a counter-resolution, but it was ruled out of order. A vote was called on the original resolution. Amid vast cheering, Indiana was bound to Lincoln.

Almost immediately following, Ohio reported a legislative caucus had endorsed the renomination of Lincoln without mentioning Chase. This was a bitter blow to Chase but illustrated the deft hand of the president, exceptionally skilled in politics as in statesmanship. While the Chase men had made every effort to delay the vote, and soon left the caucus, they were outflanked politically by the force and skill of the Lincoln men, who had orchestrated and ruled the action.[330]

The Congress approved the rank of lieutenant general, which Lincoln promptly conferred on Grant, who was ordered to Washington. Grant arrived on March 8 and registered at the Willard Hotel, unrecognized until he signed. Looking at the name, the clerk immediately upgraded his room. Grant then went to the White House, where the president's weekly reception was in progress. Grant was ushered in to meet President and Mrs. Lincoln, and was greeted with a rousing cheer as well.

The president told Grant he would the next day confer the rank on him and name him to command the armies of the nation, "I shall make a very short speech," Lincoln said, adding, "to which I desire you to reply, for an object; and that you may be properly prepared do to so I have written what I shall say, only four sentences in all, which I will read from my manuscript as an example which you may follow, and also ready your reply." Lincoln gave Grant a copy.

"There are two points that I would like to have you make in your answer: First, to say something which shall prevent or obviate any jealousy of you from any of the other generals in the service; and second, something which shall put you on good terms as possible with the Army of the Potomac." Clearly Lincoln wanted to avoid renewed contention, noting: "If you see any objection to doing this, be under no restraint whatever in expressing that objection to the Secretary of War."

At the presentation, Grant said, "Mr. President. I accept this commission with gratitude for the high honor conferred. With the aid of the noble armies that have fought on so many fields for our common country, it will be my earnest endeavor not to disappoint your expectations. I feel the full weight of the responsibilities now devolving on me and know that if they are met it will be due to these armies, and above all to the favor of Providence which leads both Nations and men."[331]

The president immediately issued Orders No. 98: "I. Major General H. W. Halleck is, at his own request, relieved from duty as General-in-Chief of the Army, and Lieutenant General U.S. Grant is assigned to the command of the Armies. … The Head Quarters … will be in Washington, and also with General Grant in the field. II. Major General H. W. Halleck is assigned to duty in Washington as Chief of Staff … under … the Secretary of War and the Lieutenant General commanding."

Halleck had written to Stanton asking that he be retired from the role as general in chief, given that Congress had created the higher rank.

The order continued: "III. Major General W. T. Sherman is assigned to the command of the Military Division of the Mississippi, composed of the Departments of the Ohio, the Cumberland, the Tennessee, and the Arkansas. IV. Major General J. B. McPherson is assigned to the command of the Department and Army of the Tennessee."[332]

Prior to Blair's return to Congress, the Pomeroy Committee formally urged that the Republican National Committee postpone until September the nominating convention scheduled for June. This was asked in a letter signed by William Cullen Bryant, a friend of Chase who was aligned with the radicals. Bryant, a poet, edited the *New York Evening Post.* Aiming to derail the renomination of Lincoln, radicals argued for delay until the results of the summer military campaigns were known.

Intermixed with renomination efforts, Lincoln struggled with radicals in Congress over reconstruction. In the wake of Lincoln's December proclamation, the radicals feared Lincoln's faction would fuse with conservatives, marginalizing the radicals and creating a more conservative party. Senator Wade of Ohio and Representative Davis of Maryland struck at Lincoln with bills designed to prevent him from receiving rebel states back into the Union except as directed by Congress.

Charles A. Dana, who had served fifteen years with Greeley's *Tribune*, had in 1862 been abruptly asked by Greeley to resign. Secretary Stanton and Dana had corresponded, and Stanton called Dana to Washington as an assistant secretary in the War Department. Dana, who came to know Lincoln well, ascribed to him two key traits: "You felt that here was a man who saw through things, who understood, and you respected him accordingly." He described Lincoln as "a supreme politician."

Lincoln, Dana said, "understood politics because he understood human nature." This was illustrated, Dana said, in the spring of 1864, when the administration decided to urge the Constitution be amended to prohibit slavery. An important military measure, the proposed amendment was intended as a means of affecting the judgment, feelings, and anticipations of those in rebellion—the equivalent of a million more men in the army that would tend to paralyze the enemy.

The question of allowing Nevada to form a state government came up that month in the House of Representatives. It faced strong opposition. Dana described how the president came into his office and shut the door. "Dana," he said, "I am very anxious about this vote. It has to be taken next week. This time is very short. It is going to be great deal closer than I wish."

Dana replied, "There are plenty of Democrats who will vote for it." He cited several whom he viewed as open to persuasion.

"But there are some others that I am not clear about," Lincoln said. "There are three that you can deal with better than anybody else … as you know them all. I wish you would send for them." Lincoln gave names, one from New Jersey and two from New York.

Dana asked, "What will they be likely to want?"

Lincoln said he did not know, adding, "Here is the alternative: that we carry this vote, or be compelled to raise another million … men and fight no one knows how long."

Dana sent for the men, one by one, finding they were afraid of their party. Two of them wanted internal revenue collector's appointments, and another wanted a very important appointment at the Custom House in New York. In each case, Dana told them they would have it. One inquired, "I understand, of course, that you are not saying this on your own authority?"

Dana was swift to reply, "Oh no, I am saying it on the authority of the President."

All three voted for Nevada statehood.[333]

Blair returned to Congress, where he disputed Representative Thaddeus Stevens: "Allow me to say to the gentleman from Pennsylvania that the President's policy of amnesty, reconstruction of the States, and the segregation of the white and black races, bears not the slightest resemblance to the doctrine of the spoliation of an entire people, the annihilation of the States, and the disfranchisement of the people of our own race, thus putting them upon equality with the blacks."

Linking Stevens to Chase, he went on the attack and declared:

> So far from being the truth that the President and the gentleman from Pennsylvania stand upon "common ground," I am apprehensive that the gentleman is anxious to saddle the President with the odium of doctrines which are known to be those of rival aspirants for the Presidency, and which have proved fatal to their aspirations. This festered a dangerous schism the President had hoped to heal rather than aggravate.
>
> It is because the President has soared above these unconstitutional and inhuman dogmas, and has shown in his whole Administration … for amnesty and the restoration of the Union as soon as the inhabitants of the evolved States would resume their allegiance and provide against the recurrence of revolt by removing its cause, that the great body of the loyal people … have responded to his words of wisdom and patriotism, and have demanded his re-nomination.[334]

Blair then called for a committee of five to investigate the Treasury Department "to report whether any frauds had been practiced on the government," any favoritism shown, or any enemy helped. Chase men retorted by asserting that Blair had bought a scandalously excessive 225 gallons of brandy, 25 half-barrels of wine and whiskey, and 225 boxes of fruit with an order signed by General Blair and eight of his staff officers while he was at Vicksburg during June.

Blair explained to the House that the letter was a forgery and that B.R. Bonner, assistant special treasury agent at St. Louis, would substantiate the fact. Then radical representative J. W. McClurg declared Blair a poor witness and quoted Bonner, putting his letter on record: "It will thus be seen that General Blair … has coolly and impudently … uttered a willful, malicious, and deliberate falsehood; and now stands branded … as a reckless and unscrupulous slanderer."

Blair entered the House and requested it appoint a committee of three to investigate the matter and report. As to Representative McClurg, "I pronounce his allegation from beginning to end a base and miserable falsehood. He has taken the place of the forger and falsifier and I pronounce him an infamous liar and scoundrel." Speaker Colfax said the rule of the House forbade such language, but Blair responded that if he were guilty as charged, he was unfit to sit in the House.

Blair leveled his full fury on Chase's use of Treasury Department patronage and power: "Now I propose to show that the Secretary of the Treasury, with all the commerce of the country in his hands, with the collection of our foreign revenues and of the vast internal revenues in his hands, is using these abandoned plantations and grasping at all power and patronage for the purpose of providing a fund to carry on his war against the administration which gave him place."

He charged that Chase was disingenuous in disavowing the Pomeroy circular and withdrawing as a candidate:

> Nobody is simple enough to believe that the distinguished Secretary has really retired from the canvass for the nomination for the Presidency, although he has written a letter declining to be a candidate. That letter was written because the "strictly private" circular of the Pomeroy

> committee unearthed his underground and underhand intrigue against the President.
>
> It was such a disgraceful and disgusting sight to make use of the patronage and power given him by the President, against his chief, that even Chase got ashamed to occupy such a position publicly. For that reason his letter was written; he wanted to get down under the ground and work there in the dark as he is now doing, and running the Pomeroy machine on the public money as vigorously as ever.

At this point Blair quoted the chief newspaper organ of the Democratic Party:

> And whereas in the [New York] World on the 28th instant, it is declared that developments of the most astounding character have just come to light in the fractional currency and printing bureaus over which Mr. Clark presides; and whereas Hon. James Brooks, a member of this house, did yesterday in his place repeat the substance of the above charges. …
>
> At an early period of the session I called on the other side of the House in this matter of printing public money, and I gave them an opportunity to correct that great evil, which, because they did not correct, has led to the sacrifice of millions and millions of the public money in the printing bureau of the treasury of the United States, and to the conversion of the Treasury Department into a house for orgies and bacchanals.

Blair demanded an investigation of Treasury. "Therefore, Resolved, That a committee of nine be appointed by the Speaker of the House to investigate and report upon the truth of the allegations above quoted, and of any other allegations which have been or may be made, affecting the integrity of the administration in the Treasury Department. … Mr. Garfield moved that the vote last taken be reconsidered, and also moved that the motion to reconsider be laid on the table; which latter motion was agreed to."[335]

Garfield had previously told Chase, "It seems clear to me that the people desire the re-election of Mr. Lincoln and I believe any movement in any other direction will not only be a failure but will tend to disturb and embarrass the unity of the friends of the Union." Garfield, no Lincoln man at that point, said, "It would be a national calamity to alienate the radical element from Mr. Lincoln and leave him to the support of the Blair and Thurlow Weed School of politicians."[336]

Representative Blair on February 9 ended his remarks by saying:

> I will say that the policy of the Administration, sanctioned and sustained by the great masses of the loyal people of the country, is silently and surely working the extinction of the rebellion and the restoration of the Union as the firm and enduring basis of universal freedom. I have seen myself how the resistless march of our victorious armies is followed and their victories secured by a peaceful tide of population, sprung from the loins of the great North, bringing with them industry and thrift to heal the wounds. …
>
> In my judgment none of these States will be excluded from their just rights in the Union. Nor will any other State when the triumph of our arms makes it possible for the loyal men on those States to assert their claim to its protection. The first State which returns to the Union under the President's proclamation of amnesty and resumes its rights under the Constitution will inflict a heavier blow upon the cause of the rebellion than a victory won by our Army.[337]

CHAPTER XII

AMNESTY AND RECONSTRUCTION

Speaking in the House on February 25, Representative Henry Winter Davis said of the bill he was supporting:

> [It] involves a subject forced on us by the events of the war, and which must be determined one way or the other—the disposition of the freed Negroes in the rebel States. Slavery is dead says the honorable gentleman. … He may be a very sick man, Mr. Speakers, but I assure the gentlemen of this House and the Country that he is not dead; and if he is not done to death he will be your master again. …
>
> Slavery is not dead in Maryland … and whether the hostile influence that presides near the President's ear will allow Maryland to become a free State, or will fail her in her hour of need, remains yet to be seen. Up to this day Maryland is under no obligations to the President … for the great strikes that the cause of emancipation has been made there.

Striking again at Blair influence, he said a convention of loyal men had expressed their confidence in the President, but then they declared: "Resolved, That this convention is in favor of the entire and immediate abolition of slavery in this State and in the States in rebellion, and is opposed to any organization of State governments in those States which do not recognize the immediate and final abolishment of slavery as a condition precedent."

In another swipe, Davis said "that this convention express their sympathy with the radical emancipationists in Missouri, and in Arkansas, Tennessee, and Louisiana."

Davis turned his attack upon the Democrats too and the question of slavery in the South. "But 'slavery is dead in the rebel States.' No sir, No, sir, far from it. If our honorable friends on the other side elect their President in the coming fall, slavery is as alive as it was the day that the first gun blazed against Sumter."

Turning to the Emancipation Proclamation, he added, "What lawyer attributes to it the least legal effect in breaking the bonds of slavery?"

Then he warned the president:

> The people of Maryland thought it wise while expressing their confidence in the President to put that significant resolution before him for his serious consideration, so as to show … their devotion is not personal, but to principles; that their interest is in the cause and not in a man, and that while they will support the man as long as the man supports the cause, if the cause fail by any failure elsewhere, there may be a revision of their judgment respecting the person. …
>
> So long as the military power is engaged in suppressing resistance, they are free. … Reestablish the old governments; allow the dominant aristocracy to repossess the State power in its original plenitude, how long will they be free? What courts will give them rights? What provision is there to protect them? Where is the writ of habeas corpus? How are the courts of the United States to be open to them? Who shall close the courts of the States against the master?

> Does the master resort to the court against the slave? No; he seizes him by the neck. The law of the last Congress freeing a few slaves provides that the act may be pleaded in defense. But when is the slave sued by his master? When is the time to plead in any such process?

He declared: "Their laws are on the statute-book, and the opinions of the dominant faction conspire to perpetuate the master's rights and the slave's wrongs."

Davis emphatically declared, "Nothing but the resolute declaration of the United States that it shall be a condition precedent that slavery shall be prohibited in their constitutions, and that the United States shall be kept under the control of men of such political views and purposes that the law will be executed as a constitutional law and imposed on reluctant people—nothing else can accomplish the death of slavery."

Davis avowed firm support for his legislation as related to avoid grave social problems for the freed.

> Let the things of the future be cared for by the future. But it is necessary now to determine our policy respecting the Negroes when freed; to form some definite ideas as to what shall be the future of the Negro race; in other words, what disposition we will make of them when we have broken the masters' yoke. ... There are on that subject two, and only two, theories. One party says, "Colonize and pay for them." Another party says, "Leave them where they are."
>
> What are the grounds? First of all ... the radical abolitionists wish to change the Constitution ... and all of our laws, and to elevate to an equality this race; and in the next place that unequal races cannot live together on terms of equality and peace, and, therefore, that it is necessary to prevent the massacre of the Negro that he should be expatriated.

Mr. Speaker, what is the foundation of this view? The Negro must be colonized if he be free, or a war of races will exterminate him!

What justified this alternative? Will gentlemen tell me where in the history of the world they find the fact upon which they base that astounding generalization? Civilized people have overborne savages, men of one religion have borne down men of a different religion, ambition has overturned one nation by another; but where in the history of the world is there any case of a nation going to work to exterminate a large portion of its people of another race living in the midst of it of the same religion, civilized in the same manner, conforming to its laws, subject to its will, willing to work for its wages, not ambitious, and not disturbing the public peace, because they are of a different race? Where is the instance in the history … of the subjugation and massacre of a different race under these circumstances? My impression is that the conquered civilized the conqueror, and that it did not end in the social war … as is contemplated here.

But we are ourselves interested a little in this question of exportation of the Negro. Who will pay for the transportation? Who will supply the depleted labor of the country? Who is going to pay increased price of bread for the poor mechanic? Who is going to pay the increased price of cotton? Who is going to fill up the enormous vacuum of labor swept away by this insane and unchristian philanthropy?

What is the Negro going to do in the mean time? You cannot take them away tomorrow or in a generation. The schemers propose to build canals and fortifications, connect the Mississippi with the lakes. … Under whose supervision, at whose expense, by what new forms of socialism will you sweep a whole region of the country of three or four

> million people, and concentrate them upon the banks of the Mississippi … while cotton fields are supplanted, and men and women starving?
>
> The master will offer the Negro more to stay. Now deal with the problem under the conditions which exist. The folly of our ancestors and the wisdom of the Almighty … having allowed them to come here and planted them here, they have a right to remain here … to the latest recorded … time. And whether they become our equals or our superiors, whether they blend or remain a distinct race, your posterity will know, for their eyes will behold them as ours do now.
>
> Let us leave such questions for gentlemen of the school of Wendell Phillips. … But I earnestly pray gentlemen in high positions, in view of the feverish state of the public mind, above all in dealing with … the welfare of millions of whites and blacks, not to add to the inherent difficulties … prejudices … which we may never be called upon to deal with, and which can only exasperate the very feeling which we ought to allay and instigate the very collision we all deprecate.
>
> Sir, I am a Marylander, not a "northern fanatic." My father was a slaveholder. I was myself for years a slaveholder. I have lived all my life in Maryland. I have lived for years in Virginia. … I know the temper of her people; I know the relations of the white and black population in those States, and I am going to state some facts to the House nearer home than those cited by dreamers. In Maryland we have more free Negroes than any other State in the Union. Virginia stands next.

Davis told the story of an 1859 convention of slaveholders called ahead of the election "to put an end to free Negroism in Maryland for the benefit of whites." An old Whig slaveholder, James Alfred Pearce, disputed the claims that free blacks were idle, vicious, and unproductive. Employed as domestics, in industry and in agriculture, he explained, in some districts they supplied nearly all farm labor. Their removal would cost some 50 percent of agricultural and household labor.

Pearce urged and the secessionist Maryland legislature heeded a convention resolution: "The committee, therefore, cannot recommend their expulsion from the State. Still more unwilling should they be to favor any measure which looked to their being deprived of the right of freedom which they have acquired by the indulgence of our laws and the tenderness of their masters, whether wise or unwise, or which they have inherited as a birthright."

Some from the convention were in the legislature, and a Mr. Jacobs introduced a law to hire free Negroes to the highest bidders. If the Negroes were disobedient, they then could be sold as slaves for life. Davis said county after county objected, but it was offered to a vote in a few. He said in Howard County, Jacobs's bill got 55 votes against 1,397; in Baltimore, 581 against 5,364; and in Kent County, 74 against 1,502. It passed in only one county, and that, Davis said, was a mistake.

Davis said emancipation was indebted to the commencement of Negro enlistments, but this created discrimination between non-slave-owning, loyal whites subject to the draft, and disloyal slave owners whose slaves were not. Davis said it was these actions, more than anything else that brought directly before the people of Maryland at the last election the burdens they were suffering from the existence of slavery, even more than the proclamations and bayonets.

Davis explained whites' views: "If we are to have a draft, and if our rich neighbor's plantation is to be cultivated while we are dragged off to fill the quota of the State, we think that an injustice. We are for slave enlistments and for the party and the men who advocate it, and if it breaks up slavery we get the benefit, and we are in favor of emancipation and in favor of relieving the white people from the disproportionate burdens of the draft."

Avowing that Americans were not the only people who had prejudices, Davis called for emphasis on economics: "Let us decide the question, not upon questions of prejudice, not on questions of hostility to race, but on the great politico-economic argument, on its political dynamics, if I may use the expressions. Those forces which must determine it will determine it peacefully if we are wise, or in blood if we are unwise. Those, and those alone, in my judgment, are the alternatives."[338]

As with the other border states, so in Maryland, Lincoln worked to support and develop a loyal government free of slavery. Representative John A. J. Creswell had been a major force in the development of the Republican party in his state, and Lincoln took special care with regard to emancipation: "I am anxious for emancipation to be effected in Maryland. … I think it probable that my expressions of a preference for gradual over immediate emancipation are misunderstood."

Lincoln's view was evolving. "I had thought the gradual would produce less confusion, and destitution, and … be more satisfactory; but if those … better acquainted … prefer the immediate … I have no objection of their … prevailing. What I have dreaded is … that by jealousies, rivalries, and consequent ill-blood—driving one another out of meetings and conventions—perchance from the polls—the friends of emancipation themselves may divide, and lose the measure altogether."[339]

Lincoln also issued another draft call to "supply the force required … for the Navy, and to provide an adequate reserve force for all contingencies,—in addition to the five hundred thousand men called for February 1st, 1864, a call is hereby made and a draft ordered for two hundred thousand men for the 'military service of the United States." He explained that the numbers required could be raised by voluntary enlistment and credit given prior to April 15, when the draft would begin.[340]

In reply to an honorary membership in the New York Workingmen's Democratic Republican Association, Lincoln said:

> You comprehend, as your address shows … the existing rebellion, means more, and tends to more, than the perpetuation of African Slavery—that it is, in fact, a war upon the rights of all working people. … None are so deeply interested to resist the present rebellion as the working people. Let them beware of prejudice, working division and hostility among themselves.
>
> The most notable feature of a disturbance in your city last summer was the hanging of some working people by other working people. It should never be so. The strongest bond of human sympathy, outside of family relations, should be one uniting all working people, of all nations, and tongues, and kindreds. Nor should it lead to a war upon property, or the owners of property. Property is the fruit of labor—property is desirable—is a positive good in the world.
>
> That some should be rich shows that others may become rich, and hence is just encouragement to industry and enterprise. Let not him who is houseless pull down the house of another; but let him labor diligently and build one for himself, thus by example assuring that his own shall be safe from violence when built.

Lincoln addressed his remarks to a presenting committee of the association, who asked his endorsement of their support for the Union and sacrifices to sustain it.[341]

With the end of the war in sight, congressional debate swirled around the method of reconstruction. Those who wished to prevent Lincoln's nomination for a second term feared that state governments reconstructed under Lincoln's plan would send delegates pledged to

Lincoln to the convention. This became entangled with questions as to whether states that seceded were in or out of the Union, confiscation of property, and giving the vote to blacks.

Radicals in Congress wanted punishment and confiscation of rebel property, taking issue with Lincoln's willingness to grant amnesty and the leniency in his plan to restore state government. Radicals wanted a new political order. Lincoln questioned the authority of Congress to ban slavery in the states, contending such a prohibition would require a constitutional amendment. Lincoln's immediate goal was to use reconstruction as a means to undermine the Confederacy and end the war.

Representatives friendly to Lincoln accepted his primary purpose was restoration of the Union by organizing loyal governments in conquered Confederate states, and putting amnesty within reach. Others in Congress denied the validity of secession and declared states could not cast off allegiance to the federal Constitution, as their territory remained within the limits of the nation. Others who contended seceded states had committed suicide said only Congress could reorganize them.

On March 22, Representative Davis of Maryland moved that the House of Representatives call up HR 244, then in the Select Committee on the Rebellious States, guaranteeing a republican form of government to certain states whose governments had been usurped or overthrown. A bitter foe of the Blair's, Davis had introduced this bill in opposition to Lincoln's call for amnesty and reconstruction. He also opposed using loyalty oaths to build a constituency among rebels.

Representative Henry L. Dawes of Massachusetts introduced a resolution calling upon Lincoln "to communicate to this House whether the Hon. Francis P. Blair, Jr., representing the first congressional district of Missouri in the present House, now holds any appointment or commission in the military … and if so, what that appointment or commission is, and when the said Blair accepted the same; and whether he is acting under the authority of any such appointment or commission."

Lincoln explained when the present Congress met, Robert C. Schenck of Ohio and Frank P. Blair Jr. of Missouri, members-elect, held commissions from the executive, by and with the consent of the Senate, as major generals in the volunteer army. General Blair, in command of a corps under General Sherman before Chattanooga, was not present when Congress assembled, and arrived late. Both resigned their commissions and were granted a promise to be able to withdraw their resignations.

Schenck did not withdraw his resignation. However, when Grant was made lieutenant general, Blair sought command of a corps and requested that his commission in the army be reactivated. At the time of Dawes's inquiry, however, the formal withdrawal and order assigning the command to Blair had yet to be consummated at the War Department. In summary, Lincoln said Blair held no other appointments as he had yet to return to the military.[342]

Blair undertook his own defense on the floor of the House on April 23. A report by Representative William Higby of California declared that liquor speculation charges against Blair resulted from an altered and forged document. The report stated that the original order for liquor, tobacco, and cigars was for $150 or $170. The order was altered by one Michael Powers, representing himself as a Treasury Department agent, in a manner that netted out at the sum of $8,651.

Blair at the time was a major general commanding a corps near Vicksburg when he and eight members of his staff placed the original order. The committee reported that Powers had altered the order as a speculation to make money for himself. Thus Blair was exonerated of all charges made against him. Blair insisted that the entire report be read, and then asked leave to comment further. Speaker Schuyler Colfax ruled that no debate was in order, but Blair protested:

"I do not propose to remain here a great while longer, and it is important to me, if I am to be allowed to make any remarks … that I should have the opportunity of making them now. I do not think the House will decline to grant me this courtesy. … I do not expect to remain in the House even until the report can be printed, and I shall therefore have no opportunity to make any remarks … unless it is given to me now by the courtesy of the gentleman from California."

A Blair antagonist, Representative Henry Winter Davis of Maryland, opined, "It seems to me that we have no special connection with this matter at all. It is due to the gentleman from Missouri, respecting whom such a report has been made, and which having been made will be published and commented upon … he should be indulged in remarks upon it. I cannot conceive how, in propriety, after allowing the report to be made, we can refuse the courtesy he now asks."

Blair then proceeded:

> Mr. Speaker, I am as loth as any other member to consume the time so necessary for the public business, but the use which has been made of this affair is of such an extraordinary character, so malicious and unjust to me, that I have been compelled to appeal … for the privilege of making a few observations. … It is shown by the report … that when this "forgery" was committed I was in the service of my country, and in the trenches before Vicksburg.
>
> When it was made public and circulated far and wide in the newspapers for the purpose of destroying my reputation, I was again absent from my home and in command of the fifteenth Army corps, leading gallant soldiers on the march from Memphis to Chattanooga to share in that memorable conflict which drove Bragg from his stronghold on the heights of Lookout Mountain and Missionary Ridge, and afterwards to the relief of our beleaguered army at Knoxville.
>
> Finding myself superseded in a command of which I was so justly proud, and unconscious of having committed any

> offense … I came here to resume my seat … to which I had been returned by a confiding constituency, and … had left eighteen months before, at the solicitation of the Administration, to raise and command troops for the defense of this country. … The malignity of those who had originated and propagated this atrocious slander … pursued me.

The speaker again ruled Blair out of order, but Representative Elihu Washburne of Illinois moved that Blair be allowed to continue.

Blair raked Representative McClurg for reiterating the calumny by presenting the forged documents on the House floor, alleging speculation. Blair said evidence showed a Treasury agent had made the document public, knowing it was false and a forgery. His anger rising, Blair contended, "These dogs have been set on me by their master … who I mean to hold … responsible."

Blair alleged the attack was made on him because in a St. Louis speech, he had assailed Treasury Department trade regulations. Thus, he said, if anyone assailed in a public speech the management and operations of the Treasury, "he lays himself open to assaults from the Secretary of the Treasury and all the hound dogs that he can set upon him, and he is to be hunted and dragged down by false charges and by forgery." He reiterated his call for an investigation.

While initially supporting Chase's appointment at Treasury, Blair said he changed his mind because statements and published reports of Chase, never denied, reported him in favor of letting states in rebellion go. "Yet Mr. Chase, I soon found, never really abandoned his determination to cut off the southern states. On the contrary, he has endeavored to work out, by another program, the very thing he was in favor of doing—of letting the South go. … He is now for making them go, so far as their condition as States is concerned. He is unwilling that they should ever return to interfere with his presidential aspirations."

Blair struck hard:

> Why, sir, it was perfectly understood in the second session … of the last Congress, that he favored the annihilation of the State governments of the South. His friends in both Houses made that proposition; those who had the most intimate relations with him, in both Houses made the proposition.
>
> And it is pressed in this House again this winter in a disguised and insidious form, and under the pretentious title of "reconstruction," but which is in fact intended for the destruction of those States; but this being the very crime of which the rebels in arms are guilty, and which the gentleman from Ohio [Mr. Ashley] charges upon them, it is thought convenient to give the operations another name.

Blair turned with animosity toward the budding Wade-Davis legislation.

> The bill reported by the distinguished gentleman from Maryland, [Mr. Davis] representing the committee on the rebellious States, which, by the way, is composed to a considerable extent of the Pomeroy private circular committee, for I understand that the gentlemen from Maryland, from Ohio [Mr. Ashley] and from Missouri [Mr. Blow] are members of both these committees, is a bill which could very properly have come from the Pomeroy [Chase for President] Committee.
>
> It is a bill which should have been entitled "a bill for the permanent dissolution of the Union, to disenfranchise the whites and enfranchise the Negroes, to prevent any of the States from coming back in time to vote for Mr. Lincoln for President, and to promote the ambition of the Secretary of the Treasury." It is a bill that requires the consent of Congress for the readmission of any of these States to the Union.

Blair drew a hard line against Chase and against the radicals too. He then took aim at the underlying purpose:

> The gentlemen proceed in their disfranchising bill upon the pretext that the usurpation of the rebels for the house has destroyed the States, or that the forces of the United States sent to drive out and overthrow the rebel power which held that State and national Governments in the South alike in abeyance, are to be considered conquering forces, extinguishing the local constitutions the nation is bound to guaranty.
>
> Looking to the root of the matter, the cause of all our disasters, proves that instead of considering the State governments abolished, Congress would best perform its functions by amending the Constitution … to eradicate slavery. … This simple remedy, which can be attained by adhering to … the Constitution itself, supersedes the revolutionary schemes of those who would convert the States into Territories and assert absolutism … in regard to their admission to the Union.
>
> The founders of the Government saw the lurking evil in admitting the slave-tolerating clause in the Constitution; they foretold its fatal tendency. Our present Chief Magistrate, before he was thought of for the place he holds, predicted that this Government "could not endure permanently half free and half slave." And can there be a better solution … than that furnished by the Senate's bill incorporating Jefferson's ordinance of freedom with the fundamental law of nation?

Blair took a strong stand against members of the House and Senate who were contending for the doctrine of state suicide and strongly allied with Lincoln's conviction that states could not constitutionally secede from the Union, which was perpetual. "Is it not better than disfranchising States and robbing loyal men of their rights, putting them on a footing with rebels already disfranchised by their bloody treason? Our soldiers invoke the loyal citizens of the South to join their ranks, and patriots everywhere would call on the loyalists of the South to renew the glorious association of free States of the North and South, by joining with its armed deliverers in the reelection of the man who first organized free government over our whole country, and has thus earned the high privilege of inaugurating the renewed and most auspicious career of the Union." Blair concluded his defense and left the House.[343]

Lincoln, on March 15, wrote to Grant, "Gen. McPherson having been assigned to the command of a new Department, could not General Frank Blair without difficulty or detriment to the service, be assigned to command the corps he commanded a while last autumn."

Grant replied, "General Sherman … consents to the transfer of General Logan to the seventeenth corps … General F. P. Blair to the fifteenth corps." On April 28, Blair returned to active duty as a major general and corps commander.[344]

CHAPTER XIII

CORRALLING RENOMINATION; CONGRESSIONAL VOICES

At this time, Lincoln, knowing Weed was upset with him, dispatched Nicolay to New York with this letter: "I have been both pained and surprised recently at learning that you are wounded because a suggestion of yours as to the mode of conducting our national difficulty, has not been followed—pained because I very much wish you to have no unpleasant feeling ... and surprised, because my impression is that I have seen you, since the last message ... feeling very cheerful and happy."

Nicolay gave the note to Weed at the Astor House. Weed said he didn't quite understand, that he had written Judge Davis but had said nothing except about custom house matters. He had expected Lincoln to make a change in there, and had no preference, but thought Barney a weak man whose four deputies were intriguing against Lincoln. Weed said men were continually turned out because—and he was explicit—they were taking part in primary meetings for Lincoln's renomination.

Nicolay's account continued: "His only solicitude, he said, was for yourself. He thought that if you were not strong enough to hold the Union men together through the next Presidential election, when it must necessarily undergo a great strain, the country was in the utmost danger of going to ruin. His desire was to strengthen you as much as possible and that you should strengthen yourself." Weed contended that to hold incapable and unworthy men in office weakened Lincoln.

"This feeling among your friends also raises the question, as to whether, if reelected, you [Lincoln] would change your Cabinet," Weed told Nicolay, who reported his remarks. "The present cabinet is notoriously weak and inharmonious—no cabinet at all—gives the President no support. Wells is a cypher, Bates a fogy, and Blair at best, a dangerous friend. Something was needed to reassure the public mind and to strengthen yourself. Chase and Fremont ... yet form and lead dangerous factions."

Weed suggested Lincoln seemed unready to act on a new customs collector, fearing he would get "out of one muss into another." Nicolay reported:

> A change in the Custom House was imperatively needed because one whole bureau in it has been engaged in treasonably aiding the rebellion. ... He [Weed] feared he did not have your entire confidence ... that you only regarded him as being not quite so great a rascal as his enemies charged him with being. ...
>
> He had just received Gov. Morgan's letter informing him of the nomination of Hogeboom to fill McElrath's place, and seemed quite disheartened. ... He had assured his friends here that when in your own good time you became ready to make changes, the new appointments would be from among your friends; but that this promotion of one of your most active malignant enemies left him quite powerless.

This was a prelude to Lincoln's final confrontation with Chase over appointees.[345]

A *New York Herald* report said one reason for Weed's absence from the White House was his desire to avoid Mrs. Lincoln. As the story goes, Weed had been in a New York hotel at a time when Mrs. Lincoln was also there. He was talking with some men, one of whom remarked that General Halleck and Stanton wanted to get Mrs. Lincoln out of Washington, and in the laughter that followed, Weed said, "She ought to have been sent away a long time ago."

A friend overheard the men talking and carried the story upstairs to Mrs. Lincoln. When Weed was next in Washington, so the *Herald* reported, he went to the White House. There Mrs. Lincoln confronted him. She accused him of talking about her, struck him with a broomstick, and ordered him to leave. Whether this was part of the wound that Weed was feeling or not, it became clear that by election time that Weed was back on the team.[346]

At the end of March, Lincoln met with Kentucky governor Thomas E. Bramlett, former senator Archibald Dixon, and Albert D. Hodges, editor of the *Frankfort Commonwealth* newspaper. They came protesting the recruitment of former slaves as Union soldiers in Kentucky. Despite proslavery views, Dixon was loyal to the Union. Chosen to fill the unexpired term of Henry Clay, he had convinced Senator Douglass to eliminate the Mason-Dixon line in the Kansas-Nebraska Act.

Dixon represented his county and his state in a number of failed conventions that sought to resolve the impending conflict before it began. According to an entry by Orville H. Browning in his diary, Browning said the president told him a delegation had called regarding the enlistment of slaves as soldiers in Kentucky, as there had been much dissatisfaction. When the meeting ended, Hodges asked Lincoln for a copy of his remarks. Lincoln agreed to write out the remarks and send them.

"I am naturally anti-slavery," Lincoln wrote to Hodges.

> If slavery is not wrong, nothing is wrong. I cannot remember when I did not so think, and feel. And yet I have never understood that the Presidency conferred upon me an unrestricted right to act officially upon this judgment and

> feeling. It was in the oath I took that I would, to the best of my ability, preserve, protect, and defend the Constitution of the United States. I could not take the office without taking the oath.
>
> Nor was it in my view that I might take an oath to get power, and break the oath in using the power. I understood, too, that in ordinary civil administration this oath even forbade me to practically indulge my primary abstract judgment on the moral question of slavery. I had publicly declared this many times, and in many ways. And I aver that, to this day, I have done no official act in mere deference to my abstract judgment and feeling on slavery.
>
> I did understand, however, that my oath to preserve the constitution to the best of my ability imposed upon me the duty of preserving, by every indispensable means, that government—that nation—of which that Constitution was the organic law. Was it possible to lose the nation, and yet preserve the constitution? By general law, life and limb must be protected; yet often a limb must be amputated to save a life; but a life is never wisely given to save a limb.
>
> I felt that measures, otherwise unconstitutional, might become lawful, by becoming indispensable to the preservation of the constitution, through the preservation of the nation. Right or wrong, I assumed this ground, and now avow it. I could not feel that, to the best of my ability, I had even tried to preserve the constitution, if, to save slavery, or any minor matter, I should permit the wreck of government, country, and Constitution all together.

Lincoln said that when General Fremont attempted military emancipation, "I forbid it because I did not then think it an indispensable necessity." He took the same position regarding proposals from then secretary Cameron and General Hunter. In March, May, and July of 1862, Lincoln appealed to the border states to favor compensated emancipation, believing indispensable military emancipation and arming of blacks would come unless averted by these measures.

> They declined the proposition; and I was, in my best judgment, driven to the alternative of either surrendering the Union, and with it, the Constitution, or of laying strong hand upon the colored element. I choose the latter. In choosing it, I hoped for greater gain than loss; but of this, I was not entirely confident. More than a year of trial now shows no loss by it in our foreign relations, none in our home population, none in our white military force,—no loss by it … any where.
>
> On the contrary, it shows a gain of … a hundred and thirty thousand soldiers, seamen, and laborers. … We have the men; and we could not have had them without the measure. And now let any Union man who complains of the measure test himself by writing down in one line that he is for subduing the rebellion by force of arms; and in the next, that he is for taking these … men from the Union side, and placing them where they would be but for the measure he condemns.
>
> If he cannot face his case so stated, it is only because he cannot face the truth. In telling this tale I attempt no compliment to my own sagacity. I claim not to have controlled events, but confess plainly that events have controlled me. … If God now wills the removal of a great wrong, and wills also that we of the North as well as you of the South, shall pay fairly for our complicity … impartial history will find therein new cause to attest and revere the justice and goodness of God.[347]

In an address to the Baltimore Sanitary Fair, Lincoln said, "Looking upon these many people … it occurs to me at once that three years ago, the same soldiers could not so much as pass through Baltimore. The change from then till now, is both great, and gratifying. Blessings upon the brave men who have wrought the change, and the fair women who strive to reward them for it. But Baltimore suggests more. … The change within Baltimore is part only of a far wider change."

Speaking to the magnitude and duration beyond what any had expected for this war, Lincoln turned to the question of slavery:

> Neither did any anticipate that domestic slavery would be much affected by the war. But here we are; the war has not ended, and slavery has been much affected. … So true is it that man proposes, and God disposes. But we can see the past, though we may not claim to have directed it; and seeing it, in this case, we feel more hopeful and confident for the future.
>
> The world has never had a good definition of the word liberty, and the American people … are much in want of one. We all declare for liberty; but in using the same word we do not all mean the same thing. With some the word liberty may mean for each man to do as he pleases with himself, and the product of his labor; while … the same word may mean for some men to do as they please with other men, and the product of other men's labor … two … incompatible things.

Lincoln illustrated his point:

> The shepherd drives the wolf from the sheep's throat, for which the sheep thanks the shepherd as a liberator, while the wolf denounces him for the same act as the destroyer of liberty, especially as the sheep was a black one. Plainly the sheep and the wolf are not agreed upon a definition of the word liberty; and precisely the same difference prevails today among us human creatures, even in the North, and all professing to love liberty.

> Hence we behold the processes by which thousands are daily passing from under the yoke of bondage, hailed by some as the advance of liberty, and bewailed by others as the destruction of liberty. Recently, as it seems, the people of Maryland have been doing something to define liberty; and thanks to them that, in what they have done, the world's dictionary has been repudiated.

Lincoln then commented upon the report of a massacre of soldiers at Fort Pillow, Tennessee, saying:

> A painful rumor, true I fear, has reached us of the massacre, by the rebel forces, at Fort Pillow … of some three hundred colored soldiers and white officers, who had just been overpowered by their assailants. There seems to be some anxiety in the public mind whether the government is doing its duty to the colored soldiers, and to the service. … At the beginning of the war … the use of colored troops was not contemplated; and how the change … was wrought, I will now … explain.
>
> Upon a clear conviction of duty I resolved to turn that element of strength to account; and I am responsible for it. … Having determined to use the Negro as a soldier, there is no way but to give him all the protection given to any other soldier. The difficulty is not in stating the principle, but in practically applying it. … We do not today know that a colored soldier, or white officer commanding … has been massacred by the rebels when … a prisoner. We fear it … but … do not know it.
>
> To take the life of one of their prisoners, on the assumption that they murder ours, when it is short of certainty that they do … might be too serious, too cruel a mistake. … If there has been the massacre of three hundred … or even the tenth

> part of three hundred, it will be conclusively proved; and being so proved, the retribution shall as surely come. It will be a matter of grave consideration in what exact course to apply the retribution; but in the supposed case, it must … come.[348]

Arkansas governor Isaac Murphy telegraphed Lincoln on April 15, "Both houses of the Legislature have organized. … The vote for Constitution 12,179 against 2,026; For Gov. 12,430. … One member killed coming here. If reinforcements are not sent soon or Gen. Steele ordered to return we are in great danger." Lincoln responded, "I am much gratified to learn that you got out so large a vote. … Whatever I can, I will do … meanwhile … do your utmost to protect yourselves."[349]

As April ended, Lincoln wrote to Grant, "Not expecting to see you again before the spring campaign, I wish to express … my entire satisfactions with what you have done up to this time. … The particulars of your plans I neither know, nor seek to know. You are vigilant and self-reliant; and, pleased with this, I wish not to obtrude any constraints or restraints." Lincoln said he was anxious that any great disaster be avoided and urged Grant to call upon him for things wanting.

Grant responded, "Your very kind letter … is just received. The confidence you express for the future, and satisfaction with the past … is acknowledged with pride. It will be my earnest endeavor that you, and the country, shall not be disappointed. … Indeed since the promotion which placed me in command of all the Armies, and in view of the great responsibility, and importance of success, I have been astonished … with which every thing asked for has been yielded."[350]

Lincoln received the report on the Fort Pillow capture and wrote to his cabinet asking that each member provide in writing his opinion of what course to take. "It is now quite certain," Lincoln said, "that large number of our colored soldiers, with their white officers, were, by the rebel force, massacred after they had surrendered." Seward,

Chase, Stanton, and Wells advised that an equal number of Confederate soldiers be set apart and executed if the massacre was acknowledged.

All agreed that the Confederate government should be called upon to avow or disavow the massacre. Usher, Bates, and Blair advised no retaliation against hostages, but advised that orders be issued to execute the actual offenders if captured. In addition, a special committee of Congress appointed Senator Benjamin F. Wade of Ohio and Representative Daniel W. Gooch of Massachusetts to a special committee to fully investigate the incident. There is, however, no record of subsequent retaliation.

Confederate Nathan Bedford Forrest—a millionaire planter and slave trader—in his report said the Confederates had captured the garrison and all supplies. He said a demand for surrender was refused. He believed the tally of losses by the Union forces would never be known, as "large numbers ran into the river and were shot and drowned. The force was composed of about 500 Negroes and 200 white soldiers. The river was dyed with the blood of the slaughtered for 200 yards.

"There was in the fort a large number of citizens who had fled there to escape the conscript law. Most of these ran into the river and were drowned. The approximate loss was upward of 500 killed, but few of the officers escaping." Forrest put his own loss at 20 killed and about 60 wounded. He then boldly declared, "It is hoped that these facts will demonstrate to the Northern people that Negro soldiers cannot cope with Southerners." Adding insult to injury, he said, "We still hold the fort."[351]

As Lincoln had explained, he was slow and deliberate in evolving his policies, thus making sure the people kept pace with him. As he contemplated and undertook actions, his moral imperatives solidified. The war had given Lincoln a firm grasp on the levers of power, while making him the common target of radicals, Democrats, and the Confederacy. His strength stemmed less from methodical administration and more from skillful political management, second to none in his time.

While he gave his cabinet officers room to maneuver, they learned that when Lincoln acted decisively, he was the deciding factor. While he stood aloof from much of what Congress did—including the efforts of the Joint Committee on the Conduct of the War—Lincoln effectively used the whip hand of patronage. Lincoln personally conceived and issued the Emancipation Proclamation, managed the military, and initiated reconstruction, actions absolutely crucial to ultimate success.

Lincoln's skillfully conceived cabinet, recognizing key states and sections and the political breadth of the nation, strengthened the developing Republican political base. Lincoln's administration evolved a vital modern economic structure. This included industrial development, expanded railroads, improved agriculture productivity, protective tariffs, increased land grants, broadened tax base, and a national banking system coupled with a national currency and monetary policy.

In contrast, the Confederacy slipped into bankruptcy. Union naval forces choked off strategic imported supplies, and the Union armies reduced Southern agricultural and war material production capabilities. Increasingly, Lincoln's hard but tempered use of his constitutional powers curbed the Southern Democrats' Northern Copperhead allies. He had suspended habeas corpus as a war measure. He also supported Stanton and the War Department in arresting and jailing disloyal citizens.

As Grant moved into Virginia, Lincoln managed his strategy for renomination as Radical Republicans and Peace Democrats at this point worked to dump him. They aimed to nominate another and undermine his reelection prospects. His reconstruction proclamation and his amnesty oath triggered this opposition. Key leaders not only fought against his plan, they argued that Lincoln had exceeded his authority because reconstruction responsibility was vested only with Congress.

In their respective houses, Senator Wade and Representative Davis framed the legislation antagonistic toward Lincoln. A majority of their colleagues voted for this legislation. Many, however, did not share the personal animosity Wade and Davis felt toward Lincoln. As the debate developed, factions on every side argued whether rebel states remained states or had committed "state suicide." This was the controversial central issue within the broader question of how to reshape the nation.

"Our democratic form of Government has suddenly and violently been put to the severest test," Representative Sidney Perham of Maine declared.

> Opponents of our system have been compelled, in view of our unparalleled prosperity, to admit its superiority in time of peace; but they have told us, tauntingly, that whenever internal commotion should arise we should find our form of government inadequate … and should go down beneath the bloody surges of battle. …
>
> The world holds it breath and waits. … Crowned heads and the devotees of despotism are exulting in the hope of our downfall; while the downtrodden, the oppressed, and the liberty-loving masses … are continually offering prayers for our success. It is a struggle between freedom and despotism, not only for us, but for the world. … All of our efforts should be directed to the success of the mutual cause—the suppression of the rebellion and the salvation of our … country. …
>
> And now, did I not feel that the course pursued by the members on the other side of the Hall is calculated to undermine the people's confidence in the Government, create discord … dishearten our friends, encourage our enemies; and prolong the war, my voice would not be heard today. … They persist in characterizing this as "Lincoln's War," "Black Republican war," "abolition war," "war for the niggers," a "hellish crusade" carried on in "violation of the Constitution."

Tracing prewar actions of the Democrats, Perham said:

> If the northern delegates [at the 1860 conventions] had been willing to yield a tithe of what they have since demanded of Congress and the Administration, the southern delegates would have been satisfied. It is said, the South has been driven out of the Union by the friends of the Administration. By the same reasoning I might say to the opponents of the Administration, you drove them out of your convention.
>
> To the declaration so often made … that the Administration and its friends are responsible for the war I answer: 1. If the South had any cause for complaint, the Democratic Party, and not the Union or Republican Party, is responsible. They had controlled the Government, with but brief interruptions, for sixty years; and when the rebel States seceded, though, a Republican President had been elected, the Democrats had a majority both in the Senate and House. …
>
> 2. There was no ground for complaint. The southern States had continued in the enjoyment of all their constitutional rights, and, so far as the election of Mr. Lincoln was concerned, they never stood on a firmer basis than at the time of secession. [Quoting Senator Douglas:] "The slavery question is a mere excuse. The election of Lincoln is a mere pretext. The present secession movement is the result of an enormous conspiracy formed … in the southern confederacy. …"
> 3. The rebel government had been organized, and through the aid and cooperation of the traitors in Mr. Buchanan's Government they had thoroughly prepared for war, and the issue—abject subjection to the malcontents, and the dismemberment of our once glorious Union, or war for the maintenance of the national unity—was fully

> made up, and transmitted from Mr. Buchanan's to Mr. Lincoln's Administration.

Perham elaborated: "In December, 1860, three months before Mr. Lincoln's term commenced, seventy thousand stand of arms in Charleston, which Mr. Floyd had placed in the care of the South Carolina rebels, were taken possession of for the rebel government." He cited other similar incidents, stating, "A more disgraceful record has not been made by any party on the face of the earth than that made by the leaders of the Democratic Party during the last four years."

> 4. I answer, this is emphatically a Democratic rebellion, inaugurated by Democrats, under a Democratic Administration, by its knowledge and consent; stimulated and encouraged by the promise of powerful aid from the Democrats of the North, and now kept alive by the hope that the "peace Democracy" of the North will come to their aid and allow them to "go in peace." In proof of this declaration, I propose to notice the part which leading Democratic officials took. …
>
> Jacob Thompson, Mr. Buchanan's Secretary of the Interior, revealed his treasons in a speech which he subsequently made in Mississippi, as follows: "I sent a dispatch to Judge Longstreet that the Star of the West was coming [to Fort Sumter] with reinforcements. The troops were then put on their guard, and when the Star of the West arrived, she received a warm welcome from booming cannon, and beat a hasty retreat."
>
> 5. All the facts that have come to light during the progress of the war show that the South commenced the rebellion with the expectation, based on the assurance of northern Democrats, that a civil strife was to be created in the northern States which would neutralize the power of

> the government there, while they would make an easy conquest of this capital, take possession of the public archives, and establish the confederate government of the United States.

Again Perham quoted Douglas: "I know they expected to present a united South against a divided North." Perham also quoted from a letter from ex-President Franklin Pearce to Davis: "Without discussing the question of right, of abstract power to secede, I have never believed that absolute disruption of the Union can occur without blood; and if, through the madness of northern abolitionism, that dire calamity must come, the fighting will not be along Mason and Dixon's line merely."

Then Perham turned to the Southern press. From the *Richmond Enquirer* he quoted. "Let not the people be downcast by the result at Gettysburg, nor the loss of Vicksburg and Port Hudson. Those losses will be more than made good to us by the disorganization of northern society by the expected triumph of the peace Democracy in the free States." From the *Chattanooga Daily Gazette*, he quoted a rebel citizen: "If Lincoln is reelected we may just as well give up the game."

"Mr. Speaker," Perham declared,

> ...much has been said on the other side of this Hall about "violated" Constitution ... while they hold Mr. Lincoln to the most limited construction ... that can possibly be given, especially in regard to his measures to crush the rebellion, but few, if any, words of complaint are uttered against the rebels who are setting at defiance every constitutional obligation. The whole purpose appears to be to limit the war powers of the President. ...
>
> But there is another class of men calling themselves Democrats to whom the country gives its highest meed of praise, and whose names are embalmed in the affections

> of the American people. I refer to those ... in the Army, in civil life, and in this and the other branch of Congress, who have ... forgotten all party prejudices in their devotion to our common country; who, scorning the scoffs and anathemas of their old party associates, have known nothing but duty.[352]

Representative Francis Kernan, a New York Democrat, first reviewed the Davis bill in detail and then sharply contended, "Mr. Speaker ... this bill is in violation and subversive of the fundamental principles upon which both our national and State governments are founded. ... The States to which the bill under consideration is to apply are existing States; the bill recognizes them as such. They are not to be readmitted to the Union; they are now in law a part of the Union."

Questions were raised both by Representative George Boutwell and Representative James Ashley. Boutwell asked if Congress "should yield up the government of these rebellious States to the people who refuse to acknowledge the Constitution and laws of the United States." Ashley said, "I desire to say to the gentleman from New York that so far as the House committee are concerned they have determined to make the same requirements apply to all State alike hereafter to be admitted."

Kernan said powers of the government were confined to national purposes, adding:

> Congress has no right to dictate to a State what shall be the provisions of its State constitution. The sole power granted to the nation in reference to State governments is ... each State is to be guarantied a republican form of government. Subject to this provision ... the right of the people of each State to retain the old or form a new State constitution and government is absolute. ...
>
> I wish to see our armies conquer the rebel armies, and drive out the usurpers. ... Sir, I am no admirer or advocate of

> slavery. I object to it, believing it to be a great moral and political evil—a wrong to the slave, and, in the long run, a curse to the master. I shall rejoice to see it abolished, if it is done without violating the Constitution of the United States or interfering with the reserved rights of the people of the States to regulate their local Institutions.
>
> I submit ... that this bill is at war with the principles upon which the Federal Government rests, and is subversive of the State governments and the reserved rights of the people of each State. If Congress may impose...conditions prescribed by this bill as conditions precedent to the exercise of their right to maintain, form or administer a State government, we may require them to ordain as a part of a State constitution almost any other provision. [353]

Following Kernan, Representative Daniel W. Gooch, a Republican from Massachusetts, jumped into the debate with his own analysis:

> Mr. Speaker, it is a grave mistake for us to suppose that the contest in which we are now engaged has been going on only since the rebels took up arms against the Federal Government. It has been going on ever since two antagonistic states of society commenced existence under our republican form of government, each striving for development and the master.
>
> I do not believe that any intelligent and reflecting man has ever believed that these two antagonistic states of society would or could ... exist permanently under the same Government. ... The leading men of both sections ... looked forward to the time when it should be peacefully, and with the consent of all parties, abolished. When ... the South came to look upon the institution as essential ...

> and to desire its permanence, they … began to look … to dissolution of the Union. …
>
> The contest between slavery and freedom … under the same Government, was inevitable, and no man or organization of men now living are responsible for it; it is … a conflict which must and will go on until truth and right shall conquer. The men who have supposed that they could stop men's thinking and talking … or by stopping them the conflict would end, are as wise as those men who stop their ears in a thunder storm that they may not be struck by lightning.

Gooch said some men would have the Union fight a shadow war:

> We hear from these men when we propose to adopt vigorous measures for replenishing our armies and giving of our noble volunteers … that they march forth to meet the enemy with hope of success; we hear from them when the President proposes to exercise the rightful belligerent power of declaring the slaves … free; we hear from them when it is proposed that colored men shall be admitted into the service. …
>
> We hear from them when the Congress … proposes to lend its power to aid in the construction of loyal governments in rebel States; we hear from them when our armies meet with defeat in the field, but they are dumb when loyal men rejoice in victory. Their watchword is "unconstitutionality," and their great fear is that the rebellion will meet with some unconstitutional injury or detriment, whereby its power to prolong its existence may be diminished. …
>
> However liberal the President may be in his amnesty proclamations, or the Congress in its legislation, for the pardon of traitors, I apprehend that rebel State governments

> will hardly find themselves in the catalogue of the forgiven. Those States must first come under the military rule and control of the United States, and how long they shall continue in that condition is a question which the United States along has the power to determine. … The question is a political one. …
>
> The conclusion to which I come is this: No matter what laws may be passed by Congress, no matter what acts may be done by the Executives, as the governments in the revolted States have by treason, rebellion, and adhesion to the southern confederacy been overthrown and destroyed, no such State can have any status in the Union for any purpose until a loyal State government shall have been established … and recognized by the Congress of the United States.[354]

Representative Nehemiah Perry, a New Jersey Democrat, made a slashing attack, not only on the bill, but upon the President and the entire Administration policy related to the war:

> Mr. Speaker, we are about entering, nay, we have already entered, upon the fourth year of the war. And this simple statement invites reflection. It should induce every man to pause, to take a careful scrutiny of the past, and to look forward with profound anxiety into the opening future. …
>
> We have witnessed stealthy strides of unlawful power; we have seen the theory of the abolition of slavery in the Territories transformed into its abolition everywhere; we have noted the transition from emancipation with compensation to emancipation without compensation, from bills striking down the rights and properties of individuals to acts crushing out the rights, the institutions, and the very existence of States as this bill we now have under consideration proposes. …

> We have seen the Negro made first a soldier, then a citizen, then a member of conventions, and we behold him now stretching out his hand to grasp the exercise of the franchise and the enjoyment of political distinction. We have seen a reign of terror, when every man become the spy and accuser of his neighbors; when men were hauled to prison without knowing their accuser or crime; when the habeas corpus was struck down by proclamation.

Perry contended that a "pliant Congress" applauded the striking down of habeas corpus. That action, he said, converted the will of one man into law and the law changed "with his capricious and fluctuating notions and ambitions." He further charged that established constitutions "were brushed aside like cobwebs, and free speech and a free ballot were crushed by the mailed hand of power," adding, "We have seen proclamation fulminated after proclamation with indecent haste. … New changes and still more violent vicissitudes are brewing, and more intolerable dislocations are being conceived as this bill proposes."

Taking firm issue with civil policy, he shifted to the military:

> He will be a bold man who will deny that whatever practical results have been attained have been secured solely by our armies in the field and by our Navy—by the indomitable resolution, and unshaken constancy, the unparalleled endurance and heroism of our brave soldiers and sailors. …
>
> But what have our rulers accomplished by their civil policy? They have not won a single stronghold. They have not detached a single State nor wrested a single acre of ground from the public enemy. … Nay, our victories would have been far greater and far more decisive; for every proclamation and every act has been firing the spirits of the Confederates and welding them so firmly together as almost to defy the frown of Deity.

As for his own conduct and in self-justification, Perry said, "I have never withheld my voice or my vote for men, or money, or means to this end. And although the Administration has been guilty of many acts which I believed to be wrong in principle and almost fatally so in practice, although much of its policy appears to be madly suicidal, neither have I felt it to be in a line with my duty to cripple them in the conduct of the war, even though their errors were certain to be repeated."

Perry contended it would be "a bootless task for me to undertake to convince the present Administration of the folly of their past policy," adding, "That task already has been attempted by one who has held upon the confidence and affection of the people." Cutting to the quick, Perry said, "If the Administration rejected the comprehensive and wise plan of military operations submitted by General McClellan to the President," then he doubted his words would bring any change.

Perry again took issue specifically with the president:

> I object in part to the bill before us, because it is drawn rather too largely from the President's plan. It leaves to a military man, a brigadier general, the organization of the new governments. Mr. Speaker, we have a simple and a better mode of governing Territories. We give them a territorial government, a Governor, secretary, judges, and the right to elect a Territorial Legislature; and provide for their forming a constitution. …
>
> We have … seen the evil effects of a departure from our territorial system and a military governor attempting to organize a State … in Louisiana. … The election was a ridiculous farce, because General Banks assumed to be governed by what did not exist—the constitution of Louisiana, which had been overthrown when she withdrew her Senators from this Capitol and her members from this House. So will it be everywhere if Congress does not provide the means of reconstruction.

> But the gentleman from New York [Mr. Wood] and others tell us that before we can establish any governments in the revolted States we must exterminate or annihilate the people of the whole wide field of the confederacy; that we cannot have peace between a conquered and a conquering people or their descendants. Sir, the … Proclamation … offers … general pardon to the people of the rebel country. … Such pardons have constitutional, congressional and judicial sanction.
>
> We carry with us to the South not alone the bayonet and cannon; we approach the people with other sounds. … Ours is not a slow age; we move with electric speed. The press is free and ever in motion. The landless and ignorant whites hail social equality. … Among the four million colored people there is not one who is not loyal. … Let us … go on conquering. In complete conquest alone can peace be found, and as a means of organizing conquest and peace let us pass this bill.[355]

Representative Fernando Wood, a Democrat and former New York City mayor, said, "If Congress can do what this bill proposes on the ground alleged, so can it disfranchise any State in the Union at pleasure on any pretext whatever. The creature would thus become greater than the creator. It would be the arrogance of concentrated centralism in his worst features, because it would attempt to deprive a people of their inalienable right to form their own organic laws."

Wood argued the proposed measure took away their ability "to determine the nature of the government under which they live. It seeks to establish a supervisory power, which, under the principle asserted, could at pleasure alter, modify, amend, annul, create, or destroy the constitution of every State in the Union, North or South, in times of war or peace. … To impose upon them a form of government of your own making, under the pretext of this bill, would be the worst kind of tyranny."

Wood charged these were the pet schemes of Representative Davis:

> He has often told us that the President's scheme was folly, that it would not accomplish the purpose, but that he had discovered the philosopher's stone, and that in this bill would be found the "magic wand" that would at once remove the cause of the evil which afflicts us and secure a permanent peace hereafter. The cause of the rebellion he says is slavery; and this is repugnant to Republicanism.
>
> He portrayed in his speech … to this House … all those horrors with his usual skill, and, I may add, without intending offense, his usual sophistry. His speech, like this bill, was founded on the one idea that slavery is the cause of the rebellion, and that where slavery exists republicanism cannot exist. He assumes that republicanism and slavery are inconsistent with each other. This is the motive for providing State governments for those which he says have been "usurped."
>
> As to the riots in the city of New York, they have been before referred to by Mr. Davis, representing the city of Baltimore. … He has scarcely made a speech … that he has not referred to the riots of last summer in New York. … The city of Baltimore, and the immediate constituency of the gentleman … has long been distinguished for its riots, and for the honor of having some of the most cruel and bloodthirsty rioters which have ever disgraced any American community.
>
> This, a war of ideas, a thoroughly revolutionary war, an unholy breaking of the seals of the constitution, in order to accomplish the reorganization of southern society, conformity to the plans of the socialist reformers of the school of pseudo-philanthropists. This is neither a slave holders rebellion or

> an office-holders' revolt, but an aggressive movement on the part of those who proclaimed that this Union could not consist of States some free and others slave.
>
> The origin of the war is that firebrand theory which sometimes phrased itself in an irrepressible conflict between "free labor" and "capital labor." When anti-slavery fanaticism entered the field of politics and tinctured the deliberations of party then commenced the growth of sectionalism, a sectionalism doubly formidable, as it not only alienated State from State, dividing the Union by geographical lines, but assailed the vital interests of the citizens of those States. …
>
> [This] threatened the existence of their most important institutions, and demanded the unconditional surrender of the whole system of social order, to be reformed to suit itself. To abolish slavery by the sword is violently unconstitutional, to wipe out of existence what counted as property … to the amount of $4 billion … to destroy the settled order of society in sixteen States … to pave the way for universal degradation, poverty, and social chaos, in the States. …
>
> I say that the principle of Negro emancipation, recognized by the bill under consideration, and on which this war is now avowedly conducted, and which assuredly was the moving and effective cause of the same, involves the total disruption of society in the South and disorganization of the Government of the North. All races, ages, and conditions of mankind in both sections are interested in opposing the accomplishment of this most disastrous experiment.

An ardent Democrat at odds not only with Republicans but with a major share of the Democratic members in New York, Wood had contested the policies of Lincoln both as the New York City's mayor and in Congress. He warned:

> We of this generation may not be able to estimate the full measure of the misery that will follow the realization of the fantastic theory which, promising to remove the yoke from every shoulder, will curse the earth with sterility and man with vice and poverty.
>
> Apart from considerations based on a common origin, language, religion, ties of blood and affiliation … and, above all, the obligations of a solemn compact, which made us as substantially one as are the parties to the matrimonial bond, we should look to the probable consequences of a war like this—a conflict nursed by discordant ideas and stimulated by the exaggeration of a social reformation, so deemed in the fanatical brains where it has been hatched.[356]

Representative George W. Julian of Indiana differed: "The fortunes of this war must inevitably sweep away the title to the great body of the land in the insurrectionary districts. Every day and every hour this rebellion is becoming more and more 'a remorseless revolutionary conflict.' There is not the slightest probability that either party to this contest will voluntarily take a single step backward, under the conceivable state of facts." Citing the Fort Pillow massacre, he said:

"Not only their personal goods and their lives, but the fee simple of their lands must be taken from them. Under existing laws of Congress on the subject of taxation and revenue, millions of acres are passing from the rebels and failing under our control. The question presented by this bill is whether these lands shall be sold to speculators to become the foundation of a stupendous system of serfdom over the poor, white and black, or parceled out in small homesteads to reward … soldiers."[357]

Representative Samuel F. Miller of New York said:

> It is objected that these measures are radical. I reply the disease is radical, and the cure must go as deep. … If slavery,

> then, was the cause of the rebellion, what remedy more rational than to remove the cause? What would there be left to fight about when the cause of the quarrel was gone? If you mean by radical that the measures are extreme and beyond what public opinion will sustain, answer that public opinion has kept step to the march of events.
>
> Those who felt no sympathy with the popular uprising, those who stood still and aside and let the tide of enthusiastic patriotism sweep by them, know little of the popular heart. The youth who fell asleep leaning against a sapling and on awaking found, it grown to a mighty tree was not more surprised than most of the sleepy politicians who turn from the small despised anti-slavery party of three years ago to the party today gigantic in numbers and determined in purpose. …
>
> The madness of the rebels has given us the opportunity to secure these great results without violating a single letter of our Constitution or a single principle of law or justice. To now neglect the necessary legislation would be one of those political blunders that are said to be worse than crimes. Let us not throw away the golden moment to save our country by planting it on eternal principles of freedom, and thus link our names to the grandest event of the century.[358]

As the debate raged in Congress and equally relentless action stirred the political cauldron, Grant moved south against Lee's Army of Virginia. Radicals and abolitionists pressed their efforts for a Republican nominee other than Lincoln. The Committee on the Conduct of the War, having dispatched Wade and Gooch to investigate the Fort Pillow massacre, traveled to Annapolis, where they met with some five hundred prisoners that Confederate authorities had recently released.

The committee went at the urging of William Hoffman, commissary general of prisoners, and Secretary Stanton. Hoffman had described the condition of the prisoners, whom the Confederate authorities had given up to alleviate crowding without a corresponding release of Confederate prisoners. The committee soon verified news accounts that described the prisoners as dirty, emaciated, listless, and suffering from frostbite and other ailments. The committee interviewed both hospital staff and many of the prisoners.[359]

Many prisoners, described as little more than living skeletons, told of meager rations. One told Representative Gooch that his ration for the day was six ounces of light bread, two spoonfuls of worm-infested black beans, and two ounces of very poor meat. Asked by Wade if they complained, one said yes, but was told it was enough. Surgeon B. A. Vanderkieft told Wade that most of those released suffered from debility and chronic diarrhea due to "exposure, privations, hardship and ill treatment."[360]

The report further inflamed the reconstruction debate in Congress. Radicals again pressed to delay the upcoming Republican Party convention scheduled for June. Representative Davis, to prevent the convention, rented the regular Baltimore convention hall for June 7. Republican leaders, however, obtained the Front Street Theater to convene as planned. The national chairman, Governor Morgan, and the national committee rejected the attempts of radicals to delay the meeting.

In his diary, Secretary Wells said that at the cabinet meeting, the president read dispatches from Grant, Butler, and Sherman, "all in good and encouraging tone. There have been some … doubts in regard to General Wadsworth, who is undoubtedly slain. … He should … have been at this moment Governor of New York, but the perfidy of Thurlow Weed and others defeated him. I have always believed that Seward was, if not implicated, a sympathizer in that business."

Wells told of comparing notes with Blair regarding a letter from Morgan asking to name a month to which the Union National Convention might be postponed, but both concurred against postponement and prevailed. Blair showed Wells a letter from Samuel L. M. Barlow, described by Wells as a Copperhead leader and also as a prominent Democratic party leader. Blair viewed Barlow as a channel to get McClellan to give up politics and return to military service.

Wells took a different view, explaining, "It was this feeling that had led to the correspondence. I do not admire the idea of corresponding with such a man as Barlow, who is an intense partisan, and Blair himself would distrust any one who should be in political communication with him. Blair had written Barlow that he would try to get McC. an appointment to the army, giving up party politics. Barlow replied that no party can give up their principles."

Wells revealed an extraordinary development. He said Barlow "quotes a letter which he says was written by a distinguished member of Mr. Lincoln's Cabinet last September, urging the organization of a conservative party on the basis of the Crittenden compromise." This, Wells said, shocked Blair, who speculated that Seward was the likely author. Wells inclined to the same opinion, adding Usher might have written it "without black perfidy," but surely Seward could not.

Later Wells noted in his diary his brother-in-law, Governor Morgan, said he sent the circular, asking views on postponing the convention in self-defense. Morgan told Wells the answers were against postponement except for (William) Spooner of Ohio. Wells noted Morgan told him "that the hall in which the convention is to meet has been hired by the malcontents, through the treachery and connivance of H. Winter Davis, in whom he had confided. Says he can get the theater." Morgan prevailed.[361]

Raymond noted, "General Grant, recognizing the fact that the strength of the rebellion lay not in the fortifications of Richmond, but in the ranks of Lee's army, aimed to place himself upon the southern communications of that army, and by heavy blows to destroy it. And with the very commencement of this movement he forced Lee to leave the entrenched line which he had so long faced the gathering storm, and make haste to attack his foe before he had reached his rear."[362]

Lincoln told the serenaders, "I am … very grateful to the brave men who have been struggling with the enemy in the field, to their noble commanders who have directed them, and especially to our Maker. Our commanders are following up their victories resolutely and successfully, I think, without knowing the particulars of the plan of General Grant, that what has been accomplished is of more importance that it first appears … but there is great deal to be done."[363]

Meanwhile Grant pressed south against Lee. In the thick second-growth scrub oak and pine forest of the Wilderness—where the Battle of Chancellorville had been fought a year earlier—Lee hit Grant's flank. Union forces suffered 18,000 casualties and the Confederates losses of 11,000. Grant viewed this as the first stage of the campaign and continued south. After the bitter and confused fighting, Grant wired Lincoln, "I propose to fight it out on this line if it takes all summer."[364]

When Meade turned the army toward Spotsylvania Court House on Brock Road, the troops cheered, realizing they were not pulling out but continuing the attack. Yet Meade poorly organized the march. He failed to order Sheridan's cavalry to block the Po Bridge. This gave Lee a more direct route to get his troops into defensive positions. Meade had ordered one cavalry regiment to guard his right flank and another to lead, but the cavalry and infantry together jammed the road.

This led to a shouting match between Meade and Sheridan, which ended when Sheridan angrily declared, "I could whip Jeb Stuart if you would only let me. But you insist on giving the cavalry directions without even consulting or notifying me, you can command the Cavalry Corps yourself, I will not give it another order." Meade told Grant of the incident, complaining and quoting Sheridan. Grant replied, "Well, he usually knows what he is talking about. Let him go ahead and do it."

By this outcome, Grant avoided having to fire either, and by nightfall Sheridan led ten thousand riders to the outer reaches of Richmond, defeating the Confederate cavalry and killing Stuart in the battle. Sheridan's raid deep into enemy territory did little to capture Spotsylvania but cost Lee heavily.

The Army of the Potomac, meanwhile, crawled through woods teeming with Confederate snipers. One fatally shot Union general John Sedgwick, the popular Sixth Corps commander.[365]

In bitter hand-to-hand fighting, during which neither side broke and ran, blood flowed in the trenches and the dead and wounded were trampled underfoot. General Hancock, aided by Sedgwick's Sixth Corps, now commanded by General Wright, captured a larger part of Confederate general Edward Johnson's division. Three thousand prisoners were taken, along with General Johnson and General Steuart. Torrents of rain fell during the prevailing raw and disagreeable weather.[366]

The Northern mood turned despondent as a staggering number of wounded were brought north to Washington, and casualty counts for the May operation passed 32,000 men. Lincoln ordered a draft for 300,000 more men: "The proportional quotas for the different wards, towns, townships, precincts, or election districts, or counties, will be made known through the Provost Marshal General's Bureau & account will be taken of … former quotas." Gold shot up from $171 to $191.[367]

Elizabeth Keckley wrote that Mary Lincoln could not tolerate Grant. She quoted Mrs. Lincoln: "He is a butcher, and is not fit to be at the head of an army."

The president replied, "But he has been very successful in the field."

"Yes," Mrs. Lincoln shot back. "He generally manages to claim a victory, but such a victory. He loses two men to the enemy's one. He has not management, no regard for life. If the war should continue four years longer ... he would depopulate the North. I could fight an army as well myself. According to his tactics, there is nothing under the heaven to do but to march a new line of men up in front of the rebel breastworks to be shot down as fast as they take their position, and keep marching until the enemy grows tired of the slaughter. Grant, I repeat, is an obstinate fool and a butcher."

Lincoln said, "Well, mother, supposing that we give you command. ... No doubt you would do ... better than any general that has been tried."

Keckley, who had lost a son fighting for the Union, reluctantly had engaged Mrs. Lincoln in a conversation at the time when Mrs. Lincoln received word one of her brothers, Confederate captain Alexander Todd, had been killed. Keckley said she was hesitant to speak of it, but Mrs. Lincoln told Keckley, "You need not hesitate. Of course, it is natural that I should feel for one so nearly related to me, but not to the extent that you suppose. He decided against my husband, and through him against me."

Keckley said she felt relieved, and told of a subsequent conversation with Mrs. Lincoln, who asserted, "Why should I sympathize with the rebels; are they not against me? They would hang my husband tomorrow if it was in their power, and perhaps gibbet me with him. How can I sympathize with a people at war with me and mine?"

Keckley said Mrs. Lincoln objected to being thought Southern in her sympathies, and she also constantly objected to Lincoln walking alone at night.[368]

Union despondency was further fueled when Union forces under General Frans Sigel were defeated at New Market in Virginia's Shenandoah Valley, and the Army of the James under General Benjamin Butler was defeated at Drewry's Bluff. Butler's army had landed at a base of operations at Bermuda Hundred, formed by the James and Appomattox Rivers. Grant ordered him to cooperate with the Army of the Potomac. Grant told General Butler, "Richmond is to be your objective point."[369]

Butler was slow to move and in conflict with his key generals. His delay permitted Confederate general P. T. Beauregard to gather sufficient force to repel the delayed attack. Butler showed a lack of military judgment. At the same time, he was flirting with radical forces intent on derailing Lincoln's nomination. A duplicitous Democrat and political intriguer, Butler was pushed by some for the presidential nomination. Lincoln sounded him out on the vice presidential nomination, but he said no.[370]

Grant on May 12 attacked Lee's line, anchored on the Mule Shoe at Spotsylvania. Grant's army ploughed into the salient. Lee, however, had effectively fortified a shorter and more easily defended position further back. Grant failed to crack the line.

Delayed five more days of rain, Grant assaulted on the right. Again he encountered well-entrenched lines effectively supported by artillery. Grant halted the attack and ordered his forces south to link up with the Army of the James.[371]

Grant balanced several goals. He hoped to keep Lee pinned down and out of the trenches around Richmond. He wanted to get between Lee and Richmond. Lee, while fighting on the defensive in raids and counterattacks, ably reduced the value of Grant's advantage. The apparent numerical advantage of Union troops was an illusion in any case. Many men were diverted to guarding and handling supply lines, communications, and policing of the vast occupied Confederate areas.[372]

As the nation waited hopefully for word on Grant's Virginia campaign and Sherman's thrust toward Atlanta, a fake presidential proclamation surfaced. The bogus proclamation declared May 26 a day of fasting and called for a draft of 400,000 men. Delivered to New York City newspapers, it was published only in the *Journal of Commerce* and the *World*. The *World* was the organ of the Democratic party and the *Journal* avowedly Southern in sympathy.

"Fellow Citizens of the United States," the proclamation began.

> In all seasons of exigency, it becomes a nation carefully to scrutinize its line of conduct, humbly to approach the throne of grace, and meekly implore forgiveness, wisdom and guidance. … With a heavy heart, but an undiminished confidence in our cause, I approach the performance of a duty rendered imperative by my sense of weakness before the Almighty, and of justice to the people. …
>
> In view … of the situation in Virginia, the disaster at Red River, the delay at Charleston, and the general state of the country, I, Abraham Lincoln, do hereby recommend that Thursday, the 26th day of May, A.D., 1864, be solemnly set apart throughout these United States as a day of fasting, humiliation and prayer.

Claiming that the service of some 100,000 enlistees would soon expire, it called forth the aggregate number of 400,000 men between the ages of eighteen and forty-five.

Major General John A. Dix, commander of the Department of the East, wired Seward and asked for proof of authenticity while beginning his own investigation. Since this was the day steamers departed for Europe, Dix moved to call back the newspapers. Reacting at the behest of Seward and Stanton, Lincoln signed an order to suppress the *World* and *Journal*. This was the only recorded suppression of newspapers by Lincoln. Both copies of the order had the signatures of Lincoln and Seward on them.

Upon receipt of Lincoln's order, Dix sent soldiers to arrest *World* editor Manton Marble and the *Journal*'s William C. Prime, but found only the *Journal*'s Gerald Hallock, who was taken to Dix's office. Marble was not located. Prime went to army headquarters, and there he learned from Dix that the arrest order had been recalled. Both Marble and Prime later went to the office of General Dix and told all they knew. Both had posted notices that the proclamation was a forgery.

But at this time Joseph Howard, city editor of the *Brooklyn Daily Eagle*, and Francis A. Mallison of the *World* were in Fort Lafayette. Howard admitted he had authored the bogus proclamation with Mallison. Both had hoped to profit in the market as gold dropped some 10 percent. This was the same Howard who had written the story about Lincoln slinking through Baltimore in the Scotch cap and cape en route to his inauguration. The jailed Mallison revealed all to authorities.

At the other newspapers, the editors had either suspected the proclamation was false or checked and learned the truth. Two days later Dix, with a written confession from Howard in hand, wired Stanton the full details. Lincoln reviewed the wire, chose not to be vindictive, and ordered the suspensions on the two offending newspapers lifted.[373]

Secretary Wells, a former editor himself, recorded in his diary:

> The seizure of the office of the World and Journal of Commerce for publishing this forgery was hasty, rash, inconsiderate, and wrong, and cannot be defended. They are mischievous and pernicious, working assiduously against the Union and the Government and giving countenance and encouragement to the Rebellion, but were in this instance the dupes, perhaps the willing dupes, of a knave and wretch.
>
> The act of suspending these journals, and the whole arbitrary and oppressive proceedings, had its origin with the Secretary of State. Stanton, I have no doubt, was willing to act on Seward's promptings, and the President, in deference to Seward, yielded to it. These things are to be regretted. They weaken the Administration and strengthen its enemies. Yet the Administration ought not to be condemned for the misdeeds of one, or at most two, of its members.[374]

The enraged Marble asserted that troops occupying the *World* office had damaged property and stolen some equipment. "Not until today has

The World been free to speak," he wrote in a letter to Lincoln published in the *World*. "But to those who have ears to hear, its absence has been more eloquent than its columns could ever be. ... Had the Tribune and the Times published the forgery ... would you ... have suppressed the Tribune and the Times? You know you would not."

Self-righteously, Marble asked, "If not why not? Is there a different law for your opponents and for your supporters? Can you, whose eyes discover equality under every complexion, be blinded by the hue of partisanship?" Marble charged that Joseph Howard was a Republican politician and, from childhood, an intimate friend of Republican Henry Ward Beecher, at whose church stump speeches followed prayer. Lincoln later released Howard from prison at the behest of Beecher.

Throughout the North, newspapers both Democratic and Republican editorialized about and gave life to the story. The *Atlas and Argus*, organ of the Democratic Regency in Albany, New York, declared, "We believe that the occasion was seized upon, and the outrage has been persisted in, for the purpose of intimidating the press. The simultaneous seizure of Governor [Samuel] Medary of the Ohio Crisis, upon some false accusation and in violation of law, confirms this suspicion."[375]

CHAPTER XIV

THE BALTIMORE CONVENTION; CHASE RESIGNS; GRANT'S RELENTLESS OFFENSIVE

As Grant pushed at Cold Harbor, a collection of pro-Fremont Germans, viewing Chase as relegated to the fringe, loudly denounced Lincoln. The Fremont men had gathered in October 1863 and adopted a platform. Again in January 1864, the Massachusetts Anti-Slavery Society met, and Wendell Phillips denounced Lincoln's reconstruction program and specifically the "nonenfranchisement" of the Negroes. Missouri Germans remained bitter over Lincoln's treatment of Fremont.

While Fremont lacked support among influential party leaders, the Democratic press kept his movement alive. An organization for a May convention in Cleveland evolved. Key names associated with the movement were Wendell Phillips, Elizabeth Cady Stanton, Lucius Robinson, Emil Pretorius, B. Gratz Brown, Karl Heinzen, and Caspar Butz. Pomeroy too was working the call, but with Chase's candidacy in mind. He sought postponement to reconvene after the Republican convention.[376]

Fewer than four hundred gathered in Cleveland one week before the Baltimore convention to launch the "Radical Democratic Party." Horace Greeley editorialized against a second term for Lincoln. Greeley, however, did not attend, nor did Phillips, who by letter charged the

Lincoln administration was "a civil and military failure." Phillips said if Lincoln was reelected, "I do not expect to see the Union reconstructed in my day, unless on terms more disastrous to liberty then even disunion would be."

Phillips contended that Lincoln's plan "puts all power in the hands of the unchanged white race soured by defeat, hating the laboring class, plotting constantly for aristocratic institutions and 'makes freedom of the Negro a sham,' and perpetuates slavery under a softer name." He urged the convention "demand a reconstruction of States as speedily as possible on the basis of every loyal man, white or black, sharing the land and the ballot." Phillips strongly endorsed Fremont.[377]

After the opening speeches, the Cleveland delegates adopted thirteen resolutions. Key resolutions called for preservation of the Union; the right of free speech; free press and habeas corpus; a constitutional amendment to ban slavery; endorsement of the Monroe Doctrine; expression of gratitude to the military; direct election of the president and vice president; congressional oversight of reconstruction; and a constitutional amendment to a one-term presidency.

Some McClellan men wanted to nominate Grant with Fremont as his running mate. Yet the overwhelming number of Western delegates prevailed and Fremont was nominated. General John Cochran was chosen as his running mate. Fremont, in a prolonged speech, tore into the Lincoln administration. Fremont blasted conduct of the war and held Lincoln responsible for division and disloyalty within the ranks of the party. He endorsed an end to slavery but opposed confiscation in the South.[378]

Meanwhile Grant, coping with heavy casualties, said, "My chief anxiety now is to draw Lee out of his works and fight him in the open field, instead of assaulting him behind his entrenchments." But Lee stayed within his fortified positions. Grant said, "On the 20th Lee showing no signs of coming out of his lines, orders were renewed for a left-flank movement, to commence at night." Like his previous movements, Grant's maneuvers were sideways but steadily toward Petersburg.

The vanguard of the Army of the Potomac marched on the night of May 31 as Sheridan's dismounted cavalry held a position near Old Cold Harbor against Fitzhugh Lee. Many of the Union horses and mules were dying of thirst yet were forced through streams and over dusty roads without halting to drink. The Confederates, who had been threatening Sheridan, pulled back within their entrenchments. By afternoon, the Eighteenth Corps, Army of the James, arrived.

Lee tactically had hoped to destroy Grant's army before he reached the James River. Anticipating Grant's movement to Cold Harbor, Lee arrived there first, fortifying his positions. Horace Porter, Grant's aide-de-camp, chronicled that on the eve of Grant's attack, many of the soldiers were "calmly writing their names and home addresses on slips of paper, and pinning them on the backs of their coats, so that their dead bodies might be recognized … and their fate known to their families."[379]

Grant, in a determined thrust to break Lee's lines, ordered a June 3 general attack on Lee's positions. All felt this would be final struggle of Grant's first campaign. It would be the culmination of the wide and winding path through the tangled Wilderness and the pines of Spotsylvania, a blood-soaked cut from the Rapidan to the Chickahominy. But no further flanking movements were possible. Richmond was dead ahead. Preparations were made and the order given.

"Promptly at the hour named … the men moved from the slight cover of the rifle pits … with steady, determined advance, and there rang out … such a crash of artillery and musketry as is seldom heard in war," Brevet Major General Martin T. McMahon reported. "The time of actual advance was not over eight minutes. In that little period more men fell bleeding as they advanced than in any other like period of time throughout the war." Enemy shell and shot had poured down.

"No troops could stand against such a fire, and the order to lie down was given all along the line," McMahon said. "At points where no shelter was afforded, the men were withdrawn to such cover as could be found, and the battle of Cold Harbor, as to its result at least, was over." A second order called for all three corps to attack, which was done sporadically and failed. A third attack ordered resulted in men "simply renewing the fire … as they lay in position."

"When night came on, the groans and moaning of the wounded, all our own, who were lying between the lines, were heartrending," McMahon said. "Some were brought in by volunteers from our entrenchments, but many remained for three days uncared for beneath the hot summer suns and the un-refreshing dews of the sultry summer nights. The men in the works grew impatient, yet it was against orders and was almost certain death to go beyond our earthworks."[380]

Representative Arnold chronicled:

> During those long days of terrible slaughter the face of the President was grave and anxious, and he looked like one who had lost the dearest member of his own family. I recall one evening late in May, when I met the President in his carriage driving slowly towards the Soldiers' Home. He had just parted from those long lines of ambulances. … He paused as we met, and pointing his hand towards the line of wounded men, he said:
>
> "Look yonder at those poor fellows. I cannot bear it. This suffering, this loss of life is dreadful."

Both Mary Lincoln and the president visited the wounded and were affected. Mary's antagonism toward Grant increased.

Arnold said he reminded Lincoln of a letter he had sent to a suffering friend using these words: "And this too shall pass away. Never fear. Victory will come."

To this Lincoln replied: "Victory will come, but it comes slowly." This, Lincoln knew, meant he would call more men to arms.[381]

While the two armies were entrenched at Cold Harbor, delegates were trooping toward Baltimore by way of Washington, headed to the Republican National Convention. Weed, Davis, and Swett had fretted because it seemed as if Lincoln was letting things run. Yet now Swett wrote to General William W. Orme, his law partner, "Lincoln, out of 150 delegates elected previous to May 25, figures them all up for him." The convention was preparing to run its course, subtly guided by Lincoln.[382]

Days before the Baltimore convention, in an attempt to head off Lincoln's nomination, a mass meeting was called for June 4 in New York City in honor of General Grant. In response to an invitation from Representative F. A. Conkling, Lincoln shrewdly replied:

> Your letter, inviting me to be present at a mass meeting of loyal citizens … for the purpose of expressing gratitude to Lieutenant General Grant for his signal services, was received. … It is impossible for me to attend.
>
> I approve, nevertheless, of whatever may tend to strengthen and sustain General Grant and the noble armies. … My previous high estimate of General Grant has been maintained and heightened by what has occurred in the remarkable campaign he is now conducting. … He and his brave soldiers are now in the midst of their great trial, and I trust that … you will so shape your good words that they may turn to men and guns, moving to his and their support.

As the opposition thrashed about for a candidate who could derail Lincoln's second-term bid, they failed to reconcile their differences or agree on an alternative. Some did not scruple to push Chase to force Lincoln out. The president, however, was ahead of them at every turn, playing his own hand, and confidently saying, "It will all come out right in the end." Yet his partisans were not passive. None of those plotting against him could match his organization, political instincts, and skill.

Ten days before the convention, Lincoln had the nomination sewed up. All the delegates except those from Missouri were pledged to him. Lincoln had skillfully developed his base, handled patronage to build loyalty, and harvested support as needed. The anti-Lincoln *Chicago Times* alleged that "wire pullers and bottle washers had arranged matters." The *New York Times* and *Harper's Weekly* held that the nation was afire with pro-Lincoln sentiment.

Without incurring political debts to Weed and Davis, the president let the thing run. He had reduced deals and pledges to a minimum, although one was a masterstroke on the road to the nomination. Former Ohio governor William Dennison led the effort by which the Ohio legislature endorsed the nomination of Lincoln for reelection. The endorsement ended the Chase candidacy. Dennison had a major role at the convention and eventually joined Lincoln's cabinet.

Taking issue with those who would postpone the convention, Representative Isaac Arnold wrote to the editors of the *New York Evening Post*:

> I am perfectly convinced that the best means of securing a result so essential to success is an early convention, and that nothing would be more likely to prevent such union than its postponement. … If the time should be changed to September, we should see the most violent controversy within … Union ranks … in the history of Politics.
>
> It is … most significant … notwithstanding the efforts made in this city and elsewhere on behalf of prominent and able men in military and civil life; notwithstanding a thoroughly organized, able, ardent, and zealous opposition to President Lincoln … embodying great abilities and abundant means;

> with the co-operation of ... leading newspapers ... and with the aid of ... distinguished ... national leaders ... yet all this has produced no perceptible effect upon public opinion.
>
> The opposition of the President in our own party, talented, eloquent, zealous, and active ... has scarcely produced a ripple on the wave of public sentiment ... so strongly running in favor of Mr. Lincoln's reelection. ... The truth is, the masses of the people, and the soldiers everywhere, trust and love the President. They know his hands are clean and his heart is honest and pure. They know that the devil has not bribe big enough ... which can seduce the integrity of Abraham Lincoln.
>
> Hence the people—the brave, honest, self-denying people ... who have furnished the men, and who are ready to pay the taxes ... to crush the rebellion, and who are determined to establish national unity based on liberty—they are more wise, less factious, and more disinterested than the politicians. Their instinctive sagacity and good sense has already settled the ... question. ... A postponement ... would not prevent ... Lincoln's re-nomination; it might possibly endanger his reelection. ...
>
> The hour is critical. We approach the very crisis of our fate as a nation. With Union and harmony our success is certain. ... We cannot safely change our leaders in the midst of the storm. ... I repeat, we cannot safely or wisely change our leader in the midst of the great events which will not wait for conventions. Such is the instinctive, nearly universal judgment of the people. Let, then, let the convention meet and ratify the choice ... the people have ... so clearly indicated.[383]

The Rev. Robert J. Breckinridge of Kentucky, temporary convention chair, proclaimed open hostility to slavery and urged overthrow of rebellion: "Nothing can be more plain than ... that you are here as representatives of a great nation—voluntary representatives, chosen without forms of law, but as really representing the feeling and principles, and, if you choose, the prejudices of the American People, as if it were written in their laws and already passed by their votes."

In Baltimore, he made it clear he would follow only a Union party to the gates of hell, adding, "For the man you will nominate here for the Presidency of the United States and ruler of a great people, in a great crisis, is just as certain, I suppose, to become that ruler as any thing under heaven is certain before it is done. Moreover ... I suppose it is just as certain now, before you utter it, whose name you will utter—one which will be responded to from one end to the other of this nation."

Governor Dennison, a Lincoln ally who would become postmaster general, was chosen convention president with twenty-three vice presidents, each from a different state, and twenty-three secretaries. By a large vote on the credentials committee report, delegates voted to seat the radical Union delegation from Missouri and delegates of Tennessee, Arkansas, and Louisiana. The dark shadow of some seven thousand Union casualties at Cold Harbor hung over the convention.

Congress had resolved that states that had been in rebellion were barred from participation in national affairs until formally readmitted to the Union. Based on this, Representative Thaddeus Stevens, Pennsylvania, asked that such state delegations not be admitted. The convention, however, agreed to admit them and gave them voting rights. Delegations from the territories of Colorado, Nebraska, and Nevada—and from the states of Florida and Virginia—were seated without voting rights.

New York's Henry Raymond, as chair of the resolutions committee, reported the declaration of principles for the platform. He led off:

> Resolved, That it is the highest duty of every American citizen to maintain, against all their enemies, the integrity of

the Union and the paramount authority of the Constitution and laws of the United States ... laying aside all differences of political opinion ... to do everything in our power ... in quelling by force of arms the rebellion.

Resolved, That we approve the determination of the Government ... not to compromise with rebels, or to offer any terms of peace except such as may be based upon an unconditional surrender of their hostility and a return to their just allegiance to the Constitution and laws of the United States. ... We call upon the government ... to prosecute the war ... to the complete suppression of the Rebellion, in full reliance upon the self-sacrificing patriotism ... of the ... people.

Resolved, that as slavery was the cause and now constitutes the strength of this rebellion, and as it must be always and everywhere hostile to the principles of Republican government, justice and the national safety demand its utter and complete extirpation from the soil of the Republic. ... We uphold ... the acts and proclamations. ... We are in favor ... of such an amendment to the Constitution ... as shall terminate and forever prohibit ... slavery within ... the United States.

Resolved, That the thanks of the American people are due to the soldiers and sailors of the army and navy, who have periled their lives in defense of their country ... that the nation owes ... some permanent recognition of their patriotism and valor, and ample and permanent provision for those of their survivors who have received disabling and honorable wounds in the service ... and that the memories of those who have fallen ... shall be held in ... everlasting remembrance.

Resolved, That we approve and applaud the practical wisdom, the unselfish patriotism, and the unswerving fidelity to the constitution and the principles of American

> liberty with which Abraham Lincoln has discharged, under circumstances of unparalleled difficulty, the great duties and responsibilities of the Presidential office … the measures he has adopted to defend the nation against its open and secret foes … especially the Proclamation of Emancipation.

The resolution also approved the "employment as Union soldiers of men heretofore held in slavery; and that we have full confidence in his determination to carry those and all other constitutional measures, essential to the salvation of the country, into full … effect." A following resolution called for harmony in national councils and declared worthy of trust only those who cordially endorse these principles "which should characterize the administration of the government."

An additional four resolutions called for full protection, in line with the laws of war, for all without regard to color; fostering of foreign immigration, adding wealth, power, and development; speedy construction of the railroad to the Pacific coast; and redemption of the public debt, kept inviolate. It went on to recommend economy and responsibility in public expenditures, and a just system of taxation that would sustain national credit and promote the use of a national currency.

The final resolution defended the Monroe Doctrine, declaring, "The people of the United Sates can never regard with indifference the attempt of any European power to overthrow by force, or to supplant by fraud, the institutions of any republican government on the Western Continent; as menacing to the peace and independence of our nation efforts to obtain footholds for monarchical government, sustained by military force, in near proximity to the United States."

This reflected the alarm felt by Congress and Lincoln over French actions in Mexico. Ferdinand Maximillian Joseph, a member of the house of Habsburg-Lorraine, was proclaimed emperor of Mexico with backing from Napoleon III and Mexican monarchists. Not all foreign governments recognized his rule. Lincoln had pressed Banks to drive westward and halt the flow of supplies into Texas. Banks did undertake from Louisiana an unsuccessful Red River campaign thrust into Texas.

After the resolutions were adopted enthusiastically and unanimously, the motion that Abraham Lincoln be nominated for reelection by acclamation created pandemonium. A vote was called. Lincoln received 497 votes, but the twenty-two votes of the Missouri delegation went for Grant. The chair of the Missouri delegation, explaining they were bound to cast a first vote for Grant, then swiftly moved to switch Missouri's votes to Lincoln, and the nomination was made unanimous.

For the vice presidency, Governor Johnson of Tennessee led off with some two hundred votes on the first call, indicating he was the likely choice. Other states fell in line, and Johnson's vote total climbed to 492, with seventeen for New York's Daniel Dickinson and only nine for Vice President Hamlin. While Lincoln disclaimed any effort to affect the decision, key operatives contended he wanted Johnson. He also had said that when Fessenden joined the cabinet, it meant two from Maine.[384]

Vice President Hannibal Hamlin had played a role in the initial cabinet selection but had little role in the subsequent administration. In 1862, he wrote to Jessie Fremont, who asked help in getting a new army command for her husband, General Fremont, "What can I do? The slow and unsatisfactory movements of the Government do not meet my approbation." The Vice President explained, "I am not consulted … nor do I think there is much disposition … to regard any counsel I may give."

The convention result indicated that Hamlin was sacrificed in 1864 because President Lincoln and Republicans wanted to present a Union face to the electorate. To do this, they turned to Andrew Johnson, a Southern Democrat. An irony of Lincoln's administration was that he worked closely with two men who had once been his severest critics, Seward and Stanton. Seward and Gideon Welles were the only two cabinet secretaries to remain in office throughout Lincoln's presidency.

Chauncey M. Depew, former New York State Republican party chair and president of the Bank of Commerce, was allied with Seward and Weed. Depew claimed a major role in the nomination of Johnson to head off a threat to Seward, because more radical New York delegates wanted favorite son Daniel S. Dickinson. If Dickinson were elected vice president, it would mean two New Yorkers in high office. This would have undermined Seward and possibly forced him out of the cabinet.

Seward conferred with Depew and Judge William H. Robertson of the New York delegation, telling them, "You can quote me to the delegates, and they will believe I express the opinion of the President. While the President wishes to take no part in the nomination of Johnson for Vice President yet he favors Mr. Johnson." Depew and Robertson relayed the message to the delegates who supported Johnson. This was accounted further evidence of Lincoln's subtle but skillful political maneuvering.[385]

Governor Dennison, with members of a special committee, called at the White House and said, "Mr. President: The National Union Convention, which closed its sittings at Baltimore yesterday, appointed a committee, consisting of one from each State, with myself as chairman, to inform you of your unanimous nomination by the convention for election to the Office of President of the United States." The Republican convention had successfully reached out evolving into the Union party.

The governor continued, "I have also the honor of presenting you with a copy of the resolutions or platform adopted by the convention, as expressive of its sense and of the sense of the loyal people of the country which it represents, of the principles and policy that should characterize the administration of the Government in the present condition of the country … the convention, in thus unanimously nominating you … gave utterance to the almost universal voice of the loyal people."

To which Lincoln replied:

> I will neither conceal … nor restrain the expression of gratitude that the Union people … to save and advance the nation, have deemed me not unworthy to remain in my present position. I know no reason to doubt that I shall accept … and yet … I should not declare definitely before reading and considering … the platform. I will say … that I approve the declaration in favor of so amending the Constitution as to prohibit slavery throughout the nation.
>
> When the people in revolt, with the hundred days' explicit notice that they could within those days resume their allegiance without the overthrow of their institutions, and that they could not resume it afterward, elected to stand out, such an amendment of the constitution now proposed became a fitting and necessary conclusion to the final success of the Union cause. Such alone can meet and cover all evils … let us labor to give it legal form and practical effect.

On the same day, the National Union League, which also had met in Baltimore, called upon the president "to congratulate you … and to assure you we will not fail at the polls to give you support." Lincoln replied that he was most grateful for the renewed confidence. As he often did, Lincoln marked the point with a story: "I am reminded in this connection of a story of an old Dutch farmer, who remarked once to a companion that it was not best to swap horses when crossing a stream."

Lincoln knew his reelection depended upon the Union armies and he kept his focus on his role as commander in chief. But there was another aspect.

Douglas Fermer, writing about the *New York Herald* and its publisher, James Gordon Bennett, analyzed another aspect of the war: "The Civil War was doubtless a profoundly individual experience for those who participated in it, but the obvious thing in retrospect is that it heightened the consciousness of nationality among Northerners because it was a communal enterprise—something which involved Americans collectively." Fermer elaborated on this view:

> To open one of the large daily papers of the time such as the [New York] Herald, with its high proportion of war news, its maps, its announcements of activities and meetings to do with the war, its lists of advertisements dealing with military enlistments and equipment, its casualty lists, is to be made aware of that collective enterprise in a tangible way.
>
> It is a truism worth repeating that what is now history was once news. The American public, and indeed government officials, knew the war chiefly through the daily press and shaped their attitude to it accordingly. The war as it happened—the "People's War"—would have been inconceivable without the newspaper.

Lincoln kept a keen eye on the press and the publishers, and his insight helped him politically as newspapers fully reported the war and the politics.[386]

Had the Baltimore convention delegates been less determined, the largely preordained outcome could have been affected by the chilling report of some seven thousand casualties at Cold Harbor. "In the opinion of a majority of its survivors the battle of Cold Harbor never should have been fought," General McMahon later reported. "There was no military reason to justify it. This was the dreary, dismal, bloody, ineffective close" of Grant's first Army of the Potomac campaign.

McMahon said, "Whether the failure was due to faults inherent in the plan, or the belief upon the part of the Lieutenant General that the Army of the Potomac had never been fought to its utmost … is useless to inquire and difficult to determine."

General Grant in his memoirs said of the battle, "Cold Harbor is, I think, the only battle I ever fought that I would not fight over and under the circumstances. I have always regretted that the last assault at Cold Harbor was ever made."[387]

Yet Grant, unbeknown to Lee, amazingly had shifted his entire army south of the James by June 17. This great mass of men, artillery, animals, and baggage had crossed the James on June 14 on a nearly seven-hundred-yards-long pontoon bridge, unprecedented in military annals. An added burden had been to corduroy the marshy approaches so the trains could move onto the bridge. Once the entire army was across the James, the bridge was taken down, and troops reached Petersburg.

As Grant moved south, Lee held and fortified a line from White Oak Swamp to Malvern Hill, remaining in place four days and wondering what had happened to Grant. Lee had been deceived. Lee could not accept Beauregard's report that Grant's whole army was before Petersburg. Except for the tardiness and mistakes of several of Grant's generals, Lee's cause would have been lost then. On June 18, Lee learned that the quick work of General Beauregard had saved Petersburg from capture.[388]

President Lincoln arrived from Washington with the aim of visiting the Union lines at Petersburg. Accompanied by General Grant, Admiral Lee, and Charles A. Dana, the president rode along the lines. Returning, the group passed among a division of black troops who had greatly distinguished themselves fighting under General Smith. Drawn up in double lines on each side of the road, they broke into hearty shouts as the president passed without his hat, knocked off by a limb.

In mid-June, Lee ordered General Jubal Early with an entire corps to drive Union forces from the Shenandoah Valley. Fortunately General Meade discovered that Early was no longer in the lines at Petersburg. A deserter came into the Union camp on July 4 and reported that Early was headed for Maryland. This posed a threat to Washington and Baltimore. The Confederates drove General Hunter's Union forces, which endangered their supply lines at Lynchburg, out of the Shenandoah Valley.[389]

Lincoln, at the Great Central Sanitary Fair in Philadelphia, declared, "War, at the best, is terrible, and this war of ours, in the magnitude and in its duration, is one of the most terrible. It has deranged business, totally in many localities, and partially in all. … It has destroyed property and ruined homes; it has produced a national debt and taxation unprecedented. … It has carried morning to almost every home, until it can almost be said that the 'heavens are hung in black. … ' The Sanitary Commission … (and) the Christian Commission … have contributed to the comfort and relief of the soldiers."

Lincoln noted that such efforts had not been known in any former war. These operations, he said, showed the soldier—"who takes his life in his hands and goes to fight the battles of his country"—was not forgotten and the efforts were voluntary. They gave proof, he said, that "the national spirit of patriotism is even stronger than at the commencement of the rebellion."

It was often asked, he said, when the war would end? "We accepted this war for an object, a worthy object, and the war will end when the object is attained. Under God, I hope it will never end until that time. … General Grant is reported to have said, I am going through on this line if it takes all summer. … I say we are going through on this line if it takes three years more" to restore national unity. When he asked if they would give him more men and equipment, cries of yes erupted.[390]

Late in June, Secretary Wells reported that Representative Moses Odell of Brooklyn handed him a very earnest letter from William C. Bryant, editor of the *New York Evening Post,* with another addressed to the president. It read:

> Mr. Isaac Henderson, who acts as publisher of the Evening Post, has been summarily dismissed from the office of Navy Agent, which he has held for the last three years, and at the same time arrested … on a charge of infamous frauds. …

> I am satisfied that Mr. Henderson will establish his entire innocence at the examination, and you will allow me frankly but respectfully to say, that I should not bear towards you the esteem that I do, did I not feel equally confident, that in that event, your sense of justice will lead you to reinstate him … without delay. … I cannot bear that the lest shadow of suspicion of corrupt or even questionable practice should rest on any person … connected with the Evening Post.

Lincoln wrote to Bryant:

> I know absolutely nothing of the case except as follows: Monday last Mr. Welles came to me with the letter of dismissal already written, saying he thought proper to show it to me before sending it. I asked him the charges. … With as much emphasis as I could I said: "Are you entirely certain of his guilt?" He answered that he was, to which I replied: "Then send the letter."…
>
> Whether M. Henderson was a supporter of my second nomination I neither know nor inquired. … While the subject is up may I ask whether the Evening Post has not assailed me for supposed too lenient dealing with persons charged of fraud & crime?—and that in cases which the Post could know but little of the facts? I shall certainly deal as leniently with Mr. Henderson as I have felt it my duty to deal with others, notwithstanding any newspaper assaults.[391]

With gold now hitting $240, Secretary Wells noted in his diary:

> The Treasury management is terrible, ruinous. Navy requisitions are wantonly withheld for weeks, to the ruin of the contractor. In the end the government will suffer greatly, for persons will not under these ruinous delays deal with the government at ordinary current rates. The pay of the sailors

> and workmen is delayed until they are almost mutinous and riotous. There is no justifiable excuse for this neglect.
>
> But Mr. Chase, having committed blunders in his issues, is now desirous of retiring certain paper, and avails himself of funds of creditors on naval accounts to accomplish this. …
>
> I am daily more dissatisfied with the Treasury management. Everything is growing worse. Chase, though a man of mark, has not the sagacity, knowledge, taste, or ability of a financier. Has expedients, and will break down the government. There is no one to check him.
>
> The President has surrendered the finances to his management entirely. Other members of the Cabinet are not consulted. Any dissent from, or doubts even, of his measures is considered as a declaration of hostility and an embarrassment of his administration. I believe I am the only one who has expressed opinions that questioned his policy … Congress surrenders to his capricious and superficial qualities as pliantly as the President and the Cabinet.
>
> If they do not legalize his projects, the Treasury is to be closed, and under a threat, or something approaching a threat, his schemes are sanctioned, and laws are made to carry them into effect; but woe awaits the country in consequence.

Wells, a hard moneyman, also noted, "Paper, which our financiers make the money standard, is settling down out of sight. This is the result of the gold bill and similar measures, yet Chase learns no wisdom. We are hurrying toward a financial abyss."[392]

Chase at the same time initiated a confrontation with Lincoln, writing, "I respectfully submit to your consideration the name of Maunsell B.

Field for the office of Assistant Treasurer of the United States at the City of New York. Mr. Field was for many years the assistant to Mr. [John J.] Cisco & is fully acquainted with the business of the office. For several months past he has been assistant Secretary of the Treasury. His person character … warrant … that he will perform the duties … well."

Lincoln responded, "Your inclosing a blank nomination for Maunsell B. Field to be Assistant Treasurer at New York was received yesterday. I cannot, without much embarrassment, make this appointment, principally because of Senator Morgan's very firm opposition to it." Lincoln said Morgan found acceptable R. M. Blatchford, Dudley S. Gregory, and Thomas Hilhouse, adding, "It will really oblige me if you will make choice among these three … and send me a nomination for him."

Chase replied immediately to Lincoln's letter. "I shall be glad to have a conversation with you on the subject of the appointment of Mr. Cisco's successor." Chase subsequently added: "I have telegraphed Mr. Cisco begging him to withdraw his resignation and serve at least another quarter. One of the gentlemen named by Senator Morgan is over seventy and the other, I think, over sixty years old, and neither has any practical knowledge of the duties."

Chase said in normal times he would acquiesce, arguing, "But my duty to you & to the country does not permit it now."

Cisco telegraphed Chase, saying, "I cannot resist your appeal & therefore consent to the temporary withdrawal of my resignation."

Chase wrote to Lincoln, enclosing Cisco's telegram and his own resignation, asserting:

> I have just received your note and I have read it with great attention. I was not aware of the extent of the embarrassment. …

> In recommending for office I have sincerely sought to get the best men for the places to be filled without reference to any other classification than supporters and opponents of your administration. Of the latter, I have recommended none, among the former I have desired to know no distinction except degrees of fitness. The withdrawal of Mr. Cisco's resignation ... relieves the present difficulty; but I cannot help feeling that my position here is not altogether agreeable to you ... and it is certainly full of embarrassment and difficulty and painful responsibility to allow in me the least desire to retain it. I think it my duty therefore to enclose to you my resignation. I shall regard it as a real relief if you think proper to accept it; and will most cheerfully tender to my successor any aid he may find useful in entering upon his duties.

Lincoln swiftly replied, "Your resignation of the office of Secretary of the Treasury, sent to me yesterday, is accepted."

A few days later, Wells noted, "All were surprised today with the resignation of Secretary Chase and the nomination of Governor David Tod as his successor."

This time around there were no members of Congress pleading, neither with Chase to withdraw his resignation nor with Lincoln not to accept it, as previously. Some members contended it would be destructive to the Republicans. Chase said Lincoln consulted none of his cabinet, acting completely on his own.

Ohio governor Brough arrived in Washington that same night. Lincoln told him of the resignation of Chase and of his intention to accept the resignation. Brough urged Lincoln to delay to see if he could get the Ohio men together and straighten things out. Lincoln explained, "But this is the third time he has thrown this resignation at me and I do not think I am called on to continue to beg him to take it back, especially when the country would not go to destruction as a consequence."

"This is not simply a personal matter," Brough responded. "The people will not understand it ... I think Ohio can close the breach." Lincoln then said, "I know you doctored the matter up once, but on the whole, Brough, I reckon you had better let it alone this time." Brough asked, "Have you settled who is to be the successor, or is the matter open to advisement?" Cautioning Brough that this was confidential, Lincoln said he had a person in mind but would not reveal a name.

Brough talked for two hours with Stanton, never revealing what he knew. Next morning he was with Stanton, who in the interim had learned of the resignation from Chase. Brough, glancing through Chase's note, discovered that Lincoln planned to name former governor Tod of Ohio. By naming Tod as secretary, Lincoln hoped to neutralize the fallout. Congressional reaction came out strongly against Tod. He was criticized for his lack of financial experience and as a hard-money man.

The next morning Lincoln advised Stanton that an Ohio man must replace Chase, and he was considering former governor Dennison. Stanton told Brough, "You must help me defeat that, Brough, or we are lost. I would not remain Secretary of War an hour after such an appointment." Stanton's concern was that both Tod and Dennison were hard-money men, while Chase had come to accept paper money as the only means of keeping the war machine going and avoiding bankruptcy.[393]

Tod wired Lincoln: "The condition of my health forbids the acceptance of the distinguished position, your offer me," thanking him for the mark of confidence.

Lincoln then nominated Maine Senator William Fessenden, whom the Senate immediately confirmed. Wells said he had the impression Fessenden was an improvement, as he had chaired the Senate Finance Committee. He noted Seward likely was not consulted, as Fessenden had been his avowed opponent of late.[394]

In a memorandum regarding his interview with Fessenden, Lincoln said, "I will keep no person in office in his department, against his express will, so long as I choose to continue him, and he has said to me, that in filling vacancies he will strive to give his wiling consent to my wishes." Lincoln said he expected to give him complete control of his department, but "in questions affecting the whole country there should be full and frequent consultations" including the secretary.[395]

CHAPTER XV

WADE-DAVIS ACT VETO; CONFEDERATE PEACE PLOYS; CONFEDERATE THRUST FROM SHENANDOAH VALLEY INTO MARYLAND

Another vital Union victory, the sinking of the Confederate raider *Alabama* off Cherbourg, France, created jubilation in the cabinet when announced by Secretary Wells. Union captain John A. Winslow of the USS *Kearsarge* had learned that the *Alabama* was at Cherbourg. He entered the harbor and circling the *Alabama*, then withdrew, patrolling outside the harbor. When the *Alabama* emerged, both opened fire, and within an hour the *Alabama* was afire and sank.

The *Alabama* was one of three Confederates warships, together with the *Florida* and *Shenandoah*, built in Scottish shipyards, which had much angered the Union. It was an uncle of future president Theodore Roosevelt, Admiral James Bullock, who successfully negotiated the building and commissioning of the ships that wreaked havoc upon the Union merchant marine. Teddy's mother and grandmother, Bullocks from Georgia, strongly supported the Confederates during the war.

Bullock also arranged for the construction of two Confederate rams in Scottish yards, which alarmed the Union. Seward issued a threat to turn lose an armada of privateers on English shipping if the ships were released. As a result, the two rams were built, but the Confederates were not allowed to take possession. The two ships were later sold to another nation. These losses and the increasing effectiveness of the Union blockade steadily constricted Confederates supply lines.

"New York's merchant marine—badly buffeted in 1857 and 1858—was finished off by Confederate Cruisers. After 284 captures by southern privateers (sixty-four by the … Alabama alone) and the … hike in insurance rates, most American and overseas traders transferred their vessels to foreign flags. The value of goods carried in U.S. vessels sank from $507 million in 1860 to $185 million in 1864. By war's end 3/4th of the commerce in New York's harbor was with foreign lines …"[396]

As Representative Isaac Arnold recorded in his book on the life of Lincoln, "Nothing occurred during the war which more incensed the American people than the ravages upon their commerce by English built cruisers sailing under the rebel flag. Avoiding armed antagonists, they long roamed the sea with impunity, robbing and destroying American merchantmen, and finding refuge and protection, and often supplies, in neutral ports, especially those of Great Britain."[397]

The first session of the Thirty-Eighth Congress adjourned July 4—a session marked by distinct differences and a heavy legislative calendar. A central focus was on both reconstruction legislation and fiscal and monetary policy underpinning the Union war effort. Before Chase's resignation and at Chase's request, Congress passed and the president signed a bill designed to stop speculation and gambling on gold. Some seventeen days later, as gold gyrated up and down, the measure was repealed.

The first half of 1864 saw gold climb from $150 to $250, creating a field day for gold gamblers and sending more gold into hiding or overseas. Lincoln was quoted as crying out that every gold gambler "ought to have his devilish head shot off," yet officials had learned they would have to coexist. Traders on the floor of the gold exchange were heard manifesting rebel sympathy as the price fluctuated with the success or failure of Union armies.[398]

Congress—after considerable debate—adopted a joint resolution imposing a special income tax duty. Representative Justin Morrill of Vermont introduced the measure he said would pay bounties for military enlistment. It provided a special income duty on gain, profits, or incomes at the rate of 5 percent. Expected to bring in some $20 million, it would tax citizens at home or living abroad. "If we enlist by bounties 200,000 men, it will require $20 million to pay bounties," he said.[399]

Representative Davis's proposed amendment to Morrill's bill would levy a 10 percent tax on the average amount of notes in circulation as currency of every bank, company, or association other than national banks. Davis's amendment failed even as he explained:

> My purpose ... is this: We are proposing now to levy an extraordinary and almost oppressive income tax, and if we are to impose additional taxes I wish to see the Government taking steps ... toward the cure of the great evil of its finances.
>
> When the Government now levies two dollars, we only get the value of one dollar. The reason ... is that there are now two or three different currencies, one or other of which has reduced the value of the currency one half or 100 per cent, and more. The reason ... in 1860 the species circulation and the circulation of the banks were about $300 million.

He said that the addition of United States notes and Treasury notes had significantly run up the money in circulation to $951 million. "These figures explain the fact that gold is now two hundred or two hundred and fifty per cent. These figures explain the fact that the enormous revenue we are raising will not pay the expenses of the government. If you will strike out half the currency you will double the value of the revenue. If you will apply the remedy I have offered in my amendment I am willing to go for the additional income tax. If we are to incur two dollars for one dollar—the tax cannot have my vote." It passed without the Davis amendment.[400]

In the wake of Lincoln's December reconstruction proclamation tied to an amnesty oath, Davis had introduced, during the following February, his bill declaring the rebel states lacked a republican form of government and therefore required reorganization. While ignoring the question of "state suicide," the bill took issue with the president, declaring authority over reconstruction was vested exclusively in Congress and not the president, challenging Lincoln's reconstruction measures.

During the acrimonious session, radical members attacked the president and persistently maneuvered to derail his renomination. By a vote of 73 to 59, the Davis bill passed the House on May 4, 1864. Wade too laced the Senate debate with sharp attacks on Lincoln. He brought his similar measure before the Senate, and it passed 18 to 14, after a conference in which the Senate acceded to the House version. The Wade-Davis bill, adopted by Congress, went to the president for his signature.[401]

As the Congress adjourned, presidential secretary John Hay reported that Lincoln was busy signing legislation and reading reported bills. Hay said Senator Sumner, in a state of intense anxiety over the reconstruction measure, and Representative Boutwell, an advocate, feared it would be vetoed. Senator Chandler asked if it had been signed and was told no. Chandler claimed that if the measure were not signed into law, it would create a terrible record on which to campaign.

Lincoln told Chandler the bill had been placed before him a few minutes before Congress adjourned and was a matter of "too much importance to be swallowed in that way." Chandler then said a veto would damage Republicans fearfully in the Northwest, especially in Michigan and Ohio, arguing, "The important point is that one prohibiting slavery in the reconstructed states." Lincoln replied bluntly to Chandler, "That is the point on which I doubt the authority of Congress to act."

Chandler: "It is no more than you have done yourself." Lincoln: "I conceive that I may in an emergency do things on military grounds which cannot be done constitutionally by Congress." Chandler replied,

"Mr. President I cannot controvert your position by argument, I can only say I deeply regret it." He left, and Lincoln said, "I do not see how any of us now can deny and contradict all we have always said, that Congress has no constitutional power over slavery in the states."

Lincoln, Hay recorded, explained what he considered the fatal flaw:

> This bill and this position … seems to me to make the fatal admission that states whenever they please may of their own motion dissolve their connection with the Union. Now we cannot survive that admission I am convinced. If that be true I am not President, these gentlemen are not Congress. I have laboriously endeavored to avoid that question … & thus to avoid confusion and disturbance in our own counsels.
>
> It was to obviate this question that I earnestly favored the movement for an amendment to the Constitution abolishing slavery, which passed the Senate and failed in the House. I thought it much better, if it were possible, to restore the union without the necessity of violent quarrel among its friends, as to whether certain states have been in or out of the Union during the war: a merely metaphysical question and one unnecessary to be forced into discussion.

The president summed up the potential political consequences: "If they choose to make a point upon this I do not doubt that they can do harm. They have never been friendly to me & I don't know that this will make any special difference as to that. At all events, I must keep some consciousness of being somewhere near right: I must keep some standard of principle fixed within myself." Lincoln could not and would not bend on a question central to the just underpinning of his position.[402]

On July 5, the president suspended the writ of habeas corpus and proclaimed martial law throughout Kentucky, stating, "Many citizens of the State of Kentucky have joined the forces of the insurgents and such insurgents have on several occasions entered the said State of Kentucky in large force, and not without aid and comfort furnished by disaffected and disloyal citizens residing therein, and have overborne the civil authorities and made flagrant civil war."

Lincoln further explained that these insurgents were "destroying property and life … and [that] combinations have been formed … with a purpose of inciting rebel forces to renew the said operations of civil war … and thereby embarrass … armies [Sherman's army and his supply lines] now operating in the States of Virginia and Georgia and even to endanger their safety." He made clear it was not to interfere with lawful elections, proceedings of the legislature, or civil actions in the courts.[403]

The president on July 8 issued a proclamation on reconstruction that explained his pocket veto of the Wade-Davis Bill. Lincoln said he was unprepared by a formal approval of the bill "to be inflexibly committed to any single plan of restoration." He further declared himself unprepared to see the free state constitutions of Arkansas and Louisiana, already adopted, set aside and held for naught "thereby repelling and discouraging the loyal citizens who have set up the same."

Lincoln objected to a provision "to declare a constitutional competency in Congress to abolish slavery in States, but am at the same time sincerely hoping and expecting that a constitutional amendment, abolishing slavery throughout the nation, may be adopted." He declared himself "fully satisfied with the system for restoration contained in the bill, as one very proper plan for the loyal people of any State choosing to adopt it," adding that he would assist any using the plan.

Wade and Davis responded with a tart manifesto: "We have read without surprise, but not without indignation, the Proclamation. … The President, by preventing this bill from becoming a law, holds the electoral votes of the Rebel States at the dictation of his personal ambition. If those votes turn the balance in his favor, is it to be supposed that his competitor, defeated by such means, will acquiesce?" If a rebel majority asserted control and sent votes, "Will we not repel his claims?"

The manifesto, in bold defense of Congress, continued, "Were it not that civil war for the Presidency, inaugurated by the votes of Rebel States? Seriously impressed with these dangers, Congress, the proper constitutional authority, formally declared that there are no State Governments in the Rebel States, and provided for their erection at a proper time; and both the Senate and House … rejected the Senators and Representatives chosen under the authority" of the president's plan.

"The President's proclamation 'holds for naught' the judgment, and discards the authority of the Supreme Court, and strides headlong toward the anarchy his Proclamation of the 8th of December inaugurated," they charged.

> If electors for President be allowed to be chosen in either of those States, a sinister light will be cast on the motives which induced the President to "hold for naught" the will of Congress rather than his Government in Louisiana and Arkansas.
>
> A more studied outrage on the legislative authority of the people has never been perpetrated. Congress passed a bill; the President refused to approve it, and then by proclamation puts as much of it in force as he sees fit, and proposed to execute those parts by officers unknown to the law of the United States and not subject to confirmation of the Senate. … The President, after defeating the law, proposes to appoint without law … Military Governors for the Rebel States.

The congressional duo angrily lectured Lincoln on limits of executive power: "The President has greatly presumed on the forbearance which the supporters of this Administration have so long practiced. … But he must understand that our support is of a cause and not of a man; that the authority of Congress is paramount and must be respected; that the whole body of Union men of Congress will not submit to be impeached by him of rash and unconstitutional legislation.

"If he wishes our support, he must confine himself to his executive duties—to obey and execute, not make the laws to suppress … armed Rebellion, and leave the political reorganization to Congress. If the supporters of the Government fail to insist on this, they become responsible … and are justly liable to the indignation of the people whose rights and security … they sacrifice. Let them consider the remedy for these usurpations and … fearlessly execute it."

Wade and Davis drew unanticipated sharp criticism from Gerrit Smith, a wealthy antislavery advocate, who declared, "I have read your protest. It is a strongly reasoned and instructive paper. Nevertheless I regret its appearance. For it will serve to reduce the public goodwill toward Mr. Lincoln; and that is what, just at this time, the public interest cannot afford. It may turn out that Mr. Lincoln is the man for whom it will be vital to the national existence to cast the largest possible vote."

Smith, who had run three times for president, declared it imperative for the Radicals to close ranks for the reelection of Lincoln. "Personally he may not be more worthy of it than Mr. Fremont or Mr. Chase or some other man, who may be nominated. But if, as the election draws near, it shall be seen that he will probably get a larger vote than any other candidate of the uncompromising opponents of the rebellion, then it will be the absolute duty of every one … to vote for him."

Smith made it clear that while some might disagree with Lincoln, the worst consequence would be a lost election:

> The election of a man who would consent to anything short of unconditional surrender of those who, without, even the slightest cause of complaint, have made war upon us, would

> not only be the ruin of our nation, but it would be also the base betrayal of that sacred cause of nationality, which they of one nation owe to those of every other nation, the earth over. …
>
> But no such consequence, nor any other fatal consequence, would there be, should a loyal man of whatever faults be elected—a man who, because he is loyal, would in no event fail to insist on the absolute submission of those who had causelessly rebelled against their country. Hence … we should nevertheless all feel ourselves urged by the strongest possible motives to cast our votes just where they will be likely to contribute most to defeat the compromising or sham peace candidate.

Smith launched into a critique of Lincoln's presidency, calling him able, honest and patriotic, but admitting grave errors on his part. "But who, in his perplexing circumstances, would have been exempt from them?" While contending Lincoln made too much of pleasing border states and peace Democrats, Smith came to his defense, saying, "But in all this he has sought not his own advantage, but the safety of his country from the harm … which … threatened her."

He said Lincoln had imprisoned too few treasonable men, suppressed too few treasonable newspapers, and imposed penalties less severe than appropriate. Smith asserted the City of New York was emphatically a theater of the war: "Thousands there with worse than Southern hearts—for Northern rebels are worse than Southern rebels—are constantly plotting war. … Why, we have immeasurably more to fear from the ever-warring disloyalty of New York and Philadelphia."

Smith declared, "I have virtually said that a treasonable press is capable of working ruin to a country. 'The forged proclamation,' for instance, was a blow at the credit and at the very life of the nation. But for the intervention of the military arm it would have done much evil, and other disloyal presses would have been emboldened to do more. I add that if it were left alone to the civil authority to watch the presses … a considerable share would be teaming with treason."

Honoring the good intentions of Lincoln, Smith would have preferred the firm action of an Andrew Jackson, but argued decisively, "The putting down of the rebellion—that is our one present work. Our absorption in it should be so entire as to leave us no time and no heart for anything which is unnecessary." He condemned Democrats arguing for slavery and abolitionists who put abolition before suppressing rebellion "for the rebellion super adds to all that is bad in slavery."

Noting his abolitionist credentials, Smith said, "I regret your protest … the unseasonable publication of it. There is much truth in it. … But the country cannot now afford to have the hold of Mr. Lincoln on the popular confidence weakened. … The election of no loyal man, however faulty he may be, can destroy the nation. But the election of whatever disloyal man will. Strong as is your dislike … you will not let it stand in the way of your voting to save the country, nor … entreating others."

Harper's Weekly said, "We have read with pain the manifesto … not because of its envenomed hostility to the President, but because of its ill-tempered spirit, which proves conclusively the unfitness of either … for grave counselors in time of national peril. … To charge him with extraordinary and dangerous assumptions of power is childish. … It is simply impossible to make the American people believe that the President is a wily despot, or a political gambler."[404]

James R. Gilmore called upon Lincoln and recommended another effort to negotiate peace. Gilmore and James F. Jacquess asked permission to visit Richmond, and Lincoln's note to Grant allowed them to pass through the lines with ordinary baggage. Lincoln provided a "To Whom It May Concern" pass that they might visit Richmond and confer with Jefferson Davis, but exclusively as private citizens representing no one but themselves. He gave a leave of absence for Col. Jacquess.[405]

Meanwhile, Democrat Samuel J. Tilden and allies arranged to link Greeley with Confederates in Canada, who wanted a meeting with Lincoln. Using Greeley as messenger, the Confederates represented themselves as peace negotiators empowered by Jefferson Davis. Lincoln saw a political trap, knowing the Confederates lacked any such authority.

Greeley wrote to Lincoln:

> I venture to enclose you a letter from our irrepressible friend, Colorado Jewett, at Niagara Falls. I think they deserve attention. Of course, I do not indorse Jewett's positive averment that his friends … have "full power" from J. D., though I do not doubt that he thinks they have. I let that statement stand as simply evidencing that anxiety of the Confederates everywhere for peace.
>
> So much is beyond doubt. … And thereupon I venture to remind you that our bleeding, bankrupt, almost dying country also longs for peace—shudders at the prospect of fresh conscriptions, of further wholesale devastations, and of new rivers of human blood. And a widespread conviction that the Government … are not anxious for Peace … is doing great harm now, and is morally certain, unless removed, to do far greater in the approaching Elections. …
>
> I entreat you … to submit overtures for pacification to the Southern insurgents which the impartial must pronounce frank and generous. If only with a view to the momentous Election soon to occur in North Carolina, and of the Draft to be enforced in the Free States, this should be done at once. I would give the safe conduct … but you may see reasons for declining. … But … do not … fail to make the Southern people comprehend that you and all of us are anxious for peace. …

> Mr. President, I fear you do not realize how intently the people desire any peace consistent with the national integrity and honor. … With United States stocks worth but forty cents in gold per dollar, and drafting about to commence on the third million of Union soldiers, can this be wondered at? I do not say that a just peace is now attainable, though I believe it to be so. But, I do say, a frank offer by you to the insurgents of terms … will … prove an immense and sorely needed advantage.

Greeley declared not only would this advantage the national cause, but "may save us from a northern insurrection. … I beg you to invite those now at Niagara to exhibit their credentials …" He enclosed a letter from William Cornell (Colorado) Jewett saying he had just left Hon. Geo N. Sanders of Kentucky on the Canada side and "that two ambassadors—of Davis & Co are now in Canada—with full & complete powers for a peace & Mr. Sanders requests that you come on immediately."

Lincoln replied explaining his position to Greeley and laying forth his views on saving thc union. "Your letter of the 7th, with enclosures, received. If you can find any person anywhere professing to have any proposition of Jefferson Davis in writing, for peace, embracing the restoration of the Union and abandonment of slavery, what ever else it embraces, say to him he may come to me with you, and that if he really brings such proposition, he shall … have safe conduct, with the paper (and without publicity if he choose) to the point where you shall have met him."

Lincoln added appropriately that if there were two or more persons with such information, the same applied.

Subsequently Greeley said he doubted the rebels would open their best terms to him, adding, "I have neither purpose nor desire to be made a confidant, far less an agent in such negotiations. But I do deeply realize that the Rebel chiefs achieved a most decided advantage in proposing … to have A. H. Stephens visit Washington as a peacemaker, and being rudely repulsed. And I am anxious that the ground lost … by that mistake shall somehow be regained in season."

This referred back to the Confederate effort, just prior to the Battle of Gettysburg, by Confederate vice president Alexander H. Stephens to proceed to Washington. That came through Admiral Samuel E. Lee. Stephens contended he was the bearer of "a communication in writing from Jefferson Davis Commander-in-Chief of the land and Naval forces of the Confederate States to Abraham Lincoln Comd'r-in-Chief of the land and Naval forces of the United States." Lincoln did meet later with Stephens.[406]

When Greeley wrote again, Lincoln dispatched his secretary, John Hay, with his answering letter. "I am disappointed that you have not already reached here with those Commissioners, if they would consent to come, on being shown my letter to you. … Show that and this [letter] to them; and if they will come on the terms stated in the former, bring them. I not only intend a sincere effort for peace, but I intend that you shall be a personal witness that it is made."

Hay wired Lincoln that Greeley did not think the letter sufficient protection. Lincoln authorized him to write a more definitive order, which Hay did. "The President of the United States directs that the four persons whose names follow, towit: Hon. Clement C. Clay, Jacob Thompson, Prof. James B. Holcombe, George N. Sanders: Shall have save conduct with the Hon. Horace Greeley … exempt from arrest … during their journey … to Washington. … By order of the President."[407]

Hay arrived at the International House at Niagara and met Greeley. Hay insisted, as Lincoln and Seward thought it necessary, that Greeley and he cross over the border to the Clifton House. At the door, they met George Saunders, described by Hay as "a seedy looking rebel with grizzled whiskers & a flavor of old cho." Greeley told the rebels, "Major Hay has come from the President of the United States to deliver you a communication in writing & to add a verbal message."

Hay said in an exchange, Saunders told Greeley, "I wanted old Bennett to come up but he was afraid to come." This referred to James Gordon Bennett, publisher of the *New York Tribune*. Obviously seeking a propaganda advantage, the Confederate intelligence group—well versed in Union government and politics as they had held prewar government posts—maintained a lively intercourse with many former political associates and with newspaper publishers and editors in the North.[408]

Jaquess, a Methodist minister commanding a Union regiment, and Gilmore, a journalist, met with Jefferson Davis, who insisted the only terms for peace were the complete independence of the Confederacy. When Gilmore reported to the president, Lincoln said it was imperative that Davis's position be made known at once: "It will show the country that I didn't fight shy of Greeley's Niagara business without a reason … this may be worth as much to us as half a dozen battles."[409]

Meanwhile Early, with General John C. Breckinridge, the nation's former vice president, among his officers, stormed through Maryland, destroying mills, workshops, and factories and driving fleeing citizens into Baltimore and Washington. On July 6, General Grant became convinced Washington was the objective. Dana was sent to Washington with orders to keep Grant informed.

General Grant wired specific instructions aimed at forcing Early back and he also told Halleck: "Forces enough to defeat all that Early has with him should get in his rear south of him, and follow him up sharply, leaving him to go north, defending depots, towns &c, with small garrisons and the militia. If the President thinks it advisable that I should go to Washington in person, I can start in an hour leaving everything here on the defensive."[410]

To this the president replied:

> Your dispatch to General Halleck, referring to what I may think in the present emergency, is shown me.

> General Halleck says we have absolutely no force here fit to go to the field. He thinks … the hundred day men, and invalids … can defend Washington … Besides these, there are about eight thousand not very reliable, under Howe at Harper's Ferry, with Hunter approaching that point. … Wallace with some odds and ends, and part of what came up with Ricketts, was so badly beaten yesterday at Monocacy, that what is left can attempt no more than to defend Baltimore.
>
> What we shall get in from Penn. & N.Y. will scarcely worth counting, I fear. Now what I think is that you should provide to retain your hold where you are certainly, and bring the rest with you personally, and make a vigorous effort to destroy the enemy's force in this vicinity. I think there is really a fair chance to do this if the movement is prompt.

He added that his letter was not an order. Grant dispatched a whole corps commanded by General Horatio G. Wright and some three thousand other troops.

Grant said the force, with another division of the Nineteenth Corps, "will be able to join Wright in rear of the Enemy. … I think on reflection it would have a bad effect for me to leave here, and with General [Edward O.C.] Ord at Baltimore and Hunter and Wright with the forces following up the enemy, could do no good. I have great faith that the enemy will never be able to get back with much of his force." Early saw the newly arrived troops file into fortifications and backed off.

Lincoln stood on the parapets of Fort Stevens as the saddled Early, leading his troops, sat not too far distant, assessing the situation. Breckinridge also watched. For the first time Lincoln witnessed Confederate fire and men fall wounded. An officer three feet from him was fatally wounded. Nicolay and Hay reported that the president held his place amidst the whizzing bullets until finally "General Wright peremptorily represented to him the needless risk he was running."

Lincoln called Grant's response "very satisfactory," adding, "The enemy will learn of Wright's arrival, and then the difficulty will be to unite Wright and Hunter, south of the enemy before he will re-cross the Potomac." As Dana explained, "The pursuit of Early proved, on the whole an egregious blunder." General Halleck declined to give orders, and the result was there was no overall command. Early escaped south with several thousand cattle, horses, and mules and large amounts of plunder.[411]

"Today," Bates recorded, "I spoke my mind very plainly, to the Prest (sec). about the ignorant imbecility of the late military operations, and my contempt for General Halleck."

Stanton was quoted as saying, "Mrs. Lincoln, I intend to have a full length portrait of your husband standing on the ramparts of Fort Stevens overlooking the fight."

She retorted, "I can assure you … Mr. Secretary, if I had had a few ladies with me the Rebels would not have been permitted to get away."[412]

Displeasure was widespread, as Stanton respectfully referred to Lincoln a letter from General Halleck that said, "I am informed by an officer of rank and standing in the military service that the Hon. M. Blair, Post Master Genl, in speaking of the burning of his home in Maryland … said, in effect, that 'the officers in command about Washington are poltroons; that there were not more than 500 rebels on the Silver Spring road and we had a million of men in arms."

Halleck alleged that Blair called the action "a disgrace" and had said, "General Wallace was in comparison with them far better as he would at least fight." Given that officers in and about Washington, as well as the War Department, had devoted their time and energy and periled their lives "it is due to them that it should be known whether such wholesale denouncement & accusation by a member of the cabinet received the sanction and approbation of the President. If so," Halleck concluded, "the names of the officers accused should be stricken from the rolls of the Army; if not, it is due to the honor of the accused that the slanderer should be dismissed from the cabinet."

The president responded to Stanton:

> The General's letter, in substance demands of me that if I approve the remarks, I shall strike the names of those officers from the rolls; and if I do not approve them, the Post Master General shall be dismissed from the Cabinet.
>
> Whether the remarks were really made I do not know; nor do I suppose such knowledge is necessary to a correct response. If they were made I do not approve them; and yet, under the circumstances, I would not dismiss a member of the Cabinet therefor. I do not consider what may have been said in a moment of vexation at so severe a loss, is sufficient ground for so grave a step. Besides this, truth is generally the best vindication against slander.

Lincoln, who was fielding a vast number of charges and countercharges, as well as assaults directed at him personally, asserted bluntly, "I propose continuing to be myself the judge as to when a member of the Cabinet shall be dismissed." The president read his statement to his assembled cabinet. This failed to temper the hostility directed by Stanton and Seward toward Blair, who also increasingly came in for harsh criticism and opposition from Republicans, chiefly radicals.[413]

In a foray into Pennsylvania, the Confederate cavalry rode into Chambersburg and made a demand for $100,000 in gold or $500,000 in greenbacks. When the residents said they could not pay that sum, an officer read an order from General Early that upon refusal to pay, the town would be burned "in retaliation for the depredations committed by General Hunter." First the town buildings were set afire, and cotton balls soaked in turpentine were used to fire shops and houses.

The Confederates, ten miles to the east of the town, rode to the ironworks of Thad Stevens. There they fired a large charcoal furnace, forge, rolling mill, and coalhouse shops worth more than $50,000. The *Chambersburg Repository* reported that when General Early was told the destruction would harm scores of poor laborers, he replied, "Mr. Stevens was an 'enemy of the South, in favor of confiscating their property and arming their Negroes, and the property must be destroyed.'"[414]

As Early moved south, Grant wired Sherman, "The attempted invasion of Maryland having failed ... they are now returning, with possibly 25,000 troops. It is not improbable, therefore, that you will find ... reinforcements in your front. ... I advise, therefore, that if you can get to Atlanta you set about destroying the railroads as far to the east and south of you ... collect all the stores ... for your own use, and select a point you can hold until help can be had."

Lincoln told Grant, "In your dispatch of yesterday to Gen. Sherman, I find the following, towit: 'I shall make a desperate effort to get a position here which will hold the enemy without the necessity of so many men.' Pressed as we are by lapse of time, I am glad to hear you say this; and yet I do hope you may find a way that the effort shall not be desperate in the sense of great loss of life." Lincoln then issued a proclamation calling for a renewed draft of 500,000 men.[415]

Sherman, chronicling the advance of his army, moved deep into Georgia, forcing Confederate general Joseph E. Johnston back across the Chattahoochee River. Sherman had this to say of Johnston: "No officer or solider who ever served under me will question the generalship of ... Johnston. His retreats were timely, in good order, and he left nothing behind." Sherman had advanced into the enemy's country 120 miles along a single-track railroad, and now Atlanta was in sight.

While Johnston's force numbered 62,000, Sherman explained that the single-track rail he used "had to bring clothing, food, ammunition, everything requisite for 100,000 men and 23,000 animals." In mid-July, the Confederate government, in the words of Sherman, "rendered us most valuable service" when Davis and Braxton Bragg, against the advice of Lee, relieved Johnston and gave the command to General John Bell Hood, who Sherman described as known to be a fighter.

Sherman was pleased with the change, noting that Hood had graduated forty-fourth in the same class with two of his generals, James McPherson and Schofield, were ranked first and seventh. Tragically, Sherman had lost McPherson, killed in battle.

While confident of his superior force, Sherman found difficulty in relying on poorly constructed railroads extending some five hundred miles back to Louisville, Kentucky. Sherman maneuvered to fight in open country rather than attacking the enemy in prepared defensive parapets.[416]

Chapter XVI

Coping with Greeley, the Herald's Bennett, and Weed; War Democrats

Still coping with Greeley, Lincoln clarified his position in a "To Whom It May Concern" statement: "Any proposition which embraces the restoration of peace, the integrity of the whole Union, and the abandonment of slavery, and which comes by and with an authority that can control the armies now at war against the United Sates will be received and considered by the Executive government ... and will be met by liberal terms on other substantial and collateral points."[417]

Lincoln picked up on Saunders's remark to Greeley, overheard by Hay, that the Confederates had tried to enlist Bennett in the negotiations. A canny Scott and one-time Roman Catholic seminarian, Bennett, who was in Charleston at the time of the Nat Turner slave rebellion, was influenced by that event. Bennett's *Herald* and Greeley's *Tribune* were the most widely read newspapers in the nation.

Thus Lincoln wrote to Abram Wakeman, in a letter marked private but for Bennett, "The men of the South, recently ... at Niagara Falls, tell us distinctly that they are in the confidential employment of the rebellion; and they tell us as distinctly that they are not empowered to offer terms of peace. Does any one doubt that what they are empowered to do, is to assist in selecting and arranging a candidate and a platform for the Chicago convention?"

Lincoln asserted confidential employment had to come from Jefferson Davis and the Confederates. "Who could have given them this confidential employment but he who only a week since declared to Jaquess and Gilmore that he had no terms of peace but the independence of the South—the dissolution of the Union? Thus the present presidential contest," Lincoln asserted, "will almost certainly be no other than a contest between a Union and a Disunion candidate, disunion certainly following the success of the later. This issue is a mighty one for all people and all time."

Lincoln closed by saying that "whoever aid the right, will be appreciated and remembered,"

Wakeman replied, "Your excellent letter was duly received. I have read it with proper explanation to Mr. B. He said … that so far as it [was] released to him, 'It did not amount to much.'" Wakeman said he hoped to avoid writing further, but would if necessary elaborate as he would be in Washington the next week.

Bennett had savaged the Lincoln administration yet despised the radicals and moved adroitly focused on the self-interest of the *Herald.* He also taunted Horace Greeley's *New York Herald* and the pro-Lincoln *New York Times* edited by Henry J. Raymond. Bennett also believed the Democrats would be helped if race was the issue, likely because of his Charleston experience. Lincoln wisely humored Bennett, although he did not hesitate to take issue with him diplomatically.

With the Democrats in power, Bennett claimed a constitutional amendment would not involve such "fallacies as Negro equality, political or social, with the white race." He joined in branding all abolitionists as "racial amalgamationists." Yet Bennett quietly backed off his opposition, as Lincoln shrewdly dangled the French ministry before him. Lincoln also reiterated that it was important to humor Bennett, given the scope and reach of the *Herald*, both in the United States and in Europe as well.

Wakeman told Lincoln, "A word on another matter. I am fearful our hold upon Mr. Weed is slight. He evidently has his eye upon some other candidate. I deeply regret this, for against him it will be difficult to carry New York. Now I don't know, precisely, what he asked when he last saw you, but I think, so far as could without compromising principle, I would yield to his wishes. Can't this be done?"

Based on information from Wakeman, Lincoln wrote this memorandum:

> Hon. Clement C. Clay, one of the Confederate gentlemen … has prepared a Platform and an Address to be adopted by the Democracy at the Chicago Convention, the preparing of these, and conferring with the democratic leaders in regard to the same, being the confidential employment of their government, in which he, and his confreres, engages. The following planks are in the platform:
>
> 1. The war to be further prosecuted only to restore the Union as it was, and only in such manner, that no further detriment to slave property shall be effected.
> 2. All Negro soldiers and seamen to be at once disarmed and degraded to menial service in the Army and Navy; and no additional Negroes to be, on any pretense whatever, taken from their masters.
> 3. All Negroes not having enjoyed actual freedom during the war to be held permanently as slaves; and whether those who shall have enjoyed actual freedom during the war, shall be free to be a legal question.

The following … are in the address: Let all who are in favor of peace; of arresting the slaughter of our countrymen, of saving the country from bankruptcy & ruin, of securing food & raiment & good wages for the laboring classes; of disappointing the enemies of Democratic & Republican Government who are rejoicing in the overthrow of their proudest monuments; of vindicating our capacity for self government, arouse and maintain these principles, and elect these candidates.

Lincoln then quoted Clay's comment about him: "The stupid tyrant who now disgraces the Chair of Washington and Jackson could, any day, have peace and restoration of the Union; and would have them, only that he persists in the war merely to free the slaves."

The Union secret service, among its successes, placed a spy who became a trusted Confederate courier of correspondence with the Canadian intelligence operation. This provided to Lincoln the reports and directions of Clay.[418]

Another spy, a peddler named Morse, went back and forth, bringing valuable information but also taking goods, properly inspected, that people wanted. In October he went to Baltimore, collecting some $25,000 of goods from Baltimore merchants. When inspected by the War Department's chief detective, the detective found uniforms and other military goods with bills showing the peddler had bought the goods. The result was that the goods were confiscated and Morse went to prison.

It turned out merchants in Baltimore had partnered with him, and Secretary Stanton said he would arrest every one. Dana sent an assistant adjutant general to Baltimore, who reported the case would involve the arrest of two hundred citizens. When Dana revealed this to Stanton, he determined to arrest them. The next morning, ninety-seven leading citizens of Baltimore were in jail. Immediately a deputation from Baltimore called on President Lincoln, demanding that the arrested be set free.

Lincoln sent the Baltimore delegation to Stanton, to whom they detailed the circumstances and objected to the outrage of what they called unjustified arrests. Dana reported Stanton then made "one of the most eloquent speeches" describing the beginning of the war, saying that being beaten in an election did not justify war to destroy a government and declaring that half a million young men had died as a result. He showed them bills for the goods. Without responding, they went away.[419]

Lincoln fielded resignations from the federal service consistent with his vigorous reelection campaign, making it clear he would not retain those who would undermine his efforts. The case of Charles Gibson, appointed solicitor of the United States Court of Claims in 1861, was a case in point. Gibson, through James C. Welling, clerk of the Court of Claims, sent a letter of resignation in which he declared that support for Lincoln's reelection was inconsistent with his principles.

Hay, writing to Welling, said he had placed the resignation before the president, noting:

> He has read the letter, and says he accepts the resignation, as he will be glad to do with any other, which may be tendered, as this is, for the purpose of taking an attitude of hostility against him. He says he was not aware that he was so much indebted to Mr. Gibson for having accepted the office at first, not remembering that he ever pressed him … or that he gave it … than … upon request.
>
> He thanks Mr. Gibson for his acknowledgment that he has been treated with personal kindness and consideration; and he says he knows of but two small draw-backs upon Mr. Gibson's right to still receive such treatment, one of which is that he never could learn of his giving much attention to the duties of his office, and the other is the studied attempt of Mr. Gilson's to stab him.

Welling said he was instructed to give a copy of Gibson's letter to the public press.[420]

General Hunter, at Harpers Ferry with his own set of problems, wired Halleck, "General [Horatio G.] Wright reports his corps so much fatigued and scattered as to be unable to move this morning. The whole command is now encamped at Halltown, but my information is so unreliable and contradictory that I am at a loss to know in which direction to pursue the enemy." Grant, concerned over the lack of direction, knew that his pressure on Lee kept Lee from providing Early vital reinforcements.

Grant had proposed to combine the departments of Susquehanna, Washington, Middle Virginia and West Virginia under General George C. Meade, prompting Lincoln to propose they meet at Fortress Monroe. Stanton wrote to Halleck:

> Grant having signified that, owing to the difficulties and delay of communication between his headquarters and Washington, it is necessary that in the present emergency military orders must be issued directly from Washington. …
>
> The President directs me to instruct you that all the military operations for the defense of the Middle Department, the Department of the Susquehanna, the Department of Washington and the department of West Virginia, and all the forces in those departments, are placed under your command, and that you will be expected to take all military measures necessary for defense against any attack of the enemy and for his capture and destruction.

He did not mention Meade.

Then on August 1, Grant took the initiative and wired to Halleck, "I am sending General Sheridan for temporary duty whilst the enemy is being expelled from the border. Unless General Hunter is in the field in person, I want Sheridan put in command of all the troops in the field, with instructions to put himself south of the enemy, and follow him to the death."

Wanting a meeting with Grant, Lincoln was unable to make a proposed trip to Fortress Monroe, but noting the order, he wrote to Grant, "I have seen your dispatch, in which you say, 'I want Sheridan put in command of all troops in the field with instructions to put himself south of the enemy, and follow him to the death. ... ' This, I think, is exactly right, as to how our forces should move. But please look over the dispatches you may have received from here, even since you made that order, and discover, if you can, that there is any idea in the head of anyone here, of 'putting our army south of the enemy. '"

Lincoln concluded forcefully, "I repeat to you it will neither be done nor attempted unless you watch it every day, and hour, and force it."

Grant wired Lincoln, "I will start in two hours for Washington & will spend a day with the Army under Genl Hunter." Sheridan arrived in Washington the next day, and was ordered to meet Grant at Monocacy Junction. This established Grant's control and took the War Department out of the middle—moves essential for success.[421]

Returning to his correspondence with Greeley, Lincoln received from Raymond a copy of a recent Greeley *Tribune* article saying he would gladly consent to the publication of the correspondence with Lincoln. Lincoln replied to Raymond, "I have proposed to Mr. Greeley that the Niagara correspondence be published, suppressing only the parts of his letters over which the red-pencil is drawn. ... He declines giving his consent ... unless these parts be published with the rest."

Lincoln explained, "I have concluded that it is better for me to submit, for the time, to the consequences of the false position in which I consider he has placed me, than to subject the country to the consequences of publishing these discouraging and injurious parts. I send you this, and the accompanying copy, not for publication, but merely to explain to you, and that you may preserve them until their proper time shall come." Greeley remained bitterly opposed to Lincoln's policy and reelection.[422]

Lincoln wrote to Greeley, "Herewith is a full copy of the correspondence, and which I have had privately printed, but not made public. The parts of your letter which I wish suppressed, are only those which, as I think, give too gloomy an aspect to our cause, and those which present the carrying to elections as a motive of action."

Turning to Greeley's persistent contention that Lincoln had rebuffed peace efforts of Confederate Vice President Alexander Stephens, Lincoln said:

> I can only say that he sought to come to Washington in the name of the "Confederate States," in a vessel of "The Confederate States Navy," and with no pretense even, that he would bear any proposal for peace, but with language showing that his mission would be Military, and not civil, or diplomatic. Nor has he … since pretended that he had terms of peace, so far as I know. … On the contrary, Jefferson Davis has … declared that Stephens had no terms of peace.
>
> I thought we could not afford to give this quasi acknowledgement of the independence of the Confederacy, in a case where there was not even an intimation of any thing for our good. Still, as the parts of your letters relating to Stephens contain nothing worse than a questioning of my action, I do not ask a suppression.

Greeley retorted, "I cannot see that you are at all implicated in my anxiety that a generous offer … be made and a kindly spirit evinced."[423]

Grant wired to Halleck, "If there is any danger of an uprising … to resist the draft or for any other purpose our loyal Governors ought to organize the militia at once to resist. If we are to draw troops from the field to keep the loyal Sates in harness it will prove difficult to suppress the rebellion in the disloyal States. My withdrawal now from the James River would insure the defeat of Sherman. Twenty thousand men sent to him at this time would destroy the greater part of Hood's army."

Grant said that reinforcing Sherman would leave men for other required needs, adding:, "General [Samuel P.] Heintzelman can get from the Governors of Ohio, Indiana and Illinois a militia organization that will deter the discontented from committing any overt act." He urged the President to call on them to "organize thoroughly to preserve the peace until after the election."

Lincoln agreed, wiring to Grant, "Hold on a with bull-dog grip, and chew & choke, as much as possible."[424]

Charles D. Robinson, editor of the Green Bay, Wisconsin, *Advocate* and a war Democrat, raised the issue of keeping war Democrats in the fold with Lincoln:

> The Niagara Falls "Peace" movement was of no importance whatever, except that it resulted in bringing out your declaration, as we understand it, that no steps can be taken towards peace ... unless accompanied with an abandonment of slavery. This puts the whole war question on a new basis ... leaving us no ground to stand upon.
>
> I venture to write you this letter ... not for the purpose of finding fault with your policy ... but in the hope that you may suggest some interpretation of it, as will ... make it tenable ground on which we War Democrats may stand—preserve our party --consistently support the government—and continue to carry also to its support those large numbers of our old political friends who stood by us up to this time.

He sent the letter through his friend, Governor Alexander W. Randall.

Lincoln quoted his Greeley letter: "I shall do more whenever I shall believe doing more will help the cause." He elaborated:

> The way these measures were to help the cause, was not to be by magic, or miracles, but by inducing the colored people to come bodily over from the rebel side to ours. … I am sure you would not desire me to say, or to leave an inference, that I am ready, whenever convenient, to join in re-enslaving those who have served us in consideration of our promise.
>
> As matter of morals, could such treachery … escape the curses of Heaven, or of any good man? As matter of policy, to announce such a purpose, would ruin the Union cause. … All recruiting of colored men would instantly cease, and all colored men … would instantly desert us … rightfully too. Drive back to the support of the rebellion the physical force which the colored people now give … and neither the present, nor any coming administration, can save the Union. …
>
> It is not the giving of one class for another. It is simply giving a large force to the enemy, for nothing in return. In addition to what I have said, allow me to remind you that no one, having control of the rebel armies, or, in fact, having any influence whatever in the rebellion, has offered, or intimated a willingness to, a restoration of the Union, in any event, or on any condition whatever. Shall we be weak enough to allow the enemy to distract us with an abstract question?[425]

In a penned but unsent reply, Lincoln tested the arguments for war Democrat support, but Frederick Douglass counseled Lincoln against sending it. Emphatically agreeing regarding the importance of black soldiers, Douglass said it "would be given a broader meaning than you intend to convey, it would be taken as a complete surrender of your anti-slavery policy, and do you serious damage." Lincoln's own convictions concurred with those of Douglas, and he did not to reply.

Confronting the dangers in a victory of Democrats, Lincoln told Douglass the "slaves are not coming so rapidly and so numerously to us as I had hoped." Douglass explained that the "slaveholders knew how to keep such things from their slaves." Lincoln appealed to Douglass, himself an escaped slave who was well educated and had become a leader in the abolitionist movement, to organize a group of black scouts to go into rebel lines and spread the word.

Sometime later, Douglass remembered Lincoln words as showing "a deeper moral conviction against slavery than I had even seen before in anything spoken or written by him." Douglass then quoted these words of Lincoln: "Douglass, I hate slavery as much as you do, and I want to see it abolished altogether." Douglass also told General John Eaton that Lincoln "treated me as a man, he did not let me feel for a moment that there was any difference in the color of our skins."

Here again, as at many junctures during his presidency, Lincoln was faced with a clear question of morality. Within his own party, political factions—including Greeley—were demanding negotiations and a return to war for the Union alone. Yet Lincoln turned to Douglass and held his ground. Rather than yield, he took up his pen in his studied method and put words on paper. At no point did he back off his reiterated conviction, calling for equality and freedom for all, regardless of race.

Lincoln made a broader appeal to the 164th Ohio Regiment: "I wish it might be more generally and universally understood what the country is now engaged in. … This form of Government and every form of human right is endangered if our enemies succeed. … There is involved in this struggle … whether your children and my children shall enjoy the privileges we have enjoyed." This was one of several speeches Lincoln made to soldiers of regiments passing through Washington.[426]

Lincoln's Robinson memorandum, as drafted, evolved from an interview with Randall and Judge Joseph T. Mills. Mills recorded the interview in his diary:

> My own experience has proven to me, that there is no program intended by the Democratic Party but that will result in the dismemberment of the Union. But General McClellan is in favor of crushing out the rebellion & he will probably be the Chicago candidate, adding the rebel armies cannot be destroyed by democratic strategy.
>
> It would sacrifice all the white men of the North to do it. … You cannot conciliate the South, when the mastery & control of millions of blacks makes them sure of ultimate success … that they see they can achieve their independence. The war Democrat depends on conciliation. He must confine himself to that policy entirely. If he fights at all in such a war as this he must economize life & use all the means which God & nature puts in his power. … We have to hold territory.

Describing Lincoln, Judge Mills asserted:

> The President appeared to be not the pleasant joker I had expected to see, but a man of deep convictions & an unutterable yearning for the success of the Union cause. His voice was pleasant—his manner earnest & cordial. As I heard a vindication of his policy from his own lips, I could not but feel that his mind grew in stature like his body, & that I stood in the presence of the great guiding intellect of the age … fit to bear the weight of mightiest monarchies.
>
> His transparent honesty, his republican simplicity, his gushing sympathy for those who offered their lives for their country, his utter forgetfulness of self in his concern for his country, could not but inspire me with confidence, that he was Heavens instrument to conduct his people thro this red sea of blood to a Canaan of peace & freedom … We parted … with firmer purpose to sustain the government,

> at who's head there stands a man who combines in his person ... all that is hopeful in progress.[427]

Radicals praised the Niagara manifesto, yet many Democrats objected strongly. Maryland senator Reverdy Johnson, a conservative Unionist, demanded, "Could there be a refusal so insane, so reckless, so inhuman, so barbarous?" Johnson had served as attorney general under President Zachary Taylor and was a legal colleague of Confederate secretary of state Judah P. Benjamin in prewar days. Johnson, ironically, was a potent voice in the Senate favoring adoption of the Thirteenth Amendment, most likely consistent with Maryland sentiment.

The Democratic *Cincinnati Enquirer* declared the manifesto "a finality which ... will preclude any conference for a settlement. Every soldier ... that is killed will lose his life not for the Union ... but for the Negro." And from New Yorker George Templeton Strong, a strong war supporter, came an assessment that it "may cost him [Lincoln] his election. By declaring that abandonment of slavery is a fundamental article ... he has given the disaffected and discontented a weapon that doubles their power."[428]

CHAPTER XVII

AUGUST GLOOM AND THE BLIND MEMORANDUM; POLITICS ESCALATES

A perceived military stalemate following a heavy flow of casualties into Washington and a call for a new draft affected the national political mood. Lincoln was plagued, as Wells explained, by "an accumulation of disheartening difficulties, internal and external in the free States—differences such as loyal and disloyal, democrat and republican, republican and radical, personal and sectional—had clouded the administration during the spring and summer."

He added:

> Whilst putting forth the utmost energies of the nation to maintain the Union, which for three years the rebels had, with immense armies, striven to dissolve, the President, from the day of his inauguration, encountered in the free States the steady opposition of the broken, but yet powerfully organized Democratic Party, which had been in political sympathy with the rebels prior to his election, and which still affiliated with its old party associates [in the Confederacy].
>
> Added to these, and quite as discouraging and more disheartening than either ... were the embarrassing intrigues of discontented and aspiring factions among Republicans,

> growing out of the approaching ... election and radical claim for legislative supremacy in the conduct of the government. The opportunity was seized, not only by personal aspirants, but by the disaffected ... who, disagreeing among themselves, had the common purpose of weakening the President. ...
>
> His ability and energy in prosecuting the war were questioned, his conciliatory policy towards the rebels and his disinclination to confiscate their property were denounced, and his amnesty and reconstruction measures were censured and condemned. The expediency of a change in the presidential office for a more resolute and arbitrary executive was urged by radical congressional leaders during the whole of the first session of Congress ... and after its adjournment.[429]

August gloom engulfed party leaders, spawning a secret movement aimed at replacing Lincoln as the nominee. Even Weed toyed with replacing Lincoln, but the movement was centered among the radicals. A meeting at the New York home of David Dudley Field drew in Mayor George Opdyke, Parke Godwin, William Curtis Noyes, Representative Davis, Theodore Tilton, Franz Lieber, and twenty others, all agreeing to call upon Lincoln to withdraw as a candidate.

A call was made for a September 8 convention in Cincinnati, with correspondence to be handled by John Austin Stevens, secretary of the National War Committee and an active Republican since the inception of the party. "Mr. Lincoln is already beaten," Greeley wrote to Mayor Opdyke. "We must have another ticket to save us from utter overthrow. If we had such a ticket as could be had by naming Grant, Butler, Sherman for President, and Farragut as Vice [President], we could make a fight yet."

Butler's chief of staff, J. W. Shaffer, said Butler went home to Lowell, Massachusetts, stopping two days at New York's Fifth Avenue Hotel, where he could be consulted. Shaffer showed concern over word that

Lincoln had copies of dispatches to Chase, Ashley, and Sprague, yet he closed by saying, "it makes little difference what Mr. Lincoln knows." Butler, showing his interest, wrote from Lowell, naming two friends who knew his views and also proclaiming his availability for the emergency.[430]

Many of Lincoln's closest political advisors were stampeded, and Weed, who had been consulted about replacing Lincoln, wrote to Seward, "When, ten or eleven days since, I told Mr. Lincoln that his re-election was an impossibility, I also told him that the information would soon come to him through other channels. It has doubtless, ere this, reached him, At any rate nobody here doubts it; nor do I see anybody from other States who authorizes the slightest hope of success.

Mr. Raymond, who has just left me, says that unless some prompt and bold step be now taken, all is lost," Weed asserted. "The People are wild or Peace. They are told that the President will only listen to terms of Peace on condition Slavery be 'abandoned.' Mr. Swett is well informed in relation to the public sentiment. He has seen and heard much. Mr. Raymond thinks commissioners should be immediately sent, to Richmond, offering to treat for Peace on the basis of Union."[431]

Weed warned, "That something should be done and promptly done, to give the Administration a chance for its life, is certain."

Prior to Weed's letter, Lincoln had received Raymond's blunt and depressing letter:

> I feel compelled to drop you a line concerning the political condition of the country as it strikes me. I am in active correspondence with your staunchest friends in every state and from them all I hear but one report. The tide is setting strongly against us.
>
> Hon. E. B. Washburne writes, "Were an election to be held now in Illinois we should be beaten." Mr. Cameron writes

> that Pennsylvania is against us. Gov. Morton writes that nothing but the most strenuous efforts can carry Indiana. This state, according to the best information … would go 50,000 against us. … And so of the rest, nothing but the most resolute and decided action on the part of the government and its friends can save the country from falling into hostile hands.
>
> Two special causes are assigned to this great reaction in public sentiment … the want of military successes, and the impression in some minds, the fear and suspicion in others, that we are not to have peace … under this administration until Slavery is abandoned. In some way or other the suspicion is widely diffused that we can have peace with Union if we would. It is idle to reason with this belief—still more idle to denounce it. It can only be expelled by some authoritative act.

Such an act, Raymond argued, need be "at once bold enough to fix attention and distinct enough to defy incredulity & challenge respect."

Then Raymond proposed:

> Why would it not be wise, under these circumstances, to appoint a Commissioner, in due form, to make distinct proffers of peace to Davis, as the head of rebel armies, on the sole condition of acknowledging the supremacy of the constitution—all other questions to be settled in a convention of the people. …
>
> If the proffer were accepted (which I presume it would not be) the country would never consent to place the practical execution … in any but loyal hands. If it should be rejected, (as it would be) it would plant seeds of disaffection in the South, dispel all the delusions about peace … silence the clamors & damaging falsehoods … take the wind

> completely out of the sails of the Chicago craft, reconcile public sentiment to the War, the draft & the tax … and unite the North.

Nicolay recorded Raymond's interview with Lincoln: "The President and the stronger half of the Cabinet, Seward, Stanton, and Fessenden, held a consultation with him and showed him that they had thoroughly considered and discussed the proposition of his letter … and on giving him their reasons he very readily concurred with them in the opinion that to follow his plan of sending a commission to Richmond would be worse than losing the Presidential contest."[432]

Days before the interview, Lincoln was made aware of an antagonizing movement by Boston friends of Chase and Senator Sumner, who displayed animus and intent against Lincoln. The movement from supposedly pronounced friends at such a time affected the president far more than the assaults of the radicals in the recently adjourned session of the Congress. It was an ungenerous and most unfriendly political act.

It came in the form of a letter, addressed to General Fremont, that read, "Sir—you must be aware of the wide and growing dissatisfaction in the republican ranks with the presidential nomination at Baltimore; and you may have seen notices of a movement, just commenced, to unite the thorough and earnest friends of a rigorous prosecution of the war in a new convention, which shall represent the patriotism of all parties." Then came the blunt demand: "To facilitate that movement it is emphatically advisable that the candidates nominated should withdraw."

What the letter asked was for Fremont and the president to leave the field entirely free for such a united effort. "Permit us, sir, to ask whether, in case Mr. Lincoln will withdraw, you will do so, and join your fellow-citizens in this attempt to place the administration on a basis broad as the patriotism of the country and as its needs." The six Bostonians who signed were George L. Stearns, S. R. Urino, James M. Stone, Elizur Wright, Edward Habich, and Samuel G. Howe.

As Secretary Wells reported, "The proposition, presumptuous and absurd, which as he and the leading minds of the administration believed, and as events proved, was made by friends of Sumner and Chase, and probably made honestly by those whose names were appended, struck the president painfully." Wells noted the letter was dated August 21. It was on August 23 that the president penned, folded, and sealed what became known as "The Blind Memorandum."[433]

It began: "This morning, as for some days past, it seems exceedingly probable that this administration will not be reelected. Then it will be my duty to so cooperate with the President-elect as to save the Union between the election and the inauguration; as he will have secured his election on such ground that he cannot possibly save it afterward. A Lincoln." He handed the sheet of paper, folded and pasted so what was inside could not be read and asked each to sign across the back. Each signed not knowing the contents of the document.[434]

On the same day Lincoln penned the Blind Memorandum, New York representative Reuben E. Fenton responded to a telegram from Nicolay saying the president wished to meet with him. Lincoln said, "You are to be nominated by our folks for Governor of your State. Seymour … will be the Democratic nominee. You will have a hard fight. I am very desirous that you should win the battle. There is some trouble among our folks over there, which we must try and manage."

Lincoln cautiously explained, "Or rather, there is one man who may give us trouble, because of his indifference, if in no other way. He has great influence, and his feelings may be reflected in many of his friends. We must have his counsel and cooperation if possible. This, in one sense is more important to you than to me, I think, for I should rather expect to get on without New York, but you can't. But in a larger sense than what is personal to myself, I am anxious for New York."

The person was Weed, and Lincoln concluded, "We must put our heads together and see if the matter can't be fixed."

Fenton, yet to be nominated, was asked to sort out the New York Customs Office patronage. Fenton, in company with Nicolay, left for New York and met Weed the next day at the Astor House. Fenton reported that Nicolay left the following afternoon with the resignation of Rufus F. Andrews. Weed's man, Abram Wakeman, was named New York port surveyor in his place.[435]

Lincoln was equally concerned with replacing Hiram Barney, collector of customs, because of his weak leadership. Another Weed ally, Simeon Draper, was named to replace him. Then Weed lieutenant James Kelly was appointed New York postmaster, replacing Wakeman. Noting the Wakeman appointment, Fenton said, "From that time forward Mr. Weed was earnest and helpful in the canvass." As a result in November Fenton carried the canvass by a thin seven thousand votes.[436]

Lincoln skillfully starved enemies such as Senator Pomeroy, but met the needs of allies. Summonsing Philadelphia postmaster Cornelius Walborn to Washington, Lincoln said complaint had been made "that you are using your official power to defeat Judge [William D.] Kelley for re-nomination to Congress." Lincoln told Walborn he could do as he chose, but warned him not to constrain any subordinate staff, as it was essential they have freedom of choice among friends.[437]

Lincoln was equally firm with Chicago postmaster John L. Scripps regarding the renomination of Representative Arnold and with Commissioner of Patents David P. Holloway regarding the renomination of Representative George W. Julian of Indiana. Lincoln also backed the return to Congress of Roscoe Conkling, who had served previously. It was readily apparent that Lincoln was wielding patronage unsparingly to reward those who had supported him and to assure support from Congress.[438]

Greeley, still sore over Lincoln outsmarting him on the Niagara fiasco, remained unconvinced that the Confederates would not negotiate. Pressing a movement for a substitute candidate for president, Greeley headed a committee of three, writing letters marked "private and confidential," asking each if he believed the election of Lincoln a probability, whether Lincoln could carry his state, and whether Union party interests required replacing Lincoln with another candidate.

These letters were signed by Greeley as editor of the *New York Tribune*, Parke Godwin, editor of the *New York Evening Post*, and Theodore Tilton, editor of the *New York Independent*. Secrecy was promised recipients. Maryland governor Bradford replied affirmatively to the first two and said that he believed Lincoln was the only candidate who could win. No candidate, he added, "brought under the auspices of the leaders most conspicuous in their objections to Mr. Lincoln" had a chance.

That very day, Greeley's *Tribune* carried a two-column editorial proclaiming, "Henceforth, we fly the banner of ABRAHAM LINCOLN for the next President. ... WE MUST reelect him, and, God helping us, we will." The abrupt change could not have been based on the replies of governors, as they could not have been received. The shift came as Lincoln, knowing Greeley's lust for public office, dangled before him appointment as postmaster general, and because Sherman captured Atlanta.[439]

William Cullen Bryant had advocated postponing the nominating convention and had taken issue with Lincoln's administrative polices, yet he brought his *New York Evening Post* into line. The *Evening Post*'s September 20 editorial declared, "He [Lincoln] has gained wisdom by experience. Every year has seen our cause more successful ... has seen abler generals, more skillful leaders ... every year has seen fewer errors, greater ability, greater energy, in the administration."

A friend of Chase with hopes of promoting his candidacy, the radical Bryant also carried baggage because the *Post*'s business manager was implicated in a nasty scandal. Bryant had moved away from Lincoln early in the war due to Lincoln's patient approach to emancipation. Bryant criticized Lincoln for his failure to free the slaves, but soon added criticism on any issue he could find. The *Evening Post* became an ardent admirer of Grant, eulogizing him for having won the most victories.[440]

Lincoln told homeward-bound men of the 148th Ohio Regiment:

> Whenever, I appear before a body of soldiers, I feel tempted to talk to them of the struggle in which we are engaged. I look upon it as an attempt on the one hand to overwhelm and destroy the national existence, while, on our part, we are striving to maintain the government and institutions of our fathers, to enjoy them for ourselves, and transmit them to our children and our children's children forever.
>
> To do this the constitutional administration of our government must be sustained, and I beg of you not to allow your minds or your hearts to be diverted from the support of all necessary measures. … Again I admonish you not to be turned from your stern purpose of defending your beloved country and its free institutions by any arguments urged by ambitious and designing men, but stand fast to the Union and the old flag. Soldiers, I bid you God-speed to your homes.[441]

All grades of politicians besieged the While House, and Mrs. Lincoln was blamed for certain men around her. "I have an object in view, Lizabeth," she told her friend, confidante, and seamstress, Elizabeth Keckley, who quoted her. "In a political canvass it is policy to cultivate every element of strength. These men have influence, and we require influence to re-elect Mr. Lincoln. I will be clever to them until after the election, and, if we remain at the White House, I will drop every one of them."

Mrs. Lincoln said she also would let them know plainly she had made tools of them. "They are an unprincipled set, and I don't mind a little double-dealing with them."

Keckley asked, "Does Mr. Lincoln know what your purpose is?"

Mary Lincoln replied, "God! No; he would never sanction such a proceeding, so I keep him in the dark, and will tell him of it when all is over. He is too honest to take the proper care of his own interests, so I feel it to be my duty to electioneer for him."

Keckley said Lincoln was far from handsome, but was admired "for the nobility of his soul and the greatness of his heart."

> His wife was different. He was wholly unselfish in every respect, and I believe that he loved the mother of his children very tenderly. He asked nothing but affection from her, but did not always receive it. When in one of her wayward impulsive moods, she was apt to say and do things that wounded him deeply. Had he not loved her, she would have been powerless. …
>
> Mrs. Lincoln was extremely anxious that her husband should be re-elected President of the United States. In endeavoring to make a display becoming her exalted position, she had to incur many expenses. Mr. Lincoln's salary was inadequate to meet them, and she was forced to run in debt, hoping that good fortune … enables her to extricate herself … She bought most expensive goods on credit, and in the summer of 1864 enormous unpaid bills stared her in the face.

Keckley, in regard to why Lincoln would be reelected, explained, "Because he has been tried, and has proved faithful to the best interests of the country. The people of the North recognize in him an honest man, and they are willing to confide in him, at least until the war has been brought to a close. The Southern people made his election a pretext for rebellion, and now to replace him by some one else … would look too much like … surrender. … So, Mr. Lincoln is certain to be re-elected."

Mrs. Lincoln told her, "You understand, Lizabeth, that Mr. Lincoln has but little idea of the expense of a women's wardrobe. He glances at my rich dresses, and is happy in the belief that the few hundred dollars that I obtain from him supply all my wants. I must dress in costly materials. The people scrutinize every article that I wear with critical curiosity. The very fact of having grown up in the West, subjects me to more searching observation … I must have money—more than Mr. Lincoln can spare."

Keckley asking if Lincoln even suspected, quoting Mary's reply, "'God no!'—This was her favorite expression—'and I would not have him suspect. If he knew that his wife was involved to the extent that she is, the knowledge would drive him mad. He is so sincere and straightforward himself, that he is shocked by the duplicity of others. He does not know a thing about any debts, and I value his happiness, not to speak of my own, too much to allow him to know anything. This is what troubles me so much.'"

With a hysterical sob, Mrs. Lincoln said in defeat, the bills would be sent to him and he would know all. Fearing politicians would use her debts against Lincoln, she said, "The Republican politicians must pay my debts. Hundreds of them are getting immensely rich off the patronage of my husband, and it is but fair that they should help me out of my embarrassment. I will make a demand of them, and when I tell them the facts they cannot refuse to advance whatever money I require."[442]

CHAPTER XVIII

DEMOCRATS: A WAR CANDIDATE ON A PEACE PLATFORM

As September came the Democrats met in Chicago and nominated General George B. McClellan for president, a war president on a peace platform with a peace candidate as his running mate, Representative George H. Pendleton. Pendleton was a friend of Jefferson Davis, and an avowed foe of the war as well as a peace advocate. McClellan and his running mate became saddled with the peace platform, engineered by the former congressman Clement L. Vallandigham, the notorious Ohio Copperhead.

As *Sacramento Union* reporter Noah Brooks left Washington for Chicago, Lincoln asked that he send reports on the Chicago convention. Brooks recalled that Lincoln said, "Write just what you would talk, but wouldn't print." Lincoln forecast a result: "They must nominate a Peace Democrats on a war platform, or a War Democrat on a peace platform; and I can't say I care much which they do." They were called to order in the Wigwam, where Lincoln had been nominated in 1860.

The convention delegates were a diverse group of peace Democrats, war Democrats, Whigs, Know-Nothings, Conservatives, states' rights extremists favoring secession, millionaires, and run-down politicians, among others. From the Confederacy and from Canada came spies. Delegates were called together by August Belmont, a wealthy New York banker, chairman of the Democratic National Committee, president of the American Jockey Club, and a former US minister in The Netherlands.

Belmont, in a bid for unity, told those assembled: "We are here not as war democrats nor as peace democrats, but as citizens of the great Republic, which we will strive to bring back to its former greatness and prosperity, without one single star taken from the brilliant constellation that once encircled its beautiful brow. … Under the blessings of the Almighty, the sacred cause of the Union, the constitution and the laws, must prevail against fanaticism and treason."

Belmont charged the Lincoln administration with "four years of misrule, by a sectional, fanatical and corrupt party" having brought the country to "the very verge of ruin." Belmont then introduced former Pennsylvania governor William Bigler as temporary chair. He defined "the first indispensable step" if the nation was to be rescued "is the overthrow, by the ballot, of the present administration." Then New York governor Horatio Seymour assumed the role of permanent chair.

Seymour told the cheering delegates the present administration could not now save the Union if it would, but "if the administration cannot save the Union, we can. Mr. Lincoln values many things above the Union; we put it first of all. He thinks a proclamation worth more than peace; we think the blood of our people more precious than the edicts of the President." In the resolutions committee, against strong opposition, Vallandigham wrote an out-and-out peace plank that carried.

In a flat-out antiwar challenge, it declared, "This convention does explicitly declare, as the sense of the American people, that after four years of failure to restore the Union by the experiment of war, during which, under the pretense of a military necessity, or war power higher than the Constitution, the Constitution itself has been disregarded in every part, and public liberty and private right alike trodden down and the material prosperity of the country essentially impaired."

In a call for peace now, it asserted, "Justice, humanity, liberty and the public welfare demand that immediate efforts be made for a cessation of hostilities, with a view to an ultimate convention of the States, or other peaceable means, to the end that at the earliest practicable moment peace may be restored on the basis of Federal Union of the States." This was a difficult straddle, and eventually General McClellan wrestled with it and disavowed this peace plank, to the ire of its proponents.[443]

McClellan's acceptance called for peace through Union: "As soon as it is clear, or even probably, that our present adversaries are ready for peace, upon the basis of the Union, we should exhaust all the resources of statesmanship practiced by civilized nations … consistent with the honor and interests of the country to secure peace, reestablish the Union, and guarantee for the future the constitutional rights of every State." He emphatically said: "The Union is the one condition of peace."[444]

As disaffected men of the Northwest mingled with Confederate spies, two planned uprisings failed to materialize. Government agents broke the subversive secret organization, the Sons of Liberty, and neutralized spies largely infiltrated from Canada. A plotted prison break, expected to free some eight thousand Confederates imprisoned at Camp Douglas near Chicago, was abandoned because Union authorities had learned of the plan and had moved to frustrate the attempt.

Operating an extremely effective counterespionage force, the federal government tracked the moves of the Sons of Liberty in Kentucky, Ohio, Indiana, Illinois, Missouri, and Wisconsin. The federal agents rounded up and jailed key officials of the organization that invited into membership all who opposed the war. As to war Democrats, a Chicago delegate declared to cheers, "They are links of one sausage, made out of the same dog."

The Sons of Liberty was organized by peace Democrats as successor to the played-out Knights of the Golden Circle and the American Knights. The national head of the organization was a newspaperman, Phineas C. Wright, who stepped aside on February 22, 1864, for Clement L. Vallandigham, who slipped back into the country the following June, returning from political exile in Canada. His work in the West finished, Wright went to New York, leaving the reins to Vallandigham.[445]

Publisher Ben Wood hired Wright, who wrote, "I have this day connected myself with the Editorial Department of the New York Daily News. You will remember that the News has advocated the principles inculcated by Jefferson & his illustrious compeers, and has fearlessly

& openly denounced the usurpations of power which have wrested from the citizens his cherished rights, and thrown down the last barrier between him & irresponsible despotism."

With regard to Wright, the former head of the Copperhead Sons of Liberty, Robert S. Harper, wrote in *Lincoln and the Press*: "To say the Wood brothers [Ben and Fernando] were not aware of Wright's connections would be nothing short of ridiculous. The war course of the News would indicate that Wright was hired because of his connections." The *New York Herald* published a report that the *News* had received $20,000 through Confederate intelligence in Canada.

Wright also elaborated: "The News will be our especial organ, and will be the medium of interchange of sentiments & opinions of the friends of peace touching the momentous concerns involved in the existing crisis. I entreat your kind offices & influence in extending the circulation of the News throughout the entire field of our labor." Confederates seeking to message their friends in the North often placed coded classified advertisements in the *News*. That came to light at this time.[446]

Belmont had appointed the *World*'s Marble to the Democratic National Campaign Committee, and Belmont and Dean Richmond gave Marble responsibility for publicity and publications for the party campaign effort. Some twenty-seven campaign documents were printed by the *World*, ranging from Samuel F. B. Morse's "Ethical Position of Slavery in the Social System" to attacks upon the Emancipation Proclamation to Union general Franz Sigel's "Why I Won't Stump for Old Abe."

The *New York World* editorialized on McClellan's letter of acceptance: "Thank God for a purified, regenerate, disenthralled, Democratic party! Thank God that every burden is lifted from its back, every impediment from its victorious path! The men who have been the curse of the party have gone out of the party. Close up the ranks. ... Now we go into the November fight without a flaw in our armor." The *World* increasingly attacked Lincoln and inflamed racial prejudice among voters.

In mid-September, some fifty antiwar men met in New York to consider an alternative candidate to McClellan. The leaders were Ben Wood and James McMaster of the *Freeman's Journal*; Fernando Wood did not join. In Ohio, Vallandigham and leaders of the Sons of Liberty met similarly. Soon party leaders persuaded Vallandigham to back McClellan and the efforts collapsed. Vallandigham, nevertheless, consistently denied that McClellan expressed party views.

J. Perkins wrote to Lamon inquiring if there was any truth to a *World* story claiming that Lincoln, while touring the Antietam battlefield with Lamon and General McClellan, had asked Lamon to sing the ditty "Picayune Butler." The *World* alleged the incident occurred as they were driving over the battlefield in an ambulance, and the men were engaged in burying the dead. The newspaper account contended that McClellan protested the singing of the song.

Perkins said, "This story has been repeated in the … World almost daily for the last three months. … That it is a damaging story, if believed, cannot be disputed. That it is believed by some … is evident by the accompanying … doggerel, in which allusion is made to it: 'Abe may crack his jolly jokes, O'er bloody fields of stricken battle, While yet the ebbing life-tide smokes, From men that die like butchered cattle; He, ere yet the guns grow cold, To pimps and pets may crack his stories,'"

Lincoln drafted a memorandum for Lamon's signature, but never released it. It explained the president and Lamon, two weeks after the battle, rode in review of the troops for two days. On the third day, they joined McClellan in an ambulance for the more distant review of General Fitz John Porter's corps. On the way, and on no part of the battlefield, Lamon wrote, Lincoln asked him to sing a little sad song. When it was over, he said, another asked him for more, and he sang "Picayune Butler."

Lamon said on the fourth day, the president and McClellan visited the wounded still in the vicinity and examined the South Mountain battleground. McClellan returned to camp, and the president to Washington, Lamon added, "This the whole story. … Neither General McClellan or any one else made any objection to the singing; the place was not on the battle field, the time was sixteen days after the battle, no dead body was seen during the whole time during the whole time."[447]

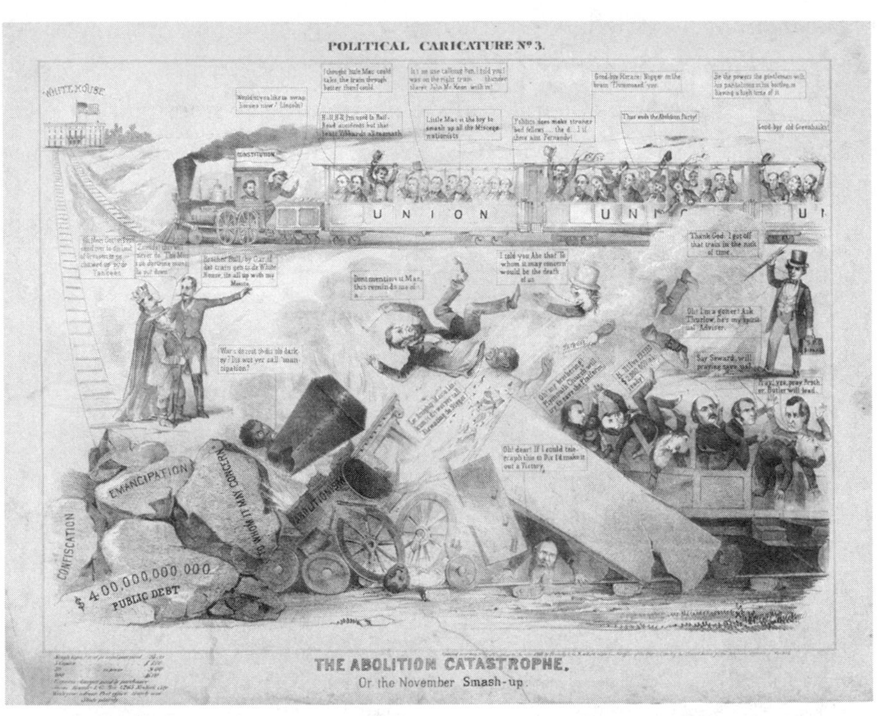

THE ABOLITION CATASTROPHE,
Or the November Smash-up.

"YOUR PLAN AND MINE".

CHAPTER XIX

ATLANTA, THE SHENANDOAH VALLEY, AND MOBILE VICTORIES; ELECTION VICTORIES IN INDIANA, OHIO, AND PENNSYLVANIA; RADICALS RECONCILED

The gloomy outlook that hung over the North lifted when General Sherman wired proudly, "Atlanta is ours and fairly won!" Union navy and army forces captured Mobile, Alabama, and closed this major Confederate gulf port. Lincoln issued a special order of thanks, praising Admiral David Farragut and Major General Edward Canby for the operation in Mobile Harbor and General Sherman and his gallant officers and soldiers before Atlanta. Northern moral soared.

Lincoln issued a "Proclamation of Thanksgiving and Prayer." "The signal success that Divine Providence has recently vouchsafed to the operations of the United States fleet and army in the harbor of Mobile and the reduction of Fort Powell, Fort Gains and Fort Morgan and the glorious achievement of the Army under Major General Sherman in the State of Georgia, resulting in the capture of the City of Atlanta, call for devout acknowledgment of the Supreme Being in whose hands are the destinies of nations."

A Negro delegation came from Baltimore and presented Lincoln a Bible. The Reverend S. W. Chase addressed the president:

> The loyal colored people of Baltimore have entrusted us with authority to present this Bible as a testimonial of their appreciation of your humane conduct towards the people of our race. … Since our incorporation into the American family we have been true and loyal, and we are now ready to aid in defending the country, to be armed and trained. …
>
> Toward you, sir, our hearts will ever be warm with gratitude. We come to present to you this copy of the Holy Scriptures, as a token of respect for your active participation in furtherance of the cause of the emancipation of our race. This great event will be a matter of history. Hereafter, when our children shall ask what mean these tokens, they will be told of your worthy deeds, and will rise up and call you blessed. The loyal colored people … everywhere will remember you.

"I can only now say … it has been a sentiment with me I have before said … that all mankind should be free," Lincoln replied. "So far as able … I have always acted as I believed to be right and just; and I have done all I could for the good of mankind. … In regard to this great book … it is the best gift God has given to man. All the good the Savior gave to the world was communicated through this book." He added, "But for it we could not know right from wrong."[448]

With Indiana governor Morton much concerned with the coming October 11 elections, Lincoln wired to General Sherman, "The loss of it to the friends of the government would go far towards losing the whole Union cause. The bad effect upon the November election, and especially the giving the State Government to those who will oppose the war in every possible way, are too much to risk, if it can possibly be avoided."

Lincoln explained, "The draft proceeds, notwithstanding its strong tendency to lose us the State. Indiana is the only important State, voting in October, whose soldiers cannot vote in the field. Any thing you can safely do to let her soldiers go home and vote … will be greatly in point.

They need not remain for the Presidential election, but may return … at once. This is in no sense an order, but it merely intended to impress you with the importance to the army … of your doing all you safely can."

Morton, members of the congressional delegation, and others had written asking aid and warned Stanton, "We express it as our profound conviction that upon the issue of the election … may depend the question as to whether the secession element shall be effectually crushed or whether it shall acquire strength enough, we do not say to take the state out of the Union, but practically to sever her from the federal government, so far as future military aid is concerned."[449]

General Sheridan on September 19 wired Grant, "I attacked the forces of General Early over the Berryville Pike at the crossing of Opequan Creek, and after a most stubborn and sanguinary engagement … completely defeated him … driving him through Winchester, capturing about 2,500 prisoners—five of artillery, nine Army flags and most of their wounded." Lincoln wired his congratulations to Sheridan: "Have just learned of your great victory. God bless you all, officers and men."[450]

The fight for the Shenandoah Valley continued through the fall into winter as Sheridan's troops moved up and down the valley. The cavalry was deployed across the valley, destroying or taking away everything of value to the enemy. The valley had been fruitfully supplying the Confederates. It served as a base for bushwhackers and guerrillas murdering Union soldiers on the roads. Sheridan's troops destroyed railroads, canals, and barns with devastating effect.[451]

Military victories reduced the political threat posed by Democrats. Radical John Murray Forbes, rather than demanding a new convention, called for key men to meet, aiming to advise Lincoln and hoping to control his campaign. They specifically feared Lincoln might listen to Raymond and others and consider negotiations with the South. Governor Andrew, agreeing with Forbes as reelection seemed sure, wanted "men of motive and ideas" to run the machine, and so told Lincoln.

The *New York Herald* declared, "Whatever they say now, we venture to predict that Wade and his tail; and Wendell Phillips and his tail; and Weed, Barney and Chase, who have no tails; will all make tracks for Old Abe's plantation, and will soon be found crowing and blowing, and vowing and writhing, and swearing and stumping ... that he alone is the hope of the nation, the bugaboo of Jeff Davis, the first of conservatives, the best of Abolitionists, and purest of patriots."[452]

In mid-September, Lincoln announced the news that Republicans had scored well in both Maine and Vermont. From Maine, James G. Blaine, Republican state central committee chair, reported, "The State Election today has resulted in a great victory for the Union cause. Governor (Samuel) Cony reelected by a large majority with the entire Cong [congressional] ticket." In a second wire, Blaine said, "The Union majority in Maine will reach 20,000. We will give you 30,000 in November."[453]

Senator Chandler undertook to reconcile Wade and Winter Davis in support of Lincoln, and get Fremont's withdrawal from the race. While often sharply critical of Lincoln, Chandler had remained on good personal terms with Lincoln. Lincoln had given Chandler his say on Michigan patronage even as Chandler held to a hard line on war and reconstruction. Chandler held with Lincoln, knowing a divided party would mean the election of McClellan on the hated peace platform of Democrats.

Wade and Davis finally agreed they would support Lincoln if Montgomery Blair was dropped from the cabinet. Fremont was equally bitter against Blair. Chandler undertook negotiations with Lincoln. In an ironic play, Fremont failed to obtain the Chicago nomination and failed to come to terms with McClellan. Even his efforts to weaken Lincoln's reelection were failing. Chandler, a fearless legislator, kept no record as he shuttled among the players, yet his efforts yielded crucial results.[454]

Lincoln wrote to Blair, "You have generously said to me more than once, that whenever your resignation could be a relief to me, it was at my disposal. The time has come. You very well know that this proceeds from no dissatisfaction of mine with you personally or officially. Your uniform kindness has been unsurpassed by that of any friend." As for Blair's stewardship of the Post Office Department, he concluded, "I remember no single complaint against you."

Blair replied, "I have received your note … referring to my offers to resign whenever you should deem it advisable for the public interests that I should do so and stating that in your judgment that time has come. I now … formally tender my resignation. … I cannot take leave without renewing the expressions of my gratitude for the uniform kindness which has marked your course toward me." Blair had stood by Lincoln consistently, speaking out strongly against Chase.

Blair's brother, Frank Blair Jr., wrote to his father, Francis P. Blair, supporting his brother's action: "Indeed, before I received your letter my instincts told me that my brother had acted his part for the good of the country and for the reelection of Mr. Lincoln in which the safety of the country is involved. I believe that a failure to reelect Mr. Lincoln would be the greatest disaster that could befall the country and the sacrifice made by the Judge to avert this is so incomparably small."[455]

On September 22, a Fremont letter was published that dropped his third-party candidacy. The circumstances resulted from effective pressure by Chandler, a Michigan dry goods merchant, real estate speculator, and forceful politician. Fremont made only a lukewarm endorsement of Lincoln, declaring, "I consider that his administration has been politically, militarily and financially a failure, and that its necessity is a cause of regret for the country."

The hard-charging Chandler had initiated his reconciliation efforts in Ohio with Wade then traveled east to bring other radicals into line. Chandler extracted the promise from Lincoln to drop Blair from the cabinet if Fremont would withdraw from the race. Chandler went to New York and, after a strenuous argument, persuaded Winter Davis to support the ticket. Fremont insisted his withdrawal was only for the good of the Republican Party, but it took his name off the ballot.[456]

On September 24, Lincoln wired former Ohio governor William Dennison, "Mr. Blair has resigned, and I appoint you Post Master General. Come immediately." Dennison, who was in southeastern Ohio at the time, wired back on September 27th, "I expect to leave for Washington Thursday so as to reach there Friday to enter upon the duties of the office with which you have honored me." Montgomery Blair headed to Maryland to campaign for Lincoln. Winter Davis also stumped for the president.[457]

Dennison, Ohio governor during the first two years of the war, was a lawyer, president of the Exchange Bank of Columbus, and president of the Columbus and Xenia Railroad Company. Adding an Ohioan who firmly advocated his renomination and a politically savvy friend of the Blairs was a win for Lincoln. As Justice David Davis had written to Lincoln when recommending Dennison to chair the Baltimore convention, "You could not get a wiser counselor." Dennison had broad support.[458]

Senator James Harlan of Iowa told Hay that the *New York Herald*'s support was vital, and suggested that Bennett, the publisher, be offered a foreign post. Hay reported that Forney also was talking with Bennett, and was asked, "Will I be a welcome visitor at the White House if I support Mr. Lincoln?" Harlan feared the *Herald*'s influence on the soldier vote. Lincoln acted, dangling the offer of a foreign post. Bennett moderated his criticism but never gave outright support for Lincoln.[459]

General Sherman told Lincoln he had positive knowledge of Confederate general Hood speaking at Macon and bitterly attacking both General Johnston and Georgia governor Joseph E. Brown. Both opposed the growing federal power of the Confederacy. Increasing inflation and potential bankruptcy pushed Brown to mobilize welfare efforts for soldiers, families, and citizens with support from Vice President Stephens and Robert Tombs, key Georgian politicians.[460]

Sherman told Lincoln, "Great efforts are being made to reinforce Hood's army and to break up my Railroads, and I should have at once a good reserve force at Nashville. It would have a bad effect if I were to be forced to send back any material part of my army to guard roads so as to weaken me to an extent that I could not act offensively." He said he had reinforced his line back as far as Chattanooga, and was asking that regiments in Indiana and Ohio to be sent to Nashville.[461]

When Lincoln told Grant "he was a little afraid lest Lee sends reinforcements to Early, and thus enables him to turn upon Sheridan," Grant replied, "I am taking steps to prevent Lee sending reinforcements to Early by attacking him here. Our advance is now within six miles of Richmond and have captured some very strong enclosed forts, some fifteen or more pieces of artillery and several hundred prisoners." Grant said he could not yet estimate the sustained Union losses in the struggle.[462]

Lincoln also issued an order of thanks to one-hundred-day troops from Indiana, Illinois, Iowa, and Wisconsin. "It was their good fortune to render effective service in the brilliant operations in the southwest, and to contribute to … victories … over the rebel forces in Georgia under command of Johnston and Hood." He commended them for performing with alacrity and courage. The draft and calls for more volunteers were essential because of the ebb and flow of short-term volunteers.[463]

Henry W. Hoffman, chairman of the Maryland Unconditional Union Committee, called upon Lincoln to join a mass meeting October 10th "in favor of the 'Free Constitution,'" explaining, "We are convinced that your presence on the occasion would ensure its success both as to harmony and point of numbers and that its influence upon the vote to be taken on the following Wednesday would be to add hundreds and perhaps thousands of votes to the free state column."

Hoffman told Lincoln that if he could not come, they would like a letter, and Lincoln wrote and sent this letter:

> I presume the only feature of the instrument, about which there is serious controversy, is that which provides for the extinction

> of slavery. It needs not to be a secret … that I wish success to this provision. I desire it on every consideration. I wish all men to be free. I wish the material prosperity of the already free which I feel sure the extinction of slavery would bring.
>
> I wish to see, in process of disappearing, that only thing which ever could bring this nation to civil war. … Argument upon the question is already exhausted by the abler, better informed, and more immediately interested sons of Maryland herself. I only add that I shall be gratified if the good people of Maryland, by their votes, ratify the new constitution.

Lincoln's letter was read to wild applause, and the constitution was ratified by a narrow margin of 30,174 to 29,799.[464]

Next came important fall elections in Pennsylvania, Ohio, and Indiana. The Union ticket carried Ohio by fifty thousand votes, capturing seventeen of the nineteen congressional seats. Among the defeated was the most prominent House Democrat, S. S. "Sunset" Cox, a key ally of Belmont, Barlow, and Marble.

In Indiana, Republicans captured eight of the eleven congressional seats while reelecting Governor Morton with twenty thousand more votes this time around. Lincoln wired: "Bravo, for Indiana, and for yourself."[465]

Pennsylvania was a squeaker, and many blamed Cameron. Lincoln wrote to Grant, who asked about the election: "Pennsylvania very close, and still in doubt on home vote. Ohio largely with us. … Indiana largely with us. … Send us what you may know of your army vote." As it turned out, the Republicans carried Pennsylvania by a slim fifteen thousand votes. The home vote margin was only 391 because Democrats garnered small majorities in a number of local and congressional races.

As McClure explained, "There was no state ticket to be elected. … McClellan, a native of Pennsylvania, was the Democratic candidate for

President, and the state pride naturally added to his strength. Simon Cameron was chairman of the Republican State Committee. He was well equipped for the position, but was so entirely confident of success that he neglected to perfect the organization."

Lincoln had asked McClure to personally strengthen the organization. "I reminded him that Cameron and I were not in political sympathy, and that he would regard it as obtrusive for me to volunteer assistance to him, in the management of the campaign." To this Lincoln replied, "Of course, I understand that, but if Cameron shall invite you can you give your time fully to the cause?"

McClure said two days later he received a cordial letter from Cameron, inviting him to headquarters to assist in the November contest.

Cameron, faced with the humiliation of the Pennsylvania result contrasted with Ohio and Indiana, opened the door. A like invitation had gone to Wayne MacVeagh, also brought about by Lincoln. MacVeagh had chaired the committee the previous year, and McClure the year before. McClure said he booked a hotel room and left headquarters only for confidential meetings, writing Lincoln every night, as requested, to give him a full report on the progress of the committee.

Given the unexpected success, Democrats were elated and developed plans to hold the state in November. "So anxious was Lincoln," McClure said, "that after I had been a week in cooperation … he sent Postmaster General William Dennison over to Philadelphia to talk over the situation more fully. … It was evident that we had gained nothing, and so I informed the Postmaster General, and expressed great doubts as to our ability to do more than hold our own."

McClure said that in another week, it could be determined if they were safe with the home vote. Seeing nothing to show the gain of any material advantage, McClure wired that he would see Lincoln at ten o'clock the next night. Exhibiting great solicitude, Lincoln met with

McClure, and McClure explained, "He knew that his election was in no sense doubtful, but he knew that if he lost New York and with it Pennsylvania on the home vote, the moral effect of his triumph would be broken."

McClure further explained, "His power to prosecute the war and make peace would be greatly impaired." When Lincoln asked what could be done, McClure said Grant was idle at Petersburg and Sheridan had won all possible victories in the valley. He suggested that five thousand Pennsylvania troops be furloughed home from each army and the election could be carried. "Surely … you can trust Grant with a confidential suggestion to furlough Pennsylvania troops?"

Lincoln hesitated and told McClure, "I have no reason to believe that Grant prefers my election to that of McClellan." McClure then suggested the order go to Meade and to Sheridan, which was done. The November result was that Lincoln carried the Pennsylvania home vote by a narrow 5,712 majority, and the overall vote by 14,363, with the army vote adding significantly to the majority. McClure left distrusting Grant because of Lincoln's unwillingness to send the order to him.[466]

At the same time, Lincoln wrote on a printed telegraph blank his predicted state-by-state tally for the election. In the "Supposed Copperhead" vote column, he listed New York, Pennsylvania, New Jersey, Delaware, Maryland, Missouri, Kentucky, and Illinois. Under the Union vote, he listed the New England states, Michigan, Wisconsin, Minnesota, Iowa, Oregon, California, Kansas, Indiana, Ohio, West Virginia, and Nevada. Simultaneously, he directed political efforts to improve these results.[467]

Pennsylvania governor Curtin wired Lincoln that he had information that the "enemy has arranged for a raid into Pennsylvania about the end of the month." He contended that Sheridan's force has been reduced by 25,000 men and would be followed by a serious disaster. Lincoln swiftly wired back, "Your information is erroneous. No part of Sheridan's force has left him, except by expiration of terms of service. I think there is not much danger of a raid into Pennsylvania."

Speaking in Auburn, New York, Seward told the audience that Lincoln had been elected president for all states but secession had prevented him from presiding over all. Opponents contended that this meant Lincoln would not relinquish the presidency even if he failed to be reelected.

Lincoln, displeased by Seward's remarks, clarified the matter. On the occasion of a serenade by loyal Maryland citizens residing in the District of Columbia, celebrating the adoption of Maryland's new constitution, Lincoln said:

> Most heartily do I congratulate you, and Maryland, and the nation, and the world, upon the event. I regret that it did not occur two years sooner, which I am sure would have saved to the nation more money that would have met all the private loss incident to the measure. But it has come at last, and I sincerely hope its friends may fully realize all their anticipations of good from it; and that its opponents may, by its effects, be agreeably and profitably, disappointed.
>
> A word upon another subject. Something said by the Secretary of State … has been construed by some into a threat that, if I shall be beaten at the election, I will, between then and the end of my constitutional term, do what I may be able, to ruin the government. Others regard … that the Chicago convention adjourned … but to meet again, if called … as the intimation of a purpose that if their nominee shall be elected, he will at once seize control of the government.
>
> I hope the good people will … suffer no uneasiness on either point. I am struggling to maintain government, not to overthrow it. I am struggling especially to prevent others from overthrowing it. … I shall remain President until the fourth

> of next March; and that whosever shall be constitutionally elected … shall be duly installed … and that in the interval I shall do my utmost that whoever is to hold the helm … shall start with the best possible chance to save the ship. …
>
> This is due to the people both on principle, and under the constitution. Their will, constitutionally expressed, is the ultimate law for all. If they … resolve to have immediate peace even at the loss of their country, and their liberty, I know not the power or the right to resist them. It is their own business, and they must do as they please with their own. I believe … they are still resolved to preserve their country and their liberty; and … in office or out … I am resolved to stand by them.[468]

Tennessee governor Andrew Johnson—the Union party vice presidential candidate—required an oath as a prerequisite to voting in his state, triggering a delegation that called on Lincoln for redress. The oath said:

> I solemnly swear that I will henceforth support the Constitution of the United States, and defend it against all enemies of the United States; that I am an active friend of the Government of the United States, and the enemy of the so-called Confederate States. …
>
> I ardently desire the suppression of the present rebellion against the Government of the United States; that I sincerely rejoice in the triumph of the armies and navies of the United States, and in the defeat and overthrow of the armies, navies, and all armed combinations … of the so-called Confederate States; that I will cordially oppose all armistices or negotiations for peace with rebels in arms, until the Constitution shall be established over all the people. …
>
> And whereas I, Andrew Johnson, Military Governor of the State of Tennessee, being anxious to cooperate with the loyal

> people of the state, and to encourage them in all laudable efforts to restore the State to law and order again, and to secure the ballot box against the contamination of treason by every reasonable restraint that can be thrown around it, I do therefore order and direct that an election for President and Vice President of the United States be opened and held at the county seat.

Lincoln responded to William B. Campbell and others in a Tennessee delegation protesting the required oath. The president noted they had laid before him a protest, with names appended. It included the Johnson proclamation and purported extracts from the Code of Tennessee. Lincoln said that prior to this, he had never seen the papers nor heard of them, and that nothing had passed between Governor Johnson or anyone else connected with the proclamation and himself.

> I have given the subject such brief consideration as I have been able to do in the midst of so many pressing public duties. My conclusion is that I can have nothing to do with the matter, either to sustain the plan as the Convention and Governor Johnson have initiated it, or to revoke or modify it as you demand. By the Constitution and laws the President is charged with no duty in the conduct of a presidential election … nor do I … perceive any military reason for … interference. …
>
> I do not perceive in the plan any menace of violence or coercion towards any one. … But you object to the plan. Leaving it alone will be your perfect security against it. It is not proposed to force you into it. Do as you please on your own account, peacefully and loyally, and Governor Johnson will not molest you, but will protect you against violence so far as in his power.

He said not the executive but another governmental department would decide if the votes were to be counted.

One of the protestors, John Lellyett, wrote his account of the meeting in a letter to the editor of the *New York World*: "I called upon the President today and presented and read to him the subjoined protest. Having concluded, Mr. Lincoln responded: 'May I inquire how long it took you and the New York politicians to concoct that paper?' I replied: It was concocted in Nashville, without communication with any but Tennesseans ... but not with New York politicians."

Lellyett continued, "'I will answer,' said Mr. Lincoln emphatically, 'that I expect to let the friends of George B. McClellan manage their side of this contest in their own way, and I will manage my side of it in my way.'" Lellyett said he asked a written answer, alleging Lincoln replied, "Not now, lay those papers down here. I will give no other answer now. I may or may not write something. ... I understand this, I know you intend to make a point of this, but go ahead, you have my answer."[469]

Given the rabid opposition of the *New York World* to Lincoln, the plausibility of its reporting is an open question. Yet William O. Stoddard, a Lincoln secretary, noted, "To such an extent was his absorbed devotion to business carried that the perpetual strain upon his nervous system, with the utter want to all exercise, began to tell seriously upon his health and spirits." Mary Lincoln said that when Lincoln was worn down, he spoke crabbedly to men.

A McClellan partisan wrote to Marble, "The conviction seems to be almost universal that no one but McClellan can control any large portion of the army vote in the field and at home: that he alone can prevent the use of the army by Mr. Lincoln."

Lincoln, however, knew the attitude of the soldiers had shifted when McClellan failed to follow up victory at Antietam. Lincoln's popularity increased, and he frequently spoke to regiments passing through Washington.[470]

William H. Osborn, chairman of the board of directors of the Illinois Central Railroad, viewed the contest differently. In a chat with several

McClellan supporters in the office of Abram S. Hewitt, a gun barrel maker, Osborn explained to those present why he believed they were mistaken in thinking McClellan would be elected. Having seen both men at close range in his position as Illinois Central president, Osborn rendered his blunt evaluation of the two presidential candidates.

Osborn described both men and then declared, "No, Lincoln will beat McClellan, for he has the courage of his convictions and does things, but McClellan, while able and great in preparation, lacks confidence in himself at critical times. Even if elected he would be a failure in the responsible position of President. He could, and did, build the best and strongest bridges on our road, but I always noticed that at the finish he hesitated to give the order to send over the first train."[471]

The Lincoln campaign used government employees as it saturated soldiers, sailors, and the general public with campaign literature. Most of these workers were patronage appointees. Democrats, especially the *New York World*, howled with rage over the use of Capitol committee rooms and the Post Office Department. Management of this task was in the hands of Raymond, effectively assisted by Weed, in his capacity as chair of the Union National Committee.

Raymond made it clear those who held government positions in the Lincoln administration would be required to contribute to the campaign. Early on he had collected $500 contributions from Seward, Interior Secretary Usher and the Postmaster General Blair. Secretary Wells expressed discomfort with the demand and protested against collecting from naval yard workers, but the collections proceeded. Raymond even gained dismissal of some who refused.

Raymond looked to the United States Custom House in New York and the post office for funds. A National Union Committee circular to all Custom House employees assessed "an average three per cent of their yearly pay." Funds poured in from throughout the Union, some directly to the White House, which turned them over to Raymond. Raymond collected from recipients of government contracts, reaching out to scores of contractors, many who supplied the military.

Phelps, Dodge and Co. of New York sent this letter to Raymond: "I enclose check for $3,000—from members of our firm who sympathize most heartily with the good cause in which your Committee is working. We shall be glad to do more if necessary. Very respectfully & truly yours etc. W. E. Dodge Junior." Recipient of favors and loyal to Lincoln personally, William E. Dodge Sr. gained the Republican Union nomination in the Eighth Congressional District in New York.

The Union Executive Congressional Committee—three Republican members of the Senate and three Republicans members of the House—raised large sums and cooperated with the Union National Committee. Members included Senators E. D. Morgan of New York, James Harlan of Iowa, and L. M. Morrill of Maine, and Representatives E. B. Washburne of Illinois (chair), R. B. Van Valkenburg of New York, and James A. Garfield of Ohio. This was a formidable group.[472]

Chairman Raymond parceled out the contributed funds among the various states and pumped money into key congressional races. As Democrats continued to rage, Raymond rolled on unfazed. The sums raised by both parties could not be calculated. Likely it was the most expensive race in the history of the nation up to that time. In running the New York campaign, Weed's highly efficient organization, coupled with effective fund raising, worked vigorously for Lincoln.

The Union League of America, formed in Illinois, spread rapidly across the North. In addition, Union clubs, strong bands, national leagues, loyal leagues, and national union associations, with a combined membership close to one million, organized for Lincoln and Johnson. The Loyal Publication Society raised $30,000 and produced ninety different pamphlets, sending out in aggregate 900,000 copies. It sent 470,000 to post exchanges, hospitals, newspapers, and ladies' societies.[473]

In preparation for canvasing the soldier vote, New York Secretary of State Chauncey Depew called on Secretary Stanton in Washington and asked for a listing of New York units and their location. Stanton raged that such information would leak to newspapers and endanger the troops. Depew encountered Representative Washburne, saying he would have to publish a card in the newspapers saying that Stanton's decision would preclude the soldier vote.

"You don't know Lincoln," Washburne told Depew. "He is as good a politician as he is a President, and if there was no other way to get those votes he would go round with a carpetbag and collect them himself." Washburne called upon Lincoln and explained the situation. Some fifteen minutes later, an orderly ushered Depew into Stanton's office, and the request was courteously granted. Depew then boarded the evening train with a full list of locations for all New York units.[474]

Chapter XX

The Reelection Campaign

Lincoln also turned to Union officers with political credentials, and leaves were granted. Perhaps the most exceptional was General John A. Logan, a former member of Congress who represented "Little Egypt," as Southern Illinois was known. "Black Jack" Logan had sponsored the black laws that curbed the rights of blacks in Illinois as a legislator, but when the Civil War broke out, he enlisted and became a highly regarded general and a devoted Republican on the stump.[475]

Early in the war, Logan had told Lincoln about weapons that often misfired, ammunition that failed, and other faulty military supplies coming from the War Department under Cameron. When Lincoln asked him to temporarily leave his command under Sherman, he complied and stumped Illinois to great effect. Other officers joined including: Carl Schurz, influential and highly regarded among Germans; and Col. Thomas O. Osborn, a former Chicago lawyer.

Lincoln prepped Schurz, explaining that as president he could do things in time of war that Congress could not do. Schurz took into the campaign his own observation that Lincoln personified the people and "that is the secret of his popularity." Schurz said his administration "is the most represented that has ever existed in world history," adding, "Lincoln's name will stand written upon the honor roll of the American Republic next to Washington, and will remain for all time."[476]

Osborn commanded the Thirty-Ninth Illinois, known as Yates' Phalanx in honor of Governor Richard Yates. A key organizer and recruiter of Chicago men, Osborn's election as colonel had been ratified by Governor Yates. It was the first Western regiment sent east. It fought first at Harper's Ferry and then on the Sea Islands off Charleston, fighting along with black units. Osborn, born in 1832 in Licking County, Ohio, graduated from the University of Ohio, studied law in the offices of General Lew Wallace, and opened a law office in Chicago.

The entire regiment had reenlisted when their three years expired while serving in the Sea Islands. After a thirty-day furlough in Chicago, the Thirty-Ninth was assigned to the Army of the James. In May, Osborn took a bullet in his elbow while maneuvering his men back to safety in the Battle of Drewry's Bluff. Called from the hospital, Osborn stumped for Lincoln in Illinois, Indiana, and Michigan. His brigade was one of two that broke Lee's rear guard at Fort Greg. His brigade then was the first infantry to reach the Lynchburg Road as Lee was attempting to break through Sheridan's cavalry, as Lee chose to surrender when he encountered infantry on that road. For this Osborn was given the rank of brevet major general at age 32.

From the Canadian side of the border, Confederate intelligence waged a constant espionage campaign with plots, explosions, robberies, spying, and propaganda. Jacob Thompson, relying on his shrinking gold supply, reported, "In order to arouse the people, political meetings, called 'peace meetings,' have been held and inflammatory addresses delivered, and wherever orators have expressed themselves … the cheers and clamor of the masses have known no bounds."

Putting his actions in perspective, Thompson said in a report to Confederate secretary Benjamin, who directed intelligence, "Lincoln had the power and would certainly use it to reelect himself, and there was no hope but in force. The belief was entertained and freely expressed, that by bold, vigorous and concerted movement … Illinois, Indiana, and Ohio could be seized and held." These attempts came to naught in the face of effective Union intelligence and swift response.[477]

Giving perspective in a nine-page report, the *Atlantic Monthly* in early November asserted:

> The war was made … because of Mr. Lincoln's election to the presidency. The North was to be punished for having had the audacity to elect him even when the Democracy were divided. … He, a mere man of the people, should never become President of the United States! The most good-natured of men, it is known that his success made him an object of aversion to the Southern Leaders.
>
> They did their worst to prevent his becoming President of the Republic, and in that way they wronged and insulted the people far more than they wronged and insulted the man whom the people had elected … and the people are bound, by way of vindicating their dignity and establishing their power, to make Mr. Lincoln President of the United States.

The *Atlantic* contended "the majesty of the law could be best served by again placing Mr. Lincoln at the head of the Republic."

The *Atlantic* noted, "The revolt of the slaveholders [was] directed against him personally as well as against that principle of which he was the legally elected representative. Many of us thought … his Emancipation

Proclamation a year too late; but we must now see that the time selected … was as skillfully chosen as its aim was laudable. That act, the noblest in Lincoln's history, secured his country against even the possibility of foreign intervention, and foreign war."[478]

In the War Department, Dana related:

> During the presidential campaign … we were busy … arranging for soldiers to go home to vote, and also for the taking of ballots in the army. There was a constant succession of telegrams from all parts of the country requesting that leave of absence be extended to this or that officer, in order that his district at home might have the benefit of his vote and political influence. Furloughs were asked for private soldiers … in close districts. …
>
> All the power and influence of the War Department, then something enormous from the vast expenditure and extensive relations of the war, was employed to secure the reelection of M. Lincoln. The political struggle was most intense, and the interest taken in it, both in the White House and in the War Department, was almost painful.

Troops were deployed in key cities, largely out of sight, and General Butler was assigned to New York City, resulting in a calm election there.

Dana was in the War Department at eight o'clock on election night and found the president and Secretary Stanton in the secretary's office. General Eckert, in charge of the War Department telegraph, reported on election returns as received. During a lull, Lincoln chose to read aloud a work by humorist Petroleum V. Nasby, which enraged Stanton. With the safety of the republic at stake, Stanton viewed the reading as nonsense. He never came to understand the relief such jests gave Lincoln.[479]

Chapter XXI

Lincoln's Decisive Victory; The Union Saved

Responding to a serenade, yet possessing only the most preliminary results of the election, Lincoln said:

> I cannot at this hour say what has been the result of the election; but, whatever it may be, I have no desire to modify this opinion—that all who have labored today in behalf of the Union organization have wrought for the best interests of their country and the world, not only for the present, but for all future ages. I am thankful to God for this approval of the people.
>
> But while deeply grateful for this mark of their confidence in me, if I know my heart, my gratitude is free from any taint of personal triumph. I do not impugn the motives of any one opposed to me. It is no pleasure to me to triumph over any one; but I give thanks to the Almighty for this evidence of the people's resolution to stand by free government and the rights of humanity.

Lincoln praised them, as he inferred they were among those who would perpetuate administration efforts.[480]

Lincoln won with an electoral college landslide of 212 to 21, losing only his birth state of Kentucky, New Jersey, and Delaware. His edge in New York and Pennsylvania was slim, but among the soldiers he had 78 percent of the vote. The final tally showed the soldier vote possibly providing the margin of victory in New York and Connecticut. His base was among the rural voters, whose pulse showed in the weekly newspapers they read and whose editors touched their views.[481]

1864 Presidential General Election Results

1864 Election for the Twentieth Term, 1865-1869

Abraham Lincoln,* President; Andrew Johnson, Vice President

For President:	AL	AR	CA	CT	DE	FL	GA	IL	IN	IA	KS	KY	LA	ME	MD	MA	MI	MN	MS	MO	NV	NH	NJ	NY	NC	OH	OR	PA	RI	SC	TN	TX	VT	VA	WV	WI	Total
Abraham Lincoln, of Illinois	-	-	5	6	-	-	-	16	13	8	3	-	-	7	7	12	8	4	-	11	2	5	-	33	-	21	3	26	4	-	-	-	5	-	5	8	212
George B. McClellan, of New Jersey	-	-	-	-	3	-	-	-	-	-	-	11	-	-	-	-	-	-	-	-	-	-	7	-	-	-	-	-	-	-	-	-	-	-	-	-	21
For Vice-President:	**AL**	**AR**	**CA**	**CT**	**DE**	**FL**	**GA**	**IL**	**IN**	**IA**	**KS**	**KY**	**LA**	**ME**	**MD**	**MA**	**MI**	**MN**	**MS**	**MO**	**NV**	**NH**	**NJ**	**NY**	**NC**	**OH**	**OR**	**PA**	**RI**	**SC**	**TN**	**TX**	**VT**	**VA**	**WV**	**WI**	**Total**
Andrew Johnson, of Tennessee	-	-	5	6	-	-	-	16	13	8	3	-	-	7	7	12	8	4	-	11	2	5	-	33	-	21	3	26	4	-	-	-	5	-	5	8	212
George H. Pendleton, of Ohio	-	-	-	-	3	-	-	-	-	-	-	11	-	-	-	-	-	-	-	-	-	-	7	-	-	-	-	-	-	-	-	-	-	-	-	-	21
Total Electoral Vote:	**AL**	**AR**	**CA**	**CT**	**DE**	**FL**	**GA**	**IL**	**IN**	**IA**	**KS**	**KY**	**LA**	**ME**	**MD**	**MA**	**MI**	**MN**	**MS**	**MO**	**NV**	**NH**	**NJ**	**NY**	**NC**	**OH**	**OR**	**PA**	**RI**	**SC**	**TN**	**TX**	**VT**	**VA**	**WV**	**WI**	**Total**
	-	-	5	6	3	-	-	16	13	8	3	11	-	7	7	12	8	4	-	11	2	5	7	33	-	21	3	26	4	-	-	-	5	-	5	8	233

*Abraham Lincoln, the sixteenth president of the United States, was shot by an assassin on the night of April 14, 1865, and died the following morning. The duties of the Presidential office devolving, in this event, upon the vice president, Andrew Johnson, he accordingly took the oath of office April 15, 1865.

Responding to another serenade two days after the election, Lincoln turned to the fundamental issue of the election:

> It has long been a grave question whether any government, not too strong for the liberties of its people, can be strong enough to maintain its own existence, in great emergencies. On this point the present rebellion brought our republic to a severe test; and a presidential election occurring in regular course during the rebellion added not a little to the strain.
>
> If the loyal people … were put to the utmost of their strength by the rebellion, must they not fail when divided, and partially paralyzed, by a political war among themselves? But the election was a necessity. We cannot have free government without elections; and if the rebellion could force us to forego, or postpone a national election, it might fairly claim to have already conquered and ruined us. The strife of the election is but human nature practically applied to … the case.
>
> What has occurred … must ever recur in similar cases. Human nature will not change. In any future great national trial, compared with the men of this, we shall have as weak, and as strong; as silly and as wise; as bad and good. Let us, therefore study the incidents of this, as philosophy to learn wisdom from, and none of them as wrongs to be revenged.
>
> The election, along with its incidental, and undesirable strife, has done good too.
>
> It has demonstrated that a people's government can sustain a national election, in the midst of a great civil war. Until now it has not been known to the world that this was a possibility. It shows also how sound, and how strong we still are. It shows that, even among candidates of the same party, he who is most devoted to the Union, and most opposed to treason,

> can receive most of the people's votes. It shows also … we have more men now, than … when the war began.
>
> But the rebellion continues; and now, that the election is over, may not all, having a common interest, reunite in a common effort, to save our common country? For my own part I … shall strive to avoid placing any obstacle in the way. So long as I have been here I have not willingly planted a thorn in any man's bosom. … May I ask those who have not differed with me, to join with me, in this same spirit toward those who have?

At this point Lincoln called for three cheers for the military.[482]

Lincoln in his December message to Congress said:

> The most reliable indication of public purpose in this country is derived though our popular elections. Judging by the recent canvass and its result, the purpose of the people, within the loyal States, to maintain the integrity of the Union, was never more firm, nor more nearly unanimous than now. The extraordinary calmness and good order with … millions of voters … at the polls give strong assurances of this.
>
> Not only all those who supported the Union ticket, so called, but a great majority of the opposing party also, may be fairly claimed to entertain, and to be actuated by, the same purpose. It is an unanswerable argument to this effect, that no candidate for any office whatever, high or low, has ventured to seek votes on the avowal that he was for giving up the Union.

Lincoln asserted:

> This firmness and unanimity of purpose, this election has been of vast value to the national cause.

> The election has exhibited another fact not less valuable ...the fact that we do not approach exhaustion in the most important branch of national resources—that of living men. While it is melancholy ... that the war has filled so many graves ... it is some relief ... that, compared with the surviving, the fallen have been so few. While corps, and divisions, and brigades, and regiments have formed, and fought, and dwindled ... a great majority who composed them are still living."

Lincoln turned to the West. "The steady expansion of population, improvement and governmental institutions over the new and unoccupied portions of our country have scarcely been checked, much less impeded or destroyed, by our great civil war, which at first glance would seem to have absorbed almost the entire energies of the nation." He said the admission of Nevada firmly established the American system across the vast area between the Atlantic and Pacific coastal states.

Lincoln urged the attention of Congress to information and recommendations relating to public lands, Indian affairs, the Pacific railroad, and mineral discoveries, as well as patents, pensions, and other key topics. He said the quantity of public land disposed of during the five quarters ending September 30 had been 4,221,342 acres. Of these, 1,538,614 acres were entered under the homestead law. He said the acreage surveyed was equal to the acreage that was disposed.

Lincoln said numerous discoveries of gold, silver, and cinnabar mines in the Sierra Nevada and Rocky Mountains were richly remunerative and teeming with labor. He said the great enterprises connecting the Atlantic and Pacific states by railways and telegraph lines were initiated. The main line of the transcontinental railway had been definitely fixed for one hundred miles from its initial point at Omaha, and in the West from Sacramento to the great bend in the Truckee River in Nevada.

Remodeling the Indian system was on Lincoln's agenda to provide proper governance of the Indians and security for advancing settlers. Regarding the liberal provisions for pensions, Lincoln said the payments were to go to invalid soldiers and sailors, widows, orphans, and dependent mothers of those who had fallen in battle. He noted the Agricultural Department was rapidly commending itself, and was most peculiarly the people's department.

Lincoln called for reconsideration of the amendment to the Constitution abolishing slavery. Noting that it had passed the Senate, yet failed of the requisite two-thirds vote in the House, "I … recommend the reconsideration and passage of the measure at the present session. … The abstract question is not changed; but an intervening election shows … that the next Congress will pass the measure if this does not." It was a question of when it went to the states for their action, he explained.

"It is the voice of the people now, for the first time, heard upon the question," Lincoln declared. "In a great national crisis, like ours, unanimity of action among those seeking a common end is very desirable—almost indispensable. And yet no approach to such unanimity is attainable, unless some deference shall be paid to the will of the majority, simply because it is the will of the majority."

He did not question the wisdom or patriotism of those who stood in opposition. "In this case the common end is the maintenance of the Union; and, among the means to secure that end, such will, through the election, is most clearly declared in favor of such constitutional amendment," Lincoln said. During the session, he identified those members opposing it whom he considered the most approachable. Dangling the carrot of patronage, each was asked to vote for its adoption, and through his personal intervention the Thirteenth Amendment passed the House.

Lincoln reinforced Secretary Fessenden's call for increased taxes needed to fund the cost of war. He said that if the war continued another year, current debt of $1,740,690,489.49 would likely increase by not far from $500 million.

He said:

> Held as it is, for the most part, by our own people, it has become a substantial branch of national, though private property. For obvious reasons, the more nearly this property can be distributed among all the people the better.
>
> With this view, I suggest ... it might not be both competent and expedient for Congress to provide ... a limited amount of some future issue of public securities might be held by any bona fide purchaser exempt from taxation, and from seizure for debt, under such restrictions and limitations as might be necessary to guard against abuse of so important a privilege. This would enable every prudent person to set aside a small annuity against a possible day of want.
>
> The national banking system is proving to be acceptable to capitalists and to the people. On the 25th day of November 584 national banks had been organized, a considerable number ... conversions from State banks. Changes ... to the national system are rapidly taking place, and it is hoped that ... soon, there will be in the United Sates, no banks of issue not authorized by Congress, and no bank-note circulation not secured by the government.
>
> That the government and the people will derive great benefit from this change in the banking systems of the country can hardly be questioned. The national system will create a reliable and permanent influence in support of the national credit, and protect the people against losses in the use of paper money. Whether or not any further legislation is advisable for the suppression of State bank issues, it will be for Congress to determine.
>
> It seems quite clear that the treasury cannot be satisfactorily conduced unless the government can exercise a restraining power over the bank-note circulation of the country.

This was a significant gain for Lincoln, who had assumed office in an atmosphere of failing state banks, a national dependence on specie that became increasingly sparse due to hoarding, and reliance on gold, which fluctuated wildly in the speculative market depending on the fortunes of the Union military.

> The public purpose to reestablish and maintain the national authority is unchanged, and, as we believe, unchangeable. … On careful consideration of all the evidence … it seems to me that no attempt at negotiation with the insurgent leader could result in any good. He would accept nothing short of severance of the Union—precisely what we will not and cannot give. His declarations to this effect are explicit and oft-repeated. He does not attempt to deceive us. …
>
> He cannot voluntarily reaccept the Union; we cannot voluntarily yield it. Between him and us the issue is distinct, simple, and inflexible. It is an issue which can only be tried by war, and decided by victory. If we yield, we are beaten; if the Southern people fail him, he is beaten. Either way, it would be victory and defeat following war. What is true … of him who heads the insurgent cause, is not necessarily true of those who follow. … He cannot reaccept the Union, they can.
>
> Some of them, we know, already desire peace and reunion. The number … may increase. They can … have peace simply by laying down their arms and submitting to the national authority under the Constitution. After so much, the government could not … maintain war against them. The loyal people would not sustain or allow it. If questions should remain, we would adjust them by … means of legislation, conference, courts, and votes … in constitutional and lawful channels.

In reiterating that general pardon and amnesty with specific terms were offered broadly, excepting certain designated classes, Lincoln declared,

"In presenting the abandonment of armed resistance to the national authority ... as the only indispensable condition to ending the war. ... I retract nothing heretofore said as to slavery." He explained that once fighting ceased, executive power would be reduced, while Congress would decide whether to seat those elected to Congress.

Lincoln firmly stated, "I repeat the declaration made a year ago, that 'while I remain in my present position I shall not attempt to retract or modify the emancipation proclamation, nor shall I return to slavery any person who is free by the terms of that proclamation, or by any of the Acts of Congress.' If the people should, by whatever mode or means, make it an Executive duty to re-enslave such persons, another, and not I, must be their instrument to perform it."

In closing, Lincoln asserted, "In stating a single condition of peace, I mean simply to say that the war will cease on the part of the government, whenever it shall have ceased on the part of those who began it."[483]

APPRECIATION

Writing this book ends a 20-year odyssey. So many have helped me with direction, suggestions, research and insight. Two, John Sellers of the Library of Congress and Michael Musick of the National Archives, stand out. Given the time lag both have retired, but remain active and are on the board of The Abraham Lincoln Institute.

Twice I have been elected president of the ALI. This, coupled with my years on the board, gave me the contacts and the benefit of learning from my distinguished board member colleagues: Douglas L. Wilson, Robert Willard, Jennifer L. Weber, Paul R. Tetreault, Ron Soodalter, David Seddelmeyer, Thomas F. Schwartz, Scott Sandage, Rodney A. Ross, Trevor K. Plante, Paul L. Pascal, the late William Lee Miller, Edna Greene Medford, Jonathan H. Mann, Gordon Leidner, Lucas E. Morel, Michelle A. Krowl, Charles M. Hubbard, Thomas A. Horrocks, William C. Harris, Stephen Goldman, Allen Guelzo, Joan E. Cashin and Terry Alford. The annual ALI symposia with a run of scholars and authors, provides access to the latest in Lincoln scholarship.

The late William Lee Miller was a special source of inspiration and insight. His work focused on Lincoln's ethics and his statesmanship. Our email exchanges and our discussions were fruitful for me. Bill understood politics, politicians and government and excelled as a writer and teacher.

Michael Burlingame, a prolific writer noted for his encyclopedic memory and Lincoln scholar and author of the two-volume, Abraham Lincoln:

A Life, readily responded to questions. Lincoln scholar Gabor Boritt provided special help, advice and shared knowledge, entertaining me at his Gettysburg home.

My much-admired friend and colleague, Karen Needles of Documents on Wheels, proved invaluable. She produced my book cover and illustrations.

My undergraduate roommate at the University of Denver, the late Dr. Frank T. Edgar, taught at Culver-Stockton College at Canton, MO. He steered me to Springfield, IL, where I had the good fortune to first meet Tom Schwartz and Kathryn Harris at the Illinois State Library. Both were generous in helping.

Dr. Edgar and I studied history under Dr. Allen D. Breck at DU. An exceptional scholar and teacher, Dr. Breck opened the doors of historical research and scholarship igniting my desire to write this book.

Home base during the last 20 years was the Institute of Governmental Studies at the University of California, Berkley. When I retired the then director, the late Nelson Polsby, invited me to become a Visiting Scholar, giving me the run of the campus, and the current director, Jack Citrin, has allowed me to continue.

At Berkeley I met Librarian Susan Koskinen who produced my bibliography and footnotes and schooled in these necessities. I combed the Bancroft Library and the Moffett Library microfiche reading Civil War era newspapers, developing into the volumes of Jefferson Davis papers and finding other source material. On line, read the Congressional Globe.

The late Representative Chalmers Wylie introduced me to the Ohio Historical Library and archives in Columbus. The late Missouri legislator, Francis M. Barnes, did the same for me in Missouri. Both were friends and mentors.

Dr. Joel Fleishman and his able assistant, Pam Ladd, provided me with access to the Duke University Library where I read the archived papers of Hershel Johnson. At the Huntington Library I combed the papers of Samuel L. M. Barlow, and am grateful for the opportunity.

At the Senior Managers in Government program at the John F. Kennedy School at Harvard gave me benchmarks for evaluating government. My year at the Church Divinity School at Berkeley deepened my knowledge of the Bible, religion, morals and ethics.

Many editors during thirteen early years as a reporter beginning at age 19 at the Denver Post and continuing at the Associated Press and the San Francisco Examiner honed my writing and reporting skills. Covering general news, politics, sports, state government, civil rights and urban affairs yielded a wealth of insight. I especially thank Ed Dooley who was managing editor both at The Denver Post and the San Francisco Examiner when I was there and Bob Eunson who hired me at the AP.

Vital insight came from the array of local, state, national and international public officials with whom I worked. It has been my good fortune to work with mayors, governors, members of Congress and even Presidents.

As a young reporter in Denver I worked as stringer for Editor and Publisher, a newspaper trade journal. The editor, Bob Brown, recruited me to report on the press corps in Denver covering the pre-inauguration White House team of President-elect Dwight D. Eisenhower.

I was surprised to learn that Carl Sandburg had been a reporter in our nation's capital. This accounts in part for the political understanding that permeates his work.

From DU I went to the Basic Infantry Officers School at Fort Benning, GA, and then to Korea. First as an infantry officer with the 24th Division and with the truce in place I was loaned to the Department of State and reassigned to the Office of Economic Coordinator, overseeing the massive US aid program for rebuilding Korea.

Reporting to William E. Warne, EOC chief, and Charles Edmundson, Public Affairs Director, I worked in public affairs and directly with the office of the president of Korea, his staff and cabinet officers.

Developing friendships with news correspondents and reporters, I volunteered evening in the office of an independent Korean English language newspaper, serving as copy editor. The news staff shared their aspirations for democracy and their interest in Lincoln.

My appreciation extends to a board range of people for whom and with whom I have worked. This cuts across a spectrum of activity, but without the experience and knowledge I could not have written this book. I benefited from teaching journalism at San Francisco State University and public policy development at Golden Gate University.

Seven years at the San Francisco Chamber of Commerce and editor of San Francisco Business put me in direct contact with mayors, supervisors and legislators. The elected Chamber board chair, Samuel B. Stewart, Senior Vice Chair of the Bank of America, recruited me to establish a public and government affairs program.

At Bank of America, first as Vice President Public Affairs, then Vice President & Washington Representative and finally Senior Vice President and Director of Governmental Relations, I was in direct contact with government officials at all levels. I also served on a number of local, state and national advisory commissions. In 1982 I led a trade mission to China for the State of California and the City of San Francisco. I traveled to Brussels and Geneva as a member of an Industry Sector Advisory Committee of the Department of Commerce. With retirement I have continued to travel in the Americas, Europe, Asia and Australia.

A key element of this book is the interaction of Lincoln and Chase, given the challenge to restore the nation's economy, build the industrial base, establish a banking system and a currency, and develop a tax structure. I owe much to banking regulators, administration officials and members of congress. The insight working in Washington in the 1980's proved a platform offering insight into Lincoln's challenges and actions.

Many close friends in succeeding administrations, in Congress in various branches of government schooled me, as did my private sector mentors. Among them I mention Ned and Dr. Jean Bandler, a member of the Lincoln Bicentennial Commission; Frederick Cannon, an economist currently Executive Vice President and Chief Equity Strategist, at Keefe, Bryette & Wood in New York; the late A. W. "Tom" Clausen, President & Chief Executive of Bank of America and former President of the World Bank; and Richard M. Rosenberg, a retired CEO of Bank of America. Fred Cannon was a reader too.

Special thanks go to my friend, Lauren Sapala, a writer who oversees a writers' workshop. An extremely intelligent young lady, she read and proofed the manuscript at various stages. She and her husband, John Price, also provide expertise in communications and the development of my web site:

http://fredjmartinjr.com

Most of all, my wife of 60 years, Shirlee A. Martin, endured and encouraged my preoccupation with Lincoln. She acquiesced as I acquired a formidable Lincoln Library. A teacher, retired after 34 years, she substitutes most days in local schools. She and my daughter, Laurie Martin Linden, both read and offered advice. And my Maine Coon cat, Lucy, boosted my morale.

BIBLIOGRAPHY

Arnold, Isaac Newton. *The Life of Abraham Lincoln*. Lincoln: University of Nebraska, 1994.

Bacon, G. W., Orville J. Victor, Joseph H. Barrett, and Henry J. Raymond. *The Life and Administration of Abraham Lincoln Presenting the Early History, Political Career, Speeches, Messages, Proclamations, Letters, Etc.: With a General View of His Policy as President of the United States, Embracing the Leading Events of the War: Also the European Press on His Death* London: S. Low, Son, and Marston, 1865.

Barton, William Eleazar. *The Soul of Abraham Lincoln*. Urbana: University of Illinois, 2005.

Basler, Roy P. "The Lincoln Legend; a Study in Changing Conceptions." PhD diss., Duke University, 1935.

———. *A Touchstone for Greatness: Essays, Addresses, and Occasional Pieces About Abraham Lincoln*. Westport, CT.: Greenwood Press, 1973.

Beveridge, Albert Jeremiah. *Abraham Lincoln, 1809–1858*. Boston: Houghton Mifflin, 1928.

Blair, Francis Preston, Remarks before the United States Congress, *The Congressional Globe*, Edited by John C. Rives, Franklin Rives, and George A. Bailey (1863).

Brooks, Noah, and Michael Burlingame. *Lincoln Observed: Civil War Dispatches of Noah Brooks*. Baltimore: Johns Hopkins University Press, 1998.

Boritt, Gabor, *Lincoln and the Economics of the American Dream*, University of Illinois Press, 1978

__________, *The Gettysburg Gospel*. Simon & Schuster, New York, 2006
___________, *The Lincoln Enigma, The changing Faces of An American Icon*, (Anthology edited by Gabor Boritt) 2001
Burlingame, Michael. *Abraham Lincoln: A Life*. Vol 1 & 2, Baltimore: Johns Hopkins University Press, 2008.
———. *The Inner World of Abraham Lincoln*. Urbana: University of Illinois Press, 1994.
Burlingame, Michael, John Hay, and John G. Nicolay. *Abraham Lincoln: The Observations of John G. Nicolay and John Hay*. Carbondale: Southern Illinois University Press, 2007.
Burlingame, Michael, and Lincoln Fellowship of Wisconsin. *Honest Abe, Dishonest Mary*. Racine, WI: Lincoln Fellowship of Wisconsin, 1994.
Burrows, Edwin G., and Mike Wallace. *Gotham: A History of New York City to 1898*. New York: Oxford University Press, 1999.
Capers, Gerald M. *Stephen A. Douglas, Defender of the Union*. Boston: Little Brown, 1959.
Carman, Harry J., and Reinhard H. Luthin. *Lincoln and the Patronage*. Gloucester, MA: Peter Smith, 1964.
Chase, Salmon P. *Inside Lincoln's Cabinet: The Civil War Diaries of Salmon P. Chase*. Edited by David Donald. New York: Longmans, Green, 1954.
Clinton, Catherine. *Mrs. Lincoln: A Life*. New York: Harper, 2009.
Coryell, Janet L. "John Minor Botts (1802–1869)." Virginia Memory, Library of Virginia. Accessed June 22, 2013. http://www.virginiamemory.com/online classroom/union or secession/people/john botts.
Croly, David G. *Miscegenation: The Theory of the Blending of the Races, Applied to the American White Man and Negro*. New York: H. Dexter, Hamilton, 1864.
Dana, Charles A. *Recollections of the Civil War: With the Leaders at Washington and in the Field in the Sixties*. New York: D. Appleton, 1902.
Davis, Jefferson, Lynda Lasswell Crist, Mary Seaton Dix, and Kenneth H. Williams. *The Papers of Jefferson Davis*. 13 vols, Baton Rouge: Louisiana State University Press, 1971.

Davis, William C. *Jefferson Davis: The Man and His Hour*. New York: HarperCollins, 1991.

Donald, David Herbert. *Charles Sumner and the Rights of Man*. New York: Knopf, 1970.

———. *Lincoln*. New York: Simon & Schuster, 1995.

———. *Lincoln at Home: Two Glimpses of Abraham Lincoln's Domestic Life*. Washington, DC: White House Historical Association in cooperation with Thornwillow Press, 1999.

———. *Lincoln Reconsidered: Essays on the Civil War Era*. 3rd ed. New York: Vintage Books, 2001.

———. *"We Are Lincoln Men": Abraham Lincoln and His Friends*. New York: Simon & Schuster, 2003.

Donald, David Herbert, and Robert Cowley. *With My Face to the Enemy: Perspectives on the Civil War: Essays*. New York: G.P. Putnam's Sons, 2001.

Donald, David Herbert, Don Edward Fehrenbacher, and Gettysburg College. *Accepting the Prize: Two Historians Speak*. Gettysburg, PA: Gettysburg College, 1998.

Donald, David Herbert, and Alfred Whital Stern Collection of Lincolniana. *The True Story of "Herndon's Lincoln."* New York: [n.d.]

Fehrenbacher, Don Edward. *The Changing Image of Lincoln in American Historiography: An Inaugural Lecture Delivered before the University of Oxford on 21 May 1968*. Oxford: Clarendon Press, 1968.

———. *The Leadership of Abraham Lincoln*. Problems in American History. New York: Wiley, 1970.

Fehrenbacher, Don E. *Lincoln in Text and Context: Collected Essays*. Stanford: Stanford University Press, 1987.

Fehrenbacher, Don E. *Abraham Lincoln: A Documentary Portrait through His Speeches and Writings*. Stanford: Stanford University Press, 1977.

Fehrenbacher, Don Edward. *Prelude to Greatness: Lincoln in the 1850s*. Stanford: Stanford University Press, 1962.

Fehrenbacher, Don Edward and Virginia. *Recollected Words of Abraham Lincoln*. Stanford: Stanford University Press, 1996.

Fehrenbacher, Don Edward, and Phillip Shaw Paludan. *The Minor Affair: An Adventure in Forgery and Detection*. Annual R. Gerald McMurtry Lecture. Fort Wayne, IN: Louis A. Warren Lincoln Library and Museum, 1979.

Fermer, Douglas. *James Gordon Bennett and the New York Herald: A Study of Editorial Opinion in the Civil War Era, 1854–1867*. New York: St. Martin's Press, 1986.

Gilmore, James R. *Personal Recollections of Abraham Lincoln and the Civil War*. London: J. MacQueen, 1899.

Graebner, Norman A., and Roy P. Basler. *The Enduring Lincoln; Lincoln Sesquicentennial Lectures at the University of Illinois*. Urbana: University of Illinois Press, 1959.

Grant, Ulysses S. *Memoirs and Selected Letters: Personal Memoirs of U.S. Grant, Selected Letters 1839–1865*. New York: Library of America, 1990.

Greeley, Horace, and Henry J. Raymond. *Association Discussed or, the Socialism of the Tribune Examined, Being a Controversy between the New York Tribune and the Courier and Enquirer*. New York: Harper, 1847. http://catalog.hathitrust.org/Record/011601353.

Guelzo, Allen C. *Abraham Lincoln: Redeemer President*. Grand Rapids, MI: W. B. Eerdmans, 1999.

Hammond, Bray. *Banks and Politics in America, from the Revolution to the Civil War*. Princeton: Princeton University Press, 1957.

Harper, Robert S. *Lincoln and the Press*. New York: McGraw-Hill, 1951.

Harris, William C. *Lincoln's Rise to the Presidency*. Lawrence: University Press of Kansas, 2007.

Hart, Albert Bushnell. *Salmon Portland Chase*. Boston: Houghton, 1899.

Hay, John. *At Lincoln's Side: John Hay's Civil War Correspondence and Selected Writings*. Edited by Michael Burlingame. Carbondale: Southern Illinois University Press, 2000.

———. *Lincoln's Journalist: John Hay's Anonymous Writings for the Press, 1860–1864*. Carbondale: Southern Illinois University Press, 1998.

Hay, John, Edited by John R. T. Ettlinger, and Michael Burlingame. *Inside Lincoln's White House: The Complete Civil War Diary of John Hay*. Carbondale: Southern Illinois University Press, 1997.

Hay, John, and Tyler, Dennett. *Lincoln and the Civil War in the Diaries and Letters of John Hay*. New York: Dodd, Mead, 1939.

Hirsch, David, and Dan Van Haften. *Abraham Lincoln and the Structure of Reason*. New York: Savas Beatie, 2010.

Isely, Jeter A. *Horace Greeley and the Republican Party, 1853–1861: A Study of the New York Tribune*. Princeton Studies in History. Princeton: Princeton University Press, 1947.

Jellison, Charles A. *Fessenden of Maine, Civil War Senator*. Syracuse, NY: Syracuse University Press, 1962.

Johnson, Robert Underwood, and Clarence Clough Buel. *Battles and Leaders of the Civil War ... Being for the Most Part Contributions by Union and Confederate Officers*. New York: Century Co., 1887.

———. *Battles and Leaders of the Civil War: Being for the Most Part Contributions by Union and Confederate Officers*. 4 vols. New York: Castle Books, 1991.

Kaplan, Fred. *Lincoln: The Biography of a Writer*. New York: HarperCollins, 2008.

Katz, Irving. *August Belmont: A Political Biography*. New York: Columbia University Press, 1968.

Keckley, Elizabeth. *Behind the Scenes, or, Thirty Years a Slave and Four Years in the White House*. Schomburg Library of Nineteenth-Century Black Women Writers. New York: Oxford University Press, 1988.

King, Willard L. *Lincoln's Manager, David Davis*. Cambridge: Harvard University Press, 1960.

Lamon, Ward Hill, and Dorothy Lamon Teillard. *Recollections of Abraham Lincoln, 1847–1865*. Chicago: A.C. McClurg, 1895.

Lewis, Lloyd. *Sherman: Fighting Prophet*. Lincoln: University of Nebraska Press, 1993.

Lincoln, Abraham. *Freedom National the Emancipation Proclamation Vindicated*. Washington, DC: Press of the National Republican, 1863. http://catalog.hathitrust.org/Record/009577068.

Lincoln, Abraham, and Roy P. Basler. *Abraham Lincoln: His Speeches and Writings*. New York: Grosset & Dunlap, 1962.

———. *Abraham Lincoln: His Speeches and Writings*. Cleveland: The World Publishing Company, 1946.

———. *The Collected Works of Abraham Lincoln: Supplement 1832–1865*. Westport, CT: Greenwood Press, 1974.

———. *Collected Works*. 9 vols. New Brunswick, NJ: Rutgers University Press, 1953.

Lincoln, Abraham, John G. Nicolay, and John Hay. *Abraham Lincoln: Complete Works, Comprising His Speeches, Letters, State Papers, and Miscellaneous Writings*. New York: Century Co., 1894.

Long, David E. *The Jewel of Liberty: Abraham Lincoln's Re-Election and the End of Slavery*. Mechanicsburg, PA: Stackpole Books, 1994.

Luthin, Reinhard H. *The First Lincoln Campaign*. Cambridge, MA: Harvard University Press, 1944.

———. *The Real Abraham Lincoln: A Complete One Volume History of His Life and Times*. Englewood Cliffs, NJ: Prentice-Hall, 1960.

Maihafer, Harry J. *The General and the Journalists: Ulysses S. Grant, Horace Greeley, and Charles Dana*. Washington, DC: Brassey's, 1998.

McClellan, George Brinton, and Stephen W. Sears. *The Civil War Papers of George B. McClellan: Selected Correspondence, 1860–1865*. New York: Ticknor & Fields, 1989.

McClure, Alexander K. *Lincoln and Men of War Times*. Philadelphia: Rolley & Reynolds, 1962.

McCulloch, Hugh. *Men and Measures of Half a Century: Sketches and Comments*. New York: C. Scribner's Sons, 1888.

McJimsey, George T. *Genteel Partisan: Manton Marble, 1834–1917*. Ames: Iowa State University Press, 1971.

McPherson, Edward. *The Political History of the United States of America, During the Great Rebellion, from November 6, 1860, to July 4, 1864; Including a Classified Summary of the Legislation of the Second Session of the Thirty-Sixth Congress, the Three Sessions of the Thirty-Seventh Congress, the First Session of the Thirty-Eighth Congress, with the Votes Thereon, and the Important Executive, Judicial, and Politico-Military Facts of That Eventful Period; Together with the Organization, Legislation, and General Proceedings of the Rebel Administration*. Washington, DC: Philip & Solomons, 1864.

McPherson, James M. *Battle Cry of Freedom: The Civil War Era*. The Oxford History of the United States. New York: Oxford University Press, 1988.

———. *Tried by War: Abraham Lincoln as Commander in Chief*. New York: Penguin Press, 2008.

Meade, Robert Douthat. *Judah P. Benjamin: Confederate Statesman*. New York: Oxford University Press, 1943.

Miller, Richard Lawrence. *Lincoln and His World*. Vol. 1, *The Early Years: Birth to First Election*. Mechanicsburg, PA: Stackpole Books, 2006.

———. *Lincoln and His World*. Vol. 3, *The Rise to National Prominence, 1843–1853*. Mechanicsburg, PA: Stackpole Books, 2006.

———. *Lincoln and His World*. Vol. 4, *The Path to the Presidency, 1854–1860*. Mechanicsburg, PA: Stackpole Books, 2006.

Miller, William Lee. *Lincoln's Virtues*. New York, Alfred A. Knofp. 2002.

———. *President Lincoln: The Duty of a Statesman*. New York: Alfred A. Knopf, 2008.

Nevins, Allan. *The Emergence of Lincoln,* Vol 1 & 2. New York, 1950.

Nicolay, John G. *A Short Life of Abraham Lincoln*. New York: The Century Co., 1921.

Nicolay, John G., and Michael Burlingame. *An Oral History of Abraham Lincoln: John G. Nicolay's Interviews and Essays*. Carbondale: Southern Illinois University Press, 1996.

———. *With Lincoln in the White House: Letters, Memoranda, and Other Writings of John G. Nicolay, 1860–1865*. Carbondale: Southern Illinois University Press, 2000.

Nolan, Alan T. *Lee Considered: General Robert E. Lee and Civil War History*. Chapel Hill: University of North Carolina Press, 1991.

Oakes, James. *Freedom National: The Destruction of Slavery in the United States, 1861–1865*. New York: W. W. Norton, 2013.

———. *The Radical and the Republican: Frederick Douglass, Abraham Lincoln, and the Triumph of Antislavery Politics*. New York: W. W. Norton, 2007.

Oberholtzer, Ellis Paxson. *Jay Cooke, Financier of the Civil War*. Vol 1 & 2, Philadelphia: G.W. Jacobs, 1907.

Office of the Federal Register. "U.S. Electoral College: Historical Election Results. Electoral Votes for President and Vice-President 1853-1869." US National Archives and Records Administration. http://www.archives.gov/federal-register/electoral-college/votes/1853_1869.html#1864.

Perret, Geoffrey. *Ulysses S. Grant: Soldier and President*. New York: Random House, 1997.

Randall, J. G. *Lincoln, the President*. New York: Dodd, Mead, 1945.

Randall, Ruth Painter. *Mary Lincoln: Biography of a Marriage*. Boston: Little, Brown, 1953.

Rawley, James A. *The Transatlantic Slave Trade: A History*. New York: Norton, 1981.

Raymond, Henry J., and F. B. Carpenter. *The Life and Public Services of Abraham Lincoln: Together with His State Papers, Including His Speeches, Addresses, Messages, Letters, and Proclamations, and the Closing Scenes Connected with His Life and Death; to Which Are Added Anecdotes and Personal Reminiscences of President Lincoln*. New York: Derby and Miller, 1865.

Rice, Allen Thorndike. *Reminiscences of Abraham Lincoln by Distinguished Men of His Time, Collected and Ed. By Allen Thorndike Rice*. Revised ed. New York: Harper & Brothers, 1909.

Ruppersburg, Hugh, and John C. Inscoe, ed. *The New Georgia Encyclopedia Companion to Georgia Literature*. Athens: University of Georgia Press, 2007.

Sandburg, Carl. *Abraham Lincoln: The War Years*. 4 vols. New York: Harcourt, Brace, 1939.

_______, *The Prairie Years*, New York, Blue Ribbon Press, 1926.

———. *Lincoln Collector: The Story of Oliver R. Barrett's Great Private Collection*. New York: Harcourt, Brace, 1949.

Sears, Louis Martin. *John Slidell*. Durham, NC: Duke University Press, 1925.

Seitz, Don Carlos. *The James Gordon Bennetts, Father and Son, Proprietors of the New York Herald*. Indianapolis: Bobbs-Merrill Company, 1928.

Smith, Donnal V. *Chase and Civil War Politics*. Columbus, OH: F.J. Heer Printing Co., 1931.

Smith, Theodore Clarke. *The Life and Letters of James Abram Garfield.* New Haven: Yale University Press, 1925.

Soodalter, Ron. *Hanging Captain Gordon: The Life and Trial of an American Slave Trader.* New York: Atria Books, 2006.

Stevens, Walter B., and Michael Burlingame. *A Reporter's Lincoln.* Lincoln: University of Nebraska Press, 1998.

Stoddard, William Osborn, and Michael Burlingame. *Dispatches from Lincoln's White House: The Anonymous Civil War Journalism of Presidential Secretary William O. Stoddard.* Lincoln: University of Nebraska Press, 2002.

———. *Inside the White House in War Times: Memoirs and Reports of Lincoln's Secretary.* Lincoln: University of Nebraska Press, 2000.

Tap, Bruce. *Over Lincoln's Shoulder: The Committee on the Conduct of the War.* Lawrence: University Press of Kansas, 1998.

Taylor, John M. *William Henry Seward: Lincoln's Right Hand.* New York: HarperCollins, 1991.

Thomas, Benjamin Platt. *Abraham Lincoln: A Biography.* London: Eyre and Spottiswoode, 1953.

Thomas, Benjamin Platt, and Michael Burlingame. *"Lincoln's Humor" and Other Essays.* Urbana: University of Illinois Press, 2002.

Thomas, Benjamin Platt, and Harold Melvin Hyman. *Stanton: The Life and Times of Lincoln's Secretary of War.* New York: Knopf, 1962.

Trefousse, Hans L. *Andrew Johnson: A Biography.* New York: Norton, 1989.

Turner, Justin G. and Linda Levitt Turner. *Mary Todd Lincoln: Her Life and Letters.* New York: Alfred A. Knopf, 1972.

United States Congress Joint Committee on the Conduct of the War. *Report on the Condition of the Returned Prisoners from Fort Pillow in the Senate of the United States. May 9, 1864.* Congressional Globe, Washington: United States Congress,1864.

Vifquain, Jean-Baptiste Victor, Jeffrey A. Smith, and Phillip Thomas Tucker. *The 1862 Plot to Kidnap Jefferson Davis.* Lincoln: University of Nebraska Press, 2006.

Waugh, John C. *Reelecting Lincoln: The Battle for the 1864 Presidency.* New York: Crown Publishers, 1997.

Weber, Jennifer L. *Copperheads: The Rise and Fall of Lincoln's Opponents in the North*. New York: Oxford University Press, 2006.
Weed, Thurlow, Harriet A. Weed, and Thurlow Weed Barnes. *Life of Thurlow Weed: Including His Autobiography and a Memoir*. Boston: Houghton Mifflin, 1884.
Weichmann, Louis J., and A. C. Richards. *A True History of the Assassination of Abraham Lincoln and of the Conspiracy of 1865*. New York: Knopf, 1975.
Weik, Jesse William, and Michael Burlingame. *The Real Lincoln: A Portrait*. Lincoln: University of Nebraska Press, 2002.
Welles, Gideon. *Lincoln's Administration, Selected Essays*. New York: Twayne Publishers, 1960.
Welles, Gideon, and Edgar Thaddeus Welles. *Diary of Gideon Welles, Secretary of the Navy under Lincoln and Johnson*. Boston: Houghton Mifflin, 1911.
White, Horace. *Money and Banking, Illustrated by American History*. Boston: Ginn and Co., 1902.
Whitman, Walt, and Roy P. Basler. *Memoranda During the War and Death of Abraham Lincoln*. Bloomington: Indiana University Press, 1962.
Wilentz, Sean, and Organization of American Historians. *The Best American History Essays on Lincoln*. New York: Palgrave Macmillan, 2009.
Wilson, Douglas L. *Lincoln's Sword: The Presidency and the Power of Words*. New York: Alfred A. Knopf, 2006.
Wilson, Douglas L., Rodney O. Davis, Terry Wilson, William Henry Herndon, and Jesse William Weik. *Herndon's Informants: Letters, Interviews, and Statements About Abraham Lincoln*. Urbana: University of Illinois Press, 1998.
Woldman, Albert A. *Lawyer Lincoln*. Boston: Houghton Mifflin, 1936.
Zornow, William Frank. *Lincoln and the Party Divided*. Norman: University of Oklahoma Press, 1954.

Index

C

D

E

F

G

H

I

J

K

L

M

N

O

P

R

S

T

U

V

W

Y

About the Book

The fate of the Union and the emancipation of slavery were at stake in the national election of 1864. It was the most important election in the history of the United States, and a beacon of hope for the world. As Abraham Lincoln explained, "The most reliable indication of public purpose in this country is derived though our popular elections." Lincoln exhibited extraordinary political skills, undergirded by a profound moral and ethical sense, which he effectively communicated to the public. He guided the nation to Victory in Civil War and overcame efforts within his own party to win a second term.

Lincoln's evolving triumph is taken step by step. Presented chiefly with words that are Lincoln's own, and the words of opponents and allies are added. Lincoln when inaugurated confronted a bankrupt nation without a currency, tax structure, functioning government, or loyal and effective military. Lincoln functioning as commander in chief restored the governing structure and led the Union victory.

Lincoln mastered language. His words changed public perspective, drove home emancipation, reignited the ideals of freedom, and saved democratic government. In all he said, Lincoln's words speak freedom to people the world over, today as in 1864. His skillful leadership provide a beacon of light for those mired in political turmoil today.

About the Author

Fred J. Martin, Jr., a 3rd generation Montanan, lives in San Francisco and is a Visiting Scholar at the Institute of Governmental Studies in Berkeley, CA. Martin worked as a night-side reporter on The Denver Post while earning a BA in History at the University of Denver. His career included work for the Associated Press, The San Francisco Examiner, the San Francisco Chamber of Commerce and Bank of America, retiring in 1993 as Senior Vice President & Director of Government Relations. His lifelong interest in Abraham Lincoln was fueled by the study of history, government and politics, and working experience in journalism, political campaigns, politics, and governmental activities. His great-great uncle, General Thomas Ogden Osborn, with a bullet-shattered elbow, took leave from the Union army and campaigned for Lincoln's reelection, returning to active duty, he was awarded a brevet major general rank at thirty-two.

Martin devoted the last twenty years to Lincoln research at the Library of Congress, the National Archives, state historical societies, archives, and libraries across the nation. He acquired an extensive library of Lincoln and Civil War books and history. He served two terms as President of The Abraham Lincoln Institute, Washington, DC.

ENDNOTES

1 Abraham Lincoln et al., *Collected Works V. 7. 1863-1864* (New Brunswick, N.J.: Rutgers University Press, 1953). p.281.
2 Abraham Lincoln, Roy P. Basler editor, *Collected Works,* vol. 7, *1863-1864* (New Brunswick, NJ: Rutgers University Press, 1953), 281.
3 Michael Burlingame, *Abraham Lincoln: A Life, Vol. 1,* (Baltimore: Johns Hopkins University Press, 2008), p. 2.
4 Albert Jeremiah Beveridge, *Abraham Lincoln, 1809-1858*, 2 vols. (Boston and New York,: Houghton Mifflin company, 1928). & Essays by Gideon Welles, p. 66-68
5 Henry J. Raymond and F. B. Carpenter, *The Life and Public Services of Abraham Lincoln, ...* (New York: Derby and Miller, 1865), 16. & Kunigunde Duncan and D. F. Nickols, *Mentor Graham, the Man Who Taught Lincoln* (Chicago: University of Chicago Press, 1944). p. xxxiii.
6 Raymond and Carpenter, *The Life and Public Services*, 16.
7 Douglas L. Wilson et al., *Herndon's Informants: Letters, Interviews, and Statements About Abraham Lincoln* (Urbana, IL: University of Illinois Press, 1998).p.36-37. Full Interview, pgs. 35-43.
8 Burlingame, *Abraham Lincoln: A Life, Vol. 1*, p.4; Reinhard H. Luthin, *The Real Abraham Lincoln; a Complete One Volume History of His Life and Times* (Englewood Cliffs, N.J.,: Prentice-Hall, 1960). p.3-5; Benjamin Platt Thomas and Michael Burlingame, *"Lincoln's Humor" and Other Essays* (Urbana: University of Illinois Press, 2002). P.7.
9 Duncan and Nickols, *Mentor Graham, the Man Who Taught Lincoln*. P. 19, 25 and 40.
10 Richard Lawrence Miller, *Lincoln and His World; V. 4. The Path to the Presidency, 1854-1860.* (Mechanicsburg, PA: Stackpole Books, 2006). p.12-13.
11 Burlingame, *Abraham Lincoln: A Life, Vol. 1*, p. 87.
12 Duncan and Nickols, *Mentor Graham*, 45.

[13] Ibid. p. 66-67.

[14] Raymond and Carpenter, *The Life and Public Services of Abraham Lincoln: Together with His State Papers, Including His Speeches, Addresses, Messages, Letters, and Proclamations, and the Closing Scenes Connected with His Life and Death; to Which Are Added Anecdotes and Personal Reminiscences of President Lincoln*. p.37-44; Miller, *Lincoln and His World; V. 4. The Path to the Presidency, 1854-1860.* P.18-19; Wilson et al., *Herndon's Informants: Letters, Interviews, and Statements About Abraham Lincoln*. p.38-39.

[15] Miller, *Lincoln and His World; V. 4. The Path to the Presidency, 1854-1860.* P.24-25.

[16] Burlingame, *Abraham Lincoln: A Life, Vol. 1*, p.29.

[17] Ibid. p. 32-36; Miller, *Lincoln and His World; V. 4. The Path to the Presidency, 1854-1860.* Chapter 20, p.45-48.

[18] Burlingame, *Abraham Lincoln: A Life, Vol. 1,* p. 48-49.

[19] Ibid.

[20] Richard Lawrence Miller, *Lincoln and His World; V. 3. The Rise to National Prominence, 1843-1853* (Mechanicsburg, PA: Stackpole Books, 2006). p.385-396.

[21] David Herbert Donald, *Lincoln* (New York: Simon & Schuster, 1995). p.42.

[22] Ibid, Richard Lawrence Miller, *Lincoln and His World; V. 1. The Early Years: Birth to First Election* (Mechanicsburg, PA: Stackpole Books, 2006).

[23] Wilson et al., *Herndon's Informants: Letters, Interviews, and Statements About Abraham Lincoln*. p. 501.; Ruth Painter Randall, *Mary Lincoln; Biography of a Marriage* (Boston, Mass.: Little, Brown, 1953). p. 10.

[24] Abraham Lincoln et al., *Collected Works V. 1. 1824-1848*, 9 vols. (New Brunswick, N.J.: Rutgers University Press, 1953). p. 10, 13.

[25] Ibid. p. 5-9.

[26] Burlingame, *Abraham Lincoln: A Life*. Vol 2, p. 79.

[27] Miller, *Lincoln and His World; V. 4. The Path to the Presidency, 1854-1860.* p.81.

[28] Raymond and Carpenter, *The Life and Public Services of Abraham Lincoln: Together with His State Papers, Including His Speeches, Addresses, Messages, Letters, and Proclamations, and the Closing Scenes Connected with His Life and Death; to Which Are Added Anecdotes and Personal Reminiscences of President Lincoln*.p, 728-30.

[29] Burlingame, *Abraham Lincoln: A Life, Vol. 1*, pg. 84, 165.

[30] Ibid. v. 1, pg. 131.

[31] Ibid. p. 112.

[32] Ibid. p. 113, fn. 168.;Miller, *Lincoln and His World; V. 4. The Path to the Presidency, 1854-1860*. p. 118.

[33] Lincoln et al., *Collected Works V. 1. 1824-1848*. p. 159-161.

[34] Miller, *Lincoln and His World; V. 1. The Early Years: Birth to First Election*.p. 223-224.

[35] Lincoln et al., *Collected Works V. 1. 1824-1848*. p. 108-115.

[36] Ibid. p. 159-179

[37] Miller, *Lincoln and His World; V. 4. The Path to the Presidency, 1854-1860*. p. 155-56.

[38] Randall, *Mary Lincoln; Biography of a Marriage*. p. 47-48.

[39] Lincoln et al., *Collected Works V. 1. 1824-1848*. p. 288-290.

[40] Miller, *Lincoln and His World; V. 4. The Path to the Presidency, 1854-1860*. p. 178.

[41] Donald, *Lincoln*. p. 90-93.

[42] Burlingame, *Abraham Lincoln: A Life, Vol. 1,* p. 194-195.

[43] Miller, *Lincoln and His World; V. 4. The Path to the Presidency, 1854-1860*. p. 212-215.

[44] Burlingame, *Abraham Lincoln: A Life*. p. 229-230.

[45] Ibid. p. 224.

[46] Miller, *Lincoln and His World; V. 4. The Path to the Presidency, 1854-1860*. p. 178.

[47] William C. Harris, *Lincoln's Rise to the Presidency* (Lawrence: University Press of Kansas, 2007).p. 38-39.

[48] Lincoln et al., *Collected Works V. 1. 1824-1848*. p. 382.

[49] Randall, *Mary Lincoln; Biography of a Marriage*. P. 107-108.

[50] Burlingame, *Abraham Lincoln: A Life*.p. 250-260 Donald, *Lincoln*.p. 135.

[51] Lincoln et al., *Collected Works V. 1. 1824-1848*. p. 420-22.

[52] Ibid. p. 446-448.

[53] Ibid. p. 448.

[54] Miller, *Lincoln and His World; V. 4. The Path to the Presidency, 1854-1860*. p. 240.

[55] Ron Soodalter, *Hanging Captain Gordon: The Life and Trial of an American Slave Trader* (New York: Atria Books, 2006). p. 175

[56] Carl Sandburg, *Abraham Lincoln; the War Years, Vol. 1,* (New York: Harcourt, Brace & Co., 1939). p. 126.

[57] Miller, *Lincoln and His World; V. 4. The Path to the Presidency, 1854-1860*. p. 234-235.

[58] Ibid. p. 232.

[59] Ibid. p. 238-239.

[60] Sandburg, *Abraham Lincoln; the War Years, Vol. 1*, p. 122-123.

[61] Miller, *Lincoln and His World; V. 4. The Path to the Presidency, 1854-1860.* p. 253-255.

[62] Luthin, *The Real Abraham Lincoln; a Complete One Volume History of His Life and Times.* p. 23.

[63] Abraham Lincoln et al., *Collected Works V. 2. 1848-1858*, 9 vols. (New Brunswick, N.J.: Rutgers University Press, 1953). p. 121-132

[64] George T. McJimsey, *Genteel Partisan: Manton Marble, 1834-1917*, [1st ed. (Ames,: Iowa State University Press, 1971). p. 6 & 7.

[65] Lincoln et al., *Collected Works V. 2. 1848-1858*. p. 247-283.

[66] Ibid. p. 283-386.

[67] Don E. Fehrenbacher, Editor, *Abraham Lincoln, a Documentary Portrait through His Speeches and Writings* (Stanford, Calif.: Stanford University Press, 1977). p. 86-88.

[68] Lincoln et al., *Collected Works V. 2. 1848-1858*. p. 398-410.

[69] Don Edward Fehrenbacher, *Prelude to Greatness: Lincoln in the 1850's* (Stanford, Calif.: Stanford University Press, 1962). p. 70-95.

[70] Lincoln et al., *Collected Works V. 2. 1848-1858*. p. 461-468.

[71] Robert S. Harper, *Lincoln and the Press* (New York,: McGraw-Hill, 1951). p. 131. Jeter A. Isely, *Horace Greeley and the Republican Party, 1853-1861: A Study of the New York Tribune, Princeton Studies in History* (Princeton, N.J.: Princeton University Press, 1947). p. 238-239.

[72] Harris, *Lincoln's Rise to the Presidency*. p. 90-92.

[73] Hugh McCulloch, *Men and Measures of Half a Century; Sketches and Comments* (New York: C. Scribner's Sons, 1888).

[74] Lincoln et al., *Collected Works V. 2. 1848-1858*. p. 498-499.

[75] Harris, *Lincoln's Rise to the Presidency*. p. 73-74.

[76] Abraham Lincoln, John G. Nicolay, and John Hay, *Abraham Lincoln; Complete Works, Comprising His Speeches, Letters, State Papers, and Miscellaneous Writings* (New York: Century Co., 1894). p. 122-123.

[77] Isaac Newton Arnold, *The Life of Abraham Lincoln* (Lincoln: University of Nebraska, 1994). p. 257-258.

[78] Abraham Lincoln et al., *Collected Works V. 3. 1858-1860*, 9 vols. (New Brunswick, N.J.: Rutgers University Press, 1953). p. 522-550.

[79] Harper, *Lincoln and the Press*. p. 45-46.

[80] Arnold, *The Life of Abraham Lincoln*. p. 161-162.

[81] J. G. Randall, *Lincoln, the President* (New York, N.Y.: Dodd, Mead, 1945). p. 150.

[82] Willard L. King, *Lincoln's Manager, David Davis* (Cambridge: Harvard University Press, 1960). p. 135-136.

[83] Alexander K. McClure, *Lincoln and Men of War Times* (Philadelphia: Rolley & Reynolds, 1962). p. 46-56.

[84] Abraham Lincoln et al., *Collected Works V. 4. 1860-1861*, 9 vols. (New Brunswick, N.J.: Rutgers University Press, 1953). p. 51.

[85] Ibid. p. 52.

[86] Irving Katz, *August Belmont; a Political Biography* (New York: Columbia University Press, 1968). p. 5-10; 23-49.

[87] Ron Soodalter, *Hanging Captain Gordon: The Life and Trial of an American Slave Trader*. p. 75-76, 176, 183-186.

[88] Robert Douthat Meade, *Judah P. Benjamin: Confederate Statesman* (New York; London [etc.]: Oxford University Press, 1943). P. 96-103.

[89] Katz, *August Belmont; a Political Biography*. p. 74

[90] Ibid. p. 83.

[91] Burlingame, *Abraham Lincoln: A Life, Vol. 1*, p. 742.

[92] Katz, *August Belmont; a Political Biography*. p. 78; King, *Lincoln's Manager, David Davis*. p. 151-153.

[93] Wilson et al., *Herndon's Informants: Letters, Interviews, and Statements About Abraham Lincoln*. p. 759-760.; Randall, *Mary Lincoln; Biography of a Marriage*. Justin G. Turner et al., *Mary Todd Lincoln: Her Life and Letters*, [1st ed. (New York,: Knopf, 1972).

[94] Carl Sandburg, *Lincoln; Lincoln Collector*, Pages 65-69, New York, Bonanza Books, 1960.

[95] Sandburg, *Abraham Lincoln; the War Years*.

[96] Benjamin Platt Thomas and Harold Melvin Hyman, *Stanton; the Life and Times of Lincoln's Secretary of War* (New York: Knopf, 1962). p. 106

[97] John M. Taylor, *William Henry Seward: Lincoln's Right Hand*, 1st ed. (New York, NY: HarperCollins, 1991). p. 131-132.

[98] John G. Nicolay and John Hay, *Abraham Lincoln: A History* (New York: Century Co., 1890). v.3, p. 73-74.

[99] Edward McPherson, *The Political History of the United States of America, During the Great Rebellion, Including a Classified Summary of the Legislation of the Second Session of the Thirty-Sixth Congress, the Three Sessions of the Thirty-Seventh Congress, the First Session of the Thirty-Eighth Congress, with the Votes Thereon, and the Important Executive, Judicial, and Politico-Military Facts of That Eventful Period; Together with the Organization, Legislation, and General Proceedings of the Rebal Administration; and an Appendix Containing*

the Principal Political Facts of the Campaign of 1864, a Chapter on the Church and the Rebellion, and the Proceedings of the Second Session of the Thirty- Eight Congress (Washington, D.C.: Solomons & Chapman, 1876). p. 37-38.

[100] William C. Davis, *Jefferson Davis: The Man and His Hour* (New York, NY: HarperCollins, 1991). p. 173.

[101] Ibid. p. 291.

[102] Congress United States et al., "The Congressional Globe," *The congressional globe.* (1833). p. 112-114. Randall, *Lincoln, the President*. p. 224-226.

[103] United States et al., "The Congressional Globe." p. 1065.

[104] Burlingame, *Abraham Lincoln: A Life, Vol. 1,* p. 10.

[105] Lincoln et al., *Collected Works V. 4*. p. 190-191.

[106] Ibid. p. 193-194.

[107] Ibid. p. 206-207.

[108] Ibid. p. 232-233.

[109] Ibid. p. 235-236.

[110] Ibid. p. 236-237.

[111] Ibid. p. 240-241.

[112] Ibid. p. 244-245.

[113] Harper, *Lincoln and the Press*. p.88-90.

[114] Sandburg, *Abraham Lincoln; the War Years, Vol. 1,* p. 75-77; Arnold, *The Life of Abraham Lincoln*. p.186-187.

[115] Lincoln et al., *Collected Works V. 4*. p. 262-271.

[116] Arnold, *The Life of Abraham Lincoln*. p. 194.

[117] Michael Burlingame, John Hay, and John G. Nicolay, *Abraham Lincoln: The Observations of John G. Nicolay and John Hay* (Carbondale: Southern Illinois University Press, 2007). p. 68.

[118] Lincoln et al., *Collected Works V. 4*. p. 180.

[119] Albert Bushnell Hart, *Salmon Portland Chase, American Statesmen* (Boston, New York,: Houghton, 1899). p. 3-13, 86-89.

[120] Allan Nevins, *The Emergence of Lincoln* (New York: Scribner, 1950). p. 446.

[121] Lincoln et al., *Collected Works V. 4*. p. 273

[122] Hart, *Salmon Portland Chase*. p. 205-207.

[123] Lincoln et al., *Collected Works V. 4*. p. 154.

[124] Harry J. Carman and Reinhard H. Luthin, *Lincoln and the Patronage* (Gloucester, Mass.: Peter Smith, 1964). p. 54-54.

[125] Gideon Welles and Edgar Thaddeus Welles, *Diary of Gideon Welles, Secretary of the Navy under Lincoln and Johnson* (Boston; New York: Houghton Mifflin Co., 1911). p. 14-15.

[126] Ward Hill Lamon, Dorothy Lamon Teillard, *Recollections of Abraham Lincoln, 1847-1865* (Chicago,: A.C. McClurg and company, 1895). p. 60-79.; Lincoln et al., *Collected Works V. 4.* p. 351-351

[127] Lincoln et al., *Collected Works V. 4.*p. 284-285.

[128] Ibid. p. 317-318.

[129] Ibid. p. 316-317.

[130] Sandburg and Stone, *Abraham Lincoln; the War Years, Vol. 1,* p. 189-193; 198-200.

[131] Lincoln et al., *Collected Works V. 4.* p. 350-351.

[132] Sandburg, *Abraham Lincoln; the Prairie Years and the War Years, Vol. 1,* p. 194-195.; Contributed by Janet L. Coryell, *Virginiamemory: Union or Secession, Virginians Decide; John Minor Botts.* (LIbrary of Vigrinia, 2001 [cited); available from http://www.virginiamemory.com/online_classroom/union_or_secession/people/john_botts.

[133] Sandburg, *Abraham Lincoln; the War Years, Vol. 1,* p. 206.

[134] Lincoln et al., *Collected Works V. 4.* mp. 332.

[135] Welles and Welles, *Diary of Gideon Welles, Secretary of the Navy under Lincoln and Johnson. Vol. 1.* p. 32-34.

[136] Gerald M. Capers, *Stephen A. Douglas, Defender of the Union,* [1st ed., *The Library of American Biography* (Boston,: Little, 1959). p. 223-224.

[137] McClure, *Lincoln and Men of War Times.* p. 129.

[138] Hart, *Salmon Portland Chase.* p. 206, 213, 215-222.

[139] Horace White, *Money and Banking, Illustrated by American History* (Boston: Ginn and Co., 1902). p. 131-138.

[140] Lloyd Lewis, *Sherman: Fighting Prophet* (Lincoln: University of Nebraska Press, 1993). p. …

[141] George Brinton McClellan and Stephen W. Sears, *The Civil War Papers of George B. Mcclellan: Selected Correspondence, 1860-1865* (New York: Ticknor & Fields, 1989). p. 1-3.

[142] Lincoln et al., *Collected Works V. 4.* p. 340-342.

[143] Ibid. p. 342-343.

[144] Ibid. p. 344.

[145] Carl Sandburg, *Abraham Lincoln; the War Years,* 4 vols. (New York,: Harcourt, 1939). p. 275.

[146] Ibid. p. 276.

[147] Sandburg, *Abraham Lincoln; the War Years, Vol. 1,* p. 278-279

[148] Ibid. p. 279-280.

[149] James M. McPherson, *Tried by War: Abraham Lincoln as Commander in Chief* (New York: Penguin Press, 2008). p. 34-35.

[150] Lincoln et al., *Collected Works V. 4*. p. 457-458.

[151] McClellan and Sears, *The Civil War Papers of George B. Mcclellan: Selected Correspondence, 1860-1865*. p. 127-128.

[152] Ibid. p. 133-134.

[153] Ellis Paxson Oberholtzer, *Jay Cooke, Financier of the Civil War* (Philadelphia: G.W. Jacobs & Co., 1907). p. 146-147.

[154] Ibid. p.150-151.

[155] Lincoln et al., *Collected Works V. 4*. p. 421-440.

[156] John G. Nicolay, *A Short Life of Abraham Lincoln* (New York: The Century co., 1921). p. 200-201.

[157] Ibid. p. 200-204.

[158] Lincoln et al., *Collected Works V. 4*. p. 506-507; 517-518.

[159] Ibid. p. 531-533

[160] Ibid. p. 538-538; 541.

[161] Ibid. p. 562.563

[162] Ibid. p. 262-263

[163] Burlingame, *Abraham Lincoln: A Life*. v. 2, p. 210.

[164] Abraham Lincoln et al., *Collected Works V. 5. 1861-1862*, 9 vols. (New Brunswick, N.J.: Rutgers University Press, 1953). p. 25-26.

[165] Ibid. p. 24.

[166] Ibid. p. 35

[167] Ibid. p. 35-53.

[168] Ibid. p. 35-53

[169] McJimsey, *Genteel Partisan: Manton Marble, 1834-1917*. p. 43-47.; Edwin G. Burrows and Mike Wallace, *Gotham: A History of New York City to 1898* (New York: Oxford University Press, 1999).

[170] Robert S. Harper and Irving Stone, *Lincoln and the Press* (New York,: McGraw-Hill, 1951). p. 116-117. Regarding Woods Only

[171] Sandburg, *Abraham Lincoln; the War Years*. p. 433.

[172] Welles and Welles, *Diary of Gideon Welles, Secretary of the Navy under Lincoln and Johnson*. v. 1, p. 57-58.

[173] United States et al., "The Congressional Globe." p. 1141-1145.

[174] Bray Hammond, *Banks and Politics in America, from the Revolution to the Civil War* (Princeton: Princeton University Press, 1957). p. 341-341; 350-352.

[175] Burlingame, *Abraham Lincoln: A Life, Vol. 1*, p. 238-239.

[176] Thomas and Hyman, *Stanton; the Life and Times of Lincoln's Secretary of War*. p. 134-135.
[177] Lincoln et al., *Collected Works V. 5*. p. 96-97.
[178] Ibid. p. 224-226.
[179] Lincoln et al., *Collected Works V. 5*. p. 240-243
[180] Thomas and Hyman, *Stanton; the Life and Times of Lincoln's Secretary of War*. p. 152-154, 169-171, 244-245.
[181] McClellan and Sears, *The Civil War Papers of George B. Mcclellan: Selected Correspondence, 1860-1865*. p. 154-155.
[182] Ibid. p. 162-171.
[183] Ibid.p. 204-205, 228.
[184] Bruce Tap, *Over Lincoln's Shoulder: The Committee on the Conduct of the War* (Lawrence: University Press of Kansas, 1998). p. 24.
[185] David Herbert Donald, *Charles Sumner and the Rights of Man* (New York: Knopf, 1970). p. 54-55.
[186] United States et al., "The Congressional Globe." p.3460-3461; Gideon Welles, *Lincoln's Administration, Selected Essays by Gideon Welles* (New York: Twayne Publishers, 1959-1960). p. 75-78.
[187] Hans L. Trefousse, *Andrew Johnson: A Biography* (New York: Norton, 1989). p. 152-153; Elizabeth Keckley, *Behind the Scenes, or, Thirty Years a Slave and Four Years in the White House, The Schomburg Library of Nineteenth-Century Black Women Writers* (New York: Oxford University Press, 1988). p. 132.
[188] Lincoln et al., *Collected Works V. 5*. p. 144-146.
[189] Ibid. p. 152-153
[190] Ibid. p. 184-185.
[191] Ibid. p. 222-223.
[192] Ibid. p. 224-225.
[193] Ibid. p. 186 & 265.
[194] Ibid. p. 128-129.
[195] Ibid. p.273-274.
[196] Ibid. p. 275.
[197] Ibid. p. 282.
[198] Ibid. p. 342-344.
[199] Ibid. p. 289-291.
[200] McClellan and Sears, *The Civil War Papers of George B. Mcclellan: Selected Correspondence, 1860-1865*. p. 332.
[201] Ibid. p. 344-345.
[202] Ibid. p.348.

[203] Raymond and Carpenter, *The Life and Public Services of Abraham Lincoln: Together with His State Papers, Including His Speeches, Addresses, Messages, Letters, and Proclamations, and the Closing Scenes Connected with His Life and Death; to Which Are Added Anecdotes and Personal Reminiscences of President Lincoln*. p. 761.

[204] Burlingame, *Abraham Lincoln: A Life*. v. 2, p. 351.

[205] Raymond and Carpenter, *The Life and Public Services of Abraham Lincoln: Together with His State Papers, Including His Speeches, Addresses, Messages, Letters, and Proclamations, and the Closing Scenes Connected with His Life and Death; to Which Are Added Anecdotes and Personal Reminiscences of President Lincoln*. p. 253; Lincoln et al., *Collected Works V. 5*.p. 388-389; 288-289.

[206] Lincoln et al., *Collected Works V. 5*. p. 388-389

[207] Ibid. p. 284 & 287.

[208] James M. McPherson, *Battle Cry of Freedom: The Civil War Era, The Oxford History of the United States* (New York: Oxford University Press, 1988). p. 532.

[209] Lincoln et al., *Collected Works V. 5*. p. 486; Nicolay, *A Short Life of Abraham Lincoln*. p. 312-313.

[210] Robert Underwood Johnson and Clarence Clough Buel, *Battles and Leaders of the Civil War … Being for the Most Part Contributions by Union and Confederate Officers*. (New York: Century Co., 1887). v.2, p. 550.

[211] Lincoln et al., *Collected Works V. 5*. p. 419-425.

[212] McPherson, *Battle Cry of Freedom: The Civil War Era*. p. 534.

[213] Robert Underwood Johnson and Clarence Clough Buel, *Battles and Leaders of the Civil War: Being for the Most Part Contributions by Union and Confederate Officers, Vol. 1-4*. (New York: Castle Books, 1991). p. 604-611.

[214] Ibid. p. 539.

[215] Lincoln et al., *Collected Works V. 5*. p. 433-436.

[216] Ibid. p. 441.

[217] Ibid. p. 460.

[218] Ibid. p. 474.

[219] Ibid. p. 485-486.

[220] Sandburg, *Abraham Lincoln; the War Years*. p. 603-604.

[221] Donald, *Lincoln*. p. 383.

[222] Lincoln et al., *Collected Works V. 5*. p. 509-510.

[223] Jennifer L. Weber, *Copperheads: The Rise and Fall of Lincoln's Opponents in the North* (Oxford; New York: Oxford University Press, 2006). p. 69-73.

[224] Lincoln et al., *Collected Works V. 5*. p. 508-509.

[225] Lamon, *Recollections of Abraham Lincoln, 1847-1865*. p. 218-219.

[226] Lincoln et al., *Collected Works V. 5*. p. 518-537.

[227] Abraham Lincoln et al., *Collected Works V. 6. 1862-1863*, 9 vols. (New Brunswick, N.J.: Rutgers University Press, 1953). p. 10.

[228] Charles A. Jellison, *Fessenden of Maine, Civil War Senator* (Syracuse, N.Y.: Syracuse University Press, 1962). p. 156-159; Burlingame, *Abraham Lincoln: A Life*. p. 451.

[229] Sandburg, *Abraham Lincoln; the War Years, Vol. 1* p. 637.

[230] Welles and Welles, *Diary of Gideon Welles, Secretary of the Navy under Lincoln and Johnson*. p. 205; Burlingame, *Abraham Lincoln: A Life*. V 2. p. 448-457

[231] Keckley, *Behind the Scenes, or, Thirty Years a Slave and Four Years in the White House*. p. 127-132.

[232] Sandburg, *Abraham Lincoln; the War Years, Vol 1*. p. 651.

[233] Lincoln et al., *Collected Works V. 5*. p. 553-554.

[234] Lincoln et al., *Collected Works V. 6*. p. 26-28.

[235] Ibid.p. 28-31

[236] Katz, *August Belmont; a Political Biography*. p. 107-108

[237] Louis Martin Sears, *John Slidell* (Durham, N.C.: Duke University Press, 1925). p. 122-123.

[238] Burlingame, *Abraham Lincoln: A Life*. p. 696-697

[239] Lincoln et al., *Collected Works V. 6*. p. 53.

[240] Ibid. p. 36-37

[241] United States et al., "The Congressional Globe." p. 52-66.

[242] Lincoln et al., *Collected Works V. 6*. p. 60-62.

[243] Ibid. p. 112-113; Thurlow Weed, Harriet A. Weed, and Thurlow Weed Barnes, *Life of Thurlow Weed: Including His Autobiography and a Memoir* (Boston: Houghton Mifflin, 1884). p. 434-435.

[244] Lincoln et al., *Collected Works V. 6*. p. 112-113; Welles and Welles, *Diary of Gideon Welles, Secretary of the Navy under Lincoln and Johnson*. v. 1, p. 235.

[245] Lincoln et al., *Collected Works V. 6*. p. 63-65; Lincoln's letter to the Manchester (England) working men.

[246] Ibid. p. 78.

[247] Ibid. p. 108.

[248] Jean-Baptiste Victor Vifquain, Jeffrey A. Smith, and Phillip Thomas Tucker, *The 1862 Plot to Kidnap Jefferson Davis* (Lincoln, Neb.; Chesham: University of Nebraska Press; Combined Academic [distributor], 2006). p. 69-73.

[249] Lincoln et al., *Collected Works V. 6*. p. 122-123.

[250] Ibid. p. 132-133.

[251] Weed, Weed, and Barnes, *Life of Thurlow Weed: Including His Autobiography and a Memoir*. v. 2, p. 428.

[252] Thomas and Hyman, *Stanton; the Life and Times of Lincoln's Secretary of War*. p. 280.

[253] Carl Sandburg, *Abraham Lincoln: The War Years. Volume 2* (New York: Harcourt, Brace, & Co., 1939). p. 157.

[254] Alan T. Nolan, *Lee Considered: General Robert E. Lee and Civil War History* (Chapel Hill: University of North Carolina Press, 1991). p. 87-88.

[255] Burlingame, *Abraham Lincoln: A Life*. v. 2, p. 505-506.; Weber, *Copperheads: The Rise and Fall of Lincoln's Opponents in the North*. p. 95.; Sandburg, *Abraham Lincoln: The War Years. Volume 2*. v. 2, p. 161-162.

[256] Lincoln et al., *Collected Works V. 6*. p. 151-152.

[257] Ibid. p. 155-156.

[258] Ibid. p. 164-165.

[259] Johnson and Buel, *Battles and Leaders of the Civil War: Being for the Most Part Contributions by Union and Confederate Officers, Vol. 1-4*. v. 3, p. 172-182.

[260] Johnson and Buel, *Battles and Leaders of the Civil War ... Being for the Most Part Contributions by Union and Confederate Officers*. v. 3, p. 172-182; McPherson, *Battle Cry of Freedom: The Civil War Era*. p. 645.

[261] Lincoln et al., *Collected Works V. 6*. p. 173-174.

[262] Ibid. p. 204.

[263] Ibid. p. 217-218.

[264] Ibid. p. 244-245.

[265] Ibid. p. 260-269.

[266] Ibid. p. 300-306.

[267] Johnson and Buel, *Battles and Leaders of the Civil War ... Being for the Most Part Contributions by Union and Confederate Officers*. v. 3, p. 240-244.

[268] Ibid. v. 3, p. 141-143.

[269] McPherson, *Battle Cry of Freedom: The Civil War Era*. p. 646-647.

[270] Nolan, *Lee Considered: General Robert E. Lee and Civil War History*. p. 114.

[271] Johnson and Buel, *Battles and Leaders of the Civil War ... Being for the Most Part Contributions by Union and Confederate Officers*. v. 3, p. 256.

[272] Ibid. v.3, p. 274-277.

[273] Ibid. v. 3, p. 293-294.

[274] Ibid. v. 3, p. 303.

[275] Ibid. v. 3, p. 318-319.

[276] Ibid. v. 3, p. 472-475.

[277] Ulysses S. Grant, *Memoirs and Selected Letters: Personal Memoirs of U.S. Grant, Selected Letters 1839-1865, Library of America* (New York, N.Y.: Library of America, 1990). Chpt 38, p. 359-381.

[278] Lincoln et al., *Collected Works V. 6*. p. 326.

[279] Sandburg, *Abraham Lincoln: The War Years. Volume 2*. p. 363.

[280] Burrows and Wallace, *Gotham: A History of New York City to 1898*. p, 876.

[281] Ibid. p. 895-896.

[282] Weed, Weed, and Barnes, *Life of Thurlow Weed: Including His Autobiography and a Memoir*. v. 2, p. 485-486.

[283] Lincoln et al., *Collected Works V. 6*. p. 269-270.

[284] Ibid. p. 389-390.

[285] Ibid. p. 391-392.

[286] Ibid. p. 406-410.

[287] Burlingame, *Abraham Lincoln: A Life*. v. 2, p. 531.

[288] Weed, Weed, and Barnes, *Life of Thurlow Weed: Including His Autobiography and a Memoir*. v. 2, p. 437-438.

[289] Ibid. v. 2, p. 438-439.

[290] Lincoln et al., *Collected Works V. 6*. p. 83-84.

[291] Ibid. p. 83-84.

[292] James R. Gilmore, *Personal Recollections of Abraham Lincoln and the Civil War* (London: J. MacQueen, 1899). p. 98.

[293] McClure, *Lincoln and Men of War Times*. p. 131-132.

[294] Weed, Weed, and Barnes, *Life of Thurlow Weed: Including His Autobiography and a Memoir*. v. 2, p. 439-440; King, *Lincoln's Manager, David Davis*. p. 214-217.

[295] Weed, Weed, and Barnes, *Life of Thurlow Weed: Including His Autobiography and a Memoir*. v. 2, p. 441-443.

[296] Lincoln et al., *Collected Works V. 6*. p. 415-416.

[297] Ibid. p. 423.

[298] Sandburg, *Abraham Lincoln: The War Years. Volume 2*. p. 404-405.

[299] Lincoln et al., *Collected Works V. 6*. p. 440.

[300] Sandburg, *Abraham Lincoln: The War Years. Volume 2*. p. 424-425. brother-in-law

[301] Lincoln et al., *Collected Works V. 6*. p. 478.

[302] Carl Sandburg, *Abraham Lincoln: The War Years. Volume 2* (New York: Harcourt, Brace, & Co., 1939). p. 426-427.

[303] Burlingame, *Abraham Lincoln: A Life*. p. 565.

[304] Lincoln et al., *Collected Works V. 6*. p. 451-452.

[305] Ibid. p. 523-524.

[306] Johnson and Buel, *Battles and Leaders of the Civil War … Being for the Most Part Contributions by Union and Confederate Officers*. v. 3. p. 681-683,

[307] Sandburg, *Abraham Lincoln: The War Years. Volume 2*. p. 454-455.

[308] Burlingame, *Abraham Lincoln: A Life*. p. 458-459.

[309] Lincoln et al., *Collected Works V. 7. 1863-1864*. p. 17-23.

[310] Ibid. p. 24-25.

[311] Lincoln et al., *Collected Works V. 6*. p. 554-555.

[312] Lincoln et al., *Collected Works V. 7. 1863-1864*. p. 39.

[313] Ibid. p. 40-41.

[314] Ibid. p. 51-56.

[315] Burlingame, *Abraham Lincoln: A Life, Vol 2,* p. 629–30

[316] Johnson and Buel, *Battles and Leaders of the Civil War: Being for the Most Part Contributions by Union and Confederate Officers, Vol. 3*. p. 710–11.

[317] Lincoln et al., *Collected Works V. 7. 1863-1864*. p. 144.

[318] Jefferson Davis, Lynda Lasswell Crist, Mary Seaton Dix, Kenneth H Williams, *The Papers of Jefferson Davis*, 1-13 vols. (Baton Rouge,: Louisiana State University Press, 1971). v. 10, p.152-153.

[319] Douglas Fermer, *James Gordon Bennett and the New York Herald: A Study of Editorial Opinion in the Civil War Era, 1854-1867* ([London]; New York: Royal Historical Society; St. Martin's Press, 1986). p. 255.

[320] Sandburg, *Abraham Lincoln: The War Years. Volume 2*. p. 537-538.

[321] Lincoln et al., *Collected Works V. 7. 1863-1864*. p. 181; Hart, *Salmon Portland Chase*. p. 193.

[322] William Frank Zornow, *Lincoln & the Party Divided*, [1st ed. (Norman: University of Oklahoma Press, 1954). p. 40-43.

[323] Carman and Luthin, *Lincoln and the Patronage*. p. 234-235.

[324] John Dennett Tyler Hay, *Lincoln and the Civil War in the Diaries and Letters of John Hay* (New York: Dodd, Mead & Co., 1939). p. 152-153; Carman and Luthin, *Lincoln and the Patronage*. p. 236.

[325] Carman and Luthin, *Lincoln and the Patronage*. p. 238-239.

[326] Burlingame, Hay, and Nicolay, *Abraham Lincoln: The Observations of John G. Nicolay and John Hay*. p. 437-438.

[327] NY Herald, Feb. 24, 1864.

[328] Welles, *Lincoln's Administration, Selected Essays by Gideon Welles* p. 141.

[329] Lincoln et al., *Collected Works V. 7. 1863-1864*. p. 200-201.

[330] Salmon P. Chase, *Inside Lincoln's Cabinet; the Civil War Diaries of Salmon P. Chase. Edited by David Donald*, [1st] ed. (New York: Longmans, Green, 1954). p.211.; Donnal V. Smith, *Chase and Civil War Politics, by Donnal V. Smith, Ph. D* (Columbus, O.: The F.J. Heer Printing Co., 1931). p.122-123.

[331] Lincoln et al., *Collected Works V. 7. 1863-1864*. p. 234-235.

[332] Ibid. p. 239-240.

[333] Charles A. Dana, *Recollections of the Civil War; with the Leaders at Washington and in the Field in the Sixties, by Charles A. Dana* (New York: D. Appleton and company, 1902). p. 174-176.

[334] Sandburg, *Abraham Lincoln; the War Years. Vol. 3*. p. 26-27; United States et al., "The Congressional Globe." p. 46.

[335] United States et al., "The Congressional Globe." p. 46-51.

[336] Zornow, *Lincoln & the Party Divided*.p. 55.; Theodore Clarke Smith, *The Life and Letters of James Abram Garfield* (New Haven: Yale university press; [etc., etc.], 1925).

[337] United States et al., "The Congressional Globe." 38th Congress, 1st Session, p. 513-514.

[338] Ibid. 38th Congress, 1st Session, Appendix, p. 44-46.

[339] Lincoln et al., *Collected Works V. 7. 1863-1864*. p. 226-227.

[340] Ibid. p. 245.

[341] Ibid. p. 259-260.

[342] Ibid. p. 319-320.

[343] United States et al., "The Congressional Globe." 38th Congress, 1st Session, Part 3, p. 44-51.

[344] Lincoln et al., *Collected Works V. 7. 1863-1864*. p. 248.

[345] Ibid. p. 268.

[346] Harper, *Lincoln and the Press*. p. 323-324.

[347] Lincoln et al., *Collected Works V. 7. 1863-1864*. p. 282-282.

[348] Ibid. p. 301-303.

[349] Ibid. p. 318.

[350] Ibid. p. 324-325.

[351] Ibid. p. 328-329.

[352] United States et al., "The Congressional Globe.", House of Representatives, 38th Congress, 1st Session, p. 2063-2067.

[353] Ibid. p. 2067-2069.

[354] Ibid. p. 2069-2071.

[355] Ibid. p. 2071-2074.

[356] Ibid. p. 2074-2081.

[357] Ibid. p. 2108.

[358] Ibid. p. 2108-2110.

[359] War United States. Congress. Joint Committee on the Conduct of the, *[Report on the Condition of the Returned Prisoners from Fort Pillow] in the Senate of the United States. May 9, 1864.--Ordered ... Printed*, ed. Senate United States. Congress and House United States. Congress ([Washington: 1864). p. 6-8, 10-14.

[360] Tap, *Over Lincoln's Shoulder: The Committee on the Conduct of the War*. p. 202.

[361] Welles and Welles, *Diary of Gideon Welles, Secretary of the Navy under Lincoln and Johnson*. p. 28-29.

[362] Raymond and Carpenter, *The Life and Public Services of Abraham Lincoln: Together with His State Papers, Including His Speeches, Addresses, Messages, Letters, and Proclamations, and the Closing Scenes Connected with His Life and Death; to Which Are Added Anecdotes and Personal Reminiscences of President Lincoln*. p. 524.

[363] Lincoln et al., *Collected Works V. 7. 1863-1864*. p. 334.

[364] McPherson, *Tried by War: Abraham Lincoln as Commander in Chief*. p. 218-219.

[365] Geoffrey Perret, *Ulysses S. Grant: Soldier & President*, 1st ed. (New York: Random House, 1997). p. 315-317.

[366] Johnson and Buel, *Battles and Leaders of the Civil War: Being for the Most Part Contributions by Union and Confederate Officers, Vol. 1-4*. p. 170-175.

[367] McPherson, *Battle Cry of Freedom: The Civil War Era*. p.732.

[368] Keckley, *Behind the Scenes, or, Thirty Years a Slave and Four Years in the White House*. p.133-136.

[369] Johnson and Buel, *Battles and Leaders of the Civil War: Being for the Most Part Contributions by Union and Confederate Officers, Vol. 1-4*. p. 491, 206-207.

[370] McClure, *Lincoln and Men of War Times*. p. 118.

[371] Perret, *Ulysses S. Grant: Soldier & President*. p.318.

[372] Ibid. p. 319-320.

[373] Harper, *Lincoln and the Press*. p.289-303.

[374] Welles and Welles, *Diary of Gideon Welles, Secretary of the Navy under Lincoln and Johnson*.

[375] Harper and Stone, *Lincoln and the Press*. p.300-301.

[376] Zornow, *Lincoln & the Party Divided*. p. 77-79.

[377] Burlingame, *Abraham Lincoln: A Life*. p. 637.

[378] Zornow, *Lincoln & the Party Divided*. p.79-83.

[379] Harry J. Maihafer, *The General and the Journalists: Ulysses S. Grant, Horace Greeley, and Charles Dana*, 1st ed. (Washington [D.C.]: Brassey's, 1998). p. 108.

[380] Johnson and Buel, *Battles and Leaders of the Civil War: Being for the Most Part Contributions by Union and Confederate Officers, Vol. 1-4.* v.4, p. 213-219.
[381] Arnold, *The Life of Abraham Lincoln*. p. 375.
[382] Carl Sandburg, *Abraham Lincoln: The War Years. Volume 3* (New York: Harcourt, Brace, & Co., 1939). p. 70-71.
[383] Arnold, *The Life of Abraham Lincoln*. p. 387-389.
[384] Raymond and Carpenter, *The Life and Public Services of Abraham Lincoln: Together with His State Papers, Including His Speeches, Addresses, Messages, Letters, and Proclamations, and the Closing Scenes Connected with His Life and Death; to Which Are Added Anecdotes and Personal Reminiscences of President Lincoln*. p. 654-658.
[385] Zornow, *Lincoln & the Party Divided*. p. 101-102.
[386] Fermer, *James Gordon Bennett and the New York Herald: A Study of Editorial Opinion in the Civil War Era, 1854-1867*. p. 205.
[387] Johnson and Buel, *Battles and Leaders of the Civil War ... Being for the Most Part Contributions by Union and Confederate Officers. Vol. 4*. p. 213, 220.; Grant, *Memoirs and Selected Letters: Personal Memoirs of U.S. Grant, Selected Letters 1839-1865*. p. 276.
[388] Dana, *Recollections of the Civil War; with the Leaders at Washington and in the Field in the Sixties, by Charles A. Dana*. p. 221-223.
[389] Ibid. p. 224-225.
[390] Lincoln et al., *Collected Works V. 7. 1863-1864*. p. 394-396.
[391] Ibid. p. 409-410.
[392] Welles and Welles, *Diary of Gideon Welles, Secretary of the Navy under Lincoln and Johnson*. p. 58-62.
[393] Thomas and Hyman, *Stanton; the Life and Times of Lincoln's Secretary of War*. p. 312-315.
[394] Lincoln et al., *Collected Works V. 7. 1863-1864*. p. 420.; Welles and Welles, *Diary of Gideon Welles, Secretary of the Navy under Lincoln and Johnson*. p. 64-65.
[395] Lincoln et al., *Collected Works V. 7. 1863-1864*. p. 423.
[396] Burrows and Wallace, *Gotham: A History of New York City to 1898*. p. 875-876.
[397] Arnold, *The Life of Abraham Lincoln*. p. 381.
[398] Sandburg, *Abraham Lincoln: The War Years. Volume 3*. p. 124.
[399] United States et al., "The Congressional Globe." p. 3527-3528.
[400] Ibid. p. 3529.
[401] Ibid. p. 3491.

[402] John Hay, John R. T. Ettlinger, and Michael Burlingame, *Inside Lincoln's White House: The Complete Civil War Diary of John Hay* (Carbondale: Southern Illinois University Press, 1997). p. 217-219.

[403] Lincoln et al., *Collected Works V. 7. 1863-1864*. p. 425-426.

[404] Carman and Luthin, *Lincoln and the Patronage*. p. 272.

[405] Lincoln et al., *Collected Works V. 7. 1863-1864*. p. 429.

[406] Lincoln et al., *Collected Works V. 6*. p. 314-317.

[407] Lincoln et al., *Collected Works V. 7. 1863-1864*. p. 435-451.

[408] Hay, Ettlinger, and Burlingame, *Inside Lincoln's White House: The Complete Civil War Diary of John Hay*. p. 226.

[409] Sandburg, *Abraham Lincoln: The War Years. Volume 2*. p. 672-673.

[410] Dana, *Recollections of the Civil War; with the Leaders at Washington and in the Field in the Sixties, by Charles A. Dana*. p. 237-238.

[411] Lincoln et al., *Collected Works V. 7. 1863-1864*. p. 437-438.; Dana, *Recollections of the Civil War; with the Leaders at Washington and in the Field in the Sixties, by Charles A. Dana*. p. 232-233.

[412] Lincoln, et al., Collected Works, V. 7. 1863-64, P. 437.

[413] Lincoln et al., *Collected Works V. 7. 1863-1864*. p. 439-440; Nicolay, *A Short Life of Abraham Lincoln*. p. 488.

[414] Sandburg, *Abraham Lincoln: The War Years. Volume 3*. p. 149-150.

[415] Lincoln et al., *Collected Works V. 7. 1863-1864*. p. 444-445, 448-449.

[416] Johnson and Buel, *Battles and Leaders of the Civil War … Being for the Most Part Contributions by Union and Confederate Officers*. v.IV. p. 252-253.

[417] Lincoln et al., *Collected Works V. 7. 1863-1864*. p. 451.

[418] Ibid. p. 459-461; Dana, *Recollections of the Civil War; with the Leaders at Washington and in the Field in the Sixties, by Charles A. Dana*.p. 239-242.

[419] Dana, *Recollections of the Civil War; with the Leaders at Washington and in the Field in the Sixties, by Charles A. Dana*. p. 237-238.

[420] Lincoln et al., *Collected Works V. 7. 1863-1864*.p. 462.

[421] Ibid. p. 469 & 476.

[422] Ibid. p. 494-495.

[423] Ibid. p. 489-490.

[424] Ibid. p. 499.

[425] Ibid. p. 499-502.

[426] Ibid. p. 504-505.

[427] Ibid. p. 506-508.

[428] Burlingame, *Abraham Lincoln: A Life*. v. 2, p. 671.

[429] Welles, *Lincoln's Administration, Selected Essays by Gideon Welles* p. 180-181

[430] Sandburg, *Abraham Lincoln: The War Years. Volume 3*. p. 203-204.
[431] Lincoln et al., *Collected Works V. 7. 1863-1864*. p. 514-515.
[432] Ibid. p. 518.
[433] Welles, *Lincoln's Administration, Selected Essays by Gideon Welles* p. 186-187.
[434] Lincoln et al., *Collected Works V. 7. 1863-1864*. p. 514.
[435] Allen Thorndike Rice, *Reminiscences of Abraham Lincoln by Distinguished Men of His Time, Collected and Ed. By Allen Thorndike Rice*, New and rev. ed. (New York, London: Harper & Brothers, 1909). p. 68-70.
[436] Carman and Luthin, *Lincoln and the Patronage*. p. 279-282.
[437] Lincoln et al., *Collected Works V. 7. 1863-1864*. p. 400 and 402.
[438] Carman and Luthin, *Lincoln and the Patronage*. p. 282-284.
[439] Harper, *Lincoln and the Press*. p. 314.
[440] Ibid. p. 315-317; Welles, *Lincoln's Administration, Selected Essays by Gideon Welles* p. 60-61.
[441] Lincoln et al., *Collected Works V. 7. 1863-1864*. p. 528-529.
[442] Keckley, *Behind the Scenes, or, Thirty Years a Slave and Four Years in the White House*. p. 145-151.
[443] Sandburg, *Abraham Lincoln: The War Years. Volume 3*. p. 226-227.
[444] McClellan and Sears, *The Civil War Papers of George B. Mcclellan: Selected Correspondence, 1860-1865*. p. 591.
[445] Harper, *Lincoln and the Press*. p. 325-326.
[446] Ibid. p. 326-328; NY Herald, 13, 16, 18, July 1864.
[447] Lincoln et al., *Collected Works V. 7. 1863-1864*. p. 548-549.
[448] Ibid. p. 543.
[449] Abraham Lincoln et al., *Collected Works V. 8. 1864-1865*, 9 vols. (New Brunswick, N.J.: Rutgers University Press, 1953). p. 11-12.
[450] Ibid. p. 13.
[451] Johnson and Buel, *Battles and Leaders of the Civil War ... Being for the Most Part Contributions by Union and Confederate Officers*. p. 512-513.
[452] Carman and Luthin, *Lincoln and the Patronage*. p. 272-273.
[453] Lincoln et al., *Collected Works V. 8. 1864-1865*. p. 2-3.
[454] Zornow, *Lincoln & the Party Divided*. p. 144-145.
[455] Lincoln et al., *Collected Works V. 8. 1864-1865*. p. 18-19.
[456] Carman and Luthin, *Lincoln and the Patronage*. p. 278.
[457] Lincoln et al., *Collected Works V. 8. 1864-1865*. p. 20.
[458] Sandburg, *Abraham Lincoln: The War Years. Volume 3*. p. 242.
[459] Hay, Ettlinger, and Burlingame, *Inside Lincoln's White House: The Complete Civil War Diary of John Hay*. p. 229-230.

[460] *The New Georgia Encyclopedia Companion to Georgia Literature*, ed. Hugh Ruppersburg and John C. Inscoe (Athens: University of Georgia Press: Published in association with the Georgia Humanities Council and the University System of Gerogia/GALILEO, 2007).

[461] Lincoln et al., *Collected Works V. 8. 1864-1865*. p. 27.

[462] Ibid. p. 29.

[463] Ibid. p. 33.

[464] Ibid. p. 42.

[465] Ibid. p. 46; Burlingame, *Abraham Lincoln: A Life*. p. 720.

[466] McClure, *Lincoln and Men of War Times*. p. 196-200.

[467] Lincoln et al., *Collected Works V. 8. 1864-1865*. p. 46.

[468] Ibid. p.52-53, Thanksgiving Proclamation, p.55-56; Burlingame, *Abraham Lincoln: A Life*. p. 716

[469] Lincoln et al., *Collected Works V. 8. 1864-1865*. p. 58-72.

[470] Carman and Luthin, *Lincoln and the Patronage*. p. 286.

[471] Sandburg, *Abraham Lincoln: The War Years. Volume 3*. p. 284.

[472] Carman and Luthin, *Lincoln and the Patronage*. p. 286-292.

[473] Ibid. p.180.

[474] Sandburg, *Abraham Lincoln: The War Years. Volume 3*. p. 284-285.

[475] Burlingame, *Abraham Lincoln: A Life*. p. 718.

[476] Ibid. p. 718-719. Reference to Shurz Papers.

[477] Sandburg, *Abraham Lincoln: The War Years. Volume 3*. p. 290.

[478] Ibid. p. 392.

[479] Dana, *Recollections of the Civil War; with the Leaders at Washington and in the Field in the Sixties, by Charles A. Dana*. p. 261-262.

[480] Lincoln et al., *Collected Works V. 8. 1864-1865*. p. 96.

[481] Office of the Federal Register., *U.S. Electoral College: Historical Election Results. Electoral Votes for President and Vice-President 1853-1869.* (U.S. National Archives and Records Administration., [cited); available from http://www.archives.gov/federal-register/electoral-college/votes/1853_1869.html#1864.

[482] Lincoln et al., *Collected Works V. 8. 1864-1865*. p. 100-101.

[483] Ibid., p. 136–152.